GUIDE TO GENEALOGICAL RESOURCES IN THE BRITISH ISLES

by
Dolores B. Owen

The Scarecrow Press, Inc.
Metuchen, N.J., & London
1989

British Library Cataloguing-in-Publication data available

Library of Congress Cataloging-in-Publication Data

Owen, Dolores B.
    Guide to genealogical resources in the British Isles /
Dolores B. Owen.
        p.   cm.
    Includes index.
    ISBN 0-8108-2153-2
    1. Great Britain--Genealogy--Archival resources--
Great Britain--Directories. 2. Great Britain--Genealogy
--Library resources--Great Britain--Directories. I. Title.
Z5305.G7094   1989
[CS434]
929'.1'02541--dc19   88-22574

To the men in my life:

Travis, Mitch, Chuck, Benjamin Franklin,

and you, too, Larry.

CONTENTS

PREFACE

Searching among the archives in record offices and libraries in the British Isles can be a delightful experience or an exercise in frustration. I hope this guide will give the information necessary to help researchers avoid at least some of the pitfalls they might encounter.

This work is not meant to instruct the genealogist or local historian in how to conduct research; that task is for other books. Travel information is also limited here in view of the abundance of guidebooks, travel advisories and tourist directories which are readily available. History, geography, and the political process and its similarities and differences are also left to other texts. Still, there are other matters that no one thinks to put in a guidebook or manual. Usually the visitor deals with these surprises, sometimes incurring expense and loss of time, and forgets all about them. If, however, visiting scholars anticipate some of these problems, they may find them easier to solve, and save both time and money.

Readers will find information designed to prepare them for some possible difficulties in Chapter 1. Chapter 2 covers the institutions with collections of interest to the genealogist, the family historian, and those concerned with local history. Facts concerning collections, opening hours, copying facilities, services, and publications are supplied. Since admission to a library or record office is not always automatic, the conditions imposed by the institutions are also given. There are three appendices: I) an Alphabetical List of Institutions; II) Associations and Societies; and III) Maps. There is a Subject Index, and separate indexes by County and by Country.

Almost all of this information was gathered through a questionnaire, correspondence, and visits to as many of the institutions as possible. Although the response to the questionnaire was most gratifying, it was not total. In those cases where no reply was received or was incomplete, and a visit was not feasible, data were sought in published sources. Catalogs, directories, and various compilations were used. Where reliable information was unavailable, it was either omitted or so noted.

I owe an immeasurable debt of gratitude to the archivists, librarians and curators who helped me. Without their advice and assistance, this endeavor would have foundered long ago. They were unfailingly cooperative, many going out of their way to provide comprehensive information concerning their institutions. They corrected drafts of my entries, and many supplied an abundance of additional detail, while others sent their publications, from which I could glean specifics concerning collections and use of the facilities. There is some variance among archivists about which words used to name various records should be capitalized. This guide follows the practice of the responding institution, so some inconsistency will be found.

The staffs of the record offices and libraries I visited were invariably courteous and helpful. Individuals at the British Library were especially accommodating and I want to thank Eve Johansson, Mary Hurworth and Peter Jones for their counsel and guidance. I feel compelled to say that without my friend Larry Robertson to negotiate curious (to Americans) directions, unfamiliar road conditions and a tiny, right-hand-drive car, I would never have managed to visit as many cities and towns in the British Isles as I did. It should also be noted that without my husband Travis, I might still be compiling this work into the 21st Century. His patience is legend, his encouragement constant, and his ability to reduce stumbling blocks to rubble, limitless.

D. B. Owen
former head of the
Documents Department,
University of Southwestern
Louisiana
Lafayette, LA

ACKNOWLEDGMENTS

Many institutions, the individuals in them and the councils that administer them, were exceedingly generous in allowing me to use their material and in supplying information. I am greatly pleased to acknowledge them:

J. McLean, Brenda R. Cluer, H. A. Hanley, R. Geraint Gruffydd, Janet Marx, Peter Grant, J. A. Cripps, Amanda Arrowsmith, R. G. Thomas, G. A. Mitchell, S. Campbell, V. M. E. Adams, Bryan Lucas, Ian Mason, A. C. J. Jones, C. Johnston, Patricia Bell, K. D. Holt, J. D. Warner-Davies, Mary E. Williams, Brian Redwood, J. T. Hopkins, S. J. Macpherson, J. Grisenthwaite, A. M. Kennett, L. Greaves, Dilys Bateman, Tim Cadogan, Patricia McCarthy, Kieran Burke, Richard Storey, David Rimmer, Anne M. Oakley, Patricia Moore, Else Churchill, Delwyn Tibbott, Gareth H. Williams, Maureen Patch, Susan Beckley, A. E. B. Owen, J. M. Farrar, D. M. Bowcock, Patricia Gill, Victor Gray, B. Barber, Miriam Cutchlan, P. Curtis, Ann Rhydderch, Hugh Jaques, D. J. Butler, B. Murphy, Brigid Dolan, Eileen McGlade, W. Darcy, Michael Hewson, David Craig, James Galbraith, George MacKenzie, E. D. Yeo, Arnott T. Wilson, Peggy Moreton, J. D. Brunton, M. M. Rowe, M. P. Shaw, D. J. H. Smith, J. Voyce, Thomas Sharkey, Patrick Conway, John Wilson, Shirley Corke, Penelope Morgan, A. G. Veysey, Peter Walne, Rev. P. J. Jagger, J. Pepler, Alan Betteridge, Alan Lawson, M. Vaglamhein, G. Oxley, David Robinson, Alison Fraser, Mary Enright, B. C. Jones, Neville Carrick, Jane Hampartumian, Kathryn Thompson, G. A. Knight, M. Weaver, R. Morgan, Murdo MacDonald, C. R. Davey, W. J. Connor, Julian Watson, Margaret Swarbrick, R. C. Yorke, C. J. Kitching, B. Curle, Martin Moir, N. M. Hunt, C. W. Harrison, V. T. H. Parry, Suzanne Burge, L. W. Lawson Edwards, S. Frilong, P. Hatfield, E. G. W. Bill, E. Nixon, David Mander, Stephen Croad, Guy Holborn, James R. Sewell, Wallace Breem, C. R. H. Cooper, E. B. Nuge, Hilary Jones, H. S. Cobb, R. Futter, Joan Sinar, S. Ferguson, Jean Ayton, D. H. Tyrell, Bruce Jackson, Alan Cameron, Adrian Henstock, C. Douglas, P. I. King, F. W. Manders, R. M. Gard, M. Y. Ashcroft, W. Seaman, Jean Kennedy, S. J. Barnes, D. G. Vaisey, John Thorn, Sarah Quail, E. A. Stuart, J. R. Elliot, K. Hall, Joe Canning, David Rilly, Michael Bott, J. A. Green, R. H. Davis, K. Hempel, Levi Fox, John Smith, Anthony M. Carr, M. Williamson, M. J.

De La Haye, Peter Bison, H. Tomlinson, D. V. Fowkes, David Postles, Christine North, H. L. Douch, D. M. M. Shuroks, E. M. Brooks, Robert Frost, L. J. Feiweles, David J. Guy, A. M. Wherry, R. J. Freedman, D. M. Smith; Dyfed Archive Service, Cumbria Record Office, Linen Hall Library, Public Record Office (Ireland), Cheshire Record Office, Hereford and Worcester County Council, Edinburgh City Council, National Library of Scotland, West Yorkshire Archive Service, York City Archives.

Chapter 1

OBSERVATIONS AND INFORMATION

Paving the Way

The British Isles lie roughly between fifty and sixty degrees
North latitude. Although they are slightly farther north than
Newfoundland, which lies between forty-six and fifty-two degrees
North latitude, they do not have the extremely cold temperature
that might be expected, because they are warmed by the Gulf Stream
which flows near their coasts. The size of all the land comprising
the British Isles is 121,356 square miles. This is about the size of
New Mexico. The variety encountered in this limited space is difficult to imagine: the rocky craigs of the Scottish Highlands, the
hills of Northumberland, the Cornish Coast, the green of Ireland,
the quiet of the villages, and the cosmopolitan bustle of the cities.

Preparation

Travelers to the British Isles from the United States are re-
quired to have a valid passport, but do not need a visa. Informa-
tion concerning these matters can be obtained from the British
Embassy and British Consulates. The Embassy is located in Washington,
D.C. and Consulates are in Atlanta, Boston, Chicago, Houston,
Los Angeles, New York, and San Francisco. Visitors to the Republic of Ireland may wish to contact the Irish Embassy in Washington,
D.C. or one of the Irish Consulates, which are found in Boston,
Chicago, New York, and San Francisco. Information is also available
from the British Information Service located at 845 Third Avenue,
New York, New York 10022, telephone: 212-752-5747; the toll-free
number for British Information Service is 1-800-223-5339. Passport
and visa information can be obtained by calling 212-752-8400.

Advice concerning travel in the British Isles can be acquired
from the British Tourist Authority at 40 West 57th Street, New York,
New York 10019, telephone: 212-581-4700. The Irish Tourist Board
is located at 757 Third Avenue, New York, New York 10017, telephone: 212-418-0800. The telephone number for the Northern Ireland Tourist Board is 212-765-5144.

Using a travel agent to make travel arrangements saves a lot of time and struggle. It is a good plan to make inquiries of several agents to be sure of getting the most advantageous flights and prices. Booking rooms in advance in the larger cities, at least for the first few days, is advisable, and is imperative during peak tourist season, i.e., the summer months and whenever there are major sporting events. Travel agents can also make recommendations concerning car rental, bus and rail travel in Britain, duty-free allowances, customs regulations, and electric current. If one wishes to use a Britrail or Eurail pass, they must be purchased in the United States. Britrail passes are accepted in the United Kingdom, but not in the Republic of Ireland, where a Eurail pass is necessary.

Currency

Travelers checks can be purchased in the United States in pounds sterling. If this is done, fluctuations in the value of the dollar in relation to the pound will make no difference, because the checks would have been bought at the rate on the day of purchase. At the same time, if the exchange rate becomes more favorable, it is not then possible to take advantage of it. British currency is accepted all over the United Kingdom, but not in the Republic of Ireland, nor is Irish currency accepted outside Ireland. When changing currency, the best rate will be obtained in a bank. If it is necessary to send money to the United Kingdom, it is possible to do so by International Money Order. There is a fee for this service and it can be quite high, although a ten dollar charge seems to be common. If the amount to be sent is small (Ł5 or less, for example), one might consider purchasing pound notes and sending these, in spite of admonitions not to send money through the mail. Banks that deal in foreign currency have staff who can give advice and can also quote the current exchange rate. Credit cards that are readily accepted overseas are American Express, MasterCard (connected in Britain with Access) and VISA (connected with Barclaycard).

Credentials

Many institutions require a letter of introduction in order for a visiting scholar to be allowed to use the collections. It would be wise, therefore, to go to the British Isles armed with some kind of academic credentials. A letter from someone of standing who attests to the individual's seriousness of purpose and the need to use archival resources in libraries and record offices should be acquired. (I had a letter from my library director, which was sufficient.)

Composition and Administration of the British Isles

"British Isles" is a geographical term for the group of islands

lying off the northwest coast of Europe. These islands consist of
Great Britain (England, Scotland and Wales), Ireland (Northern
Ireland and the Republic of Ireland), and several smaller islands in
the waters surrounding these. Northern Ireland and Great Britain
form the United Kingdom, the full name of which is the United
Kingdom of Great Britain and Northern Ireland. The Republic of
Ireland, an independent nation, has twenty-six counties and
Northern Ireland has six. Northern Ireland is sometimes referred
to as Ulster, although that province had more than six counties.
England and Wales, outside of Greater London, have fifty-three
counties and Scotland is divided into nine regions which are sub-
divided into fifty-three districts. The smaller islands include the
Channel Islands, which are largely self-governing but are crown
territories and therefore have ties to Great Britain. This is also
true of the Isle of Man. The Bailiwick of Jersey includes Ecrehou
Rocks and Les Minquiers. The Bailiwick of Guernsey includes
Alderney, Great Sark, Little Sark, Herm, Jethou and Lihou, and
associated islets. The Isles of Scilly, which are part of Cornwall
County, the Isle of Wight, Anglesey, the Orkneys, the Shetlands,
the Western Islands and others fringing Scotland are much more
closely connected administratively to the United Kingdom. The head
of state is the reigning king or queen and the head of government
is the Prime Minister. It is fair to say that England, Scotland,
Wales, and Northern Ireland, though bound together, regard themselves as separate nations in many ways, and one will find a degree
of national identity among them. As has already been pointed out,
the Irish Republic is, indeed, an independent nation.

Climate

The climate of the British Isles has been described as moderate
and the weather as unpredictable. There are mild, sunny days in
winter and wet, chilly days in summer. There can be blizzards and
there can be heat waves, and change in the weather can come quickly. Guidebooks lead one to believe that the temperature is rarely
above ninety degrees Fahrenheit or below fourteen degrees Fahrenheit.
The rainfall is over sixty inches per annum in the west and north,
and less than thirty inches in the central and eastern parts of Great
Britain. Rainfall is evenly distributed throughout the year, but
generally September to January are the wettest months and March
to June are the driest. Visitors should be prepared with rain gear.
They should also be aware that air-conditioned buildings are less
widespread than in America and many public buildings, even restau-
rants and theaters, may not have this equipment. In addition, the
heating systems may be found to be less warming than an American
is used to. Finally, if one is accustomed to using an abundance of
ice, its generous use is rare.

Language

English is, of course, the official language, but do not expect to hear it exclusively. On the Channel Islands, French is spoken, and in Scotland, Scottish Gaelic may be heard. In Northern Ireland and the Irish Republic one finds Irish Gaelic, and Manx is sometimes spoken on the Isle of Man. Welsh is widely used in Wales and one will hear it in record offices and libraries. Signs are in both Welsh and English. In the Republic of Ireland and Northern Ireland, signs are also bilingual. One should be prepared for very old church records to be in Latin.

Currency Revisited

The basic unit of currency in Britain and Ireland is the pound --either the pound sterling or the Irish pound. Again, British currency is accepted all over the United Kingdom, and the Islands, but not in the Republic of Ireland, nor will currency from there be accepted in the United Kingdom. The Channel Islands and the Isle of Man issue their own notes and coins which are not accepted elsewhere. It has already been noted that the best rate of exchange for foreign money is found in a bank. Banking hours vary from place to place, but in general they are 9:30 AM to 3:30 PM, Monday through Friday. Some banks will be open on Saturday, 9:30 AM until noon, and some will close every day during lunch-time. They all close for official holidays, which are listed below.

Holidays

A number of official holidays are observed in the British Isles. For England and Wales these are:

New Year's Day
Good Friday
Easter Monday
First Monday in May (May Day)
Last Monday in May (Spring Bank Holiday)
Last Monday in August (Summer Bank Holiday)
Christmas Day
Boxing Day (December 26)

If Christmas Day and Boxing Day fall on a weekend, the following Monday, or Monday and Tuesday will be holidays. In Scotland official holidays are:

New Year's Day
January 2
Good Friday
First Monday in May (May Day)

Last Monday in May (Spring Bank Holiday)
First Monday in August (Summer Bank Holiday)
Christmas Day
Boxing Day (December 26)

In Northern Ireland the holidays are:

New Year's Day
St. Patrick's Day (March 17)
Good Friday
Easter Monday
First Monday in May (May Day)
Last Monday in May (Spring Bank Holiday)
July 12 (Orangeman's Day)
Last Monday in August (Summer Bank Holiday)
Christmas Day
Boxing Day (December 26)

In the Irish Republic holidays are:

New Year's Day
St. Patrick's Day (March 17)
Good Friday
Easter Monday
First Monday in June (Spring Bank Holiday)
First Monday in August (Summer Bank Holiday)
Last Monday in October
Christmas Day
Boxing Day (December 26--usually observed, but not truly
    official)

One can expect record offices and libraries to be closed on these
days, and sometimes this is noted in their entries in this book.
College and university holiday schedules vary and should be requested from the schools themselves. In addition, there are local
holidays that may result in closure; for example, the Monday beginning the Glasgow fair, and market days, which differ
from town to town. One might also wish to know that
public houses (pubs) are open only during certain hours
of the day. Opening hours vary according to the country
and area concerned.

Time

The British Isles are on Greenwich Mean Time (GMT), which
is five hours ahead of Eastern Standard Time, except from the end
of March to late October when this changes to European Summer
Time, which is six hours ahead of Eastern Standard Time.

Metric System

All of the British Isles are on the metric system. Great
Britain has used this system since it joined the European Community
on January 1, 1973. One result of this change is in the size of
paper. Instead of 8½" by 11" for standard letter size, and 8½" by
14" for legal size, one finds paper designated as "A4" (8.2" by
11.69"), B4 (9.8" by 12.9"), etc. This is important because photocopying charges are frequently made on the basis of the size of
the paper.

Telephones

Every place has a telephone area code which can have up to
six numbers. These are not used for local calls, but must be used
when calling from outside the area. There is a zero preceding the
area code which is used when calling from within the country, but
not from overseas. A long-distance call is referred to as a trunk
call. Most international calls can be dialed direct from public tele-
phones, but if there is a difficulty, the operator can be reached by
dialing 100 for assistance. When using a pay telephone, do not in-
sert coins until the number has been dialed and the call answered.
There are a series of beeps which will be repeated when more coins
are necessary. It is a good idea to have the money ready, because
the call will be cut off in just a few seconds if money is not deposited.

Correspondence and Mail

When corresponding with individuals or institutions in the
British Isles, it is wise to use the British Postal Code. This will
help insure that the letter finds its mark. The code is a combination
of letters and numbers which indicate geographic units. The largest
of these is the Post Code Area and is represented by one or two
letters at the beginning of the post code. Post Code Areas are
divided into districts represented by numbers. Districts are divided
into sectors which are also indicated by numbers and begin the
second half of the code. Finally, there are two letters which denote
a street or part of a street. There is some variation in this for
London, but for similar addresses in different parts of town, it is
very important--even taxi drivers may ask for it. It may also be
useful to avoid using abbreviations in your return address, and to
use your own zip code. My experience was that LA for Louisiana
was often mistaken for Los Angeles, but the zip code directed the
letter to the proper place. It will be considered a courtesy if a
self-addressed envelope is included, along with international reply
coupons to cover postage, whether this is required or not.

The visitor to Britain may wish to know that letters addressed to him marked <u>Poste restante</u> and sent to the central post office of a town will be held for him for one month, much the same as general delivery. Proof of identity must be presented to collect this mail. Post offices are usually open 9:00 AM to 5:30 PM, Monday through Friday, and 9:00 AM to 12:30 PM, Saturday.

Tourist Information Centres

Tourist Information Centres, located all over Great Britain and Ireland, can help locate addresses, advise about distances within a city and between cities, provide brochures and pamphlets, and give touring information. They can also help find accommodations, and those that display the Local Bed and Breakfast Service sign have a booking service for individuals who personally call at the centre. Some will book a room in another town, but they also display a special sign. There is a small fee for these services. Obviously the earlier in the day this service is solicited, the better the chances of success, especially in the South of England over the summer months. Other crowded times are over bank holiday weekends or when there is a major local sporting event. There are more than seven hundred centres throughout Britain and they all display an official sign, which is easily recognizable, to designate their location. The British Tourist Authority provides a directory of centres which also indicates their services.

Locating Addresses

Addresses in the British Isles can be a real puzzle for a visitor. Streets may change names in the middle of a block, street names are often found on buildings rather than street signs, and there is a one-way system of streets used in towns, and occasional pedestrian areas where no cars are allowed. Sometimes an address is simply "County Hall," with no street or number. There are also wonderful terms, unfamiliar to Americans, such as Castle Precincts, The Close, or The Wellgate. Reproductions of maps supplied by record offices, libraries, and county and city councils, which may help alleviate difficulties, will be found in Appendix III.

Reorganization

A major reorganization of local government took place in April of 1986. The Greater London Council (GLC) and the metropolitan councils of Greater Manchester, Merseyside, South Yorkshire, Tyne and Wear, West Midlands and West Yorkshire were abolished. Most of their functions were transferred to smaller units, metropolitan district councils and, in the case of the GLC, to London Borough Councils. This should be considered when reading the particulars concerning institutions in these areas. It is believed that details

concerning location, collections, hours, etc., will not be very much
affected. Another upheaval occurred in 1974 when county boundary
lines were changed. At that time collections, locations, names of
counties and jurisdictions were altered. There are maps (p. 346 and
347) which show the counties in England, Scotland and Wales before
this change and another map (p. 348) which indicates the counties of
England and Wales and the regions of Scotland after the change.

The Institutions and Their Use

If there is one constant concerning record offices and libraries
in the British Isles, it is that things change. Telephone numbers,
hours of opening, even addresses and collections can be altered in
the blink of an eye. Administrative reorganization is not at all un-
common (see above). Expecting these developments and being prepared for them may help save time and ward off frustration.

Appointments

One way to defend against the unexpected is to call or write
ahead of a visit. Many record offices and libraries require an
appointment in advance, and some want a letter of introduction or
recommendation as well. Whether they do or not, it is always best
to call or write ahead. And again, sending along a self-addressed
envelope and postage is appreciated.

Equipment

One should go to a record office fully prepared with pencils,
paper, and money with which to purchase publications, photocopies,
or microfilm. Pens are not allowed and if one wants to use a tape
recorder or typewriter, it should be determined whether this is ap-
propriate beforehand. Researchers who wish to purchase photocopies or microfilm of records should not assume that they will be
made available immediately. There can be very long delays in some
institutions.

Access

Most record offices require that researchers sign their visitor's
book, and in doing so the individual agrees to abide by the regulations of that office. The scholar should also remember that there
are restrictions on certain public records and some cannot be viewed
for thirty years, some for fifty years, and some for one hundred
years. It is also possible that the owner of records privately donated will have placed restrictions on them that preclude their use.

Photocopying and Copyright

Copying of documents is not necessarily automatic. Material that is protected by copyright cannot be copied except under the terms of the copyright law. In the United Kingdom, copyright protection is automatic and the term is for the life of the author plus fifty years. It is "an infringement of copyright to reproduce or make an adaption of a substantial part of a work in any material form, or to publish a work, without the copyright owner's permission; the term 'substantial' is not defined in the Act and whether the copy would be so considered would have to be determined by the courts."[1] It is not an infringement of copyright to make a single copy for research purposes or for private study. Archivists will not allow fragile documents or those which might come to harm for whatever reason to be copied. Sometimes they can be photographed or filmed, but these are matters that must be decided on site.

Research for the Patron

Most record office staffs will not undertake extended research for a patron. "Brief inquiries," mentioned so often under "Other services" in the institutions entries of Chapter 2, means just that. Specific questions that can be dealt with quickly are answered and those concerning use of the facilities usually receive a response. Practice varies, of course, and sometimes research will be conducted, usually for a fee. In any event, lists of agents who do research are almost always available (and are sometimes specifically mentioned in the entries in Chapter 2), with the proviso that fees must be negotiated by the agent and the requesting party.

Research in Ireland

Those whose research will be centered in Ireland will be confronted with the complication caused by a fire in 1922 which destroyed the Public Record Office in Dublin. Many secondary sources are available, however, so research is not impossible. Among these sources is Griffith's Valuation (or the Primary Valuation), a survey of land taken between 1847 and 1865 which gives the names of those occupying the land and buildings, and tithe applotment books, created at the same time, which also give the names of those occupying land. These were prepared in order to ascertain the amount of tithe payments owed the Church of Ireland.

Attitude

Institutions are often understaffed and one must be prepared

---

1. Correspondence with K. J. Ingram, Department of Trade and Industry, Industrial Property and Copyright Department.

for delay. Some record offices supply requested documents only at set times, and sometimes one finds that the documents he wishes to consult are stored away from the premises and may take several days to retrieve. Also, the researcher should be as specific as possible and be prepared to use the indexes provided by the institution so that the request can be precise. The researcher should also gather as much information as possible before leaving home so his inquiry can be explicit. The more knowledge accumulated in advance, the less likely one is to be disappointed.

Chapter 2

INSTITUTIONS

ABERDEEN (map)

1	Institution Address	Aberdeen City Library Rosemount Viaduct Aberdeen AB9 1GU
	Telephone	0224 634622

Holdings — Genealogical material includes family histories and family trees, both printed and manuscript; old parochial registers, Aberdeen, Aberdeenshire, Banffshire and some parishes in Kincardineshire; detailed census returns for Aberdeen and Aberdeenshire, 1841, 1851, 1861, 1871, and 1881. There are also burial records and monumental inscriptions for many parts of Scotland. Also found are valuation rolls for Aberdeenshire, Banffshire, and Kincardineshire. Directories include the Aberdeen Almanac from 1734 to 1955 and Aberdeen Directory (which has ceased publication), 1824 to 1982/83. There are electoral rolls for Aberdeen and Aberdeenshire, school and university records, and 19th-century ordinance survey maps for the counties of Aberdeen, Banff, Caithness, Clackmannan, Elgin, Forfar, Kincardine, Orkney and Shetland, Perth, Ross and Cromarty, and Sutherland. Modern maps are available for the Aberdeen City District and for the Grampian Region. A detailed list of the holdings is found in the library's publication, Links in the Chain.

Conditions of admission and access — The library is open to the public, but the material must be used on the premises. Inquiries should be addressed to the City Librarian.

Hours — 9:00 AM - 9:00 PM, Monday-Friday; 9:00 AM - 5:00 PM, Saturday.

Duplicating facilities — Photocopying service is available.

Other services — Reference service is provided and inquiries are answered by telephone and by mail, but detailed searches cannot be undertaken.

Publications	Links in the Chain, compiled by Moira Henderson, 1984.

ABERDEEN (map)

2 Institution Address	City of Aberdeen District Archives The Town House Aberdeen AB9 1AQ
Telephone	0224 642121, ext. 513
Holdings	Older registers of burial grounds in the charge of Aberdeen Town Council are found in this collection. These include St. Peter's, 1769-1951; St. Nicholas, 1855-1925; St. Clements, 1855-1927; John Knox, 1837-1894; and Old Machar, 1863-1906. Minutes and reports of Aberdeen Parish Council and of St. Nicholas Parochial Board are also found here.
Conditions of admission and access	An appointment must be made to use the collection. Inquiries should be directed to the City Archivist. The material must be used on the premises.
Hours	9:30 AM - 12:30 PM, 2:00 PM - 4:30 PM, Monday-Friday.
Duplicating facilities	Photocopy services are available and photographic reproductions can also be made. Copying is done at the discretion of the Archivist.
Other services	Reference help is provided and brief questions by telephone or post are answered.
Publications	None.

ABERDEEN (map)

3 Institution Address	Grampian Regional Archives Woodhill House Ashgrove Road West Aberdeen AB9 2LU
Telephone	0224 682222, ext. 2130
Holdings	Valuation Rolls from the late 19th century to date are held and include Aberdeen City from 1974/75; Aberdeenshire from 1859/60; Banffshire from 1877/78; Kincardineshire from 1862/63. Parochial Board and Parish Council records for Aberdeenshire, Banffshire and Kincardineshire are found in the collection and include records of applications for relief and registers of poor. (Records of Banffshire Parishes now within the Moray District are found in the Moray District Record Office, listed under Forres, Entry no. 104.) School Admission

Registers and Log Books for Aberdeen and the Counties of Aberdeen, Banff and Kincardine are located here.

Conditions of admission and access	An appointment must be made to use the collection. Inquiries should be made to the Regional Archivist. The material may be used only on the premises.
Hours	9:00 AM - 5:00 PM, Monday-Friday.
Duplicating facilities	Photocopy services are available and photographic reproductions can also be made.
Other services	None.
Publications	None.

ABERDEEN

4 Institution Address	North-east of Scotland Library Service 14 Crown Terrace Aberdeen
Telephone	0224 572658
Holdings	Newsletters and minutes of Community Council meetings are held from 1975, as well as voters' rolls and valuation rolls. Records and plans of the Stricken Estate and papers from the Auchmedden Estate are found. Records of local societies, maps, plans, and photographs of the area are kept.
Conditions of admission and access	The library service is open to the public and no appointment in advance is required. Inquiries should be directed to the Local History Librarian. The collection must be used on the premises.
Hours	9:00 AM - 5:00 PM, Monday-Friday.
Duplicating facilities	Photocopying equipment is provided.
Other services	Brief questions by post or telephone are answered and reference help is available. Microform equipment is also provided.
Publications	None.

ABERYSTWYTH (map)

5 Institution Address	Cardiganshire Area Record Office County Offices Marine Terrace Aberystwyth SY23 2DE

The Cardiganshire Area Record Office is part of the Dyfed Archive Service. See also: Carmarthen (Carmarthenshire Record Office) and Haverfordwest (Pembrokeshire Record Office).

Holdings

The record office is the repository for the records of the former Cardiganshire County Council, the municipal boroughs of Aberystwyth, Cardigan and Lampeter, urban and rural district councils and some parish councils. Official and private documents of local and historical interest are retained here and include records of some Cardiganshire schools and material relating to statutory bodies, such as the Welsh Water Authority. Public records include Coroners' records, records of the Petty Sessions, Aberystwyth hospital and Local Medical Committee, shipping registers, and some crew agreements and log books of ships registered at Aberystwyth. Access to this class of records is restricted for at least thirty years (and in some instances, seventy-five or one hundred years). Electoral registers dating from the nineteenth century are found here. No original parish registers are held, as the repository for the ecclesiastical records for the Cardiganshire Area is the National Library of Wales (also at Aberystwyth). The office does, however, have indexes and transcripts of some parish registers of St. Michael's, Aberystwyth and St. Padarn, Llanbadarn-fawr, microfilms of some parish registers of Henfynyw and Llanddewi Aberarth Nantewnlle, Llanbadorn Trefeglwys, and Cilcennin, and microfilms of Cardiganshire non-parochial registers at the Public Record Office. Census returns for Cardiganshire for 1841-1881 (at ten-year intervals) are also held on microfilm, and transcripts and indexes of the census returns, 1841-1871, for Aberystwyth and the North Cardiganshire Rural Districts are available for consultation.

Conditions of admission and access

The record office is open to the public and no prior appointment is required, but is advisable for those requiring the use of microform readers. Inquiries should be made to the Records Assistant. All material must be used on the premises.

Hours

9:00 AM - 1:00 PM, 2:00 PM - 4:45 PM, Tuesday and Thursday.

Duplicating facilities

Full-size and microcopying facilities are available. A list of charges is provided on request.

Other services

Brief questions are answered by mail and telephone and reference help is available in the office. Limited searches are undertaken by staff, and longer searches may be conducted for a fee. Lectures are given and exhibits are arranged whenever feasible. Schedules of most of the collections housed at the record office are available for consultation in the search room. Copies of schedules of records deposited in the offices at Carmarthen and Haverfordwest are also provided, and at those offices the Cardiganshire office schedules are found.

Publications

There are a number of publications both for sale and issued without charge by the Dyfed Archive Service. These include Carmarthenshire Record Office; A Survey of Archive Holdings, by S. Beckley (1980); A Guide to Parish Registers in St. Davids Diocese; A Guide to Local Newspapers in Dyfed; An Introduction to Local Maps on Dyfed; Notes for Searchers; Tracing Your Ancestors; List of Record Agents; History of Houses; Summaries of Main Collections: Cardiganshire Record Office, Carmarthenshire Record Office, Pembrokeshire Record Office; and Topic Lists. These Lists give an indication of material available concerning different subjects. Those relating to documents in Aberystwyth are: Education in Cardiganshire, Railways in Cardiganshire, Cardiganshire Roads and Bridges, Lampeter, Cardiganshire Shipping and Harbour Records, Cardigan. A list of publications is available on request.

ABERYSTWYTH

Institution

Dyfed Archive Service
See: ABERYSTWYTH, Cardiganshire Area
Record Office

ABERYSTWYTH (map)

6 Institution
   Address

National Library of Wales
Aberystwyth SY23 3BU

Telephone

0970 3816, ext. 216

Holdings

The library is a copyright library and holds the world's largest collection of books in the Welsh language or books relating to Wales. It also contains special material relating to other Celtic countries. It is of interest to the genealogist that the library is a repository for manorial and estate records. These include those of Badminton (estates of the Duke of Beaufort in South Wales), Bronwydd (Southwest Wales), the Marquis of Bute (Cardiff area), Carreglwyd (Anglesey), Chirk Castle (Northeast Wales), Llanfair and Brynodol (Caernarfonshire), Penrice and Margam (Glamorgan and Gwent), Wynnstay (North Wales, especially Denbighshire). Some of these archives relate to industrial as well as landed property.
    The diocesan and capitular records of the Church

in Wales, records of many of the Welsh parishes and tithe maps and awards for Wales are part of the collection. The archives of the Welsh Church Commissioners (relating to the temporalities of the Church) and pre-1858 Welsh probate records are held in the library. Post-1660 subsidiary classes of the records of the Court of Great Sessions in Wales have been in the library since 1909 and in 1962 it received the main body of the records of the Court, which for some counties cover the whole period of the life of the Court from 1542 to 1830. The library also is the depository for the Quarter Sessions records of the former counties of Brecon, Montgomeryshire and Radnor. Official county records once deposited in the library have been transferred to the county record offices. Unofficial records and parish records may still be found either in the library or in the county record offices. Non-conformists' records and archives, notably those of the Presbyterian Church of Wales, are preserved from the 1730s. Other non-conformist denominations are represented to a greater or lesser extent. Institutions, businesses, political groups and individuals have also left their papers and records to the care of the library.

Conditions of admission and access	Admission is by reader's ticket and an application form can be obtained from the Librarian. Visiting scholars should have a letter of introduction specifying the kinds of material they wish to use. The material does not circulate and must be used on the premises. The user should know that the library is divided into three parts: the Department of Printed Books, the Department of Manuscripts and Records (which holds the genealogical material described above), and the Department of Pictures and Maps.
Hours	9:30 AM - 6:00 PM, Monday-Friday; 9:30 AM - 5:00 PM, Saturday.
Duplicating facilities	Full-sized and microcopies are available and photographic reproduction and photostating can be provided.
Other services	Reference service is provided and information will be given by telephone or by mail. Ultra-violet lamps for reading manuscripts are provided, as well as equipment for using microforms.

Publications	Bibliotheca Celtica, A Register of Celtic Publications (annual); Subject Index to Welsh Periodicals (annual); Llyfryddiaeth Cymru: A Bibliography of Wales (this supersedes the first two publications listed); National Library of Wales Journal (semi-annual); Handlist of Manuscripts; Annual Reports (containing preliminary descriptions of accessions), and A Nation's Treasury, 1982.

ABERYSTWYTH (map)

7 Institution Address	The Royal Commission on Ancient and Historical Monuments in Wales National Monuments Record Edleston House Queen's Road Aberystwyth SY23 2HP
Telephone	0970 4381/4382
Holdings	The collection includes thousands of plans and photographs of buildings in Wales. Photographs from the Welsh section of the National Building Record and copies of listed buildings are also found. There are Ordnance Survey maps and several special collections, including that of Herbert L. North which relates to arts and crafts movements in Wales. The material acquired by the field work of the staff forms the major part of the holdings.
Conditions of admission and access	The public may use the collection on the premises without prior arrangements. Inquiries should be directed to the Secretary.
Hours	9:30 AM - 12:30 PM, 2:00 PM - 5:00 PM, Monday-Friday.
Duplicating facilities	Photocopying facilities are available and photography can be provided.
Other services	Brief questions by post or telephone are answered and reference help is available. Finding aids and indexes are provided.
Publications	Inventories are published through Her Majesty's Stationery Office. HMSO has a list of those available.

AIRDRIE

8 Institution Address	Monklands District Local Collection Airdrie Library Wellwynd Airdrie ML6 0AG
Telephone	02364 63221

Holdings	The local history collection contains material from Airdrie and Coatbridge and the surrounding area, and includes maps, photographs, pamphlets, substantial works, and ephemera. The Gartsherrie estate minute books and the Weavers' Society minutes are also held.
Conditions of admission and access	The library is open to the public and an appointment in advance is not required. Inquiries should be directed to the Local History Librarian. The collection must be used on the premises.
Hours	9:30 AM - 7:30 PM, Monday-Tuesday, Thursday-Friday; 9:30 AM - 12:30 PM, 1:30 PM - 5:00 PM, Saturday; closed Wednesday.
Duplicating facilities	Full-sized copying facilities are available and photography can be provided.
Other services	Microform equipment is available and brief questions by post or telephone are answered. Reference help is provided.
Publications	Monklands, 1980.

ALDERNEY, CHANNEL ISLANDS   See: ST. ANNE'S

ANDOVER

9 Institution Address	Hampshire County Library Andover Borough Archives Chantry Way Andover SP10 1LT
Telephone	0264 52807
Holdings	The collection is composed of the records acquired while the Andover Borough Council functioned. It includes Town Council minutes, legal records, papers of local bodies, court records, charity groups, archives and royal charters.
Conditions of admission and access	Permission must be obtained to use the collection. Researchers should apply to: The Borough Secretary and Solicitor, Test Valley Borough Council, Beech Hurst, Weyhill Road, Andover SP10 3AJ. Other inquiries should be directed to the Senior Librarian. The collection must be used on the premises.
Hours	10:00 AM - 7:00 PM, Monday-Tuesday, Thursday-Friday; 10:00 AM - 4:00 PM, Saturday; closed Wednesday.
Duplicating facilities	Full-size copying facilities are available.

Other services	Brief questions by post or telephone are answered and reference help is available. A catalogue of the material is provided.
Publications	Pamphlets, brochures, and guides are produced.

ANGUS COUNTY See: DUNDEE

ANGUS DISTRICT

Institution	Angus District Libraries and Museums See: ARBROATH, Arbroath Library and Art Gallery ARBROATH, Signal Tower Museum BRECHIN, Public Library and Museum FORFAR, Forfar Public Library MONTROSE, Montrose Public Library

ARBROATH

10 Institution Address	Angus District Libraries and Museums Arbroath Library and Art Gallery Hill Terrace Arbroath
Telephone	0241 72248 (See also: ARBROATH, Angus District Libraries and Museums, Arbroath Signal Tower Museum)
Holdings	The collection includes town council records (1741-1891), business records and those concerning local labor movements. Papers of societies and associations and charitable organizations are kept. Private archives and maps and plans date from the 18th century.
Conditions of admission and access	Researchers must make application in writing to be allowed to use the collection. Inquiries should be directed to the Librarian. The collection must be used on the premises.
Hours	9:30 AM - 6:00 PM, Monday-Saturday.
Duplicating facilities	Arrangements can be made for photocopying.
Other services	Brief questions by post or telephone are answered and reference help is provided. Lists of the archives are available.
Publications	None.

ARBROATH

11 Institution	Angus District Libraries and Museums

Address	Arbroath Signal Tower Museum Ladyloan Arbroath DD11 1PU
Telephone	0241 75598 (See also: ARBROATH, Angus District Libraries and Museums, Arbroath Library and Art-Gallery)
Holdings	The records of Arbroath Burgess, 1790-1849, are held, as well as private papers which date from the 18th century. The Arbroath Museum Society records, 1843-1918 are held and archives of the Alex Shanks Dens Ironworks, including catalogs of equipment from the 19th century are found.
Conditions of admission and access	Researchers should make a written request to use the collection. Inquiries should be directed to the Curator. The collection must be used on the premises.
Hours	9:30 AM - 1:00 PM, 2:00 PM - 5:00 PM, Monday-Saturday.
Duplicating facilities	Copying facilities are not available.
Other services	Brief questions by post or telephone are answered and reference help is provided. A list of the material has been produced.
Publications	None.

ARMAGH

12 Institution Address	Armagh County Museum The Mall, East Armagh BT61 9BE, Co. Armagh
Telephone	0861 523070
Holdings	The museum holds several volumes of Armagh pedigrees (compiled by T. G. F. Paterson), specimen leases, but no grants, and an Armagh Freeholders book (1753). There are volumes of early 19th-century voter lists, militia and yeomanry lists and records and army lists. One also finds a Poll Book of 1753, a Hearth Money Roll of 1664 and a Museum Roll of 1630. Abstracts from Parish Registers are held, as are Griffith's Valuation and Index and the Census of Armagh City, 1770.
Conditions of admission and access	Research students have access to manuscripts at the discretion of the Curator. The records must be used on the premises. Inquiries should be addressed to the Curator.
Hours	10:00 AM - 1:00 PM, 2:00 PM - 5:00 PM, Monday-Saturday.

Duplicating facilities	Photocopying facilities are available.
Other services	Telephone and postal inquiries are answered and reference help is available.
Publications	None.

ARMAGH

13 Institution Address	Armagh Public Library Armagh, Co. Armagh
Telephone	Unknown (Requests for information from this library failed to elicit a response, therefore many details are lacking.)
Holdings	The library contains court records, Armagh manorial rolls and rent rolls, visitation books, military records, and corporation records. The census of Kilmore, County Armagh (1821) is located here. Family papers and the archives of individuals include those of John Lodge, and the Walter Harris manuscripts. Abstracts of wills, family histories, and pedigrees are also held.
Conditions of admission and access	Details are unknown except that inquiries should be addressed to the Director.
Hours	Unknown
Duplicating facilities	Unknown
Other services	Unknown
Publications	Catalogue of Manuscripts in the Public Library of Armagh, by J. Dean (1928).

AYLESBURY

14 Institution Address	Buckinghamshire Archaeological Society County Museum Church Street Aylesbury HP20 2QP
Telephone	0296 82158
Holdings	The museum holds manorial documents and deeds, mainly medieval, relating to Buckinghamshire. There are also copies of parish registers available.
Conditions of	Members of the society are admitted at any time

admission and
access

during opening hours, but non-members must make
an appointment to use the material. It is necessary
for visiting scholars to call ahead of time. All
records and documents must be used on the
premises. Inquiries should be made to the Hon.
Archivist.

Hours

Members of the society may use the library from
10:00 AM - 12:30 PM, and 1:30 PM - 4:45 PM,
Monday-Friday; 10:00 AM - 12:30 PM, 2:00 PM -
4:00 PM, Saturday. Non-members are admitted
on Wednesday from 10:00 AM - 12:30 PM and
1:30 PM - 3:30 PM.

Duplicating
facilities

Copying facilities are not available.

Other services

Information is given to the public as well as to
members by telephone and by mail.

Publications

Records of Buckinghamshire (annual); Newsletter
(three times a year). These publications are sent
to members.

AYLESBURY

15 Institution
Address

Buckinghamshire Record Office
County Hall
Aylesbury HP20 1UA

Telephone

0296 5000, ext. 587

Holdings

The collection contains official records of the county
and private papers. It is the Diocesan Record Office for the county of Buckingham and thus the approved place of deposit for parish registers and
records, including those of parishes now in other
counties. The office also holds the older records
of the archdeaconry proper. Records of the Bucks
peculiars, formerly at Oxford, were transferred to
this office in 1981. Official records include Quarter
sessions (from 1678), County Council (from 1889),
and Lieutenancy. Among the transferred records
of official bodies functioning within the county are
Archdeaconry of Buckingham, Parish, Coroners,
Poor Law Guardians, District Councils, Petty Sessions, School Board, Constabulary, and non-
conformist. The non-conformist church records include Baptists, Independents or Congregational,
Wesleyan, Primitive Methodists (thirty-three congre-
gations in all), registers of birth or baptisms and
burials, 1765-1837. Some post-1837 records are
also held. Parish registers of christenings, marriages and burials from 1538 survive in varying
degrees of completeness. Microfilm copies of some
registers not deposited are also found. Entries in

earlier registers are not in any set order and may be in Latin. Bishop's Transcripts are also found in the collection. Wills, Letters of Administration, title deeds, manorial records, settlement certificates and apprenticeship records are also kept. There are private deposits of personal, family, estate, and business records.

Conditions of admission and access

The record office is open to the public, but it is strongly advised that searchers reserve a seat in the reading room at least a week before their intended visit, and two weeks during school holidays. If microfilm of a record is held, this is usually produced in order to reduce wear on the original. Inquiries should be addressed to the County Archivist. Those from countries other than Great Britain should be accompanied by three international reply coupons to cover postage. All material must be used on the premises.

Hours

9:00 AM - 5:15 PM, Tuesday-Thursday; 9:00 AM - 4:45 PM, Friday. There is extended opening to 7:45 PM on the first Wednesday of each month, but only by prior appointment. Closed Monday.

Duplicating facilities

Full-sized copies and microcopies can be supplied, and photographic reproduction can be arranged in consultation with the record office. Orders for photostatic copies of large documents cannot be executed at the office, but arrangements can be made for the work to be done professionally; a delay of up to six weeks is entailed. A leaflet giving details of reprographic services and prices is available.

Other services

Postal inquiries can be answered only if they do not involve extensive research. There are guides, indexes and catalogs available to help the searcher in the use of the material (described in the leaflet Notes for the Guidance of Genealogists), and also a small selection of general reference works available. Reference help is provided and a list of record searchers will be supplied on request. The record office is equipped with microfilm readers and ultra-violet lamps, and manuscript repair facilities are available.

Publications

Buckinghamshire Sessions Records, 1678-1730, Vol. I-VII, 1933-1953; A Handlist of Buckinghamshire Enclosure Acts and Awards, by W. E. Tate, 1946; Education Records, 1961; Archdeaconry Records, 1961; Catalogue of Maps, 1961; Parliamentary Enclosure; Parliamentary Elections in Bucks to 1832; An Eighteenth Century Squire; Dr. Lee of Harwell, 1783-1866, by H. A. Hanley, 1983; Notes for the Guidance of Genealogists; Annual Report and List of Accessions. Facsimiles of maps, posters,

handbills, railway timetables, and other documents
are also obtainable. A list of these publications,
their availability, price and ordering information,
is provided.

AYR

16	Institution Address	Ayrshire Sub-region Archives County Buildings Wellington Square Ayr KA7 1DR
	Telephone	0292 266922, ext. 348 (See also: GLASGOW, Strathclyde Regional Archives)
	Holdings	The holdings include family collections covering Kirkmichael and North Ayrshire farms and valuation rolls from 1892 onward (excluding burghs). There are copies of the census for Colmowell for 1871 and 1881 and baptismal register copies for Colmowell for 1759 and 1800-1854. Also found are copies of bap- tismal registers of Girvan for 1820-1854. A large collection of Ayrshire Poor Law records dating from 1845 is also held.
	Conditions of admission and access	The archives are open to the public without prior appointment. Inquiries should be directed to the Archivist. The collection must be consulted on the premises.
	Hours	9:30 AM - 1:00 PM, 2:00 PM - 4:30 PM, Wednesday only.
	Duplicating facilities	Facilities are available for photocopying, photog- raphy and dyelining.
	Other services	Postal inquiries and those by telephone are answered.
	Publications	Family History--A Guide to Ayrshire Sources, ed. by Jane Maclean (1984).

BALBY   See: DONCASTER

BANGOR

17	Institution Address	University College of North Wales The Library Department of Manuscripts Bangor LL57 2DG
	Telephone	0248 51151, ext. 316

Holdings	The collection includes Quarter Sessions records for the Borough of Beaumaris, family and estate papers and business and trade archives, including those for mines and quarries. There are manuscript records relating to Beaumaris and Anglesey, Baron Hill, Bodrhyddan, Bodorgan, Maesyneuadd, Mastyn, Kinmel, Nannau, Plas Cock and Plas Newydd, Porth yr aur, and Penrhyn Castle. Ordnance Survey maps are also held.
Conditions of admission and access	Visiting scholars are welcome to use the collection but an appointment should be made in advance. Inquiries should be addressed to the Archivist and Keeper of Manuscripts. The collection must be used on the premises.
Hours	9:15 AM - 4:45 PM, Monday-Tuesday, Thursday-Friday; 9:15 AM - 8:50 PM, Wednesday, during the term. 9:15 AM - 4:45 PM, Monday-Friday during vacation.
Duplicating facilities	Full-size copying facilities are available and photography can be provided.
Other services	Brief questions by post or telephone are answered and reference service is provided. Microform equipment is available and there are catalogs and indexes to help the researcher.
Publications	Guides, brochures, and lists.

BARKING   See: LONDON, London Borough of Barking and Dagenham

BARNET   See: LONDON, London Borough of Barnet

BARNSLEY

18 Institution Address	Barnsley Central Library Local Studies Department Barnsley S70 2JF
Telephone	0226 83241
Holdings	Minutes, rate books and other papers for the borough are held from the early 19th century. There are also non-conformist records from local Methodist churches and papers of societies, charitable organizations, and businesses available. In addition, there are photographs and a collection of postcards.
Conditions of admission and access	The collection is open to the public and while no prior appointment is required, advance notice of a visit is preferred and strongly urged for a

Saturday visit. Inquiries should be made to the Local History Librarian. The material must be used on the premises.

Hours   9:30 AM - 8:00 PM, Monday, Wednesday; 9:30 AM - 6:00 PM, Tuesday, Thursday-Friday; 9:30 AM - 5:00 PM, Saturday (with advance notice).

Duplicating   Photocopying facilities are available.
facilities

Other services   Brief questions by post or by telephone are answered and reference service is available. Microform equipment is provided. There are finding aids to further help the scholar and lists of the material are in preparation.

Publications   Lists are produced.

BARROW-IN-FURNESS
(map)

19 Institution   Cumbria Record Office (Barrow)
   Address   140 Duke Street
                     Barrow-in-Furness LA12 1XW

   Telephone   0229 31269
                     (See also: CARLISLE, Cumbria Record Office;
                     KENDAL, Cumbria Record Office)

   Holdings   Church registers for Southwest Cumbria, which includes most of Furness, are found here. Parish registers include (but are not limited to) Aldingham, St. Cuthberts (1539-1978); Barrow-in-Furness, St. George's (1861-1969), St. James' (1867-1963), St. John's (1876-1946), St. Paul's (1870-1960), St. Mark's (1878-1962), St. Matthew's (1878-1971), St. Luke's (1878-1976), St. Perran's (1894-1972); Millom, Holy Trinity (1590-1960); Dalton-in-Furness, St. Mary's (1565-1883); Lowick, St. Luke's (1718-1947); Broughton-in-Furness, St. Mary Magdalene (1634-1971); Pennington, St. Michael's (1612-1979); Seathwaite, Holy Trinity (1684-1975); Ulverston, St. Mary's (1545-1975); Woodland, St. John's (1735-1956). There are also Bishop's Transcripts and some Methodist, Quaker, and Presbyterian registers. Records from local authorities, schools, businesses and solicitors are also kept, and records of several Furness manors (approximately from 1740 to 1928) will be found. The office is a repository for manorial and tithe documents and for ecclesiastical records of the Archdeaconry of Furness. Many records of the Furness estates of the Dukes of Buccleuch (ca. 1820-1960) are located in the record office. These relate particularly to local iron mining. Also

available here are Barrow Borough Council
Records, 1867-1970s, Barrow Quarter Sessions
records, 1962-1971 (these are subject to restric-
tion for up to one hundred years), Vickers' (shipbuilders) gun-mounting drawings, 1890-1950, and
many other business and family records.

Conditions of admission and access	No appointment is necessary to use the search room, but patrons requiring any special service are advised to notify the office ahead of their visit. All material must be used on the premises. Inquiries should be directed to the Archivist-in-Charge.
Hours	9:00 AM - 5:00 PM, Monday-Friday.
Duplicating facilities	Full-size copies can be made at the office. Microcopies and other copying processes are available by arrangement.
Other services	Reference help is provided and short inquiries will be answered by mail or telephone, but detailed or lengthy searches are not undertaken. There is a small library of reference books in the record office, and the Barrow Central Library (where copies of local census returns are held) is next door.
Publications	Leaflets are provided which serve as guides to the record office and a list of the register holdings is available. A Genealogical Guide, planned for publication in the near future, will include all three Cumbria Record Offices. Also available is a map, "Church of England Parishes in Cumbria," which is sold by all three offices.

BATH (map)

20	Institution Address	Bath City Record Office Guildhall Bath BA1 5AW
	Telephone	0225 61111, ext. 201
	Holdings	The City records held by the record office include (but are by no means limited to): Charters, 1189-1973; Commissions, etc., 1275-1662; Deeds, 1218-1900; Hall Notice Books, 1776-1895; Freemen's Rolls, 1712 to date; Freemen's Accounts, 1776-1880; Militia Orders, Papers and Lists (St. James), 1795-1830; Quarter Sessions sessions Books, 1683-1785, Court Rolls, 1776-1971, Court Papers, 1786-1835. The Petty Sessions record extends from 1851 to 1933. There is no index of personal names for either the Quarter Sessions or Petty Sessions records. Rate Books and Valuation Lists from 1766

(City Parishes), 1775 (Walcot), 1777 (St. Michaels), 1779 (St. James), 1784 (Abbey), 1796 (Lyncombe and Widcombe), 1818 (Bathwick), 1821 (Twerton) are found, and minutes and other records of Council Committees, many of which include sub-committee records, are also kept. Among these are Baths and Pump Room, 1774-1969; Fire Brigade, 1891-1968; Housing of Working Classes, 1894-1968; Markets, 1837-1960; and Parks and Cemeteries, 1891-1973. The Bathwick Police records, 1835-1851 and Walcot Police records, 1766-1822 are found as are maps and plans from the 18th to the 20th century, and Bath Poor Law Union records. Transcripts and indexes of registers of Bath parishes include St. Peter and St. Paul (Abbey), 1569-1840; St. James, 1569-1840; St. Michael, 1679-1840; Lyncombe and Widcombe, 1813-1840; Twerton, 1538-1942; Weston, 1538-1969. There are also records of the Methodist Churches (the earliest of which is 1792) and the Trinity Presbyterian Church, 1920-1973. There is a small collection of Office copy wills (17th-20th century), which are indexed, and among the title deeds are the Bath Corporation leases, 1581-1900, which are also indexed. There are smaller collections of deeds which are not indexed. Private deposits include the Bathwick Estate Company (deeds, 1780-1910); Royal Bath and West and Southern Counties Society (Minutes, 1777-1960; Correspondence, 1777-1960; Accounts, 1777-1805; Sub-Committees' Minutes, 1777-1954). The Library of the Society, which contains many valuable items, has been placed in the University of Bath Library.

Conditions of admission and access	The office is open to the public and no appointment is necessary. All material must be used on the premises. Inquiries should be directed to the City Archivist.
Hours	9:00 AM - 1:00 PM, 2:00 PM - 5:00 PM, Monday-Thursday; 9:00 AM - 1:00 PM, 2:00 PM - 4:30 PM, Friday.
Duplication facilities	Full-sized copies can be provided at the Record Office. Photographic reproductions can also be made.
Other services	Ultra-violet lamps are available for reading manuscripts. Reference help is given and short questions are answered on the telephone or by mail.
Publications	The office has issued no publications of its own, but a list of the principal holdings can be found in Avon Local History Handbook, by J. S. Moore (1979).

BATHGATE

21	Institution Address	West Lothian District Library Wellpark Majoribanks Street Bathgate EH48 1AN

Telephone   0506 52866/630300

Holdings   Town Council minutes for Bathgate, Linlithgow, Armadale, and Whitburn and County Council minutes for West Lothian are held (19th and 20th century). District Council minutes found include East Calder, West Calder, Uphall and Whitburn, and Torphichen and Bathgate (19th and 20th century). There is also a collection of local newspapers dating from 1883.

Conditions of admission and access   The library is open to the public and no prior arrangements to use the collection are required. Inquiries should be directed to the Chief Assistant. The collection must be used in the Library.

Hours   8:30 AM - 5:00 PM, Monday-Thursday, 8:30 AM - 4:00 PM, Friday.

Duplicating facilities   Photocopying facilities are available.

Other services   Brief questions by telephone or post are answered and reference service is available. Microform equipment is provided. There are catalogs, lists and indexes to further aid the scholar.

Publications   None.

BEDFORD (map)

22	Institution Address	Bedfordshire County Record Office County Hall Bedford MK42 9AP

Telephone   0234 63222, ext. 276

Holdings   The record office holds county records and is a repository for manorial and tithe documents and for ecclesiastical records for St. Albans (Archdeaconry of Bedford). Parish Registers for all old parishes are kept and those before 1812 are typed and indexed. The wills proved in the Archdeaconry of Bedford up to 1857 are also found.

Conditions of admission and access   The collection is open to all searchers, but restrictions are placed on certain types of (mainly recent) documents. Neither a letter of introduction nor a previous appointment is usually required, but certain depositors request their written permission before allowing photocopying. All material must be used on the premises. Inquiries should be made to the County Archivist.

Hours

9:15 AM - 1:00 PM, 2:00 PM - 5:00 PM, Monday-Friday.

Duplicating facilities

Full-sized and microcopies can be provided. There is a minimum charge of Ł2 for all items sent by post. Photographic reproductions can also be made.

Other services

Microform equipment is available and reference help is provided. Brief questions will be answered by mail. There are facilities for the repair of manuscripts and in some cases this service is available to outside bodies or individuals.

Publications

Guide to the Bedfordshire Record Office (1957); Supplements (1962, 1966).

BELFAST (map)

23 Institution Address

Belfast Library and Society for Promoting Knowledge
Linen Hall Library
17 Donegall Square, North
Belfast BT1 5GD

Telephone

0232 221707

Holdings

The collection includes a Register of Births, Marriages and Deaths extracted from the Belfast Newsletter, 1738-1840 (which is presently being updated). The Blackwood collection of about six hundred family histories in manuscript, mainly of County Down families; indexes to wills; records of different churches; published genealogies; army lists; information concerning landed gentry; hearth money rolls; and lists of voters are also found.

Conditions of admission and access

The collection is open to the public and no advance appointment or letter of introduction is necessary. The records may be consulted only on the premises.

Hours

9:30 AM - 6:00 PM, Monday-Wednesday, Friday; 9:30 AM - 8:30 PM, Thursday; 9:30 AM - 4:00 PM, Saturday.

Duplicating facilities

Full-sized copies can be provided on the premises.

Other services

Reference help is available and brief questions will be answered by mail or telephone.

Publications	A catalogue of the genealogical collection is in preparation.

BELFAST (map)

24 Institution	Belfast Public Library
Address	Irish and Local Studies Department
	Royal Avenue
	Belfast BT1 1EA
Telephone	02 43233
Holdings	A large collection of biographies and family histories gives comprehensive coverage of Irish genealogy. There is a major collection of news-papers both in paper and on microfilm and a fully indexed series of cuttings books which complement it. Complete sets of minutes for thirteen of the twenty-six District Councils in Northern Ireland, for three of the four Health and Social Services Boards, and for all the Library and Education Boards are found, and a complete set of Belfast District Council minutes and the minutes of the Old Belfast City Corporation are held. There is a col-lection of early maps dating from the 16th to the early 19th century. The archives of F. J. Bigger, J. S. Crone, A. S. Moore, A. Riddell, and W. S. Ryan are kept here. A photographic collection is expanding rapidly and contains several major de-posits. Political ephemera, material on the theatre and cinema, literary manuscripts, directories, and government publications are also held.
Conditions of admission and access	The collection is stored in areas of the library closed to the public, but will be retrieved for use in the reading rooms as requested. Use of some material is restricted to those engaged in serious research and with appropriate credentials. An ap-pointment in advance is strongly recommended. Some works are stored outside the main building and arrangements for their use should be made ahead of time to avoid inconvenience. The collec-tion must be used on the premises. Inquiries should be directed to the Librarian.
Hours	9:30 AM - 8:00 PM, Monday, Thursday; 9:30 AM - 5:30 PM, Tuesday-Wednesday, Friday; 9:30 AM - 1:00 PM, Saturday.
Duplicating facilities	Photocopying facilities and full-size copies from microfilm are provided.
Other services	Postal and telephone inquiries are welcome and reference help is available.
Publications	Catalogues, guides, including Guide to Irish and

Local Studies Department, lists and brochures are produced.

BELFAST

25	Institution	General Register Office
	Address	Department of Health and Social Services
		Oxford House
		49-55 Chichester Street
		Belfast BT1 4HL

Telephone   0232 235211

Holdings   The collection contains records of births, deaths, marriages, and adopted children's certificates as follows: Birth and Death Registers, 1864 to date; Marriage Registers, 1922 to date (Marriage Registers, 1844-1921 are held by District Registrars); and Adopted Children's Registers, 1931 to date--but these are not available to the public. It holds the Registrar General's Annual Reports for Ireland, 1864-1921 and the Annual Reports for Northern Ireland; Vital Statistics of Northern Ireland since 1922; Census of Population as follows: 1841, 1851, 1861, 1871, 1881, 1891, 1901, 1911, 1926, 1937, 1951, 1961, 1966, 1971, and 1981. The Medical Sections contain material relating to diseases and methods of coding deaths.

Conditions of admission and access   The office is open to the public, but an appointment in advance is required to use the collection. Access is allowed to the Indexes and a photocopy verification of any entry can be obtained. Inquiries should be directed to the Registrar General.

Hours   9:30 AM - 3:30 PM, Monday-Friday.

Duplicating facilities   Facilities for full-sized copying are available.

Other services   No reference help is provided, but brief questions will be answered by mail or telephone.

Publications   Quarterly Returns; Registrar General's Annual Report.

BELFAST

Institution   Linen Hall Library
See: Belfast Library and Society for Promoting Knowledge, Linen Hall Library

BELFAST

26 Institution   Presbyterian Historical Society of Ireland

Address	Church House Fisherwick Place Belfast BT1 6DU
Telephone	0232 323936
Holdings	The principal interest reflected by this collection is in the history of ministers and congregations in the Presbyterian Church in Ireland. Some baptismal and marriage records are held. Information concerning the location of records is provided for a fee.
Conditions of admission and access	The collection is open to the public, but an appointment in advance is advisable. Inquiries should be directed to the Hon. Secretary. The material may be consulted only on the premises.
Hours	10:00 AM - 12:30 PM, Monday-Tuesday, Thursday-Friday; 10:00 AM - 1:00 PM, 2:00 PM - 4:00 PM, Wednesday.
Duplicating facilities	Photocopying facilities are available.
Other services	Very brief questions by telephone are answered. Postal inquiries will be answered if accompanied by a self-addressed airmail envelope, two international reply coupons and a fee. Some reference help is provided.
Publications	Indexes and lists are produced for in-house use.

BELFAST

27		
	Institution Address	Public Record Office 66 Balmoral Avenue Belfast BT9 6NY
	Telephone	0232 661621 or 663286
	Holdings	The Public Record Office receives the records of the Northern Ireland Government departments and of the Supreme Court of Judicature and all inferior courts. The collections include works on historical, political, social and economic development of Northern Ireland. The period covered is from ca. 1650. Unfortunately many 1900 Irish papers were destroyed in 1922. The surviving ones are the basic source and post-1920 records of the Northern Ireland administration reflect every function of the government. Ecclesiastical collections include administrative records for the Church of Ireland dioceses of Down and Connor and Dromore, Clogher, Armagh, and Derry. Also there is material from the Roman Catholic Diocese of Clogher which

includes correspondence dealing with political events in the nineteenth century. (Part of this archive may be examined only with the written consent of His Lordship the Bishop.) The archive of the Society of Friends contains a number of registers of births, deaths, marriages, wills and inventories dating from the seventeenth century. Copies of the microfilms of Roman Catholic registers made by the National Library of Ireland are available. There are registers, vestry minute books, etc. for Church of Ireland churches such as that for the parish of Blaris, 1675 to 1794, and registers and minute books for over two hundred Presbyterian Churches (on microfilm); manorial court records, material from eighty different councils, Urban district, Rural district, Borough and County, most of which dates from 1898 (some are subject to the thirty-year closure law). Records of business and industry form one of the most important and substantial classes of records in the office and range from hundreds of account books and ledgers of large firms to a few documents of one-man concerns. Some collections reflect the growth of the mercantile business in Ireland as well as other forms of industry and trade from the late seventeenth century. An interesting collection relative to trade is the thousand documents, commercial correspondence, and accounts which belonged to Sir Robert Cowan, a Governor of Bombay for the East India Company, 1723-1741. The Foster/Massereene Papers (concerning the politics of the 1798 Rebellion and the passing of the Act of Union); the diaries of William Johnston of Ballykilbeg (1847-1870 and 1873-1902); the political papers of Frederick, First Marquis of Dufferin and Ava (about 80,000 documents and 750 volumes including correspondence) are also found in the collection. Other records concern roads, canals, railways, shipping, property, land, agriculture, the poor, medical provisions and hospitals, education, politics, and newspapers.

Conditions of admission and access

Researchers are welcome to use the collection. Inquiries should be addressed to the Director, preferably by letter. All material must be used on the premises.

Hours

9:30 AM - 4:45 PM, Monday-Friday. The office is closed the first two weeks in December.

Duplicating facilities

Both full-sized and microcopies can be provided. Photographic reproductions can also be made.

Other services

Brief inquiries are answered by telephone and mail, but letters are preferred. Reference material is available to aid the searcher and there are three sets of indexes: personal name, place name, and subject. Reference help is also provided.

Publications	Annual Reports (with abstracts of manuscript material acquired during the year); Local History Studies; Eighteenth Century Irish Official Papers in Great Britain; Private Collections, Volume 1- ; Aspects of Irish Social History, 1750-1800; Letters of a Great Irish Landlord (a selection from the estate correspondence of the Third Marquess of Downshire, 1809-1845); The Extraordinary Career of the Second Earl of Massereene, 1743-1805; The Asbourne Papers, 1869-1913; Irish Unionism, 1885-1923; and Registrom Johannis Mey; The Register of John Mey, Archbishop of Armagh, 1443-1456, by W. G. H. Quigley and E. F. D. Roberts. These publications (except the Annual Report, which is offered by the office) are produced by the Record Office and published by Her Majesty's Stationery Office. The following are published by the Northern Ireland Public Record Office: Ballymoney: Sources for Local History; Problems of a Growing City: Belfast, 1780-1870; Isaac Corry, 1755-1813 'An Adventurer in the Field of Politics,' by A. P. W. Malcomson; Northern Ireland Town Plans, by G. Hamilton (a catalogue); An Anglo-Irish Dialogue: a Calendar of the Correspondence Between John Foster and Lord Sheffield, 1774-1821, by A. P. W. Malcomson; Letters from an Ulster Land Agent, comp. by W. H. Crawford; Balleer School, Copy-Book of Letters, 1827-29, comp. by S. McMenamin; James Orr, Bard of Ballycarry, Local Poets and Social History, by D. H. Akenson and W. H. Crawford; The Ulster Textile Industry: a Catalogue of Business Records in PRONI Relating Principally to the Linen Industry in Ulster, by P. M. Bottomley; The Poor Law and the Workhouse in Belfast, 1838-1948, by M. Farrell; Macartney in Ireland, 1768-72: A Calendar of the Chief Secretaryship Papers of Sir George Macartney, by T. Bartlett; The Graham Indian Mutiny Papers, by A. T. Harrison; The Fottrell Papers, by Rev. Hugh Fenning; Lord Shannon's Letters to his Son: a Calendar of the Letters Written by the Second Earl of Shannon to his Son, Viscount Boyle, 1790-1802, comp. by E. Hewitt; Road Versus Rail, by P. E. Greer; A Register of Trees for County Londonderry, 1765-1911, by Eileen and Donal McCracken.

BELFAST

28	Institution	The Queen's University of Belfast
	Address	The Library
		Belfast BT7 1LS
	Telephone	02245133, ext. 3607

The response from this library indicated that the

genealogical collection is limited and inquiries are usually directed to the Public Record Office of Northern Ireland or to the Linen Hall Library.

BERWICK-UPON-TWEED

29	Institution Address	Berwick-upon-Tweed Record Office Berwick-upon-Tweed Borough Council Office Wallace Green Berwick-upon-Tweed TD15 1ED
	Telephone	0289 306332
	Holdings	The office holds the archives of Berwick-upon-Tweed and Glendale, Norham, and Islandshire rural district councils. The census returns for Berwick are held on microfilm, 1841-1881. Also found are Berwick-upon-Tweed and Tweedmouth parish registers.
	Conditions of admission and access	Visiting scholars may use the collection on the premises. Inquiries should be addressed to the County Archivist, Northumberland County Record Office, Melton Park, North Gosforth, Newcastle-upon-Tyne NE3 5QX
	Hours	10:00 AM - 1:00 PM, 2:00 PM - 5:00 PM, Thursday.
	Duplicating facilities	Facilities for photocopying are available.
	Other services	Reference help is available during open hours and brief postal or telephone inquiries are answered.
	Publications	Berwick Borough Records: Brief Guide. A detailed catalogue for local use is in progress.

BEVERLEY (map)

30	Institution Address	Humberside County Record Office County Hall, Champney Road Beverley HU17 9BA
	Telephone	0482 867131, ext. 3393 (Archivist); 3394 (Searchroom)

See also: GRIMSBY, South Humberside Area Record Office

	Holdings	The collection includes official and semiofficial records of the county and of its predecessor authority, the East Riding County Council. Family and estate papers from the same area are included, notably those of the Chichester Constable family of Burton Constable from the 13th century, and

Beaumont of Carlton Towers, which contains a confirmation of an exchange of lands from the 11th
century. Title deeds, maps, plans, and surveys
are also included. Parish records from the Archdeaconry of East Riding include baptism, marriage,
and burial registers from nearly two hundred
parishes and date from the 16th century. A list
of these parishes with the dates of the earliest
and latest entries is available. (It should not be
assumed that consecutive registers between these
dates are held.) The office is a repository for
manorial and tithe documents and is the Diocesan
Record Office for the Archdeaconry of the East
Riding. School Board minutes and accounts are
held as are school log books, title awards, Beverley
Borough Muniments, and Hedon Borough Muniments.
In addition, there are varied collections which contain many interesting items. Among these is an
Inspeximus of the annexation of the Hospital of
St. Giles, Beverley to Warter Priory (1286), Selby
Abbey Kitchener's court roll (1411-1413), and plans
of the manors of Warter (17th century), Howsham
(1705), and Fraisthorpe (1716).

Conditions of
admission and
access

The record office is open to the public but because
of limited space it is necessary to make an appointment in advance. This can be done by mail or
telephone. Inquiries should be made to the County
Archivist. Records are produced for use at the
following fixed times: 10:00 AM, 11:00 AM, 12:00
Noon, 2:00 PM, 3:00 PM, and 4:00 PM (except
Friday). In addition, up to six items will be provided upon arrival if they have been ordered in advance. Records required for use on Tuesday
evening must be ordered by 4:30 PM Tuesday after-
noon. All records must be used on the premises.

Hours

9:15 AM - 1:00 PM, 2:00 PM - 4:45 PM, Monday,
Wednesday-Thursday; 9:15 AM - 1:00 PM, 2:00 PM -
8:00 PM, Tuesday; 9:15 AM - 1:00 PM, 2:00 PM -
4:00 PM, Friday. The office is closed on all public
holidays, on the Tuesdays following the Spring and
late Summer Bank Holidays, and the last complete
week in January.

Duplicating
facilities

Full-sized copies can be provided.

Other services

Reference help is available in the search room and
brief questions will be answered by mail and telephone. There are ultra-violet lamps accessible
and a small reference library for the use of staff
and researchers. Numerous indexes and calendars of collections are available to aid patrons locate information.

Publications

Brief Guide to the Contents of the Humberside

County Record Office (1974); List of Parish Registers on Deposit; List of Non-Anglican Church Records on Deposit; Summary Listing of Education Records.

BEXLEY	See: LONDON, London Borough of Bexley

BILSTON

31 Institution Address	Wolverhampton Borough Archives Bilston Branch Library Mount Pleasant Bilston WV14 7LV
Telephone	0902 42097
	See also: WOLVERHAMPTON, Wolverhampton Borough Archives
Holdings	The collection includes the Bilston local archives, local government records, estate papers, maps, and photographs.
Conditions of admission and access	The collection may be consulted by appointment only. Inquiries should be made to the Archivist at the Central Library (Wolverhampton Borough Archives, Central Library, Snow Hill, Wolverhampton SV1 3AX; telephone: 0902 773824) or to the Branch Librarian at the address above. The material must be used on the premises.
Hours	An appointment must be arranged to consult the archives.
Duplicating facilities	Photocopies and photographs can be provided.
Other services	Brief questions by post or telephone are answered and reference help is provided.
Publications	None.

BIRKENHEAD

32 Institution Address	Wirral Archives Service Birkenhead Reference Library Borough Road Birkenhead L41 2XB
Telephone	051 652 6106/6107/6108
Holdings	The Wirral Archives Service has been approved by the Lord Chancellor as the local repository for public and local records and as such collects and preserves historical records of the locality. The

holdings are comprised mainly of 19th and 20th
century administrative records of local government
bodies, companies, societies and such institutions
as hospitals, workhouses, and schools. Microfilm
copies of some local parish registers, local newspapers (from 1860) and the Wirral Census returns,
1841-1881 are held. There are also records of
superseded local authorities, including Birkenhead
Improvement Commission (1833-1877), Hoylake and
West Kirby Gas and Water Company (1878-1926),
and Poulton-Cum-Seacombe School Board (1889-
1903). The local government records held by Wirral
Archives usually include Council and Committee
minutes, accounts, ratebooks, valuation lists, maps
and plans, correspondence, reports, departmental
records, school log books and registers. Deposited
records include archives of local companies, solicitors' papers, records of tradesmen, and private
business correspondence.

Conditions of admission and access	The Archives are open to the public and may be consulted in the Reference Library of the Central Library. Some classes of records are legally sub-ject to restriction. Also, as a large proportion of the collection is stored in other buildings, three days' notice of an intended visit is requested to avoid delays and disappointments. Inquiries should be addressed to the Archivist.
Hours	10:00 AM - 8:00 PM, Monday-Tuesday, Thursday-Friday; 10:00 AM - 1:00 PM, 2:00 PM - 5:00 PM, Saturday; closed Wednesday.
Duplicating facilities	Photocopying facilities are available, including microform copying.
Other services	Brief questions by telephone or post will be answered and reference help is available. A large collection of local history is provided in the Reference Library, which includes maps, street directories, photographs, and the standard reference works used by genealogists.
Publications	Lists, indexes, and brochures are produced.

BIRMINGHAM (map)

33 Institution Address	Birmingham Public Libraries Archives Department Central Libraries Chamberlain Square Birmingham B3 3HQ
Telephone	021 235 4217
Holdings	The library includes among its holdings the minutes

of the Birmingham City Council and the former Sutton Coldfield Borough Council and departmental records relating to education, the fire service, health, parks and baths, planning, public works and rating. The records of the Birmingham Court of Quarter Sessions, the City Coroner's Court and some hospital records are available (in part for public use). Copies of wills proved at Birmingham are held from 1858 to 1941 and Wills' Index from 1858 to 1931 for England and Wales. Parish Registers from 1538 for the Birmingham area are kept and other records have been deposited by Anglican Churches within the City of Birmingham (excluding Sutton Coldfield). The Methodist Church has deposited material from many of its churches within the same area. Several other non-conformist denominations are represented, including Unitarians and Congregationalists. Business records and those of commerce, charities, individuals, industry, institutions, landed families, and professions are kept as well as private deeds and personal archives, and date from ca. 1150. The Reference Library Archives Department is the official repository for archives and records in the Birmingham Metropolitan District, for manorial and tithe documents, and the Birmingham Diocesan Record Office is based in the Department.

Conditions of admission and access

The Library is open to the public and no advance appointment or letter of introduction is necessary. The material is in the Archives Department on the seventh floor of the Central Library and all material must be used in the department. (The department is reached by a spiral staircase from the floor below.) Inquiries should be directed to the Principal Archivist.

Hours

9:00 AM - 6:00 PM, Monday-Friday; 9:00 AM - 5:00 PM, Saturday.

Duplicating facilities

Full-sized and microcopies and photographic reproductions can be provided, but this work is only undertaken by the staff and at the discretion of the Archivist.

Other services

Reference help is provided and brief inquiries will be answered by mail or telephone. There are ultraviolet lamps available to aid the user. The indexes include personal name, place name, and subject. There are special indexes of apprenticeship documents, occupations and trades, and seals. Some of these may be consulted only on request.

Publications

There is an introductory guide to the use of the department and its collections.

BOLTON

34	Institution Address	Bolton Metropolitan Borough Archives Central Library and Museum Le Mans Crescent Bolton BL1 1SE
	Telephone	0204 22311, ext. 318
	Holdings	The collection includes official and nonofficial records relating to the borough. Among these are found Poor Law Unions, Water Board (Irwell Valley), Bolton Borough Quarter Sessions and Magistrates' Court. Religious papers include Methodist and the North East Lancashire Unitarian Mission. Family and estate records include those of the Heywood family of Bolton (ca. 1784-1938) and Crompton of Hall i'th Wood and Bolton. There are also business papers, notably the records of Hick, Hargreaves and Co. (ca. 1819-1959), and the archives of local organizations, trade unions, societies, and charities.
	Conditions of admission and access	The library is open to the public and an appointment in advance is not required. Archives are not produced without prior arrangement from 12:00 Noon to 2:00 PM, after 4:30 PM or on Saturday (except on Thursday, when one may request documents until 7:15 PM).
	Hours	9:30 AM - 7:30 PM, Monday-Tuesday, Thursday-Friday; 9:30 AM - 1:00 PM, Wednesday; 9:30 AM - 5:00 PM, Saturday.
	Duplicating facilities	Facilities for photocopying and for making full-size copies from microforms are available and photography can be arranged.
	Other services	Brief questions by post or telephone will be answered and reference service is available. Microform equipment is provided.
	Publications	Archives Services; Tracing Your Ancestors at Bolton.

BOSTON

35	Institution Address	Boston Borough Council Municipal Buildings West Street Boston PE21 8QR
	Telephone	0205 64601
	Holdings	The collection includes committee and council minutes dating from 1545. There are also deeds,

conveyances, other contracts, and a collection of printed books of use to the researcher.

Conditions of admission and access

The researcher must obtain permission to use the collection. Inquiries should be directed to the Chief Executive. The material must be used on the premises.

Hours

9:30 AM - 12:30 PM, 2:30 PM - 4:30 PM, Monday-Friday.

Duplicating facilities

Photocopying equipment is not provided.

Other services

Brief questions by post or telephone are answered. There is an extensive index available.

Publications

None.

BRADFORD (map)

36 Institution
Address

West Yorkshire Archive Service
Bradford District Archives
12 Canal Road
Bradford BD1 4AT

Telephone

0274 731931

The West Yorkshire Archive Service was formed from several separate agencies; see also: HALIFAX, HUDDERSFIELD, LEEDS, and WAKE-FIELD.

Holdings

The collection contains parish records, including registers for parishes within the Bradford Metropolitan District. Many Church of England parishes are represented, the earliest being Keighley, which dates from 1562. Non-conformist records include those for Methodist, Baptist, and United Reform churches. Family and estate records include the Spencer Stanhope papers (some of which are held by the Sheffield City Library), the Tong manuscripts (which relate to the Tempest family who lived at Tong Hall), the Eshton Hall papers (which deal with the Keighley area), and the Bardsley-Powell papers which relate to the Francis Sharp Powell family of Little Horton Hall. Official records come mostly from the Borough and District Councils (which amalgamated in 1974 to form the Metropolitan Bradford Council) and contain information on housing, sanitation, health, recreation, sport, leisure, culture, and education. Records of school boards and Boards of Guardians are also held. Business records include those for the Heaton family of Ponden Hall, Fisons of Burley-in-Wharfedale and James Drummond of Bradford. Bradford

Chamber of Commerce papers, and archives of
the Bradford Manufacturers Association and the
Wool Textile Manufacturers Association are also
available. The records of George Hattersley and
Son, the world's oldest loom manufacturer, are
among the holdings. Trade union records are extensive and include material on the 1825 strike.
Political records contain material relating to working class agitation in the 1830s and 1840s, particularly the Ten Hours Movement. Records of societies, organizations, charities, and the personal
letters, diaries, reminiscences, and autobiographies
of individuals are also found.

Conditions of   The collection is open to the public, but an appoint-
admission and   ment in advance is necessary. Inquiries should be
access   addressed to the District Archivist. The material
                     must be used on the premises.

Hours   9:30 AM - 1:00 PM, 2:00 PM - 5:00 PM, Monday-
                     Friday.

Duplicating   Photocopying facilities are available.
facilities

Other services   Brief questions by post or telephone are answered
                     and reference help is available in the search room.

Publications   Guides, brochures, and lists are produced by the
                     West Yorkshire Archive Service as well as the fol-
                     lowing: The West Riding Council, 1889-1974:
                     Historical Studies, by B. J. Barber and M. W.
                     Beresford (1978); Search Guide to the English Land
                     Tax, by R. W. Unwin (1982); Guide to the West
                     Yorkshire Archive Service for Family Historians
                     (1984); Guide to the Quarter Sessions of the West
                     Riding of Yorkshire 1637-1971 and Other Official
                     Records, by B. J. Barber (1984); Guide to the
                     Archive Collection of the Yorkshire Archaeological
                     Society 1931-1983 and to Collections Deposited with
                     the Society, by S. Thomas (1985).

BRECHIN

37 Institution   Angus District Libraries and Museums
   Address   Brechin Public Library and Museum
                     St. Ninean's Square
                     Brechin

   Telephone   03562 2687

   Holdings   The collection includes Burgh Charters, 1306-
                     1685, Burgess rolls from 1710, Roll of Honor,
                     1914-1951, and Town Council papers from 1805 to
                     1906. There are also business and trade records
                     and those of local organizations, charitable

associations and societies, and private individuals. Maps and plans are also held.

Conditions of admission and access	The researcher should make arrangements in advance in writing to use the collection. Inquiries should be directed to the Librarian. The collection must be used on the premises.
Hours	9:30 AM - 6:00 PM, Monday-Saturday.
Duplicating facilities	Arrangements can be made for photocopying.
Other services	Brief questions by telephone or post are answered and reference service is provided.
Publications	None.

BRISTOL (map)

38 Institution Address	Bristol Record Office The Council House College Green Bristol BS1 5TR
Telephone	0272 26031, ext. 441/442
Holdings	The office is the official repository for the records of the City (and former County) of Bristol. These include archives of the Corporation of Bristol and of the Diocese of Bristol, as well as public records of a local nature, manorial and tithe documents, and private archives. Among the Official Archives are Charters and Custumals, records relating to Lieutenancy and Shrievalty, administrative records, financial records, judicial records, and the records of various statutory authorities, such as the Local Board of Health, School Boards, and Urban and Rural District Councils. Unofficial deposited archives include Ecclesiastical Records, family archives, business and trade archives, and records of societies and institutions.
Conditions of admission and access	The record office is open to the public, but an appointment in advance is required. All material must be used on the premises. Inquiries should be addressed to the City Archivist.
Hours	8:45 AM - 4:45 PM, Monday-Thursday; 8:45 AM - 4:15 PM, Friday; 9:00 AM - 12:00 Noon, the first two Saturdays (generally) in each month, by appointment in advance ONLY.
Duplicating facilities	Full-sized and microcopies can be provided.
Other services	Brief inquiries are answered by mail and by

telephone. Reference help is available, but visitors are encouraged to carry out their own research or employ a record agent. Talks are given on sources, and exhibitions of archives are mounted quarterly in the City Museum. Microform equipment and ultra-violet lamps are available.

Publications   Guide to the Parish Records of the City of Bristol and County of Gloucester, ed. by Irvine Gray and Elizabeth Ralph (1963); Diocese of Bristol: A Catalogue of the Records of the Bishop and Archdeacons and of the Dean and Chapter, ed. by I. M. Kirby (1970); Guide to the Bristol Archives Office, ed. by Elizabeth Ralph (1970); Government of Bristol, 1373-1973, by Elizabeth Ralph (1973). At one time details of accessions acquired since the publication of the Guide were published in the Transactions of the Bristol and Gloucestershire Archaeological Society. This is no longer the case, but a supplement to the Guide is included in Avon Local History Handbook, ed. by J. S. Moore (Phillimore, 1979).

BROMLEY   See: LONDON, London Borough of Bromley

BURTON-ON-TRENT

39 Institution   Burton-on-Trent Library
    Address   Riverside
                High Street
                Burton-on-Trent DE13 9HD

    Telephone   0283 43271

    Holdings   The records of the local Councils and of the former County Borough of Burton and Tatbury District Councils are held. Also in the collection are papers of the Marquess of Anglesey concerning Burton Abbey. In addition there are non-conformist (Methodist) records, Board of Guardians documents and papers relating to education.

    Conditions of   Researchers wishing to use the archives should
    admission and   give advance notification of a visit. Inquiries
    access   should be directed to the Librarian. The archives may be used only on the premises.

    Hours   9:30 AM - 6:00 PM, Monday-Tuesday, Thursday-Friday; 9:30 AM - 1:00 PM, Wednesday, Saturday.

    Duplicating   Photocopying can be arranged.
    facilities

    Other services   Brief questions by post or telephone will be answered and reference help is available in the library. There are also lists and indexes to aid the researcher.

Publications   <u>Historical Collection of Staffordshire</u>.

BURY ST. EDMUNDS
(map)

40 Institution   Suffolk Record Office
   Address   Raingate Street
                    Bury St. Edmunds IP33 1RX

   Telephone   0284 63141, ext. 2522

                    <u>See also</u>: IPSWICH, Suffolk Record Office

   Holdings   Records of the County Council and those of official bodies, churches and chapels, businesses, societies, families and estates of the western area of the county are held here. It is a repository for manorial and tithe documents and for ecclesiastical records of the St. Edmundsbury and Ipswich Archdeaconry of Sudbury. Collections date from the twelfth century to the present day.

   Conditions of   The record office is open to the public and no advance appointment is necessary. Inquiries should be directed to the County Archivist. All material must be used on the premises. Records for use on Saturday must be requested by 1:00 PM on Friday.

   Hours   9:00 AM - 5:00 PM, Monday-Thursday; 9:00 AM - 4:00 PM, Friday; 9:00 AM - 1:00 PM, 2:00 PM - 5:00 PM, Saturday.

   Duplicating   Full-sized and microcopies can be provided. Photographic reproductions can also be made.

   Other services   Brief inquiries by telephone and by mail will be answered. An education service is provided for students from schools and colleges to work under the guidance of an archive education officer, and exhibitions and talks are given to local groups. There are facilities for the repair of manuscripts and ultra-violet lamps are provided.

   Publications   There are guides for the record office user and other publications based on the record office's holdings, and a <u>Guide to Genealogical Sources in Suffolk</u> (2nd ed., 1985).

CAERNARFON

41 Institution   Gwynedd Archives Service
   Address   Caernarfon Area Record Office

County Offices
Victoria Dock
Caernarfon LL55 1SH

Telephone	0287 4121, ext. 2095

The Caernarfon Area Record Office is part of the Gwynedd Archive Service (which comprises the former Anglesey, Caernarfon, and Merionethshire Record Offices). See also: DOLGELLAU (Dolgellau Area Record Office) and LLANGEFNI (Llangefni Area Record Office)

Holdings	The collection contains a comprehensive range of material on Welsh history (particularly North Wales local history and local newspapers). The holdings include official county records (Quarter Sessions from 1541); private deposited records from 1176 (family, estate, and business papers); local authority papers (including Guardians of the Poor and police), and a large accumulation of quarrying records. The office also holds microforms of records found elsewhere. It is a repository for manorial and tithe documents and for certain ecclesiastical records, namely the parish records of Caernarfonshire parishes in Bangor and St. Asaph dioceses.
Conditions of admission and access	The record office is open to the public. Appointments in advance are advised to assure space in the search rooms as they are frequently full. Inquiries should be directed to the Area Archivist. All material must be used in the search rooms.
Hours	9: 30 AM - 12: 30 PM, 1: 30 PM - 5: 00 PM, Monday-Tuesday, Thursday-Friday; 9: 30 AM - 12: 30 PM, 1: 30 PM - 7: 00 PM, Wednesday.
Duplicating facilities	Full-sized and microcopying facilities are provided.
Other services	Brief questions by mail and telephone are answered (but not those on census entries), and reference help is available in the office. An education service for liaison with schools and colleges can be arranged.
Publications	Guide to the Caernarvonshire Record Office, by W. O. Williams (1952); Gwynedd Archives Services: Bulletin (annual); Miscellaneous calendars, guides, reproductions of documents, postcards, and general books on local history.
CALDERDALE	See: HALIFAX

CAMBRIDGE (map)

42 Institution	County Record Office, Cambridge
Address	Shire Hall
	Castle Hill
	Cambridge CB3 0AP
Telephone	0223 317281
	See also: HUNTINGDON, Cambridgeshire Record Office
Holdings	The record office contains the historical records of ancient Cambridgeshire and the Isle of Ely, including the archives of Quarter Sessions and administrative papers until 1889. These records begin in the time of Charles II (1630-1685) and concern crime and its punishment and also such matters as poor relief, bridges, ale-houses, turnpikes, militia, dissenters' meeting houses, houses of correction, local rates and about 250 plans (beginning in 1826) made in connection with projected roads, docks, railways, and water-works. They also include a series of inclosure awards and maps made between 1776 and 1889 which cover most parishes. Road, school, and public health records of the County Councils and their predecessors are held from the 18th century, including minutes, accounts, and other records of the Board of Guardians from 1836 to 1930. Also deposited in the office are the records of the City of Cambridge and other District Councils. Parish records found in the record office include registers of baptisms, marriages, burials, vestry minutes, churchwardens' accounts, rate books, poor law papers, and apprenticeship indentures. For some parishes there are tithe apportionments and plans made after 1836. Non-conformist records include documents of the Society of Friends in Cambridgeshire, the Isle of Ely, and Huntingdonshire, and also records of Methodists and others. The Office has extensive land drainage records, including those of the Bedford Level Corporation, the principal drainage authority in the southern fens, from 1635 to 1920. These include proceedings, accounts, reports, lot books and maps. Family and estate records date from the late 12th or early 13th century, and include deeds of title, estate maps, correspondence, legal papers, and manorial documents. The archives of the Tharp family of Chippenham contain court rolls, deeds, letters and accounts concerning Chippenham and Snailwell from 1287 to the 20th century and many papers about plantations in Jamaica between 1670 and 1870 which contain several lists of slaves. The Gape family records relating to Croydon and Caxton (1499-1907) include the Caxton market charter of 1668. Other family or

estate collections include those of the Baumgartners
of Milton, the Beldams of Royston, the Birds of
Linton, the Cottons of Landwade and Madingley,
the Briscoes of Longstowe, the Chafys of Chatteris,
the De Frevilles of Shelford, the Delmé-Radcliffes
of Litlington, the Huddlestons of Sawston, the
Nash-Woodhams of Shepreth, the Ruck-Keenes of
Linton, the Townleys of Fulbourn and the Yorkes,
Earls of Hardwicke, of Wimpole. Antiquarians'
papers include the Mundy collection concerning
Ickleton and the Maynard collection regarding
Whittlesford and nearby parishes. Solicitors'
papers deposited (on loan) in the record office
provide accounts, rentals, letters, and manor court
papers. There are also manuscript maps which date
from the seventeenth century, microfilm of records
relating to Cambridgeshire and the Isle of Ely deposited elsewhere, including parish records and
census records, 1841-1881. Diocesan and probate
records are at the University Library, West Road,
Cambridge. The branch office at Huntingdon
(County Record Office, Grammar School Walk,
Huntingdon, PE18 6LF; telephone 0480 57734) contains records for the former county of Huntingdonshire.

Conditions of
admission and
access

The record office is open to the public and no
appointment is necessary except for Tuesday evening. It is helpful, however, if researchers write
or telephone ahead to arrange visits when extended research is contemplated. Inquiries should
be addressed to the County Archivist. All material
must be used on the premises.

Hours

9:00 AM - 12:45 PM, 1:45 PM - 5:15 PM, Monday-
Thursday; 9:00 AM - 12:45 PM, 1:45 PM - 4:15 PM,
Friday; 5:15 PM - 9:00 PM, Tuesday, by appoint-
ment only.

Duplicating
facilities

Full-sized copy services, which include the ability
to enlarge or reduce and print-out from microfilm,
are available, usually on demand. Other forms of
copying are available to order.

Other services

There is a reference library available for researchers' use and reference help is available. There
are many lists and indexes provided to aid the
scholar in his work. These include indexes to marriages in Cambridgeshire and the Isle of Ely,
1538-1625, 1676-1837, and in Huntingdonshire,
1754-1837, indexes to persons in the 1851 census,
and to wills proved in the local courts before
1858, and many indexed transcripts of parish
registers. The staff is happy to arrange exhibitions
and give lectures whenever possible.

Publications

Annual Reports, 1965-   , including lists of

accessions; Guide to Educational Records in the County Record Office, Cambridge (1972); Genealogical Sources in Cambridgeshire, by J. M. Farrar (1979), out of print at present, but a new edition is planned.

CAMBRIDGE (map)

43 Institution Address	Cambridge University Library Manuscripts Department West Road Cambridge CB3 9DR
Telephone	0223 61441
Holdings	Ely Diocesan, Chapter archives, and probate records are held as well as manorial and tithe documents. The Ely Diocesan Records, which include the medieval records of the bishops and a number of genealogical sources, are described in Ely Records by D. M. Owen (1971). The Ely Chapter Records of the medieval Cathedral monastery and post-reformation Dean and Chapter are described in the Library and Muniments of Ely Cathedral, by D. M. Owen (1973).
Conditions of admission and access	In general, a visiting scholar must have permission and a prior appointment to use these resources. A letter of introduction is recommended. Inquiries should be directed to the Head of Manuscripts Department and if a visit is planned by a non-member of the University, to the Admissions Officer. The Admissions Office is open 9:30 AM - 12:30 PM, 2:15 PM - 4:15 PM, Monday-Friday; 9:30 AM - 12:30 PM, Saturday. User's tickets can be issued or requested only at these times. No material from the Manuscripts Room may be borrowed. Use of the archives found here is restricted to the room.
Hours	9:00 AM - 6:45 PM, Monday-Friday; 9:00 AM - 12:30 PM, Saturday. A list of holidays observed by the university for which the library closes is available. Admissions Office hours are noted under "Conditions of admission and access."
Duplicating facilities	Full-size and microcopying facilities are available, but permission may be required to copy these resources.
Other services	Reference help is available and leaflets giving further information are provided. There are indexes and catalogues to aid the researcher. Guide to Reader Services No. 9 gives helpful information and there is a Readers Handbook for Cambridge University Library.

Publications	Catalogue of the Manuscripts Preserved in the Library of the University of Cambridge, 6 volumes, 1856-67 (reprinted, 1980); Summary Guide to Accessions of Western Manuscripts (Other than Medieval) Since 1867, by A. E. B. Owen (1966); Ely Records: A Handlist of the Records of the Bishop and Archdeacon of Ely, by D. M. Owen (1971); Archives of the University of Cambridge, by H. E. Peek and C. P. Hall (1962).

CAMDEN   See: LONDON, London Borough of Camden

CANTERBURY (map)

44 Institution   Cathedral Archives and Library, Canterbury
   Address   8 The Precincts
                     Canterbury CT1 2EG

   Telephone   0227 63510 (for Archives); 0227 58950 (for
                     Printed Books)

   Holdings   The collection includes records from the Dean and
                     Chapter, the City, and the Diocese of Canterbury.
                     (The researcher should be aware that the records
                     of the Archdiocese of Canterbury are kept in
                     London at Lambeth Palace Library (see entry no.
                     170). The Dean and Chapter records date from
                     the 8th century and contain ecclesiastical suits,
                     financial records, inventories, manorial financial
                     records from ca. 1280-1536, obedientiary accounts,
                     professions of obedience, property deeds, 742-1540,
                     registers, sede vacante records (wills), Chapter
                     Acts, Dean's books, lease books, manuscript music
                     books dating from the 17th to the 20th century,
                     offertory books (these have a gap from ca. 1628-
                     1670 because of a fire in 1670); patent confirmation
                     registers, precentors' books, receivers' books,
                     treasurers' books, bills and vouchers, rentals, seal
                     books, service registers, surveys, and tithe books.
                     Among the city records will be found charters,
                     1155-1974, minute books, 1536 to the present, finan-
                     cial records (accounts, 1393-1836, fragments and
                     abstracts of accounts, 1875-1974, lease books,
                     1575-1841, rate books for individual parishes, 1842-
                     1911 [with many gaps], city rate books, 1866,
                     1867, 1908 to the present). Court records are
                     also here and contain Borough Sessions, 13th-18th
                     century, Quarter Sessions, ca. 1461-1972, Court
                     of Summary Jurisdiction, 19th century. Records
                     for civil defence, 1939-1945, pavement commissions,
                     1787-1841, registers of freemen, 13th-20th century,
                     and apprentice books, 1765-1835, vehicle licences
                     and numbers, 1904-1936, workhouse minute books,
                     1728-1929, and various taxation records from the
                     13th century can be consulted here. The Diocesan

records include Bishop's transcripts for the whole diocese from ca. 1561-1639, and 1661-ca. 1880, church court records (clergy books, visitation records, deposition books, instance business books, comperta and detecta, 14th-18th century), tithe maps, churchwardens' presentments, 1700-ca. 1800, Compton census, 1676, curates' licenses, 1667, 1716-1723, 1813-1961, faculties, 1694-1899, general licences, 1568-1937, marriage bonds and allegations, 1700-1937, meeting house certificates, 1789-1852, ordinations, 1777-1961, presentations, 1633-1918, terriers, 17th-19th century. In addition, there are school records in which will be found minutes of the Society for the Education of the Children of the Poor, 1811-1839, Local Board minutes, 1839-1863, Diocesan School minutes, 1867-1932, Canterbury Diocesan Education Society Minutes, annual reports, and trust returns from 1838-1920, St. Paul's Canterbury School log books, 1863-1957, and others; Church commissioner records, and chapter manorial records. There are also deposited collections which include the Fordwich Borough Archives, the Irby Collection (Hasted Papers), St. John's, Eastbridge, and Jesus Hospitals, Canterbury Congregational and Huguenot Church records, and the Hales Collection which includes the Throckmorton Diaries. There are literary and other manuscripts which contain such diverse items as a 13th-century bestiary, a catalogue of the benefactors of the library from 1628 to the 18th century, a burnt breviary of the 12th century and a list of goods sold at Canterbury Cathedral by the Royal Commissioners at the Dissolution, 1540. The printed books contain resources in early theology, history, paleography, law, natural sciences, travel, 17th to 19th century pamphlet material, early government publications, bibles and prayer books. (This information is taken from "Canterbury Archives Source List.")

Conditions of admission and access

The collection may be used only on the premises and an appointment in advance is required. Also, researchers must have a letter of introduction on their first visit. Inquiries should be directed to the Archivist or Keeper of Printed Books. It is appreciated if correspondence is accompanied by a stamped, self-addressed envelope or the envelope with international reply coupons. Fees are charged, and there is an explanation of these available in the library.

Hours

9:30 AM - 12:45 PM, 2:00 PM - 4:30 PM, Monday-Friday. The library is closed the third week in January, July, and October, and occasionally for exhibitions.

Duplicating facilities

Photocopying is available for archival material, but

not for printed books. Photographs can be arranged.

Other services

There is limited staff available for reference help,
but there are many catalogs and indexes available
to aid the researcher. These are described in
"Canterbury Archives Source List," which may be
obtained in the library. Only brief questions are
answered by telephone or post. An ultra-violet
lamp is provided.

Publications

In addition to the "Source List for Archives,"
there are Source Guides to Oxford and Anti-Slavery
Movements, guides, leaflets, and brochures.

CANTERBURY

45 Institution
    Address

The Institute of Heraldic and Genealogical Studies
79-82 Northgate
Canterbury CT1 1BA

Telephone

0227 68664/462618

Holdings

The volumes in the Institute's Library are almost
all related to genealogy, heraldry, and general,
family and local historical background material.
There is a collection of armorial and heraldic works
which has strong coverage of foreign sources.
There are also books on social and economic history, occupations, etymologies of names and peer-
ages, and many complete collections of periodicals
and journals, with over ninety from Britain and
thirty foreign received. Included in the collection
is a large group of topographical materials relating
to the British Isles, transcripts of parish registers,
census indexes, monumental inscriptions, marriage indexes and licences, immigration lists, commercial directories, professional directories, army
and navy lists, and such series as the British
Record Society and Harleian Society. The International Genealogical Index and Pallot Index of marriages, mainly for London, are found in the library
but are not on open access (see below, "Conditions
of admission and access"). Finally there is an
archive collection of some 20,000 genealogical cases
kept (also on closed access, but an abstract can be
made with permission), and some other collections
specifically related to London, Kent, Sussex, and
Hampshire, and there are armorials.

Conditions of
admission and
access

Members of the Institute, both qualified genealogists
and unqualified supporting members, have use of
the library. Non-members must pay a fee to gain
access. All visitors to the library should make an
appointment in advance. Inquiries should be addressed to the Librarian. Some material, such as

the International Genealogical Index and the Pallot Index of Marriages in London are not available for consulting by researchers, but the staff will do so and will send the results to the requesting party by post. Fees are charged for this service. Material may not be removed from the library (with some exceptions). Duplicate copies of books may be borrowed for use in research rooms.

Hours

10:00 AM - 4:30 PM, Monday, Wednesday-Friday; other times by arrangement.

Duplicating facilities

Full-size and microcopying facilities are available.

Other services

Reference help is provided in the library and brief questions are answered by telephone or post. A research service is available for those who cannot visit the library personally, details of which should be obtained from the Librarian. It is worth noting that the staff is prepared to search printed works, microforms, or manuscripts on a world-wide basis and supply photocopies or other prints of pages required. A form is provided for requests for such searches and will be forwarded upon receipt of a stamped self-addressed (foolscap) envelope, as will a schedule of fees. It may be necessary to send international reply coupons. A program of lectures and events is available from the Registrar. Searches in the Index to the 1851 census of Kent will be made for a fee and those requesting this service must also supply a self-addressed envelope with stamps.

Publications

The publications of the Institute include, but are not limited to the following: Anglo-Norman Armory, by C. R. Humphery-Smith; Arms of Oxford and Cambridge Colleges; Elephant Hunt--an Educational Exercise, by G. M. Swinfield; Heraldic Notes on the Issue of Postage Stamps, by C. J. Holyoake; Heraldry, by C. R. Humphery-Smith; Heraldry in Canterbury Cathedral, by E. E. Thoyts; Index of Baronetage Creations, by C. J. Parry; Kennedy's Book of Arms, by Patrick Kennedy; Our Family History, by C. R. Humphery-Smith; Thirteenth International Congress of Genealogical and Heraldic Sciences. Proceedings. Up the Beatles Family Tree, by C. R. Humphery-Smith; Atlas and Index of Parishes of England and Wales; Parish Map Book; Index to Irish Wills; Genealogist's Bibliography; Family Historian's Pocket Book, by C. R. Humphery-Smith; Guide to Marriage Licences; Introduction to Medieval Genealogy; and Family History, the Institute's journal, published six times a year since 1961. A complete list and a price list of these and other publications for sale in the Institute's shop are available.

CARDIFF (map)

46 Institution	Glamorgan Record Office
Address	County Hall
	Cathays Park
	Cardiff CF1 3NE

Telephone   0222 820282

The Glamorgan Record Office is part of the Glamorgan Archive Service and covers Mid, South and
West Glamorgan. See also: SWANSEA (West Glamorgan Area Record Office)

Holdings   The records include those of the County Council,
Quarter Sessions, Petty Sessions, Turnpikes, Local
Boards of Health, and Boards of Guardians. There
are also estate papers, industrial records, maps,
some newspapers, and the Transactions of local
history societies. Among the special collections are
Swansea Gaol Journals of Governor, Surgeon, and
Chaplain, 1729-1878 (thirty-three volumes); the
Minutes of the South Wales and Monmouthshire
Branch of the British Medical Association, 1871-
1943 (six volumes); annual Return of Medical Officers of Health of District Councils and Boroughs
to County Medical Officer of Health, 1892-1910 (sixteen volumes); and the Cardiff Medical Society
Minutes, 1870-1948 (six volumes). Indexes to
Grants of Probate in England and Wales, 1858-1928;
Indexes to pre-1858 wills proved at Llandaff (original wills from Llandaff are at the National Library
of Wales at Aberystwyth) are held. The office is
a repository for Society of Friends records for
Wales and border counties, for manorial and tithe
documents, and for ecclesiastical (parish) records
of Llandaff, and Swansea and Brecon dioceses.
The parish records which are found come from
parishes within Llandaff diocese and from that part
of Swansea and Brecon diocese which lies within
West Glamorgan. Complete sets are found here,
even for parishes within West Glamorgan. The
record office also administers the archive collection of the former Cardiff City Library.

Conditions of   The office is open to the public and no advance
admission and   appointment is required. Inquiries should be ad-
access   dressed to the Archivist. All material must be
used on the premises.

Hours   9:00 AM - 5:00 PM, Tuesday-Thursday; 9:00 AM -
4:30 PM, Friday.

Duplicating   Full-size and microcopying facilities are provided.
facilities

Other services   Brief inquiries by post or telephone are answered.

Reference help is available in the search room, and an ultra-violet viewer is provided.

Publications

Iron in the Making; Dowiais Iron Company Letters, 1762-1860, ed. by M. Elsas (1960); Annual Report; accessions lists; Glamorgan, 1536-1974: Aspects of a Changing County (1974), and guide sheets on various subjects such as Sources of Education History, Parts I-II, Notes for the Guidance of Colleges of Education and Schools, and Ordnance Survey Maps.

CARLISLE (map)

47 Institution
Address

Cumbria Record Office (Carlisle)
The Castle
Carlisle CA3 8UR

Telephone

0228 23456, ext. 2416

See also: BARROW-IN-FURNESS, Cumbria Record Office; KENDAL, Cumbria Record Office

Holdings

The record office holds Quarter Sessions records including all enclosure awards and deposited parliamentary plans from 1686, minutes of the County Council and its committees from 1889 and all the Clerk's letter books, files, and working papers from 1889. Architects' letter books, school managers' minute books and log books of closed schools and Treasurer's account books from 1889 are also found. Absorbed or defunct authority records include Public Assistance Committee minute books and minute books and papers of the North Cumberland Water Board. Lieutenancy records are incomplete, but include militia books and returns for Cumberland and Eskdale Wards, 1796-1830. Carlisle City records include all extant records prior to 1835 except some title deeds of corporate property. There are absorbed authority records, Lighting and Watching Commissioners, 1803-86, records of the local Board of Health and Burial Board from 1850 and of the Gas and Waterworks companies, 1818-1869, minutes of the Corporation and its committees, 1835-1950, and Town Clerk's letter books, files, and legal papers, 1836-ca. 1950. Engineer and Surveyor's books, files, and Building Inspectors' plans, including town files and plans, ca. 1850-1950. Chief Fire Officer's Reports and station log books, 1867-1936, letter books and miscellaneous books and papers of the Medical Officer of Health, 1893-1953. Turnpike Trusts, Boards of Guardians, and some school boards are found, and many parish councils' records are now deposited. Dalston Parish Council records at Carlisle include vestry and overseers' minutes, accounts and

papers, and a series of letters addressed to the
overseers from or on behalf of migrants who left
the parish, 1811-1835. Comparable series are found
among the records deposited by Greystoke parish
church. Bishop's transcripts of parish registers
and tithe awards and plans for Cumberland are
found here. Probate records are those of Carlisle
Consistory Court, 1558-1858, and the manorial peculiar court records of Ravenstonedale, 1691-1851,
and Temple Sowerby, 1580-1816. Original Dean
and Chapter estate leases from the 17th century
are at the record office, and other Dean and
Chapter records can be made available there, but
it is best to make prior application. These include
the monastic registers of Holme Cultram (13th century) and Wetheral (14th century). The Chapter
registers, which date from the 16th century and
other records which begin after 1660 and include
lease books, manor books, and a variety of papers
relating to the Chapter's ecclesiastical and estate
functions, are in this group. Also included are
the Machell manuscripts (17th century), Nicolson
manuscripts and the Hill manuscripts (19th century),
family papers of the Machell family of Crackenthorpe,
13th century to 1768, letter books of Bishop Walde-
grave (late 19th century), and the manuscripts of
18th century local histories. Records of parish
churches have been deposited at Carlisle and include parish registers, churchwardens' and overseers' accounts, vestry minutes, settlement papers,
and charity accounts. Records of the Society of
Friends in Cumberland from 1670, minutes, accounts and some registers of the Carlisle Methodist
Circuit (Primitive Methodist from 1823, Wesleyan
Methodist from 1863, and United Methodist from
1854) are found, as are records of Congregational
and Presbyterian churches in Cumberland. Lecon-
field Estate records are housed at Cockermouth
Castle, but are administered from the Carlisle office, where they can be made available. They com-
prise the local administrative records of the Earls
of Northumberland to 1682, of their successors, the
Dukes of Somerset, 1682-1750, and the Earls of
Egremont (Wyndham family) from 1750. Court rolls
and estate accounts from the 15th century relating
to the Honour of Cockermouth, and the Baronies of
Allerdale, Egremont and Wigton in West Cumberland
are available. The coal, lead, iron, and slate industries are well documented here. The records
of the Earl of Lonsdale found at the office include
estate accounts, rentals, plans and manorial records
for Lowther, Hackthorpe, and other Westmorland
properties in the Eden Valley, Maulds Meaburn,
Shap, Crosby Ravensworth, Kirkby Londsdale and
the Barony of Kendal, the Barony of Burgh by
Sands, and other Cumberland properties in Carlisle,
Penwith, Holme Cultram, Flimby, Wythop, Cardew

and Warnell, ca. 1500-1875. There are also
family and estate correspondence, estate agents'
correspondence, poll and canvassing books; Barbados Council minute and order books, 1711-1720;
and Carleton of Hillbeck family papers, 1425-1806,
which contain letters, bills, accounts of Yosegill
cotton factory, 1786-1793, and colliery and limekiln
records, 1784-1789. Other family and estate
records are Senhouse of Netherhall, Maryport (correspondence, records relating to Ellenborough and
Broughton collieries, Carlisle to Maryport railway,
shipping, Dominica Plantation (from the 16th century), Fleming family records, 1671-1749 (correspondence of Sir George Fleming, Bishop of
Carlisle, 1734-1747), Curwen of Workington from
ca. 1768 to the early 20th century, Fletcher Vane
of Hutton in the Forest, Musgrave of Edenhall,
Pennington of Muncaster, and Stanley of Dalegarth--
medieval deeds found from ca. 1200-1550 are found in
these. Other records include Lamplugh of Lamplugh, Lawson of Isel, and solicitors' and business
records.

Conditions of admission and access	The office is open to the public and no prior ap-pointment is necessary, but visitors requiring large numbers of records should notify the record office in advance. Also, access to Lord Egremont's estate records at Cockermouth Castle requires one week's notice. Dean and Chapter records can be made available, but advance notice is advisable. Inquiries should be directed to the County Archiv-ist. All material must be used in the search room.
Hours	9:00 AM - 5:00 PM, Monday-Friday, except public holidays.
Duplicating facilities	Full-size and microcopying facilities are available. Photographs can be provided.
Other services	A reference library and reference help is avail-able in the search room. Brief questions by post or telephone are answered, but detailed searches are not undertaken. Leaflets on copying facilities and on the educational use of records are provided. Names of recommended searchers and details of the Cumbria Family History Society can be supplied on request.
Publications	Bibliography of the History and Topography of Cumberland and Westmorland, by H. W. Hodgson (1969); Fleming-Senhouse Papers, by E. Hughes (1961); Records at a Glance (1979); Subject Guides for enclosure, genealogy, hospitals, health and medicine, Leconfield and Lonsdale estate, Sources for Family History, Sources for School Records, Sources on World Wars One and Two, Inclosure Awards List, Tithe Awards List, Guide to the

Records of Lord Egremont at Cockermouth Castle. A map of Church of England parishes in Cumbria is also available. The following articles are about the record office: "Local Archives of Gt. Britain XXVIII. Cumberland, Westmorland, and Carlisle Record Office, 1960-1965," by B. C. Jones, Archives, Vol. VII, no. 34; "Cumberland and Westmorland Record Offices, 1968," The School of History, University of Leeds. Reprinted in Archives, Vol. VII, no. 34 (from which much of the material in "Holdings" was taken).

CARMARTHEN (map)

48	Institution Address	Carmarthenshire Area Record Office County Hall Carmarthen SA 31 1JP
	Telephone	0267 233333, ext. 4182, or 0267 230837

The Carmarthenshire Area Record Office is part of the Dyfed Archive Service.
See also: ABERYSTWYTH (Cardiganshire Area Record Office) and HAVERFORDWEST (Pembrokeshire Area Record Office)

Holdings	The record office is a repository for manorial and tithe documents and for ecclesiastical records such as the parish records of St. Davids. There is also manuscript material here that relates to the former county (Carmarthenshire) area and also to official authorities. There are agricultural and business records as well as those of local historical interest to be found, including extensive holdings of estate papers.
Conditions of admission and access	The record office is open to the public and no prior appointment is required except for a Saturday visit (see "Hours" below). Inquiries should be made to the Archivist-in-Charge. The material may be consulted only in the search room.
Hours	9: 00 AM - 4: 45 PM, Monday-Thursday; 9: 00 AM - 4: 15 PM, Friday; 9: 30 AM - 12: 30 PM, on the first and third Saturday of each month (except bank holiday weekends), by appointment only.
Duplicating facilities	Full-size and microcopying facilities are available.
Other services	Brief questions by mail or telephone are answered and reference help is available in the office. Exhibitions and lectures are arranged by the staff when possible.
Publications	There are a number of publications both for sale

and issued without charge by the Dyfed Archive
Service. These include Carmarthenshire Record
Office: A Survey of Archive Holdings, by S.
Beckley (1980); A Guide to Parish Registers in
St. Davids Diocese; A Guide to Local Newspapers
in Dyfed; Notes for Searchers; Tracing Your
Ancestors; List of Record Agents; History of
Houses; Summaries of Main Collections: Cardigan-
shire Record Office, Carmarthenshire Record Of-
fice, Pembrokeshire Record Office; and Topic Lists.
These Lists give an indication of material available
concerning different subjects. Those relating to
documents in Carmarthen are: The Rebecca Riots,
Maps of Carmarthen Town, Cardiganshire Views and
Engravings, The French Invasion of Pembrokeshire,
Carmarthenshire Roads, Poor Law, The Eisteddfod
in Carmarthenshire, Llanelli Coalfield--Bitumious
Region, Amman and Gwendraeth Coalfield--Anthra-
cite Region, Laugharne, Carmarthenshire Police,
Scouts and Guides, in Carmarthenshire.

CARMARTHEN

Institution
Dyfed Archive Service
See: CARMARTHEN, Carmarthenshire Record
Office

CASHEL

49 Institution
Address
The GPA Bolton Library
(Cashel Diocesan Library)
John Street
Cashel, Co. Tipperary

Telephone
062 61944

Holdings
The collection includes baptisms, confirmation lists,
marriages, and burials from about 1664. There is
also a selection of legal documents, letters, and
maps dating from 1668 which were still unsorted
in 1986. Printed books in the library date from
1473 and the oldest manuscript is from 1168.

Conditions of
admission and
access
Those not wishing to consult the collection may
view it behind glass. Bona fide scholars may
handle the material only under supervision. A letter
of introduction is required and an appointment in
advance is recommended. Access to the collection
is allowed only on the premises. Inquiries should
be made to the Dean of Cashel (at the Deanery in
Cashel).

Hours
9:30 AM - 5:30 PM, Monday-Saturday; 2:30 PM -
5:30 PM, Sunday.

Duplicating facilities	Duplicating facilities are not available.

Other services — Postal inquiries are answered, but questions by telephone are not encouraged. The recent installation of a computer should make access to information more timely.

Publications — None.

CHANNEL ISLANDS

See: ST. ANNE'S, Alderney
ST. HELIER, Jersey
ST. PETER PORT, Guernsey

CHELMSFORD (map)

50 Institution
    Address

Essex Record Office
County Hall
Chelmsford   CM1 1LX

Telephone

0245 267222, ext. 2104
See also: SOUTHEND-ON-SEA, Essex Record
Office; COLCHESTER, Essex Record Office

Holdings

The office holds the administrative records of the County of Essex and of towns and districts within it. Also found are local court records, probate records of local jurisdictions, parish records of the diocese of Chelmsford, including registers of baptisms, marriages, and burials, tithe records, poor law records, privately deposited records, including title deeds, manorial, family and business records. The County Council records held begin in 1888 and are preceded by Court of Quarter Sessions records from the 16th century. There are also records of local societies and organizations, maps and plans, photographs and engravings, sale catalogs of numerous properties, and a collection of books and local newspapers, and pamphlets on local history. The record office is a depository for public records, manorial and tithe documents, and parish records of Chelmsford diocese.

Conditions of
admission and
access

The office is open to the public and an appointment in advance is usually necessary as the search room is often crowded. Also the staff appreciates the opportunity to prepare material ahead of time and certain records may need to be brought in from outside storage, so a previous indication of requirements is desirable. Inquiries should be made to the County Archivist. All material must be used in the record office.

Hours

10:00 AM - 8:45 PM, Monday; 9:15 AM - 5:15 PM, Tuesday-Thursday; 9:15 AM - 4:15 PM, Friday.

| Duplicating facilities | Photocopies, copies from microfilm, photographs, and microfilm can all be provided. A price list is available in the record office. |

Other services — Brief questions by telephone or post will be answered and reference help is available in the search room. There is also an extensive reference library for researchers' use. Detailed indexes by personal name, place, and subject provide a further help to those using the record office. Microform readers and ultra-violet lamps are provided. There is a schools service which assists and encourages the teaching of local history. Students with school projects are given special attention, but advance appointments are necessary in these cases.

Publications — The Essex Record Office has an extensive publication program and produces books on local themes. There is a catalogue available and the publications are on sale at a Bookshop within the office. Among these publications one finds Catalogue of Maps in E.R.O., 1566-1855 (reprint, 1969); First Supplement (1952, out-of-print); Second Supplement (1964); Third Supplement (1968); Essex Parish Records, 1240-1894 (1966); Guide to Essex Record Office, by F. G. Emmison (1969); Elizabethan Life (5 vols. 1970-1980, vol. 3 out-of-print); Essex People, 1750-1900, by A. F. J. Brown (1972); Essex and the Industrial Revolution, by John Booker (1974, out-of-print); No. 1 Essex Quarter Session Book, 1652-1661, ed. by D. H. Allen (1974); Handlist of Parish and Non-conformist Registers in the Essex Record Office (revised annually); Medieval Essex Community: Lay Subsidy of 1327, ed. by Jennifer C. Ward (Essex Historical Documents, vol. 1, 1983). There is also a series of teaching portfolios which consist of plates with teaching notes relating to the illustrations. These are taken from manuscripts, maps, and pictures in the record office collection. In addition there are picture booklets, reproductions of maps, and a gramophone recording.

CHELSEA — See: LONDON, Chelsea Library

CHESTER (map)

51 Institution — Cheshire Record Office
Address — Duke Street
Chester CH1 1RL

Telephone — 0244 602574

Holdings — The office holds a variety of archival groups,

among which are County Council records (19th
and 20th century); private collections (13th to 20th
century); Diocesan records (16th to 20th century);
Ecclesiastical Commissioners' records (15th to 20th
century); Society of Friends: Cheshire Monthly
Meeting records (17th to 19th century); Methodist
records (18th to 20th century); Congregational
records (18th to 20th century); Unitarian records
(17th to 20th century); Baptist records (18th to
20th century); Statutory Authorities (Poor Law
Guardians, Borough, Urban, and Rural District
Councils); Weaver Navigation (18th to 20th century); Township and Civil Parish records (17th to
20th century); Quarter Sessions (16th to 20th century); militia records (18th to 19th century); public records (Coroners, Hospital Management Committees, Insurance Committees, Land Tax Commissioners, crew lists and log books of merchant ships
registers at Runcorn, 19th to 20th century); Probate records (from the 15th century); school records
(from the 16th century); military records and an extensive collection of private papers.

The office is a repository for manorial and tithe
documents and ecclesiastical records for Chester
and for Liverpool (marriage licences and bonds
granted at Chester for Liverpool parties while the
city was in Chester diocese; Liverpool had its own
diocese from 1880). Also found are the parish
records of the deaneries of Warrington and Farn-
worth. The collection also includes records on
microfilm, among which are census returns, 1841 to
1881 at ten-year intervals; the Ecclesiastical Census,
1851; non-conformist Registers, 1648-1837; Chester
Eyre and Quo Warranto Rolls, 1299-1499; Hearth Tax
Returns, 1663, 1664, 1668, 1674; Diocese of Chester
Visitation records, 1578, 1694; Diocese of Lichfield
Bishop's Registers, 1298-1553; Thomas Bulkeley of
Bulkeley's Civil War Memoranda Book, 17th century;
and Randle Holme's genealogical and historical
manuscripts collection. Also included are printed
maps, among which are Cheshire: Saxton, 1577;
Blaeu, 1645; Speed, 1662; Bowen, 1763; Burdett,
1777; Greenwood, 1819; Swire and Hutchings, 1830;
Bryant, 1831; Chester: Lavaux, 1745; Weston, 1789;
Wood, 1833; and Ordnance Survey maps, one-inch,
two-inch, six-inch, and twenty-five-inch from 1833.
There is also a small collection of source material.

Conditions of   The record office is freely open to the public, but
admission and   an appointment of at least a week in advance is
access   usually necessary. Inquiries should be made to
                       the County Archivist. The collection must be used
                       on the premises. Where microfilm records are avail-
                       able, these are shown rather than the deposited
                       originals.

Hours   9:45 AM - 4:30 PM, Monday-Friday.

Duplicating facilities	Full-sized and microcopies are provided. "Microcopies" indicate print-offs from individual entries on microfilmed parish registers, not actual reels of microfilm. A price sheet is supplied (minimum charge Ł1) by the record office.
Other services	Specific reference questions will be answered and limited searches of up to two hours duration are undertaken if specific instructions are provided (names, dates, places and records to be searched). An hourly fee is charged for this service. Reference help is available in the search room. Microform readers and ultra-violet lamps are provided. Visits by schools or colleges can be arranged and talks, working sessions, and teaching packages are offered.
Publications	County Record Office and Chester Diocesan Record Office (revised periodically); a Summary Guide composed of the following Source Sheets: County Council Records, Private Collections, Diocesan Records, Ecclesiastical Commissioners' Records, Society of Friends: Cheshire Monthly Meeting records, Methodist records, Statutory Authorities, Ecclesiastical Parish records, Township and Civil Parish records, Quarter Sessions records, Militia records, Public records, Probate records, School records, records on Microfilm, Printed Maps, Congregational (United Reformed Church) records, Unitarian records, Baptist records.

CHESTER (map)

52 Institution Address	Chester City Record Office Town Hall Chester CH1 2HJ
Telephone	0244 40144, ext. 2108
Holdings	The office contains the official records of Chester Corporation (from ca. 1175) which include material relating to most aspects of the city's history and the records of the Chester Rural District Council and Tarvin Rural District Council. Records of private families, businesses, and institutions, relating mainly to the city of Chester, are also held. Notable special collections are the records of the Chester Blue Coat Hospital (1700-1951); Chester Council of Social Welfare (1872-1960); Chester Royal Infirmary (1755-1947); Chester College of Education (1839-1967). There is a reference library containing works about Chester, Cheshire, and neighboring counties, general historical publications, and general reference material. The 1881 census for Chester is available on microfilm. The record office is a repository for manorial and tithe documents.

The Chester Archaeological Society Library and manuscripts are also housed in the record office.

Conditions of admission and access

The office is open to the public and no prior appointment is necessary. The collections may be consulted only in the students room. Inquiries should be directed to the City Archivist.

Hours

9:00 AM - 1:00 PM, 2:00 PM - 5:00 PM, Monday-Friday. The office is open Monday to 9:00 PM by appointment.

Duplicating facilities

Full-size copying facilities are available.

Other services

Telephone and postal inquiries will be answered. Reference aid is available and an ultra-violet lamp is provided. In some cases, repair of manuscripts can be offered to individuals or outside bodies, but the record office must be reimbursed for expenses.

Publications

Guide to the Charters, Plate and Insignia of the City of Chester, by M. Groombridge; The Chester Mystery Plays, by H. Boulton; Chester, 1066-1971: Contemporary Descriptions by Residents and Visitors, by D. M. Palliser; Chester Schools: a Guide to the School Archives with a Brief History of Education in the City from 1539 to 1972, by A. M. Kennett (1973); Loyal Chester: A Brief History of Chester in the Civil War Period, ed. by A. M. Kennett; Archives and Records of the City of Chester: A Guide to the Collections in the Chester City Record Office, ed. by A. M. Kennett.

CHESTERFIELD

53 Institution
Address

Derbyshire Library Service
Chesterfield Library
Local Studies Department
New Beetwell Street
Chesterfield S40 1QN

Telephone

0246 209292, ext. 38

Holdings

The collection contains family and estate papers, records of businesses and trades, local records, including education records, Chesterfield School Board and Education Committee and school log books. Specifically found are the archives of the Barnes family with material, including bills and accounts, relating to the Grassmoor Colliery (18th and 19th century) and papers of the Twigg family with records concerning local mining (18th century). There are non-conformist records for Methodist and Unitarian churches. The library

holds the census returns for 1841 to 1881, maps
of the area and local newspapers (<u>Derbyshire
Times</u> from 1854, and its predecessor, the <u>Derby-
shire Courier</u>, from 1828-1922 and <u>Derby and
Chesterfield Reporter</u>, 1826-1930). The Mormon
International Genealogical Index for Great Britain
is also available.

Conditions of admission and access	An appointment in advance is not required. Inquiries should be directed to the Librarian. The archives must be used on the premises.
Hours	9:30 AM - 7:00 PM, Monday-Friday; 9:30 AM - 4:00 PM, Saturday.
Duplicating facilities	Photocopying equipment is available for microfilm, microfiche, and printed resources.
Other services	Brief questions by post or telephone are answered and reference help is available. There are indexes and guides provided to further aid the scholar.
Publications	<u>Derbyshire Local Studies Collection: A Guide to Resources</u> (reprinted 1982).

CHICHESTER (map)

54 Institution Address	West Sussex Record Office County Hall (John Edes House) West Street Chichester PO19 1RN
Telephone	0234 777983
Holdings	The record office is the official repository for the records of the West Sussex County Council, and all former local authorities whose powers it has assumed. These include Urban and Rural District Councils, Chichester City Council, Boards of Health, Sanitary Authorities, Boards of Poor Law Guardians and School Boards. It is also recognized by the Lord Chancellor as a place of deposit for public records, and holds the records of the local courts of Quarter Sessions and Petty Sessions, and of all the administrative work done by Quarter Sessions. Plans of road, railway and canal schemes for the county are also in the collection, as are probate records. It is also a repository for manorial and tithe records. Tithe maps for nearly every parish in West Sussex are available in the Map Room, and for most of both West and East Sussex are available on microfilm. It is the Diocesan Record Office for the Diocese of Chichester, and the Dean and Chapter of Chichester, and of all the property which they owned. Among the Bishops' records

are the transcripts of the parish registers which
were sent to the Bishop from every parish in both
West and East Sussex. The office holds the original
registers of baptisms, marriages and burials, and
other records of the majority of the parishes in
West Sussex. There are also records deposited by
private individuals and organizations. These include the records of local solicitors, and of the
Goodwood, Cowdray and Wiston estates, and of
several of the smaller West Sussex estates. The
records of the Petworth estate are administered by
the office, and can be consulted only at the record
office with two weeks' notice being given. There
are also a number of collections of correspondence
of national importance, including the correspondence
of the 5th Duke of Richmond, Richard Cobden,
John Hawkins, and L. J. Maxse. In addition there
is a very fine collection of maps of the county,
ranging from late sixteenth-century estate maps to
inclosure awards, tithe maps, and Ordnance Survey
maps. (This information is found in A Guide to the
Use of the West Sussex Record Office.)

Conditions of admission and access

The material is available for use in the office but
is not loaned. With some exceptions documents less
than thirty years old may not be seen, and for
some classes of records there is a limit for availability of one hundred years. The Petworth House
Archives and former Rural and Urban District
Councils' records are not stored on the premises
and advance notice must be given for their consultation. Although the record office is open to the
public, visitors should ring the bell by the front
door and wait to be admitted. They are required
to sign the register, which implies agreement to
follow the regulations concerning use of the records.
It is advisable to telephone or write in advance of
a first visit. Inquiries should be made to the
County Archivist. Record office accommodations do
not allow for the admission of young children or
babies in the company of those undertaking research.

Hours

9:15 AM - 12:30 PM, 1:30 PM - 5:00 PM, Monday-
Friday.

Duplicating facilities

Copies from paper (subject to the condition of the
document) and from microforms can be provided.

Other services

Brief telephone and mail inquiries are answered and
reference help is available in the office. Microform
readers and ultra-violet lamps are provided.

Publications

Genealogists' Guide to the West Sussex Office, ed.
by P. M. Wilkinson (1983); Local History in West
Sussex: A Guide to Sources, by K. C. Leslie and
T. J. McCann (1975); A Catalogue of Sussex

Estate and Tithe Award Maps Vols. I-II, comp. by
Francis W. Steer (1962, 1968; published as Vol. 61
and 66 in the Sussex Record Society's series);
Arundel Castle Archives, Vol. I comprised of 12
Handlists, Vols. II-IV ed. by Francis W. Steer
(1972, 1976, 1980); Roots of America: An Anthology
of Documents Relating to American History in the
West Sussex Record Office, ed. by Kim C. Leslie
(1976); Goodwood: Royal Letters. Mary Queen of
Scots to Queen Elizabeth, ed. by Timothy J.
McCann (1977); West Sussex Probate Inventories,
1521-1834, comp. by Timothy J. McCann (1981);
The Wiston Archives, Vol. I ed. by John M. L.
Booker (1975), Vol. II ed. by Stephen Freeth
(1982), and many others; The Goodwood Estate
Archives, Vol. I (1970), Vol. II (1972), ed. by
Frances and J. E. Amanda Venables, and Vol. III
(1985), ed. by Timothy J. McCann. A list with
prices and in-print status is available. Among the
publications planned for the future is Records of
the Royal Sussex Regiment, ed. by A. E. Read-
man. There are a number of typescript lists and
indexes which include: "List of the Number of
Persons within the City of Chichester, 31 December 1740" (1954); "Index to the Comber Papers"
(1955); "Index to the Consecrations and Faculties
in the Diocese of Chichester before 1850"; "Ancient
Charters of the Dean and Chapter of Chichester,
689-1674," 2nd ed. (1976); "Index of Persons
Mentioned in Records of Chichester by T. G. Willis"
(1964); "Index to Sussex Pedigrees in the Challen
Papers" (1964); "Handlist of Parish Registers,
Bishops' Transcripts and Modern Transcripts in
the Diocesan Record Office" (1973); "Index to Hay's
History of Chichester" (1974); "Index of Emigrants
and Transportees from West Sussex, 1778-ca. 1874"
(1980). In 1954, A Descriptive Report on the
Quarter Sessions, Other Official, and Ecclesiastical
Records in the Custody of the County Councils of
East and Est Sussex ... was issued jointly by the
Clerk of the East Sussex County Council (Lewes)
and the Clerk of the West Sussex County Council
(Chichester).

CLEVELAND	See: MIDDLESBROUGH

COLCHESTER

55 Institution	Essex Record Office
Address	Colchester and Northeast Essex Branch
	Stanwell House
	Stanwell Street
	Colchester CO2 7DL
Telephone	0206 572099

See also: CHELMSFORD, Essex Record Office;
SOUTHEND-ON-SEA, Essex Record Office

Holdings

The office holds records which relate to the areas
administered by the Colchester Borough and Tend-
ring District Councils. Records of local administrations include the Colchester Borough records from
the early 14th century as well as the more modern
deposited records of those councils and their
predecessor bodies. Also held are parish records,
including registers of baptisms, marriages and
burials, records of non-conformist churches, business, charity, Petty Sessional and Poor Law Union
records, all for the parts of Essex previously described. The office has catalogues of the collections
held at the Chelmsford and Southend-on-Sea offices,
and indexes to locally relevant records retained at
the Chelmsford (Headquarters) office. Microfilm of
census returns is available at the Local Studies
Department of the Colchester Library.

Conditions of
admission and
access

The office is open to the public; an appointment is
always preferred and is essential if microform is to
be consulted. Prior indication of records required
is also helpful. All material must be used on the
premises. Inquiries should be directed to the
County Archivist or to the Branch Archivist.

Hours

9:15 AM - 5:15 PM, Monday-Wednesday; 9:15 AM -
5:15 PM, Thursday; 9:15 AM - 4:15 PM, Friday.
Thursday and Friday hours are by appointment
only.

Duplicating
facilities

Photocopies can be made for searchers and
arrangements can be made for microfilming,
photography or print-outs from microfilm.

Other services

Brief inquiries about archive holdings and appoint-
ments for visits can be accepted by telephone.
More detailed inquiries should be made in writing.
Reference help is available in the search room.

Publications

The Essex Record Office has an extensive publication program and produces books on local themes.
There is a catalogue available and some publications
are for sale at the branch office. Among these
publications are: Catalogue of Maps in E.R.O.,
1566-1855 (reprint, 1969); First Supplement (1952,
out-of-print); Second Supplement (1964); Third
Supplement (1968); Guide to Essex Record Office,
by F. G. Emmison (1969); Essex Parish Records,
1240-1894 (1966); Elizabethan Life (5 vols., 1970-
1980, Vol. 3 out-of-print); Essex and the Industrial Revolution, by John Booker (1974, out-of-
print); No. 1 Essex Quarter Session Order Book
1652-1661, ed. by D. H. Allen (1974); Handlist of
Parish and Non-conformist Registers in the Essex

Record Office (revised annually); Medieval Essex
Community: Lay Subsidy of 1327, ed. by
Jennifer C. Ward (Essex Historical Documents,
Vol. 1, 1983). There is also a series of teaching
portfolios which consist of plates with teaching
notes relating to the illustrations. These are
taken from manuscripts, maps, and pictures in the
record office collection. In addition there are picture booklets, reproductions of maps, and a gramophone recording.

CORK

56	Institution Address	Cork Archives Institution Christ Church South Main Street Cork, Co. Cork

Telephone: 021 509012

Holdings

Various records relating to Cork City and County
found here include records transferred by Cork
Corporation and Cork County Council. There are
also many private collections concerning business
and political interests, social and family matters,
and trade unions. Although most of the records
date from the 19th century, some collections, such
as the records of Youghal Corporation, date from
the early part of the 17th century. In general,
the collection is of more interest to the general and
the local historian rather than to the genealogist.

Conditions of admission and access

Scholars are strongly advised to make an appointment in advance of a visit and all readers are required to complete an application form stating the
purpose of their research. The Archivist's permission must be received before research can com-
mence. Inquiries should be made to the Archivist.
All material must be consulted on the premises.

Hours

10:00 AM - 1:00 PM, 2:30 PM - 5:00 PM, Monday-
Friday.

Duplicating facilities

Photocopies can be made available.

Other services

General telephone and postal inquiries are answered
as soon as possible, but extensive research is not
undertaken by the staff. Reference help is available.

Publications

As yet there are no publications available other
than "Rules Governing Access to Material at the
Cork Archives." Box lists and some full descriptive lists and index systems make up the main finding aids. There are articles on the formation of
the Archival Service in Cork which appeared in

past issues of the <u>Journal of the Irish Society for Archives</u>.

CORK

57	Institution Address	Cork City Library Grand Parade Cork, Co. Cork
	Telephone	021 504110
	Holdings	The library contains land valuations, directories, published lists of emigrants and published family histories. There are also indexes and abstracts of wills and indexes to marriage license bonds. Eighteenth, nineteenth and twentieth century local newspapers are found and there are biographical indexes to newspapers. In addition there are bibliographies and genealogical handbooks.
	Conditions of admission and access	The library is freely open to the public and arrangements in advance of a visit are not required. The collection must be used on the premises. Inquiries should be directed to the Local History Librarian.
	Hours	10:00 AM - 6:00 PM, Monday-Saturday.
	Duplicating facilities	Photocopying of some material can be arranged and off-prints from microfilm can be produced.
	Other services	Telephone and postal inquiries are answered and reference help is available.
	Publications	None.

CORK

58	Institution Address	Cork County Library Farranlea Road Cork, Co. Cork
	Telephone	021 46499/46485/46383
	Holdings	The library's collection is chiefly related to County Cork and does not include original records. Among the material found is "O'Kief, Coshe Mang" series of volumes. Also held are Griffith's Valuation for County Cork, City and County directories, and tithe books (on microfilm). There are also family histories, gravestone inscriptions, edited genealogical records, and indexes.
	Conditions of admission and access	No appointment is necessary to use the collection, but microfilm readers should be booked in advance

to avoid delays. The material must be used on the premises. Inquiries should be directed to the Reference Librarian.

Hours   9: 00 AM - 5: 30 PM, Monday-Friday.

Duplicating   Photocopying facilities are available and copies
facilities   from microfilm can be provided.

Other services   Telephone and postal inquiries are answered when
                     possible, but there is not usually sufficient staff
                     available for prompt replies. Reference help is
                     always accessible.

Publications   Although no guide or index is currently provided,
                     indexes of collections and local studies is in prog-
                     ress. This includes indexes of births, deaths, and
                     marriages from local newspapers.

CORK (map)

59 Institution   University College
    Address   Boole Library
                      Cork, Co. Cork

    Telephone   021 276871

    Holdings   The library holds the Ffolliott Index to announce-
                      ments of births, marriages, and deaths in the
                      counties of Cork and Kerry appearing in Cork
                      newspapers, 1753-1827 (compiled by Rosemary
                      Ffolliott). The 1901 Census of Ireland is found
                      here and the acquisition of a complete set of in-
                      dividual household returns for Co. Cork is in
                      process. Also available is Griffith's Valuation of
                      Ireland (1848-1864) for Cork (incomplete), Clare,
                      Kerry, Limerick, Tipperary, and Waterford.
                      The Name Indexes are not held. The Munster
                      Printing Collection is housed here and contains
                      about one thousand items, mostly from the 19th
                      and 20th centuries.

    Conditions of   If the visiting scholar anticipates lengthy re-
    admission and   search, application should be made to the Sub-
    access   Librarian for Reader Services. For a single
                      visit an appointment in advance is desirable. The
                      material may be used only in the library. Inquiries
                      should be addressed to the Librarian.

    Hours   9: 30 AM - 5: 00 PM, Monday-Friday.

    Duplicating   Photocopying and full-size copies from microforms
    facilities   can be provided.

    Other services   Reference help is available and postal and tele-
                      phone inquiries are answered.

Publications	Library Guide.

COVENTRY

60 Institution Address	University of Warwick Library Modern Records Centre Coventry CV4 7AL
Telephone	0203 523523, ext. 2014
Holdings	The collection includes records of trade unions, employers and trade associations, and other organizations. Some interest groups and business records, especially those of the motor industry, are held. Also found are papers of political parties and groups, those of some members of parliament and prominent public figures. Trade union membership and benefit records are kept but are not available for all unions. The kinds of records found among these collections are minutes, financial records, correspondence, diaries, press cuttings, photographs and statistics.
Conditions of admission and access	The centre is open to all serious researchers. Advance notice of a visit is not required, but is helpful. The material must be used on the premises and some deposits are subject to restrictions on their use for research. Inquiries should be addressed to the Archivist.
Hours	9:00 AM - 1:00 PM, 1:30 PM - 5:00 PM, Monday-Thursday; 9:00 AM - 1:00 PM, 1:30 PM - 4:00 PM, Friday.
Duplicating facilities	Photocopying facilities are available.
Other services	Brief questions will be answered by post or by telephone and reference help is available in the search room.
Publications	Guide to the Modern Records Centre, University of Warwick Library, by R. Storey and J. Druker (1977); Supplement (1981); Consolidated Guide to the Modern Records Centre, by R. Storey and A. Tough (1986); The Taff Vale Case: A Guide to the ASRS Records (1978); The Osborne Case Papers and Other Records of the Amalgamated Society of Railway Servants (1979); Trade Union and Related Records (3rd ed., 1983); Women at Work and in Society (1980); A Shop Steward at Oxford (1980); A Postman's Round, 1858-1861 (1982); The First Labour Correspondent and the Board of Trade Library (1983); The Confederation of British Industry Predecessor Archive (1984); The International Transport Workers' Federation Archive

(1985); British Employers' Confederation Archive: List and Indexes (microfiche no. 1, 1983); Information Leaflets.

COVENTRY (map)

61	Institution Address	Coventry City Record Office George Eliot House Bayley Lane Coventry CV1 5RG
	Telephone	0203 25555
	Holdings	The office is a repository for the Archives of the Borough of Coventry, including charters, title deeds and Council minute books, ca. 1120-1835. Departmental records of Coventry City Council are held from 1836. Also found are archives of superseded authorities, manorial and tithe documents, local public records and records purchased by, deposited with or donated to Coventry City Record Office. These include archives of solicitors' practices, non-conformist churches, craft guilds, manufacturing firms, charities, charity schools, antiquarians, and societies. Records of particular interest to genealogists include the archives of the Mayor's (now the Lord Mayor's) Court from 1722 and the London Road Cemetery from 1847.
	Conditions of admission and access	A prior appointment is necessary to use the resources of the record office. Inquiries should be directed to the City Archivist. All the material from the collection must be used on the premises.
	Hours	8:45 AM - 4:45 PM, Monday-Thursday; 8:45 AM - 4:15 PM, Friday.
	Duplicating facilities	Full-size and microcopying facilities are available. Photographs can also be provided.
	Other services	Reference help is available and brief questions by telephone or post are answered.
	Publications	None.

CRAIGAVON   See: PORTADOWN

CROYDON   See: LONDON, London Borough of Croydon

CUMNOCK

62	Institution Address	Cumnock and Doon Valley District Library Headquarters

Bank Glen
Cumnock KA18 1PH

Telephone	0290 22024

Holdings

The collection includes District Council minutes for Dalmellington from 1932, and records from local departments dating from 1887. The parochial records for Mauchline, New Cumnock and Sorn (19th and 20th century) are also found. Photographs, prints, pamphlets and a collection of glass negatives are kept as well.

Conditions of admission and access

The library is open to the public and no arrangements in advance of a visit are necessary. Inquiries should be directed to the District Librarian. Archives and reference works must be used in the library.

Hours

9:00 AM - 4:30 PM, Monday-Friday.

Duplicating facilities

Photocopying facilities are available.

Other services

Brief questions by post or telephone are answered and reference help is provided.

Publications

None.

CWMBRAN

63 Institution
Address

Gwent County Record Office
County Hall
Cwmbran NP44 2XH

Telephone

06333 67711, ext. 214

Holdings

The record office contains the original records of local authorities in Gwent, including the official records of the Court of Quarter Sessions, the Monmouthshire County Council and District Councils in the county. The office is a designated repository for public, manorial and tithe documents, and for ecclesiastical parish records (including registers of baptisms, marriages and burials from the sixteenth century to ca. 1980) in the diocese of Monmouth and the diocese of Swansea and Brecon. Turnpike Trusts, Highway Boards, health and services records are found and there are also privately deposited collections of documents.

Conditions of admission and access

The office is open to the public and a prior appointment is not necessary. Inquiries should be made to the County Archivist.

Hours

9:30 AM - 5:00 PM, Tuesday-Thursday; 9:30 AM - 4:00 PM, Friday. Closed on Monday.

Duplicating
facilities

Full-size and microcopying facilities are provided.

Other services

A small reference library is available for researchers' use. There is also an ultraviolet lamp and a
microform reader. Inquiries by mail or telephone
are answered if extensive research is not required.
A fee is charged for this service. Reference help
is available in the search room.

Publications

Annual Reports; Guide to Monmouthshire Record Office, by W. H. Baker (1959); Guides to research
of Poor Law, Education, Coal, Iron and Steel,
History of Houses, Harbors, Docks and Shipping,
Crime and Punishment, and Family History.

DAGENHAM

See: LONDON, London Borough of Barking and
Dagenham

DARLINGTON

64 Institution
Address

Durham County Record Office
Darlington Branch
Darlington Library
Crown Street
Darlington DL1 1ND

Telephone

0325 469858

See also: DURHAM

Holdings

The holdings include archives relating to the
Darlington District of County Durham. Among
those found here are Bishop's Borough Court
Books, 1612-1633, 1710-1769, Board of Guardians,
Board of Health, Burial Board, and District Highway Boards. Borough records include minute
books, Committee minute books, and departmental
records. Also found are School Board Minute
Books, 1871-1904 and school records. Rural District records, Parish Council records, Parish
records, tithe maps, and non-conformist church
records are among the holdings. Family papers
include Pease (diaries, letters and miscellaneous
papers), Allan (deeds), and Brigham (papers relating to the wool trade and public duties of George
and Robert Brigham of Hutton Rudby). Business
records, Turnpike Trusts papers and the archives
of clubs and societies are also kept.

Conditions of
admission and
access

The archives are open to the public and advance
booking is essential only for Saturday and evening
visits. Inquiries should be directed to the Archivist. The collection must be used on the
premises.

Hours	9:00 AM - 1:00 PM, 2:15 PM - 7:00 PM, Monday-Friday; 9:00 AM - 1:00 PM, 2:15 PM - 5:00 PM, Saturday.
Duplicating facilities	Photocopying services are available.
Other services	Reference help is available and brief questions by post or telephone can be answered.
Publications	Durham County Record Office; The Londonderry Papers: Catalogue of Documents (1969); Streatlam and Gibside: The Bowes and Strathmore Families in County Durham (1984); Guide to the Darlington Branch (1985); Handlists, Subject Guides.

DEESIDE   See: HAWARDEN

DERBY

65 Institution Address	Derbyshire Library Service Derby Central Library Local Studies Department The Wardwick Derby DE1 1HF
Telephone	0332 31111, ext. 2184
Holdings	The history of Derbyshire is well covered by this collection and one finds family and estate records, notably those of the Pares, Cotton, and Mundy families and the family libraries known as the Devonshire and Bemrose libraries. There are also Borough Court records, Board of Guardians papers, Corporation deeds (17th-19th century), and the archives of the Canal Company, 1793-1914. Other business papers include the Wyatt papers concerning lead mining and the Duesbury Collection which consists of records of the Derby China Factory.
Conditions of admission and access	The library is open to the public and prior arrangements to use the collection are not required. Inquiries should be directed to the Local Studies Librarian. The archives must be used in the library.
Hours	9:00 AM - 7:00 PM, Monday-Friday; 9:00 AM - 1:00 PM, Saturday.
Duplicating facilities	Photocopying and full-size copies from microforms can be provided.
Other services	Brief questions by post or telephone are answered and reference help is provided in the library. There are also indexes and guides to further aid the scholar.

Publications   Derbyshire Local Studies Collection (1976); guides, lists, brochures.

DOLGELLAU

66 Institution   Gwynedd Archives Service
Address   Dolgellau Area Record Office
Cae Penarlag
Dolgellau LL40 2YB

Telephone   0341 422341, ext. 261

The Dolgellau Area Record Office is part of the Gwynedd Archives Service (which comprises the former Anglesey, Caernarfonshire, and Merioneth-shire Record Offices). See also: CAERNARFON (Caernarfon Area Record Office) and LLANGEFNI (Llangefni Area Record Office)

Holdings   The record office houses certain public records and is a repository for manorial and tithe documents. The collection includes official county records, parish, estate, industrial, and business papers, newspapers, photographs, oral history tapes, and microfilm copies of the census returns, 1841-1881.

Conditions of   The office is open to the public and no advance
admission and   appointment is required except for evening hours.
access   Inquiries should be made to the Area Archivist. All material must be used on the premises.

Hours   9:00 AM - 1:00 PM, 2:00 PM - 5:00 PM, Monday-Friday. The office is open until 7:00 PM on Wednesday. On Thursdays, the office will open until 7:00 PM, by appointment.

Duplicating   Full-size and microcopying facilities are available,
facilities   and photographs can be provided.

Other services   Brief questions by telephone or post are answered. Reference help is available in the search room and services to schools are provided.

Publications   Gwynedd Archives Services Bulletin (annual); Calendar of the Merioneth Quarter Sessions Rolls, by K. Williams-Jones (1965); miscellaneous other calendars, guides, reproductions of documents, postcards, and books on local history are produced.

DONCASTER

67 Institution   Doncaster Metropolitan Borough
Address   Doncaster Archives Department
King Edward Road, Balby
Doncaster DN4 0NA

Telephone	0302 859811
Holdings	Records of parishes within the Archdeaconry of Doncaster in the Diocese of Sheffield include baptisms, and for most parishes, marriages and burials. Records of the Borough of Doncaster (1193-1974) and other local authorities in the area are also found. Family and estate collections include Cromwell (formerly Copley) of Sprotbrough, Davies-Cooke of Owston, and Battie-Wrighton of Cusworth. Methodist records for the Doncaster area are also available.
Conditions of admission and access	The archives department is open to the public without a prior appointment, although notice of a visit is appreciated. The records must be consulted in the public reading room only. Inquiries should be directed to the Archivist.
Hours	9: 30 AM - 12: 30 PM, 2: 00 PM - 5: 00 PM, Monday-Friday.
Duplicating facilities	Photocopies can be provided subject to the condition and format of the document.
Other services	Reference help is available and brief questions by post or telephone are answered. An ultra-violet lamp is provided. Lists and finding aids to further assist the researcher are available.
Publications	Guide to the Archives Department (2nd ed., 1981); List of Parish Records, List of Local Record Agents.

DORCHESTER (map)

68	Institution Address	Dorset Record Office County Hall Dorchester DT1 1XJ
	Telephone	0305 63131, ext. 4411
	Holdings	The record office holds the Parish registers of Dorset from the 16th to the 20th century. These include registers of christenings, marriages, and burials. There are probate records for the Dorset Archdeaconry, Corfe Castle, Wimborne Minister, Sturminster, Marshall, Milton Abbey, Canford Magna and Poole, Stratton peculiars, manors of Frampton and Burton Bradstock and the Dorset Probate Registry, 1660-1941. Also found are Dorset Quarter Sessions, 16th-20th century, and Petty Sessions, 16th-20th century, and large numbers of manorial, estate, business, and family papers from the 10th to the 20th century, inclosure and tithe records, and the archives of some boroughs. The record office is a repository for manorial and tithe

documents and for ecclesiastical records (Salisbury: parish records of Archdeaconries of Dorset and Sherborne).

Conditions of admission and access	An appointment in advance is highly recommended or the researcher risks finding no space available for his use. Documents are requested by means of a request slip and usually only four items per table are issued at one time. All material must be used in the search room under supervision. Inquiries should be made to the County Archivist.
Hours	9:00 AM - 1:00 PM, 2:00 PM - 5:00 PM, Monday-Friday.
Duplicating facilities	There are facilities for full-size and microcopies available. Some items in the record office may not be copied and all copying is at the discretion of the County Archivist. A leaflet is available which gives details of prices.
Other services	Reference help is available in the search room and there are catalogues and indexes to aid the researcher. An ultra-violet lamp is provided. Brief questions will be answered by telephone or post, and more extensive searches are conducted for a fee.
Publications	Index to the Dorset County Records, by A. C. Cox (1938); Leaflets explaining the use of the record office, search room, etc.; A Guide to the Location of Dorset Parish Registers (in preparation).

DOUGLAS

69 Institution Address	Isle of Man General Registry Finch Road Douglas, Isle of Man
Telephone	0624 73358
Holdings	The general registry includes among its holdings the High Court Records, original Acts and Resolutions of Tynwald, Grants of Representation to the estates' decedents, original plans and valuation of Manx estates and many other documents relating to the history and development of the Isle of Man. The registry also contains statutory records of births registered in the Isle of Man (from 1878); records of the Church of England baptisms (1611-1878); statutory records of marriages registered in the Isle of Man (from 1884); Church of England marriage records (1629-1849); Church of England and Dissenters marriage records (1849-1883); statutory records of deaths (from 1878); records of Church of England burials (1610-1878); adopted

children registers (from 1928); wills (from 1911);
deeds to property in the Isle of Man (from 1911),
and maintains the Deeds Registry of Wills admitted
to probate. (Earlier wills and deeds are at the
Manx Museum. See entry no. 70.)

Conditions of admission and access	The registry is open to the public and researchers are permitted to use the records. Inquiries should be addressed to the Chief Registrar. All material must be used on the premises.
Hours	9:00 AM - 1:00 PM, 2:00 PM - 4:30 PM, Monday-Friday.
Duplicating facilities	Full-size copying facilities are available.
Other services	Reference help is available for scholars and brief inquiries by telephone or mail will be answered.
Publications	Census Reports; Chief Registrar's Annual Report ... of Births, Marriages and Deaths.

DOUGLAS

70	Institution Address	The Manx Museum Library Kingswood Grove Douglas, Isle of Man
	Telephone	0624 75522
	Holdings	The library holds many of the public records of the Isle of Man and the ecclesiastical records of the diocese of Sodor and Man as well as private and business papers. These records include property deeds from ca. 1700 to 1910, wills, ca. 1600 to 1916, census returns, 1841-1881, and parish register copies to 1884. The printed collections include books relating to the Isle of Man, Manx newspapers from 1793, and maps. There is also a large photograph collection.
	Conditions of admission and access	Visitors are welcome to use the library. Inquiries should be made to the Archivist, and all material must be used on the premises.
	Hours	10:00 AM - 5:00 PM, Monday-Saturday.
	Duplicating facilities	Photocopying facilities are available and photographs can be provided.
	Other services	Reference help is available and brief inquiries by telephone or post will be answered.
	Publications	Journal of the Manx Museum (annual); Guide to the Manx Museum (6th ed., 1983); Guide to Cregneash,

Open-Air Folk Museum (1985); Brief Guide to the
Nautical Museum, Castletown; Guide to "The Grove"
Rural Life Museum, Ramsey (1981); The Gibbs of the
Grove: Stowell Kenyon (1979); Ancient and
Historical Monuments of the Isle of Man (5th ed.,
1981); The Art of the Manx Crosses, by A. M.
Cubbon (3rd ed., 1983); Birds of the Isle of Man,
by J. P. Cullen and D. J. Slinn (4th ed., 1983);
The J. D. Clucas Coin Collection of Manx Coins:
a Check List with Notes (1980); Early Maps of the
Isle of Man: Guide to the Collection in the Museum,
by A. M. Cubbon (4th ed., 1967); The Medieval
Chapel of St. Mary's, Castletown: Later the
Castletown Grammar School, by A. M. Cubbon;
Prehistoric Sites in the Isle of Man, by A. M.
Cubbon (3rd impr., 1984); The Collected Poems of
T. E. Brown (2nd ed., 1976); The History of Kirk
Maughold, by William and Constance Radcliffe
(1979); Manx Archaeological Survey, by J. R. Brice
(6th Report, 1968); Three Iron Age Round Houses
in the Isle of Man, by G. Bersu (1977); Cronica
Regum Mannie and Insularum, transcribed by
George Broderick (1979); Deer's Cry, Illuminated
Lettering by Archibald Knox (1983); Views of the
Isle of Man of 1795, John Warwick Smith (set of
six views); The History of the Isle of Man, by
A. W. Moore (2 vols., 1900, reprinted, 1977, out-
of-print); Calf of Man Bird Observatory Report
(1966-   ).

DOVER	See: MAIDSTONE, Kent County Archives Office

DUBLIN

| 71 | Institution
Address | Church of Ireland Representative Church Body
Library
Braemor Park
Dublin 14 |
|---|---|---|

No additional information from this library was
obtained.

DUBLIN (map)

| 72 | Institution
Address | The Genealogical Office (Office of Arms)
The Castle
Dublin, Co. Dublin |
|---|---|---|
| | Telephone | Unknown |
| | Holdings | The records include freeholders rolls for Northern
Ireland Counties of Armagh and Fermanagh and for
Ireland Counties, Clare, Donegal, Kilkenny, Lime-
rick, Longford, Meath, Roscommon, and Tipperary.
These are not complete and the earliest date is 1753. |

There are also abstracts of wills, obituaries gathered from newspapers (17th and 18th century), marriage licences and directories. Lists of freemen (City of Dublin), army lists, hearth money rolls, and poll taxes are found. Transcripts of the religious census (1766) are held for parishes in several counties and there are family histories and pedigrees, land records, and visitations.

Conditions of admission and access

The Heraldic Museum is open to the public. The collections in the Genealogical Office, because of their age and condition, are not available for research. The staff will undertake a search of the records for a fee, and a scale of fees is available. Inquiries should be addressed to the Director.

Hours

9:30 AM - 5:00 PM, Monday-Friday.

Duplicating facilities

Copying facilities are available.

Other services

The staff will conduct research among the records for visiting scholars upon payment of a fee. Copies of pertinent material will be provided for an additional fee. A scale of these fees is available.

Publications

Forms, indexes, lists, guides.

DUBLIN (map)

73 Institution
    Address

General Register Office
(Oifig An Ard-Chlaraitheora)
Joyce House
8-11 Lombard Street, East
Dublin 2

Telephone

01 711000

Holdings

The office holds registers of births and deaths registered in all Ireland on and after January 1, 1864 to December 31, 1921, and in Ireland (exclusive of the six northeastern counties) from that date. Also held are registers of marriages in all Ireland from April 1, 1845 to December 31, 1863 (except Roman Catholic) and marriages registered in all Ireland on and after January 1, 1864 to December 31, 1921 and in Ireland exclusive of the six northeastern counties from that date. Registers of births at sea of children with at least one Irish parent (January 1, 1864-December 31, 1921; after that, children belonging to parents of the six northeastern counties are excluded) and of deaths at sea of Irish-born persons (January 1, 1864-December 31, 1921; excluding the six northeastern counties after that date) are kept. Registers of births of children born of Irish parents and deaths of Irish-born persons certified by British Consuls abroad, original certificates of marriages by special license, adopted children registers and other registers of births, deaths and marriages are available.

Conditions of admission and access	The search room is open to the public and readers may undertake searches of the indexes to the records upon payment of an appropriate fee. Forms are available for the request of copies of particular certificates. This also requires a fee. Inquiries should be directed to the Registrar General.
Hours	9:30 AM - 4:40 PM, Monday-Friday.
Duplicating facilities	Photocopying facilities are available.
Other services	Searches are carried out subject to a fee. Brief postal or telephone inquiries are answered.
Publications	Lists, forms, finding aids, indexes.

DUBLIN (map)

74	Institution Address	King's Inn Library Henrietta Street Dublin 1
	Telephone	01 747134
	Holdings	The library contains the admission papers of barristers and law students from 1607 to date. There are ninety volumes of printed Irish appeals to the British House of Lords, records of rentals (concerning the areas auctioned off in the thirty years following the Encumbered Estates Act of 1849) and manuscripts in the Irish language, two of which pertain to medieval genealogies. Griffith's Valuation is held, as are Ordnance Survey maps, legal directories and Dublin street directories. There are reports of trials and cases, parliamentary debates, papers, and journals, six hundred volumes of 17th, 18th, and 19th century pamphlets, and there are paintings.
	Conditions of admission and access	This is a private library for the use of members of the Honourable Society of King's Inns. Researchers may be permitted to use the library if the Library committee considers their work of a bona fide nature. Requests to use the collection should be addressed, in writing, to the Librarian. The material must be used on the premises.
	Hours	2:00 PM - 6:00 PM, Monday; 11:00 AM - 6:00 PM, Tuesday-Friday; 10:00 AM - 1:00 PM, Saturday.

The hours vary slightly at different times of the year.

Duplicating
facilities

Photocopying facilities are available with enlargement and reduction capability.

Other services

The library staff offers reference help and postal inquiries are usually answered gratis. However, difficult questions and requests for copies receive response upon receipt of a fee for search services, copying, and postage.

Publications

King's Inn Admissions Papers, 1607-1867, ed. by Edward Keane, P. Beryl Phair, and Thomas Sadler (published in Dublin by the Irish Manuscripts Commission, 1982); A Catalogue of the Portraits in the Hall of the King's Inns (published by the Authority of Benchers and printed in Dublin by A. Thom and Co., N.D.); Catalogue of Irish Manuscripts in King's Inns Library, Dublin, by Pádraig de Brún (published by the Institute for Advanced Studies in Dublin, 1972).

DUBLIN (map)

75 Institution
    Address

Marsh's Library
St. Patrick's Close
Dublin 8

Telephone

01 753917

Holdings

The library contains 17th-century rare books, works on religious controversy, mathematics, law, science, travel, philosophy, medicine, music and the classics. There is some material relating to the Huguenots and the intellectual disputes in France in the 17th century. Some of the books contain annotations by Jonathan Swift. Name books for several counties and the Poll Money Ordinances are found here.

Conditions of
admission and
access

Researchers must have an appointment in advance and a letter of introduction. (Visitors not wishing to use the collection have no such requirements.) Inquiries should be addressed to the Librarian.

Hours

10:00 AM - 12:00 noon, 2:00 PM - 5:00 PM, Monday, Wednesday-Friday; 10:30 AM - 12:30 PM, Saturday; closed Tuesday.

Duplicating
facilities

Arrangements can be made for microfilming and for photocopying.

Other services

Questions by mail or telephone are answered, but otherwise help is limited.

Publications	All Graduates and Gentlemen: Marsh's Library, by Muriel McCarthy (O'Brien Press, 1980); Galen Remembered; Medical Exhibition Catalogue (1986).

DUBLIN (map)

76 Institution Address	National Archives Head Office Four Courts Dublin 7
Telephone	01 733833
Holdings	The Head Office of the National Archives (formed by the amalgamation of the Public Record Office of Ireland and the State Paper Office in accordance with section three of the National Archives Act, 1986) holds archives accessioned from government departments, courts, and private sources. Complete census returns for 1901 and 1911 are held, with returns for a few areas for 1821, 1831, 1841, and 1851. No manuscript returns survive for 1861, 1871, 1881, and 1891. Returns or transcripts of returns of the religious census of 1766 survive for some areas, chiefly counties Cork, Limerick, Londonderry, Louth, and Tipperary. Tithe applotment books and valuation records are held and provide a partial substitute for missing census records. Tithe applotment books, compiled between 1823 and 1837, give the name of land occupier, the amount of land held, and the sum to be paid in tithes to the Church of Ireland. Copies of the books for Northern Ireland are also kept. The Primary Valuation, also known as Griffith's Valuation, was carried out between 1847 and 1864. There is a printed valuation book for each barony or poor law union, which shows the names of occupiers of land and buildings, the names of persons from whom these were leased, and the amount and value of the property held. Records of wills and administrations held are: 1) Original wills and administration papers lodged in the Principal and District Registries since 1904; 2) Will books containing copies of most wills proved in District Registries since 1858; 3) Grant books; 4) Betham's abstracts; 5) Sadleir's abstracts; 6) Inland Revenue registers of wills and administrations, 1828-1839; 7) Charitable Donations and Bequests will extract books; 8) Other copies of extracts of wills and administrations. The office holds some Church of Ireland parish registers and has a list of all the surviving registers specifying their location. It also has a copy of the National Library's list of Catholic parish registers. Genealogical abstracts relating to particular families are available. Directories, Catholic qualification rolls

and convert rolls, Rentals of the Incumbered Estates Court and Landed Estates Court, Voters'
lists and free-holders' registers, records of police
and of teachers are also found.

Conditions of
admission and
access

The office is open to the public and no prior appointment is required. Inquiries should be made
to the Director. The archives must be used in
the reading room.

Hours

10:00 AM - 5:00 PM, Monday-Friday, excluding
public holidays.

Duplicating
facilities

Photocopying and microfilming facilities are available.

Other services

Brief questions by post and telephone are
answered, but staff does not undertake extended
research. Reference help is provided. Finding
aids, lists and indexes are available.

Publications

Information Leaflet for Genealogists; Short Guide
to the Public Record Office of Ireland; The Public
Record: Sources for Local History.

DUBLIN (map)

77 Institution
Address

National Library of Ireland
Kildare Street
Dublin 2

Telephone

01 765521

Holdings

This is one of the great libraries of the world and
as such contains a wealth of information on Ireland,
its history and its people. There are original
manuscripts and printed sources from earliest times
to the present day covering literary, social,
genealogical, and historical matters and with information in all areas of learning. The researcher
finds genealogies, pedigrees and family histories,
early newspapers, directories, histories of
counties, towns, and regions, reports, maps, surveys, copies of state papers, and letters regarding
the people and affairs of Ireland. Transcripts of
wills, marriage records, rent rolls, muster rolls,
freeman rolls, cemetery records, and lists of county
officers are among the records. Many resources
are on microfilm and many were copied from original
documents. There are also historical and genealogical periodicals and diocesan and parish histories.
Microfilm copies of the 17th-century Books of Survey and Distribution (from the Annesley Collection)
are held for every county of Ireland except County
Meath. There is also a microfilm copy of part of
the Genealogical Office Manuscript Collection. The

Freeman's Journal Index, Names Index and Land
Index from the Roman Catholic Parish Registers,
Griffith's Valuation (survey and valuation in the
1850s) with indexes by county to Griffith's Valuation and Tithe Applotment Books are also in the
collection.

Conditions of
admission and
access

The library is open to the public and advance
notice of a visit is not required. Inquiries should
be addressed to the Director. The collection must
be used on the premises.

Hours

10:00 AM - 9:00 PM, Monday-Thursday; 10:00 AM -
5:00 PM, Friday; 10:00 AM - 1:00 PM, Saturday.

Duplicating
facilities

Facilities for copying material from the collection
are available.

Other services

Brief postal or telephone questions are answered.
Reference help is provided.

Publications

The Manuscript Sources for the History of Irish
Civilization, by R. J. Hayes (11 vols., 1965);
Supplement (3 vols., 1979); Guide to Articles in
Irish Periodicals, by R. J. Hayes (9 vols., 1970).

DUBLIN

Institution

Public Record Office
See: DUBLIN, National Archives

DUBLIN (map)

78 Institution
Address

Registry of Deeds
Henrietta Street
Dublin 1

Telephone

Unknown

Holdings

There is information on families in a wide range of
social situations from the very wealthy to those in
modest circumstances. Among the records are
deeds of sales, mortgages, deeds in trust, releases,
leases, assignments, marriage settlements, business
agreements, and wills. These papers are valuable
for reconstructing families through land records
when other sources are unavailable. There is a
names index which lists the principal for whom the
instrument was drawn.

Conditions of
admission and
access

The registry is open to the public and an appointment in advance is not required. A fee is requested for consulting some records. Inquiries
should be directed to the Registrar of Deeds. The
material may be used only on the premises.

Hours	9:00 AM - 4:00 PM, Monday-Friday.
Duplicating facilities	Photocopying facilities are available.
Other services	Reference help is available in the search room, but the staff does not undertake research for the visiting scholar. Telephone or postal inquiries are answered.
Publications	Lists, indexes, guides, brochures.

DUBLIN (map)

79	Institution Address	The Royal Irish Academy Library 19 Dawson Street Dublin 2
	Telephone	01 762570/764222
	Holdings	The library's collections include records of land holdings such as books of survey and distribution and a 17th-century book of postings and sale. The genealogies in the Irish Manuscript Collection include the John Windele Manuscripts (Cork genealogies), the De La Ponce Manuscripts (Irish Brigades in France), the Marquess of MacSwiney of Mashanaglass papers (military records of the Swiss Guard at the Vatican), and the Upton papers (copies of wills, etc., County Westmeath). There are also published histories of families.
	Conditions of admission and access	Members of the Academy may use the library and readers recommended by a member are also admitted. A letter of introduction is required for scholars visiting from overseas. Appointments should be made with the Librarian. Other inquiries should also be directed to the Librarian. The material may be consulted only on the premises.
	Hours	9:30 AM - 8:00 PM, Monday; 9:30 AM - 5:30 PM, Tuesday-Friday.
	Duplicating facilities	Photocopying is available and photographs and microfilm can be provided by arrangement. Photocopying is allowed only if the physical state of the material is satisfactory.
	Other services	Telephone and postal inquiries are answered and reference help is available.
	Publications	Catalogue of Irish Manuscripts in the Royal Irish Academy (28 Fasciculi) (1926-1970); Index to First Lines (1948); General Index (1958); "Checklist of Other Manuscripts" (typescript). Also concerning this collection is Hayes, R. J. Sources for the

History of Irish Civilization, Vol. XI, pp. 272-322 (Boston, 1965).

DUBLIN (map)

80	Institution	University of Dublin
	Address	Trinity College Library
		College Street
		Dublin, 20
	Telephone	01 772941

The response from this library indicated that genealogical holdings are limited. Library policy is to direct inquiries of this kind to the Genealogical Office in Dublin or to commercial institutions which engage in this type of research.

DUDLEY

81	Institution	Dudley Central Library
	Address	Dudley Archives and Local History Department
		3 St. James's Road
		Dudley DY1 1HR
	Telephone	0384 55433, ext. 5541/5526; after 5:00 PM and on Saturday: 0384 56321
	Holdings	The collection includes material relating to the area of the present Metropolitan Borough and the surrounding areas of the Black Country, with information on a wide range of local topics. Records of the Dudley Court of Quarter Sessions (1909-1971), records of Dudley Magistrates' Court (1848-1972), records of Kings Winford and Wordsly Petty Sessional Division (1872-1966) are held. Also local government papers, school board and school records are found. The Dudley Estate Archive (the Earls of Dudley), 12th to the 20th Century, is kept and includes title deeds, manorial records, estate records, maps, and mining records. Business archives, records of societies and organizations, solicitors' and historians' manuscripts and transcripts are also found. The department is a recognized repository for parish records in the Deanery of Dudley (except Romsley) and the Deanery of Stourbridge (parishes within the Dudley Metropolitan Borough, Diocese of Worcester), and the Deanery of Himley (Diocese of Lichfield) and numbers of parishes have deposited their records. Nonconformists church records are also available and include Methodist, Baptist, Unitarian, Congregational and some Society of Friends and Roman Catholic. The Census enumerations, 1841-1881 for the area of the present Metropolitan Borough are

held on microfilm and there is a microfiche copy
of the International Genealogical Index for Staffordshire and Worcestershire. A large collection
of photographs and slides of the area is also held.

Conditions of admission and access	The department is open to the public, but prior notice of a visit is advisable. Some material is stored away from the department and there may be a delay before it can be produced. An appointment is required for those who wish to consult the collection on Saturday. The material must be used on the premises. Inquiries should be directed to the Archivist.
Hours	9:00 AM - 1:00 PM, 2:00 PM - 5:00 PM, Monday, Wednesday, Friday; 2:00 PM - 7:00 PM, Tuesday, Thursday; 9:30 AM - 12:30 PM, first and third Saturday of the month by appointment only.
Duplicating facilities	Photocopying facilities are available and photographs can be provided by arrangement.
Other services	Brief questions by telephone or post are answered and reference help is available in the search room. An ultra-violet lamp is provided, as are microform readers. These must be booked in advance. Lectures and small exhibitions can be arranged if sufficient notice is given.
Publications	Dudley the 16th Century Town; Dudley the 17th Century Town; Dudley in the 18th Century; Russell's Hall; Notes on Stourbridge Glass; Dudley Official Map; Dudley as It Was; Historical Maps; Himley Hall and Park; Joe Darby; Sports Organizations; Youth Organizations; Local Organizations and Societies; Dudley Visitors' Guide; Real Ale in the Black Country; Dudley Art Gallery; George Dunn; Francis Brett Young. Also, leaflets, brochures, and postcards are produced by the department.

DUMBARTON

82 Institution Address	Dumbarton Library Strathleven Place Dumbarton G82 1BD
Telephone	0389 63129
Holdings	The collection contains local newspapers dating from 1851 and photographs, plans, and maps of the area. There are records of associations and societies and businesses including those of the Dennystown Forge Company. Burgh records are kept for Dumbarton (1599-1975) and Helensburgh (1807-1975). Also found are charters, correspondence, and papers of private individuals.

Conditions of admission and access	The library is open to the public and visiting scholars are not required to make advance arrangements to inspect the records. Inquiries should be directed to the Librarian.
Hours	10: 00 AM - 5: 00 PM, Monday-Saturday.
Duplicating facilities	Photocopying equipment is available.
Other services	Brief questions by telephone or post are answered and reference help is available. Various finding aids and indexes are provided to aid the scholar.
Publications	None.

DUMFRIES

83	Institution Address	Dumfries and Galloway Regional Council Library Service Ewart Library Archives Catherine Street Dumfries DG1 1JB
	Telephone	0387 3820/2070
	Holdings	The records of the area are kept here, including those for the Councils and other authorities. Family papers concerning the region are found, as well as papers of individuals.
	Conditions of admission and access	The library is open to the public and whereas no formalities are required to use the collection, advance notice of a visit is appreciated. Inquiries should be directed to the District Librarian or to the Reference and Local Collection Librarian. The archives must be used in the library.
	Hours	10: 00 AM - 7: 30 PM, Monday-Wednesday, Friday; 10: 00 AM - 5: 00 PM, Thursday, Saturday.
	Duplicating facilities	Photocopying and full-size copies of microforms can be provided.
	Other services	Brief questions by telephone or by mail are answered, and reference help is available.
	Publications	None.

DUMFRIES

84	Institution Address	Dumfries Archive Centre 33 Burns Street Dumfries DG1 2PS

Telephone	0387 69254
Holdings	The centre holds the Town Council minutes for the Royal Burgh of Dumfries and assorted records relating to public bodies in Dumfries.
Conditions of admission and access	The centre is open to the public, but an appointment in advance is advisable. Inquiries should be directed to the Archivist. The material must be used on the premises.
Hours	Information on opening hours is not presently available.
Duplicating facilities	Photocopying facilities are available.
Other services	Brief questions by post or telephone are answered, and reference help is available. Information on other services is not presently available.
Publications	None.

DUMFRIES

85 Institution Address	Dumfries Museum The Observatory Church Street Dumfries DG2 7SW
Telephone	0387 53374
Holdings	The collection contains Burgess Lists for Dumfries town, Graveyard lists for Nithsdale and parts of Annandale. There are also Annan Parish census records for 1801-1821 and Register of Testaments for Dumfrieshire. Also found are indexes of local newspapers and magazines from 1773; local manuscript diaries from the mid-18th century; almost complete runs of Burgh Court books, Town Council minutes, and related material from 1563; almost complete sets of accounts, jail books, anchorage books from 1631; some 20,000 loose documents, boxed and calendared according to subjects (petitions, accounts, jail documents, military documents, etc.), up to 1720. Documents between 1720 and 1900 are arranged by bundles and subject in record boxes. Microfilm of some of this material may be obtained from the University of Edinburgh Library.
Conditions of admission and access	The visiting scholar must make an application to use this collection and admission is with the permission of the Curator of Museums, to whom inquiries should be directed. An appointment in advance and a letter of introduction are recommended. The material must be used on the premises.

Hours	10:00 AM - 1:00 PM, 2:00 PM - 5:00 PM, Monday-Friday.
Duplicating facilities	Full-size copying facilities are available.
Other services	Some reference help may be provided for the researcher and information, work space, and other accommodations are made available and the documents are provided. Brief inquiries by post or telephone are answered.
Publications	Papers in Transactions of Dumfries and Galloway Natural History and Antiquarian Society (since 1862); leaflets.

DUNDEE

86	Institution Address	City of Dundee District Archive and Record Centre City Chambers 14 City Square Dundee DD1 3BY
	Telephone	0382 23141, ext. 4494
	Holdings	The holdings include the official records of the City of Dundee District Council and of the former Corporation of Dundee. The centre also administers (on an agency basis) the official records of Tayside Regional Council, which include those relating to the former Angus County and Perth and Kinross County Councils. For the City of Dundee, these include (but are not limited to) Burgh Court books, 1520-1898, Register of Deeds, 1626-1908, Council minute books, 1553 to date and account books, 1586 to date, school records, police board and commission minutes, and Parish Council minutes. Angus County Council records include County Council minutes, school records, lieutenancy records and free holders records. Perth and Kinross County Council records include highway authorities, County Council minutes, school records, lieutenancy records, and free holders records. Family, estate, and business records have also been deposited.
	Conditions of admission and access	Scholars or authorized persons wishing to consult the records must send an application to the Archivist at least three days before an intended visit. It should state the purpose for which access is desired and the classes of documents to be consulted. Access to the records is free of charge except for consultation of documents subject to payment of statutory fees. Some records are subject to restrictions because of age or condition, or the wishes expressed by the depositor. The material must be used in the search room.

Hours	9:15 AM - 4:45 PM, Monday-Friday, by appointment.
Duplicating facilities	Photocopies can be supplied if the original is in good condition.
Other services	Reference help is available and brief questions are answered by post or telephone. An ultra-violet lamp and an illuminated magnifier are provided.
Publications	Charters, Writs and Public Documents of the Royal Burgh of Dundee, 1292-1880 (1880); Roll of Prominent Burgesses of Dundee, 1513-1880 (1887); A Bibliography of the County of Angus (1975).

DUNDEE

87	Institution Address	Dundee District Libraries Central Library The Wellgate Dundee DD1 1DB
	Telephone	0382 23141
	Holdings	The library holds the Dundee Trades Council Collection of manuscript and printed works. Correspondence of individuals from the area (including William McGonagall, Edwin Scrymgeour, and Mary Slessor) and papers relating to organizations and societies. There are also maps, plans, and photographs (notably the Wilson Collection, ca. 1888-ca. 1910), prints, posters, and newspapers.
	Conditions of admission and access	The library is open to the public, but researchers wishing to make use of a specific collection should make arrangements in advance. Inquiries should be directed to the Chief Librarian. The archives and reference collection must be used in the library.
	Hours	9:30 AM - 9:00 PM, Monday-Friday; 9:30 AM - 5:00 PM, Saturday.
	Duplicating facilities	Full-size copying facilities are provided.
	Other services	Brief questions by post or telephone are answered and reference help is provided in the library.
	Publications	A Brief Guide to the Old Dundee Historical Collection, by J. MacLauchlan (1901); guides, brochures.

DUNFERMLINE

88	Institution Address	Dunfermline District Library Central Library Abbot Street Dunfermline KY12 7NW

Telephone	0383 23661/23662
Holdings	The collection includes parish records from 1561 to 1685, valuation and voters rolls, municipal records and extracts from Burgh records. Church records and those of associations and societies are also kept. The papers of the Dunfermline Incorporation of Weavers are also found. Prints and drawings, photographs, and maps, mostly of the West Fife area, are housed here.
Conditions of admission and access	The library is open to the public and prior arrangements to use the material are not required. Inquiries should be addressed to the Director of Libraries, Museums, and Art Galleries. The archives, manuscripts and reference works must be used in the library.
Hours	10:00 AM - 7:00 PM, Monday-Tuesday, Thursday; 10:00 AM - 1:00 PM, 2:00 PM - 5:00 PM, Wednesday, Saturday.
Duplicating facilities	Photocopying equipment is available and full-size copies from microfilm can be provided.
Other services	Brief questions are answered by mail or by telephone and reference help is provided.
Publications	Guide to Local History Room (rev. 1976); A Guide to Local Maps and Plans (1978); Coal Mining in West Fife: A Bibliography of Material Held in Dunfermline Central Library (1979).

DURHAM (map)

89 Institution Address	Durham County Record Office County Hall Durham DH1 5UL
Telephone	0385 64411, ext. 2474, 2253
	See also: DARLINGTON
Holdings	The record office contains many official and public records. It is also designated by the Bishop of Durham as the Diocesan repository for parish records. The official records include County Council, Quarter Sessions, Clerk of the Peace (including enclosure awards and plans), Petty Sessions, Coroners, manorial, Municipal Corporation, Urban District Council and Local Board of Health, Rural District Council and Rural Sanitary Authority, Civil Parish, Highway Administration (including Turnpike Trust), Ecclesiastical Parish (including records of parish officers), Board of Guardians, Hospital Management Committee, National

Coal Board (including records of old colliery companies), School Board, school log books, and school
building plans. The private record collection contains records of families, estates, industries, and
non-conformist churches. These include baptism,
marriage, and burial registers from Methodist,
Baptist, Presbyterian, Congregational, one Roman
Catholic parish, a few Society of Friends, and
other church records. The parish records begin
in 1538 (but many early registers have been lost)
and include baptism, marriage, and burial records.
Civil registration records are not held. The search
room contains a library of local history books and
other works of reference, and is intended to assist
people using the documents. The record office is
a recognized repository for manorial and tithe documents and for ecclesiastical records for the diocese
of Durham and the diocese of Ripon.

Conditions of admission and access	Because of limited space in the search room, an appointment in advance is necessary for researchers to consult the documents or microfilm. A separate booking is necessary for Wednesday evening and documents for use at that time must be requested the preceding day. All material must be used on the premises. Inquiries should be directed to the County Archivist. Documents are obtained for consultation by means of a request form and no more than three documents are allowed a user at one time. If a microfilm copy of a document is held by the office, the original is not usually produced.
Hours	8:45 AM - 4:45 PM, Monday-Tuesday; 8:45 AM - 8:30 PM, Wednesday; 8:45 AM - 4:45 PM, Thursday; 8:45 AM - 4:15 PM, Friday. The record office is closed on all public holidays.
Duplicating facilities	Full-size and microcopying facilities are available. It is not possible to copy parish registers, bound newspapers, parts of large maps, those documents in poor condition, and those restricted by the owners of the documents.
Other services	Reference help is available for the visiting scholar and there are a number of indexes, guides, cata- logues, and lists which aid in conducting research. Brief queries by telephone or mail are answered.
Publications	Durham County Record Office; The Londonderry Papers: Catalogue of Documents (1969); Streatlam and Gibside: The Bowes and Strathmore Families in County Durham (1984); Handlists, Sub- ject Guides.

DURHAM (map)

90 Institution	Durham University

Address	Department of Paleography and Diplomatic 5 The College Durham DH1 3EQ and The Prior's Kitchen The College Durham DH1 3EQ
Telephone	0385 61478/64561
Holdings	The collection includes the Dean and Chapter muniments and records of Durham Cathedral, 11th to the 19th century. Family and estate papers and business records are also found. These generally concern Durham and North Gorshim for the 18th and 19th centuries. There are also the papers of Howard of Naworth relating to Cumberland and Northumberland, 18th and 19th centuries, and the estate records of private papers of the Greys of Howick, 18th to the 20th century. The Diocesan, Bishopric (financial and estate) and probate records for Durham Diocese are found. Ordnance Survey maps, photographs, stud books, and pamphlets are kept.
Conditions of admission and access	Visiting scholars are welcome to use the collection. Arrangements in advance do not normally have to be made. Inquiries should be directed to the Reader in Palaeography and Diplomatic. The collection must be used on the premises.
Hours	10:00 AM - 1:00 PM, 2:00 PM - 5:00 PM, Monday-Friday; 9:30 AM - 12:30 PM, Saturday during the term. The department is closed for one week at Christmas and at Easter and for three weeks during the summer.
Duplicating facilities	Photocopying facilities are provided.
Other services	Questions by post or telephone are answered if they do not require extended research. Reference help is provided. There are lists, indexes and other finding aids to further aid the scholar.
Publications	Lists, guides, and brochures are produced.

EDINBURGH (map)

91 Institution Address	The City of Edinburgh District Council Archives Department of Administration City Chambers High Street Edinburgh EH1 1YJ
Telephone	031 225 2424, ext. 5196

Holdings	The archives contain the records created over the centuries by the City and Royal Burgh of Edinburgh or by other municipal authorities operating in the same area. These include the Burgess Roll, which survives from the 15th century. There is a printed index to this, published by the Scottish Record Society, which is widely available and which gives much of the information contained in the original. Many records series contain names of persons resident in Edinburgh from the 16th century.
Conditions of admission and access	The archives office is open to the public by prior appointment. Inquiries should be directed to the City Archivist. All records must be used on the premises.
Hours	9:00 AM - 12:30 PM, 2:00 PM - 4:30 PM, Monday-Friday, by prior arrangement.
Duplicating facilities	Photocopying facilities are available.
Other services	Brief questions will be answered by telephone and so will those received by mail. The staff will give general advice on historical sources.
Publications	None.

EDINBURGH (map)

92	Institution Address	Edinburgh City Libraries Edinburgh Room and Scottish Library George IV Bridge Edinburgh EH1 1EG
	Telephone	031 225 5584
	Holdings	The collection includes maps and plans dating from the 16th century, photographs, prints and drawings, and press cuttings. There are also school log books and school board minutes, letters and account books. Papers of trade unions, societies, and associations are also found.
	Conditions of admission and access	Scholars are welcome to use the collection, but there are restrictions on some categories of material. Inquiries should be directed to the City Librarian. Archives and reference works must be used in the library.
	Hours	9:00 AM - 9:00 PM, Monday-Friday; 9:00 AM - 1:00 PM, Saturday.
	Duplicating facilities	Photocopies and full-size copies from microforms can be provided and arrangements can be made for photography.

Other services	Questions by post or telephone are answered, but the staff does not undertake extensive research. Reference help is available in the library.
Publications	Guides and brochures are produced.

EDINBURGH (map)

93 Institution Address	General Register Office for Scotland New Register House Edinburgh EH1 3YT
Telephone	031 566 3952
Holdings	The office contains original records of population and vital statistics relating to Scotland, supplemented by printed reports for the United Kingdom, and some British Commonwealth and foreign countries. The records include civil registers of births, deaths, and marriages in Scotland from 1855; old parish registers, 16th century to 1854; decennial census enumeration books from 1841. Census records are available up to 1891.
Conditions of admission and access	No advance appointment is necessary but payment of a fee is required to use the material. Inquiries should be directed to the Registrar General for Scotland. The collection may be used only on the premises.
Hours	9:30 AM - 4:30 PM, Monday-Thursday; 9:30 AM - 4:00 PM, Friday.
Duplicating facilities	Copying facilities are available only in the form of extracts or certified copies, which may be typewritten from the original record or in some cases photocopies from microfilm. Microfilm of the Old Parish Registers and of the census records is available for sale in complete reels.
Other services	Inquiries relating to Scottish vital statistics or census records are answered. Analyses of vital statistics will be prepared. Information from the registers and the open census records is issued in the form of official extracts of individual entries. Copies of the Genealogical Society of the Church of Jesus Christ of Latterday Saints' Computer Index to the Marriages and Baptisms in the Old Parish Registers is available for sale on microfiche. Coverage of the whole of Scotland is expected by 1988.
Publications	Reports of the Registrar General for Scotland (weekly, quarterly, and annual); Estimates of the Population of Scotland (annual); Reports on Censuses of the Population of Scotland (after each census).

EDINBURGH (map)

94	Institution	National Library of Scotland
	Address	George IV Bridge

Edinburgh EH1 1EW
and
National Library of Scotland Map Room
137 Causewayside
Edinburgh EH9 1PH

Telephone 031 226 4531 (National Library)
031 667 7848 (Map Room)

Holdings The library has been a copyright deposit library since 1710. It receives all British and Irish Publications, including Parliamentary Papers and publications of the United Nations and some other international agencies. In consequence, it can provide material on a wide range of subjects within the province of British publishing, supplemented by selected foreign purchases. The library contains a rich collection of manuscripts dealing with Scottish history and civilization and an almost complete run of Ordnance Survey maps of Scotland and England. Among the notable collections are the following: Alva (16th and 17th century law); Walter B. Blaikie (Jacobite pamphlets, broadsides, proclamations and books on Jacobitism); Blair (Celtic or Scottish interest); Ferguson (books from the 16th to 18th century); Lauriston Castle (Scottish books, pamphlets and chapbooks); Payne (books relating to Francis Bacon); Rosebery (early Scottish books and pamphlets); Keiller (books on witchcraft and demonology from the 15th century); Lyle (books on ships and shipping); Macdonald (books on heraldry); Newhailes (library of an 18th century Scots lawyer); Wordie (polar exploration). In addition, Blairs College Library (books from the libraries of Catholic institutions in Scotland and the Continent) and Accountants (antiquarian collection of the Institute of Chartered Accountants of Scotland) have been placed on deposit in the Library. The Manuscripts Department also contains a wide range of material relating to the history and civilization of Scotland, including family papers, business archives, charter material, trade union records, church mission papers, and, particularly, material relating to all aspects of Scottish literature, from authors' correspondence and manuscripts (Drummond of Hawthornden, Scott, Carlyle, Stevenson, and the authors of the 20th century are particularly well represented) to the records of printers and publishers (Blackwood, Constable, and Oliver and Boyd).

Conditions of admission and access Visiting scholars must acquire a reader's ticket to use the collection. Inquiries should be directed to the Keeper, Readers' Services. All material must be used on the premises.

Hours | 9:30 AM - 8:30 PM, Monday-Friday; 9:30 AM - 1:00 PM, Saturday. The Map Room is open 9:30 AM - 5:00 PM, Monday-Friday.

Duplicating facilities | A full photographic service including microfilming, photocopying, prints and slides can be provided. A price list will be furnished on request.

Other services | Brief inquiries by telephone or post will be answered and reference help is provided in the library. Ultra-violet lamps and microform equipment are available.

Publications | A Guide to the National Library of Scotland, (1976); Bibliography of Scotland (annual); Catalogue of MSS Acquired Since 1925, Vols. 1-4, 6 (1938/1984); Summary Catalogue of the Advocates' Manuscripts (1970); Short-title Catalogue of Books Published Abroad to 1600; List of Books Printed in Scotland Before 1700, by H. G. Aldis, rev. ed.; and catalogues of exhibitions and facsimiles (list available).

EDINBURGH

95 Institution Address | Royal Commission on the Ancient and Historical Monuments of Scotland (including The National Monuments Records of Scotland) 54 Melville Street Edinburgh EH3 7HF

Telephone | 031 225 5994

Holdings | The holdings include the Burn Collection and the Lorimer Collection of architectural drawings and the Society of Antiquaries of Scotland collection of manuscripts and drawings from the 19th century. There is an extensive collection of photographs of archaeological and architectural sites and drawings of ancient monuments and historic buildings.

Conditions of admission and access | The public is allowed to use the collection. Inquiries should be addressed to the Curator. The material must be used on the premises.

Hours | 9:30 AM - 5:00 PM, Monday-Friday.

Duplicating facilities | Photocopies and full-size copies from microforms can be provided and arrangements can be made for photographs.

Other services | Only brief questions can be answered by telephone or mail, but reference help is provided.

Publications	Lists, catalogs, and inventories are produced.

EDINBURGH (map)

96 Institution Address	Scottish Genealogy Society 21 Howard Place Edinburgh EH3 5JY
	and Library Address: 9 Union Street Edinburgh EH1 3LT
Telephone	031 556 3844 (after 6:00 PM)
Holdings	The society holds a complete set of Scottish History Society, Scottish Record Society, and Scottish Genealogy Society publications to date. There is also a large collection of monumental inscriptions for individual graveyards, mainly pre-1855. Many volumes of history and topography of Scotland are found here, and the Mormon International Genealogical Index for Scotland and Ireland (1894), Old Parish Registers (1855), and births and marriages for the north of Scotland are on microfiche.
Conditions of admission and access	Members may use the collection and visiting scholars are allowed to consult records on payment of a fee appropriate for the services required. The material must be used on the premises. Inquiries should be directed to the Hon. Secretary at 21 Howard Place, Edinburgh EH3 5JY.
Hours	3:30 PM - 6:30 PM, Wednesday.
Duplicating facilities	Copying facilities are not available at this time.
Other services	Reference help is available and brief questions are answered by telephone or post.
Publications	The Scottish Genealogist (quarterly); Library Catalogue (1964); Library Accessions, 1964-1966; Monumental Inscriptions, pre-1855: Angus 1, Angus 2, Angus 3, Angus 4, Kilmarnock Loudoun District, Speyside, Isla Munda; Register of Members Interest, 1978-1981; Supplement, (1982); Scottish Ancestry Research, by D. Whyte. Other Monumental Inscription volumes which were out-of-print are being reprinted by the Society. A list is available.

EDINBURGH

97 Institution Address	Scottish Record Office HM General Register House Princes Street Edinburgh EH1 3YY

                              and
                              Annex
                              West Register House
                              Charlotte Square
                              Edinburgh EH2 4DF

Telephone   031 556 6585

Holdings   The office holds the public records of Scotland,
                              government and legal, from the 13th century;
                              records of nationalized industries in Scotland;
                              records of court, including registers (wills) and
                              inventories; certain local authority records; records
                              of the Church of Scotland (except registers of
                              birth, marriage, and death) and of other denomina-
                              tions; private muniments; and special collections.
                              There is also a reference library of books, periodi-
                              cals, and pamphlets relating to Scottish records
                              and the work of the Scottish Record Office. The
                              main legal and older historical records are preserved
                              in HM General Register House. Modern records
                              and special collections are housed in the branch re-
                              pository at the West Register House.

Conditions of   Visiting scholars are permitted to consult any
admission and   records which are open to public access in the
access   Historical Search Room in HM General Register
                              House or in the West Register House search room.
                              Researchers are issued a reader's ticket on perso-
                              nal application only. Inquiries should be addressed
                              to the Keeper of the Records of Scotland. Records
                              may be consulted only in the search rooms.

Hours   9:00 AM - 4:45 PM, Monday-Friday.

Duplicating   Full-size and microcopying facilities are available.
facilities   Details of current fees are provided on request
                              from the Keeper of the Records of Scotland.

Other services   Brief postal or telephone inquiries will be answered.
                              For persons unable to make a personal search in
                              records, the Scottish Record Office may conduct
                              searches over such periods and subject to such
                              conditions as the Keeper of the Records of Scotland
                              may prescribe for particular classes of records.

Publications   Guide to the Public Records of Scotland Deposited
                              in HM General Register House, Edinburgh, by M.
                              Livingstone (1905); List of Gifts and Deposits in
                              the Scottish Record Office Vol. 1, 1971, Vol. 2,
                              1976. For a complete list of publications, see HMSO
                              Sectional List, No. 24, British National Archives.

ENFIELD   See LONDON, London Borough of Enfield

EXETER (map)

98	Institution Address	Devon and Cornwall Record Society West Country Studies Library Devon Library Services Central Library Castle Street Exeter EX4 3PQ

Telephone   0392 53422

Holdings   The society holds an impressive list of parish registers and Bishop's transcripts, too lengthy for elaboration here. An alphabetical list is available from the society. Many of the registers date from the 16th century. In the case of many Cornish parishes the society's register copies are of baptisms and burials only, and are intended to be complementary to Phillimore's Marriages series (Phillimore's Parish Register Series [Marriages]; Vols. 1-24, London, 1896-1938). The society owns microfilm copies of non-conformist registers of Baptist, Independent, Presbyterian, Moravian, and the several Methodist churches, 1837 and before (deposited at the Public Record Office, London) for Devon and Cornwall. These cover 171 churches or chapels. In addition, one finds Diocese of Exeter Marriage Licences and/or allegations, 1523-1837, with indexes. There are also transcripts of churchwardens' accounts from the 15th century, a large collection of local and family history source material, including transcripts of deeds, charters, wills, inquisitions post mortem, subsidies, pedigrees, and other material.

Conditions of admission and access   This collection is available only to members of the society. Application forms with a fee schedule are available from the Hon. Secretary, 7 The Close, Exeter EX1 1EZ or from the West Country Studies Library. Temporary membership for the use of the library is offered for a period of three months on payment of a fee at the West Country Studies Library. All material must be used on the premises.

Hours   Hours for the library are 9:30 AM - 8:00 PM, Monday-Tuesday, Thursday-Friday; 9:30 AM - 6:00 PM, Wednesday; 9:30 AM - 4:00 PM, Saturday.

Duplicating facilities   Full-size photocopying facilities are available. Extensive photocopying (i.e., more than ten pages) requires the permission of the Council of the Society.

Other services   Only very brief inquiries are answered by post or telephone. A list of approved record searchers is maintained by the society for those who cannot come to Exeter. Fees are arranged between searcher and client.

Publications	Devon Monastic Lands: Calendar of Particulars for Grants 1536-1558, ed. by Joyce Youings (1955); Exeter in the Seventeenth Century: Tax and Rate Assessments 1602-1699, ed. by W. G. Hoskins (1957); The Diocese of Exeter in 1821: Bishop Carey's Replies to Queries Before Visitation, ed. by Michael Cook (Vol. 1, 1958, Vol. 2, 1960); The Cartulary of St. Michael's Mount, ed. by P. L. Hull (1962); The Exeter Assembly: Minutes of the Assemblies of the United Brethren of Devon and Cornwall, 1691-1717, as transcribed by the Reverend Isaac Gilling, ed. by Allan Brockett (1963); The Register of Edmund Lacy, Bishop of Exeter 1420-1455, ed. by G. R. Dunstan (Vol. 1, 1963, Vol. 2, 1966, Vol. 3, 1968, Vol. 4, 1971, Vol. 5, 1972); The Cartulary of Canonsleigh Abbey, calendared and ed. by Vera C. M. London (1965); Benjamin Donn's Map of Devon 1765, with an introduction by W. L. D. Ravenhill (1965); Devon Inventories of the Sixteenth and Seventeenth Centuries, ed. by Margaret Cash (1966); Plymouth Building Accounts of the Sixteenth and Seventeenth Centuries, ed. by Edwin Welch (1967); The Devonshire Lay Subsidy of 1332, ed. by Audrey M. Erskine (1969); Churchwardens' Accounts of Ashburton 1479-1580, ed. by Alison Hanham (1970); The Caption of Seisin of the Duchy of Cornwall 1377, ed. by P. L. Hull (1971); A Calendar of Cornish Glebe Terriers 1673-1735, ed. by Richard Potts (1974); John Lydford's Book: The Fourteenth Century Formulary of the Archdeacon of Totnes, ed. by Dorothy M. Owen (1975) (with the Historical Manuscripts Commission and available from HMSO); A Calendar of Early Chancery Proceedings Relating to West Country Shipping 1388-1493, ed. by Dorothy A. Gardiner (1976); Tudor Exeter: Tax Assessments 1489-1595, ed. by Margery M. Rowe (1977); The Devon Cloth Industry in the Eighteenth Century, ed. by Stanley D. Chapman (1978); The Accounts of the Fabric of Exeter Cathedral 1279-1353, ed. by Audrey M. Erskine (Pt. 1, 1981, Pt. 2, 1983); The Parliamentary Survey of the Duchy of Cornwall, ed. by N. J. G. Pounds, Pt. 1, 1982, Pt. 2, 1984; Crown Pleas of the Devon Eyre of 1238, ed. by Henry Summerson (1985).

EXETER

Institution	Devon and Exeter Institution See: EXETER, University of Exeter, The University Library

EXETER (map)

99 Institution Address	Devon Record Office

Castle Street
Exeter EX4 3PU

Telephone	0392 53509

See also: PLYMOUTH, West Devon Record Office

Holdings

The record office holds the parish registers for most (but not all) Devon parishes and these date from the 16th century. They give baptisms, marriages, and burials. Bishops transcripts of Parish Registers are available for almost all Devon and Cornwall parishes; however, they do not give coverage for every year. They date from the late 16th century to ca. 1850. There are 75 wills, 1555-1765, among the records of the Orphans Court of the City of Exeter and some earlier wills are included among the city archives. For the period 1796-1812, copies of Devon wills are available at the Public Record Office, Chancery Lane, London, and from 1812 to 1857, a complete series of copies is at the Devon Record Office. Voters lists are found from 1832 to date. These are arranged by parish, but are not indexed. The office holds Exeter City records, 11th-20th century; Exeter Diocesan Records, 1257 to the 20th century; Devon County Records, 1592 to the 20th century; former District Council records, ca. 1870 to the 20th century; family, estate, and business records, ca. 1100 to the 20th century; and Borough records for Dartmouth, Totnes, Bideford, and Barnstaple. Quarter Sessions records, County Council, and records of other authorities (hospitals, Poor Law Unions, Turnpike Trustees, and Highway Boards) are held. The record office is a repository for manorial and tithe documents and for ecclesiastical records (Exeter).

Conditions of admission and access

The record office may be used on payment of a daily or an annual fee. There are some exceptions to this condition, such as scholars using the records as part of a course of studies (written evidence must be given of this at the time of the visit; special authorization forms are provided), a depositor wishing to see his own records, and those exercising statutory right of free access. No appointment is necessary. Inquiries should be directed to the County Archivist. All material must be used on the premises and some records must be requested forty-eight hours in advance. Those for use on Saturday must be ordered on Friday by 10:30 AM.

Hours

9:30 AM - 5:00 PM, Monday-Thursday; 9:30 AM - 4:30 PM, Friday; 9:30 AM - 12:00 noon on the first and third Saturday of the month. A list of these dates is available from the record office.

Duplicating   Full-size and microcopying facilities are available.
facilities

Other services   Very brief questions will be answered by telephone
                     or mail. More extensive searches are undertaken
                     for a fee. There are lists, indexes, and catalogues
                     provided to aid the researcher and reference help
                     is available. Ultra-violet lamps are found, as is
                     microform equipment.

Publications   Assizes and Quarter Sessions in Exeter, 1971;
                     Exeter Guildhall (1936); Nos Voisins d'Outre
                     Manche; Oakum, Being Strands Drawn from the
                     Maritime History of Devon (1970); Parish, Non-
                     Parochial and Civil Registers in the Devon Record
                     Office (1983); Records of the Bishop of Exeter's
                     Consistory Court to 1660 (Devon Handlist no. 1)
                     (1980); Methodism in Devon: A Handlist of
                     Chapels and Their Records (Devon Record Office
                     Handlist no. 2, 1983); Annual Report; Devon
                     Record Office: Brief Guide: Pt. I, Official and
                     Ecclesiastical (1969); Guides to Sources, which are
                     leaflets available on Family History, House History,
                     Maritime History, Transport History, Farming
                     History, Mining History, Crime and Punishment,
                     and Land Tax Assessments.

EXETER

Institution   Exeter Cathedral Library
                     See: EXETER, University of Exeter, The
                     University Library

EXETER

100 Institution   University of Exeter
    Address   The University Library
                     Stocker Road
                     Exeter EX4 4PT

    Telephone   0392 263263

    Holdings   The main library holds material on sociology,
                     politics, economics, economic history, geography,
                     and history. There are separate libraries for
                     law and education. Included are the Dodderidge
                     Theological Library and the Totnes Parochial Li-
                     brary. The Librarian provides administrative
                     assistance to the Exeter Cathedral Library
                     (Bishop's Palace, Exeter EX1 1HX; telephone:
                     0392 72894). Here is found historical material and
                     the archives of the Dean and Chapter, which in-
                     clude documents dating from the 10th century.
                     This library also contains works on early medicine
                     and science from the 16th century; English

history, medieval ecclesiastical history; 15th, 16th, and 18th century political history; and important collections on local history. It is designated as a repository for ecclesiastical records of the Archdeaconry of Exeter. The library of the Devon and Exeter Institution (7, Cathedral Close, Exeter EX1 1EZ; telephone: 0392 51017) contains an interesting local history collection and files of local newspapers.

Conditions of admission and access	The main library is open to visiting researchers on application to the Librarian. Inquiries may also be directed to the Sub-Librarian, Readers' Services. An archivist is available for the Cathedral Library and an appointment is necessary to use this collection. A letter of introduction is recommended. The material must be used by visiting scholars on the premises.
Hours	9:00 AM - 10:00 PM, Monday-Friday; 9:00 AM - 5:00 PM, Saturday during the academic year. During vacation, opening times vary. The library of the Devon and Exeter Institution is open 9:00 AM - 5:00 PM, Monday-Friday. The Cathedral Library is open 2:00 PM - 5:00 PM, Monday-Friday by appointment.
Duplicating facilities	Full-size and microcopies can be provided.
Other services	Brief inquiries by telephone and by post will be answered and reference help is available. Microform equipment and ultraviolet lamps are provided.
Publications	The library has published an Index to Theses Submitted to Exeter University Since 1955; The Devon Union List: A Collection of Written Material Relating to the County of Devon, by A. Brockett (1977); A Catalogue of Italian Books, 1471-1600, in the Libraries of Exeter University, Exeter Cathedral, and the Devon and Exeter Institution, by Roberto L. Bruni and D. Wyn Evans (1978); A Catalogue of Italian Books, 1601-1700, in Exeter Libraries, by Roberto L. Bruni and D. Wyn Evans (1982); A Catalogue of Binding in Exeter Cathedral Library, 2 Vols., by D. Wyn Evans (1979), typescript only; A Catalogue of Bindings in Exeter University Library, by D. Wyn Evans (1979), typescript only. The Cathedral Library has issued the Library of Exeter Cathedral, by L. J. Lloyd, with descriptions of the archives by A. M. Erskine.

FOLKESTONE

101	Institution Address	Kent Archives Office, South East Kent Branch

Folkestone Central Library
Grace Hill
Folkestone   CT 20 1HD

Telephone	0303 57583
Holdings	Folkestone Borough Records, 1515-1974 are held here and also the Urban District Council records for Cheriton and Shadgate (1850-1934) and Rural District Council records for Elham (1875-1974) and Romney Marsh (1861-1974). The Folkestone Parish records from ca. 1763 to 1886 are held but there are no registers. The Folkestone Township Parish records from ca. 1676 to 1911 are also held with no registers. The Folkestone Methodist circuit records, ca. 1815-1964 and the Dover and Deal Methodist circuit records, ca. 1794-1967 are found. The Deal Congregational church records, 1802 to 1975 are also here. In addition, there is a wide range of private and unofficial collections relating to Folkestone and its environs. Elham and Romney Marsh Poor Law Union records are available.
Conditions of admission and access	The office is open to the public, and whereas no prior appointment is required, visitors are strongly advised to contact the Archivist before calling at the office. The Archivist is not available on Wednesday or Saturday and may be away on other days of the week. The collection must be used on the premises. All inquiries should be directed to the Archivist.
Hours	9:00 AM - 6:00 PM, Monday, Thursday; 9:00 AM - 7:00 PM, Tuesday, Friday; 9:00 AM - 1:00 PM, Wednesday; 9:00 AM - 5:00 PM, Saturday.
Duplicating facilities	Facilities are available for full-size copying.
Other services	Reference aid is provided and brief questions by telephone or by mail will be answered. Administrative assistance is given to Dover, Hythe, Lydd, and New Romney Town Councils and to Shepway District Council, but control is not exercised over records held by other Councils.
Publications	None.

FORFAR

102	Institution Address	Angus District Council County Buildings Forfar
	Telephone	0307 65101

Holdings	The collection includes the records of the former Burghs of Arbroath (1530-1975), Brechin (1672-1975), Carnoustie (1884-1975), Forfar (1666-1975), Kirriemuir (1834-1975), and Montrose (1458-1975). Also held are the records of the District Council from 1975.
Conditions of admission and access	Visiting scholars are permitted to use the collection, but arrangements must be made in advance. Inquiries should be addressed to the Director of Administration. The material must be used on the premises.
Hours	9:00 AM - 5:00 PM, Monday-Friday.
Duplicating facilities	Photocopying can be provided.
Other services	Questions by telephone or mail are answered if they are brief and do not require extensive research. Some reference is provided.
Publications	None.

FORFAR

103	Institution Address	Angus District Libraries and Museums
Forfar Public Library
Meffan Institute
West High Street
Forfar DD8 1BB
	Telephone	0307 63468
	Holdings	The library holds genealogical collections from several families, including Erskine, Campbell, Duncan, Scrymgeour, Thomas, Seton, Gray, Whyte, Skinner, and Ogilvie. These date from the 15th to the 20th century. Also found are maps and plans, trade and business records and the Glenprosen parish records (1794-1954), and papers of local societies.
	Conditions of admission and access	Scholars should make written application to use the collection. Inquiries should be addressed to the Librarian. The material must be used on the premises.
	Hours	9:30 AM - 7:00 PM, Monday-Wednesday, Friday-Saturday; 9:30 AM - 5:00 PM, Thursday.
	Duplicating facilities	Arrangements can be made for photocopying, but advance notice is needed.
	Other services	Short questions by telephone are answered as well as those by mail if the research is not too extensive. Reference help is available.

Publications   None.

FORRES

104   Institution   Moray District Record Office
      Address   The Tolbooth
                      High Street
                      Forres IV36 0AB

      Telephone   0309 73617

      Holdings   The office holds the archives of the former local authorities within the District and documents from private sources. Among the official archives are Burgh records for Aberlour, Banff, Buckie, Burghead, Cullen, Dufftown, Elgin, Findochty, Forres, Keith, Lossiemouth, Portknockie, and Rothes. County records are for Banffshire, Elginshire and Moray, and Moray and Nairn. There are District archives for Buckie, Cromdale, Cullen, Dufftown, Duffus and Drainie, Elgin, Fochabers, Forres, Keith, Rothes, and Knockando. Also found are Justice of the Peace of Moray, Lieutenancy of Moray, Parochial Board and Parish Council, Morayshire Union Poor's House, and Old Age Pension Committee records. Police, public assistance, regality, School Board, School Management Committee, and other school records are available as are those of certain special authorities, and special water supply, drainage and scavenging district. Ecclesiastical records include Kirk Session and Presbytery. Privately deposited collections are comprised of business papers (commerce and industry), solicitors' accumulations, family muniments, estate papers, maps and plans, private diaries, and literary manuscripts.

      Conditions of admission and access   The office is open to all researchers and no appointment in advance is necessary. Documents are available only in the record office search rooms. Inquiries should be directed to the Archivist.

      Hours   9:00 AM - 12:30 PM, 1:30 PM - 4:30 PM, Monday-Friday.

      Duplicating facilities   Photocopies can be provided and arrangements can be made for photography.

      Other services   Reference help is available in the search room and brief questions by post or telephone can be answered. There are descriptive catalogues of the collections and extensive card indexes of persons, places, and subjects provided. A reference library is available and includes directories, year books and legal works. There is an ultra-violet lamp as well as other optical aids. Lectures and exhibitions can be arranged in the office or at meeting places of local clubs and societies, and illustrated lectures suitable for school children can be provided on certain subjects. Teachers are encouraged to use the archives for school project work.

Publications   Moray District Record Office Guide (1985).

GALWAY

105 Institution   Galway County Library Headquarters
    Address   Island House
                      Cathedral Square
                      Galway, Co. Galway

    Telephone   091 62471 or 091 7039

    Holdings   The library holds old Galway (City and County) newspapers which date from 1823, on microfilm. The Journal of the Galway Archaeological and Historical Society is also held and Griffith's Valuation for County Galway is found in book form. There are photocopies of the tithe applotment books, books of survey and distribution, and an index to the 1901 census for County Galway.

    Conditions of   There are no restrictions on access to the collec-
    admission and   tion, but it must be used on the premises. In-
    access   quiries should be addressed to the Librarian.

    Hours   9:30 AM - 1:00 PM, 2:00 PM - 5:00 PM, Monday-Friday.

    Duplicating   Facilities are available for copying material.
    facilities

    Other services   Brief questions by telephone or post are answered and reference help is provided. Extensive research is not carried out for patrons.

    Publications   A Bibliography of the County Galway, by Mary Kavanagh (1965); Galway Authors, by Helen Baker (1976).

GALWAY

106 Institution   University College Galway
    Address   Library
                      Galway, Co. Galway

    Telephone   091 24411

                      The response from this library indicated that the

genealogical material in the collection is limited.
No significant details were furnished.

GATESHEAD

107	Institution Address	Central Library Prince Consort Road Gateshead NE8 4LN
	Telephone	091 4773478, ext. 31

Holdings

The library is a repository for manorial and tithe
documents and contains a collection of local photographs, prints and maps, and many works on the
history of the area. The Archives Section holds
the records of local government authorities,
churches, and industry. Among the many important special collections are the Cotesworth Manuscripts and the Ellison Manuscripts. These are
18th-century family papers relating to the early
history of the coal trade. (Among the papers one
finds deeds [County Durham, Northumberland,
Newcastle-Upon-Tyne], marriage and family settlements, wills, and probate documents, legal cases,
colliery accounts, and rentals and other material
relating to the coal trade and the salt trade,
estate papers, business papers, family and household papers, and correspondence.) Also found
are the Bell Manuscripts; Nelson Collection of
Letters, which are letters and other documents collected by Robert Nelson of Bishop Auckland; the
Oxberry Manuscripts, which are documents collected
by John Oxberry (1857-1940); and the Philipps
Manuscripts. There are papers of institutions and
societies held by the library among which can be
found the records of the King James' Hospital,
Gateshead, the Mechanics Institute at Gateshead
and at Wrekenton, and the Society for the Prose-
cution of Felons at Gateshead. Also held are
business records, trade companies' papers, music
manuscripts, deeds, archives relating to education
and some Methodist Church Papers. There are local newspapers dating from 1744, early pamphlets,
and literary works which relate to the area. Parish
records include registers of baptisms, marriages,
and burials from the 16th century for St. Mary's
Gateshead (on microfilm) and registers of baptisms
(1825-1918), registers of marriages (1825-1929),
registers of burials (1825-1924), index to burials
(1884-1901) for St. John's Gateshead Fell. Transcripts of other parish registers and of wills are
also found.

Conditions of
admission and
access

The library is open to the public and visiting
scholars would be able to use the collection. No
prior appointment is required. Inquiries should

be made to the Librarian or the Local Studies
Librarian. The collections mentioned in the
"Holdings" do not circulate and may be used only
on the premises.

Hours

9: 30 AM - 7: 30 PM, Monday-Tuesday, Thursday-
Friday; 9: 30 AM - 5: 00 PM, Wednesday; 9: 30 AM -
1: 00 PM, Saturday.

Duplicating
facilities

Full-size copying facilities are available and
photography can be provided. Arrangements can
be made for microcopying, but there is some delay.

Other services

Brief inquiries by telephone or post are answered
and reference help is available. There are indexes, guides, and catalogues provided to aid the
researcher.

Publications

The Brandling Junction Railway (1973); A History
of Gateshead (1973).

GLASGOW (map)

108 Institution
Address

Glasgow District Libraries
The Mitchell Library
North Street
Glasgow   G3 7DN

Telephone

041 221 7030

Holdings

The Mitchell Library is a major research library
and holds more than a million volumes covering
all subjects and all periods. There are important
works on history, geography, archeology, travel,
a collection of over 15,000 Ordnance Survey Maps,
atlases, street plans, material on Scottish topography and history, particularly clan and family
history and local history other than Glasgow.
There are special collections on Scottish Regimental
History and Trade Unions (including the Linwood
Collection), and the North British Locomotive Company Collection, which contains about 10,000 glass
negatives and photographs (including nearly every
type of locomotive built for railway companies and
industrial firms at home and abroad), weight
diagram books, and miscellaneous items donated to
the library following the firm's liquidation in 1962.
The Baillie's Library has been incorporated in the
Mitchell Library, which contributed important ad-
ditions. The Glasgow Collection is comprised of
more than 20,000 books and pamphlets, and illustrations, maps, engravings, photographs (including
the Graham Collection of glass negatives, ca.
1900), newspapers (from 1740), watercolors, and
other illustrations. Within the Glasgow Collection
is the Wotherspoon Collection, "In the Track of

the Comet," which traces in forty-one volumes of unique scrapbook material the history of Clyde-built steamships. The Glasgow Collection also contains voters' rolls, registers of baptisms, marriages, deaths, and copies of some census returns. Also of interest are the Shawfield Papers, and the Bogle Family Papers (dating from the 17th century), which relate to the city's mercantile life, the Chamber of Commerce Papers, the High School Papers (concerning early education), the Scottish Women's Hospital Collection and the Glasgow and West of Scotland Association for Women's Suffrage Papers. There are city directories from 1783, 18th-century maps, voter registration lists from 1858, and valuation rolls from 1913. The Strathclyde Regional Archives, now housed in the Mitchell Library, contain material relating to the Strathclyde region and former counties of Argyllshire, Ayrshire, Buteshire, Dunbartonshire, Lanarkshire, and Renfrewshire. The archives are connected administratively with the Strathclyde Regional Council and not with the District, other than as tenants (in the library) and as agents for their historical records. There are also local authority records (Burgh, County and Parish, Civil), Public Deeds Registers, 1542-1927, Clyde Port Authority (harbour and navigation), 18th-20th century, City of Glasgow records, 16th-20th century, City Institutions and Guilds, 15th-20th century, landed family records, industrial and commercial (especially Clyde Shipbuilders and Engineers) 19th-20th century, legal firms' records and social, welfare, and recreational records. Church records include Church of Scotland, and Presbytery of Glasgow (official depository) 17th-20th century. The former Glasgow City Archives are incorporated in the Strathclyde Regional Archives. A dependent repository is the Ayrshire Sub-region Archives, County Building, Wellington Square, Ayr.

Conditions of admission and access	There are no restrictions on the use of the library, but the collections must be used on the premises. Inquiries should be directed to the Librarian or to the Principal Archivist for matters concerning the Strathclyde Regional Archives.
Hours	The library is open 9:30 AM - 9:00 PM, Monday-Friday; 9:30 AM - 5:00 PM, Saturday. The Strathclyde Regional Archives are open 9:30 AM - 5:00 PM, Monday-Thursday; 9:30 AM - 4:00 PM, Friday.
Duplicating facilities	Full-size and microcopying facilities are available. There are coin operated machines and a photographic department with facilities for every kind of reproduction.

Other services	Telephone and postal queries are answered and reference help is available in all the library departments. Ultra-violet lamps and microform equipment are available. There are indexes, some computer-based aids, and guides to aid the visiting scholar. There are descriptions available to tell the researcher where in the library the various collections are found. The Mitchell Library is associated with forty-three district libraries with a lending stock of over a million volumes.
Publications	The Mitchell Library Catalogue of Additions, 1915-1949, 2 vols. (1959); Catalogue of Robert Burns Collection in the Mitchell Library (1955); The Mitchell Library Catalogue of Periodicals (1962); Catalogue of Incunabula and STC Books in the Mitchell Library (1964); Glasgow Public Libraries, 1874-1966 (1966); The Mitchell Library, Glasgow, 1877-1977 (1977); The Mitchell Library, Glasgow (1982); Census Returns and Old Parochial Registers: A Directory of Public Library Holdings in the West of Scotland (1982). From the Strathclyde Regional Archives: Catalogue of Exhibitions; Panoramic Bird's Eye View of Glasgow; Notes for Teachers; Guide for Genealogists.

GLASGOW

Institution	Strathclyde Regional Archives See: GLASGOW, Glasgow District Libraries The Mitchell Library

GLOUCESTER (map)

109 Institution Address	Gloucestershire County Record Office Worcester Street Gloucester GL1 3DW and Shire Hall Westgate Street Gloucester GL1 2TG
Telephone	0452 425295 (County Record Office) 0452 425289 (Shire Hall)
Holdings	The main search room for historical and genealogical records, including the collection of local history books, photographs, pictures and maps, is at the Worcester Street address. Public and local government records, including courts, local boards, and councils, hospitals, and schools, may be consulted only at Shire Hall. The collection includes the judicial and administrative records of both county and city quarter sessions, 1660-1971; records of

ancient boroughs from ca. 1200; County and District archives from 1889; records of Petty Sessions, Coroners, School Boards and Poor Law Unions from the 19th century; the archives of River Boards from 1543, hospitals from 1754, Turnpikes from 1702; Diocesan archives from 1541; Cathedral archives from ca. 1188; Anglican parish and Free Church registers from 1538; the muniments of Gloucestershire families from ca. 1145; business records of solicitors, estate agents and architects, canal and gas companies, and old established firms of clothiers, engineers and tradesmen from ca. 1750 and records of professional associations, trade unions, societies and clubs. Non-conformists' records include those of Baptists, Congregationalists, Countess of Huntingdon's Connexion, and Society of Friends. Among family and estate papers can be found those of Agg and Agg-Gardner of Cheltenham, Chamberlayne of Maugersbury, Codrington of Dodington, Guise of Elmore, Hyett of Painswick, Kingscote of Kingscote, Sotheron-Estcourt of Shipton Moyne, and Strickland of Deerhurst. Muniments of Gloucestershire families contain documents relating to local history, national affairs, medieval monasteries, the Elizabethan navy, West Indian plantations, politics and many other subjects. There are also solicitors' deposits, including (but not limited to) the records of Brookes and Badham, Tewkesbury; Goldingham and Jotcham, Wotton-under-Edge; Kendall and Davies, Bourton-on-the-Water; Mullings, Ellett and Company, Cirencester; and Ticehurst, Wyatt and Company, Cheltenham. Business records contain industrial and handicraft records, commercial records and estate agents' papers. The office is a repository for manorial and tithe documents and for ecclesiastical records (Gloucester).

Conditions of
admission and
access

With some exceptions (depositors inspecting their own records, volunteers compiling indexes, those with statutory right, local authorities pursuing official inquiries, students consulting material in connection with their curricula), researchers must pay a fee on either a daily or semi-annual basis to use the collection. It is helpful if scholars telephone or write in advance of their visit. An appointment is necessary to use the collection at Shire Hall. Inquiries should be directed to the County Archivist. Material from the collection may not be removed from the premises. Documents may not be obtained after 4:30 PM except on Thursday, when they will be produced until 7:00 PM. Certain documents must be thirty to fifty years old to be seen and use of those in fragile condition may be refused. In some cases, the reader may be required to use microfilm or photocopies rather than the original document.

Hours

9:00 AM - 1:00 PM, 2:00 PM - 5:00 PM, Monday-Wednesday, Friday; 9:00 AM - 1:00 PM, 2:00 PM - 8:00 PM, Thursday at the Worcester Street address. The search room at Shire Hall is open by prior appointment only.

Duplicating facilities

Full-size and microcopying facilities are available and will accommodate most documents (except parish registers).

Other services

Brief inquiries by telephone or post are answered but for those requiring more extensive research a fee is charged. Reference help is available and there are many catalogues, lists, and indexes provided to aid researchers. Lectures and talks are given either in the lecture room at the record office or at schools or local societies. Exhibits are arranged periodically.

Publications

Many of the publications of the record office are now out-of-print, but those which are available may be obtained from the record office at the Worcester Street address. An asterisk indicates those which can still be provided. The list of publications is as follows: Catalogue of Gloucestershire Books (Hyett Collection) (1946); Guide to Gloucestershire Quarter Sessions Archives, 1660-1889: A Descriptive Catalogue, by I. E. Gray and A. T. Gaydon (1958); Guide to the Parish Records of Bristol and Gloucester (1963); Diocese of Gloucester: A Catalogue of the Dean and Chapter, by I. M. Kirby (1967)*; Diocese of Gloucester: A Catalogue of the Records of the Bishop and Archdeacon, by I. M. Kirby (1968)*; A Short Handlist of the Gloucestershire Record Office (1968), updated by Annual Reports (from 1969)*; Gloucestershire Family History (2nd ed.)*; Handlist of Genealogical Sources; The Country House in Gloucestershire: A Short History*; Ladybellegate House, Gloucester, and Robert Raikes; Education in Gloucestershire: A Short History; Map of Gloucestershire Parishes; Map of Ancient Churches and Chapels in Gloucestershire; Archives for Schools; Archive Teaching Books* (Cloth Industry, Turnpike Roads, Waterways, Crime and Punishment, Towns); A Calendar of the Records of the Corporation of Gloucester, by W. H. Stevenson (1893); Wills Proved in Gloucestershire Peculiar Courts (1960)*; Gloucester Diocesan Terriers (1959); Bishop's Transcripts, 1569-1812 (1968); Guide to the Parish Records of Bristol and Gloucester, by I. Gray and E. Ralph (1963); Gloucestershire Marriage Allegations, 1637-1680 and 1681-1700, by B. Frith (Vol. 1, 1954, Vol. 2, 1970); Gloucestershire, a Local History Handbook, by A. Jamieson and B. S. Smith (new ed., 1975); Diary of a Journey Through

North of England Made by William and John Blathwayt of Durham Park in 1703; Four Hundred Years
of Gloucestershire Life, by A. M. Wherry (1971).
The County Council also sponsors with the University of London the publication of the Victoria
County History of Gloucestershire. Volumes II
(ecclesiastical and economic history), VI, VIII and
X (histories of parishes in N. Cotswolds, Vale of
Tewkesbury and Severnside) have been published
and are available only through booksellers.

GRAVESEND

110 Institution Address	Kent County Library Gravesend Division Central Library Windmill Street Gravesend DA12 1AQ
Telephone	0474 65600/52758
Holdings	Records of the former Gravesend Borough Council date from 1568. There are also Chamberlain's accounts from the 17th century and Town minutes from 1571. Also found here is the George Arnold Collection, which includes scrapbooks, artifacts, and printed material (late 19th century). In addition, there are numerous engravings and photographs.
Conditions of admission and access	The library is open to the public, but a prior appointment to use the collection is requested. Inquiries should be directed to the Area Librarian. Archives and reference works must be used in the library.
Hours	9:30 AM - 6:00 PM, Monday-Tuesday, Thursday; 9:30 AM - 1:00 PM, Wednesday; 9:30 AM - 6:30 PM, Friday; 9:30 AM - 5:00 PM, Saturday.
Duplicating facilities	Photocopying can be arranged, with some limitations.
Other services	Questions are answered by post or telephone, but only if they are brief. Reference help is available.
Publications	None.

GREENWICH   See: LONDON, London Borough of Greenwich

GRIMSBY (map)

111 Institution   South Humberside Area Record Office
    Address

Town Hall
Town Hall Square
Grimsby DN31 1HX

Telephone	0472 53481

<u>See also</u>: BEVERLEY, Humberside County Record Office

Holdings	The office holds official and private records for the area of South Humberside. It is the repository for the historical archives created by Great Grimsby Borough, which date from the 13th century onwards, and by Barton on Humber Urban District Council, Brigg Urban District Council, Cleethorpes Municipal Borough Council, Glanford Borough Council, Grimsby Rural District Council, and Scunthorpe Borough Council. Also found are the papers of the local Board of Health and Urban Sanitary Authority, the Grimsby Burial Board, the Poor Law Union, and the Grimsby Borough Police and Fire Brigade. There are also some Board of Trade records such as merchant navy crew lists (1863-1913) and fishing vessel crew lists (1884-1914). The office holds Quarter Sessions records and is a repository for manorial and tithe documents. Archives formerly in the custody of the Scunthorpe Borough Museum and Art Gallery (Oswald Road, Scunthorpe, DN15 7BD) are deposited with the office, but arrangements can be made with the Keeper of Local History there for their return to the museum for study. In addition, many archives deposited by local families, businesses, societies, clubs, and landed estates are available for use.
Conditions of admission and access	The office is open to the public, but an appointment in advance is advisable. Inquiries should be directed to the Archivist in Charge. The collection may be used only on the premises.
Hours	9:30 AM - 12:00 noon; 1:00 PM - 5:00 PM, Monday-Thursday; 9:30 AM - 12:00 noon, 1:00 PM - 4:15 PM, Friday.
Duplicating facilities	Arrangements for photocopying can be made.
Other services	Brief inquiries by telephone or post will be answered and reference help is available to the researcher in the search room. Inquiries from overseas should be accompanied by an international reply coupon. There are also guides, lists, and indexes provided to aid the scholar in his work. The staff is prepared to give talks when requested and exhibits can be arranged either on or off the premises. There are facilities for group visits by schools and organizations.

Publications	<u>South Humberside Area Record Office: Summary Guide</u> (1977); leaflets, pamphlets designed to help the user in consulting the records.

GUERNSEY, CHANNEL ISLANDS   <u>See:</u> ST. PETER PORT

GUILDFORD (map)

112 Institution Address	Surrey Record Office, Guildford Muniment Room Castle Arch Guildford GU1 3SX
Telephone	0483 53942
	See also: KINGSTON-UPON-THAMES, Surrey Record Office
Holdings	In general records relating primarily to south-western Surrey are held at Guildford, and those relating to other parts of the county are found at Kingston-upon-Thames. The collection includes the official records of Guildford Borough Corporation dating back to 1514. Also found are family and estate papers (including manorial records), business papers (including Wey and Godalming Navigations and Billing and Sons, Ltd., Printers of Guildford). Anglican parish registers for most of the Diocese of Guildford and a few non-conformist records are also found, which record baptisms, marriages, and burials. There are also some transcripts. The record office is a repository for manorial and tithe documents.
Conditions of admission and access	The record office is open to the public, but an appointment in advance is essential because of limited seating space in the search rooms, and shortage of staff. This sometimes makes it impossible to produce documents without notice. Material to be used on Saturday must be requested in advance. Inquiries should be directed to the County Archivist. The collection may be consulted only on the premises.
Hours	9:30 AM - 12:30 PM, 1:45 PM - 4:45 PM, Tuesday-Thursday; 9:30 AM - 12:30 PM, 1st and 3rd Saturday in the month, by appointment.
Duplicating facilities	Full-size copying facilities are available; however, copying is done at the Archivist's discretion. Parish Registers are not copied.
Other services	Brief questions by telephone or post will be answered and reference help is available in the search room. There are indexes and guides

available to further aid the researcher. An ultra-
violet lamp is provided.

Publications   Summary Guide to Guildford Muniment Room (out-
of-print, 1967); Guide to Parish Registers Deposited in Surrey Record Office and Guildford
Muniment Room (1984).

HACKNEY

Institution   Hackney Archives Department
See: LONDON, Hackney Archives Department,
Rose Lipman Library

HALIFAX (map)

113 Institution   West Yorkshire Archive Service
     Address   Calderdale District Archives
Calderdale Central Library
Northgate House, Northgate
Halifax HX1 1UN

Telephone   0422 57257, ext. 2636

The West Yorkshire Archive Service was formed
from several separate agencies. See also:
BRADFORD, HUDDERSFIELD, LEEDS, and
WAKEFIELD

Holdings   The official archives of local government bodies
include the records of civil townships from the
late 17th century forward. Improvement Commissions from the late 18th century, Local Board of
Health and Boards of Guardians, and Borough,
Parish, and Urban District Councils from the 19th
century are represented in the collection.
Business records relate heavily to the textile
industry, but also include coal mining (from the
early 17th century), stone quarrying, brewing,
and engineering for the 19th and 20th centuries.
The 18th-century letter books of Samuel Hill of
Soyland and Joseph Halroyd of Halifax are found,
as well as the papers of the late-18th-century
Halifax attorney, Robert Parker. The original
records of over one hundred-fifty non-Anglican
Churches are deposited here and pre-1837 Anglican registers of baptisms, marriages, and burials
are available on microfilm. Also available are
microcopies of the Bishops' transcripts deposited
at the Borthwick Institute of Historical Research
in York. The parish records of Shelf, Diocese
of Bradford, 1850-1982 are held. Papers of political and labor organizations include records of the
Chartist movement for the 1830s, friendly societies
from the 1790s, trade councils from the 1860s, and

local political parties from the 1870s. Family and estate papers include medieval documents relating to the area and letters, diaries, and other records from the 17th century. The papers of Oliver Heywood, Cornelius Ashworth, and Anne Lister are housed here. Also found are census returns, 1841-1881; records concerning culture and leisure, education, law and order, public health, social welfare, transport and communications; title deeds; maps and plans and transcripts of graveyard inscriptions.

Conditions of admission and access

The archives are open to the public, but advance notice of a visit should be given whenever possible. Inquiries should be addressed to the District Archivist. Readers are advised to order original documents at least one day in advance whenever possible. Orders may be made by telephone, letter, or in person. It is also possible to reserve the use of a microfilm reader which may avoid delay.

Hours

10:00 AM - 5:30 PM, Monday-Tuesday, Thursday-Friday; 10:00 AM - 12:00 noon, Wednesday. Documents on microfilm may also be consulted 5:30 PM - 8:00 PM, Monday-Tuesday, Thursday-Friday, and 10:00 AM - 5:00 PM, Saturday in the Central Reference Library.

Duplicating facilities

Photocopying facilities are available and requests should be submitted in advance. Photocopying is done by staff members and will not be undertaken where there is risk of damage to documents.

Other services

Brief inquiries are answered by telephone or post and reference help is available in the search rooms. Many lists, guides, indexes, calendars, and other finding aids are provided to aid the researcher.

Publications

Brochures, lists, and guides are published by the West Yorkshire Archive Service as well as the following: The West Riding County Council 1889-1974: Historical Studies, by B. J. Barber and M. W. Beresford (1978); Search Guide to the English Land Tax, by R. W. Unwin (1982); Guides to the West Yorkshire Archive Service for Family Historians (1984); Guide to the Quarter Sessions of the West Riding of Yorkshire 1637-1971 and Other Official Records, by B. J. Barber (1984); Guide to the Archive Collections of the Yorkshire Archaeological Society 1931-1983 and to Collections Deposited with the Society, by S. Thomas (1985).

HAMILTON

114 Institution   Hamilton District Libraries

Address	98 Cadzow Street Hamilton ML3 6HQ
Telephone	0698 282323, ext. 143
Holdings	The library contains records of the Police Commission, Road Trustee minute books dating from the 19th century and Burgh Council minute books, 1701-1975. There are also Registers of Electors and abstracts of accounts, County Council records and Poor House minute books. The estate papers of the Duke of Hamilton are also kept. In addition, there are photographs and maps of the area and local newspapers dating from 1862. The census returns for Hamilton are held on microfilm.
Conditions of admission and access	The library is open to the public and formal arrangements to use the collection are not required. Inquiries should be directed to the Chief Librarian. Archives and reference books must be used on the premises.
Hours	9:00 AM - 7:30 PM, Monday-Tuesday, Thursday-Friday; 9:00 AM - 5:00 PM, Wednesday, Saturday.
Duplicating facilities	Photocopying equipment is available.
Other services	Brief inquiries by telephone or post are answered, and reference help is provided.
Publications	None.

HAMMERSMITH See: LONDON, London Borough of Hammersmith

HARINGEY See: LONDON, London Borough of Haringey

HAVERFORDWEST

Institution	Dyfed Archive Service See: HAVERFORDWEST, Pembrokeshire Record Office

HAVERFORDWEST

115 Institution Address	Pembrokeshire Area Record Office The Castle Haverfordwest SA61 2EF
Telephone	0437 3707

The Pembrokeshire Area Record Office is part of

the Dyfed Archive Service. See also: ABERYST-
WYTH (Cardiganshire Area Record Office) and
CARMARTHEN (Carmarthenshire Area Record
Office)

Holdings

Among the official records held by the record office are Quarter Sessions of Pembrokeshire and of
Haverfordwest, which include minutes, orders,
indictments and recognizances, calendars of
prisoners, lists of jurors, commissions of the peace,
registration of non-conformists, lists of innkeepers,
returns of lunatics, plans of roads and bridges,
police diaries and other papers. These date from
1734 to 1971. There are also the records deposited
with the Clerk of the Peace which include land
tax returns, 1786-1831; electoral registers from
1832; plans of railways, harbors, oil refineries
and other public undertakings, 1829-1964; inclosure acts and awards, 1786-1868; prison registers
and accounts with committal and discharge papers
of prisoners, 1812-1863; minutes and accounts of
Pembrokeshire, Fishguard and St. Davids Turnpike
Trusts, 1771-1833; account books and papers of
insolvent debtors, ca. 1795-1874; rules of Friendly
Societies and Savings Banks, 1772-1864; returns
of Freemasons, 1873-1945. From Petty Sessions
records (restricted for thirty years after the closing date) one finds minutes, registers, evidence
books and miscellaneous files, 19th and 20th centuries. The Boards of Guardians records include
minutes, accounts, correspondence, workhouse
registers, plans and other papers relating to poor
relief in Haverfordwest, Narberth, and Pembroke
Unions, from 1837 to the 1940s and in Cardigan
Union for the twentieth century. The Hospital
records (some of which are restricted for thirty
or one hundred years after the closing date)
include those for the County War Memorial Hospital (minutes, registers of patients, admission and
discharge books, report books and other papers,
1870-1979), Kensington Hospital (plans, staff
registers, minutes, etc., 1904-1973), Tenby Cottage Hospital (minutes, admissions and report
books, registers of patients and of treatments,
1884-1971), and Pembroke and District Cottage
Hospital (minutes, etc., 1913-1948). There are
Water Authority records which are comprised of
minutes, annual reports and accounts of the
Prescelly Water Board, the South West Wales River
Board, the South West Wales River Authority, and
the Pembrokeshire Water Board and date from
1948 to 1974. There are also registers of ships
in the port of Cardigan, 1824-1856, registers of
ships and fishing boats in the port of Milford,
1827-1930, and log books and crew agreements for
ships' registers in Milford and Cardigan, 1863-
1914. Borough records for Haverfordwest contain

deeds from the thirteenth to the twentieth century,
charters, 1378-1694, minutes, memoranda, correspondence, lists of freemen, bylaws, financial
papers, etc. from the 16th to the 20th century.
In those of Pembroke are found charters, 1378-
1527, court minutes, 1661-1835, minutes, accounts,
lists of burgesses, etc., from 1678 to the 20th
century. The Tenby records have minutes, 1946-
1973, Town Clerk's files, 1895-ca. 1970, leases,
conveyances, etc., of corporation property, 1870-
1968, and accounts, 1885-1973. The Acts of
Parliament, correspondence, deeds, accounts, and
papers concerning the construction of the bridge
and the administration of the tolls by the Haverfordwest Bridge Commissioners date from 1831-
1925. The County Council minutes, accounts and
correspondence, 1889-1974, managers' minutes,
plans, etc. from ca. 1870-1970, departmental files
of the twentieth century, police records of the
nineteenth and twentieth centuries, maps and plans
for the nineteenth and twentieth centuries and
motor vehicle licensing records from 1899-1978 are
held by the record office, as are the District Councils' minutes, rate-books, accounts, correspondence,
plans, etc., for Haverfordwest Rural District Council (RDC), Narberth RDC and Urban District Council (UDC), Pembroke RDC, Cemaes RDC, Fishguard
UDC, Milford UDC, and Neyland UDC from the
1880s to the 1970s. There are also minutes,
registers of electors, 1975-1982, rate books, 1974-
1975 from the South Pembrokeshire District Council,
and minutes, registers of electors, press cuttings
and some plans from Preseli District Council, 1973-
1981. The Parish Council records include minutes,
papers and accounts of about fifty Parish Councils
from 1894 to 1970 and some tithe maps. The
record office also holds records of the Church in
Wales, which consist of registers of baptisms, marriages, and burials of about eighty parishes from
the 16th to the 20th century, vestry minutes,
churchwardens' accounts, overseers' papers and
rate books of the 18th to the 20th century for
about sixty parishes. These also include tithe
maps. The non-conformist records are copies (including microfilms of registers held in the Public
Record Office in London of various non-conformist
registers of the late 18th to the 20th century).
There are associated minutes, accounts, deeds,
etc., of the 19th to the 20th century. Also found
in the record office are valuation lists and maps
made under the Finance Act, 1910 by the Commissioners of Inland Revenue. Family and estate
records contain collections relating to the estates
of Angle (John Mirehouse); Bush (Meyrick family);
Carew Court (Carew family); Dale Castle (Lloyd-
Phillips); Court estate; Lawrenny estate (Lord
Phillipps); Pentre (Saunders-Davies); Scolton

(Higgon); Henllan (Lewis). These contain title
deeds, rentals and maps from the 16th to the 20th
century, and also personal papers, diaries, correspondence, etc., 18th-20th centuries. The
business records are those of the Milford Docks
Company, 1874-1972; files and papers of J. Roch,
estate agent of Pembroke, 1914-1961; papers of
R. K. Lucas, estate agent of Haverfordwest, ca.
1800-1960s; papers of Messrs. Pritchard, Read and
Co., accountants, Haverfordwest, 1920s-1960s;
records relating to Porthgain Quarries, 20th
century (access with owner's permission only);
records of the Pembrokeshire Building Society,
19th-20th century; Saundersfoot Railway and
Harbour Company records, 1828-1933. Many
smaller collections include papers about coal mining at Hook, Saundersfoot, Nolton and Roch,
19th-20th century and account books, ledgers and
correspondence of smaller businesses and tradesmen, 18th-20th century. Among the solicitors'
records held by the office one finds the records
of the firms of R. T. P. Williams, Haverfordwest
and Milford branches; Eaton and Lowless of Pembroke and Pembroke Dock; Walter Williams and
Sons of Fishguard; Lewis and James of Narberth;
Price and Kelway of Milford (access with firm's
permission only); Penhale and Co., formerly
Philipps Williams and Co. of Haverfordwest. These
include office and agency papers, accounts, 19th-
20th century, and clients' papers which can include deeds, estate papers, probate papers and
accounts. Many large estates are covered, including Picton Castle, Bush and Orielton, also
Haverfordwest Borough and various businesses
and charities, 16th-20th century. There are also
a wide variety of smaller collections of documents,
volumes, postcards and photographs covering a
large number of different topics; these include
the following collections: minutes, annual reports
and pamphlets of NALGO, 1936-1975; minutes, correspondence and files of N.F.U. (some items
closed for up to fifty years), 1917-1977; minutes,
scrapbooks, correspondence and accounts of
several women's institutes, 20th century; aerial
photographs of most of Pembrokeshire taken ca.
1956-1958; Ordnance Survey maps, one-inch, six-
inch, twenty-five-inch scales, 1819-1964, and a
number of newspapers. Microfilm of the Pembroke
census returns, 1841-1881 (at ten-year intervals)
are available here for searchers' use.

Conditions of
admission and
access

The record office is open to the public and no
prior appointment is necessary. Inquiries should
be directed to the Archivist-in-Charge. All material must be used on the premises.

Hours

9:00 AM - 4:45 PM, Monday-Thursday; 9:00 AM -

4:15 PM, Friday; 9:30 AM - 12:30 PM, first and
third Saturday in each month except bank holiday
weekends.

Duplicating facilities	Full-size and microcopying facilities are provided.

Other services
Brief questions are answered by mail and by
telephone and reference help is available in the
office. There is a small reference library for the
use of researchers. Lectures and exhibitions
will be arranged by staff when possible.

Publications
There are a number of publications, both for sale
and issued without charge by the Dyfed Archive
Service. These include Carmarthenshire Record
Office: A Survey of Archive Holdings, by
S. Beckley (1980); A Guide to Parish Registers
in St. David's Diocese; A Guide to Local News-
papers in Dyfed: Notes for Searchers; Tracking
Your Ancestors; List of Record Agents; History
of Houses; Summaries of Main Collections:
Cardiganshire Record Office, Carmarthenshire
Record Office, Pembrokeshire Record Office; and
Topic Lists. These Lists give an indication of
material available concerning different subjects.
Those relating to documents in Haverfordwest are:
Haverfordwest Castle, Coal Mining in Pembroke-
shire, Railways in Pembrokeshire, Turnpike
Trusts and Rebecca Riots, Slate and Limestone
Quarrying in Pembrokeshire, Rugby Football,
Skokholm Island, Shipping Records, Coal Mining
in Pembrokeshire, Rebecca Riots, The Oil Industry
in Pembrokeshire, Politics, and Parliamentary Elec-
tions.

HAVERING
See: LONDON, London Borough of Havering

HAWARDEN

116 Institution
Address
Clwyd Record Office
The Old Rectory
Hawarden, Deeside CH5 3NR

Telephone
0244 532364

See also: RUTHIN, Clwyd Record Office

Holdings
The Clwyd Record Office has custody of the public
and official records of Flintshire and Denbighshire
from the 16th century. The collection contains
commercial directories which give a description of
towns and parishes and list principal inhabitants
for the following years and districts: 1828-1829,
1835 (all North Wales), 1841, 1856, 1868, 1874,
1886 (Flintshire and Denbighshire), 1889-1890 (all

North Wales), 1912 (Flintshire). Microfilm copies
of the census of Flintshire are held for the
years 1841, 1851, 1861, 1871, and 1881. These
are arranged by parishes, list the members of
each household and give age, relation to head of
house, occupation and, from 1851, place of birth.
Parish registers, which record baptisms, marriages
and burials are found. These were required from
1538, but for most parishes, survive only from the
17th century. Although most registers will be
found in the record office, a few have been deposited in the National Library of Wales at Aberystwyth. There are also printed transcripts of some
registers. A summary list is available at the
record office and information on the location of any
parish. Also located in the record office are tithe
maps for Flintshire, dating mainly between 1839
and 1849; Poor Law records of Holywell and St.
Asaph Union (1837-1930); school records for Flintshire, taxation records (on microfilm) of Flintshire
lay subsidies, 1544-1628, and Hearth Tax returns,
1666, 1670; shipping records, 1863-1913, include
lists of the crew of ships from Flintshire ports on
the River Dee. Electoral registers are held for
Flintshire for 1832, 1855, 1868-1869, 1912 onwards.
Non-conformist records for Flintshire, 1796-1837
include Wesleyan and Primitive Methodist Chapels
in the Buckley and Deeside Circuit, 1840-1971.
Quarter Sessions records for Flintshire are found
from 1720, and also highway and Borough and
District Council records. The office holds the archives of local families and estates, some dating
from medieval times, and collections of business
and industrial records, mostly for Flintshire, but
including some Denbighshire material. The office
is a recognized repository for manorial and tithe
documents and is designated to receive ecclesiastical records (St. Asaph parish records).

Conditions of admission and access	Researchers with limited research time or long-term projects are advised to make an appointment in advance of their visit. Most documents can be produced with no prior notice, but access to papers at St. Deiniol's Library requires at least two days' notice (see entry no. 117). Documents are not produced between 12:00 noon and 1:30 PM unless ordered in advance. All material must be used on the premises. Inquiries should be addressed to the County Archivist.
Hours	9:00 AM - 4:45 PM, Monday-Thursday; 9:00 AM - 4:15 PM, Friday.
Duplicating facilities	Full-size and microcopying facilities are available, and photographs can be provided.
Other services	Brief inquiries by mail or telephone are answered.

Reference help is available for visiting scholars, and there are lists, indexes and an extensive library of printed sources on local history and topography. The staff are available for illustrated talks and will arrange exhibits. The County Archivist acts as Hon. Archivist to St. Deiniol's Library, Hawarden.

Publications   Guide to the Flintshire Record Office (out-of-print, 1974); Hand List of the County Records (1955); Calendar of the Flintshire Quarter Sessions Rolls, 1747-1752 (1983); Clwyd in Old Photographs (1975); Historic Ruthin (1979); Clwyd Archives Cookbook (1980); Wrexham Directory (1981); Mr. Gladstone and Hawarden (1982); Parish Map (1982); Handlist of the Denbigh Borough Records (1975); Handlist of the Topographical Prints of Clwyd (1977); Guide to Parish Records of Clwyd (1984); Archive Teaching Units (collections of about fifteen facsimiles of documents with introduction and explanatory notes) which include The River Dee (1981), Coal Mining (1975), Daniel Owen (1975); illustrated booklets are as follows: Ruthin Gaol (1977), The Mold Riots (1977), The Tithe War (1978), Rhyfel y Degwm (1978), facsimiles of maps and prints; postcards.

HAWARDEN

117 Institution   Saint Deiniol's Library
    Address   Hawarden, Deeside CH5 3DF

    Telephone   0244 532350

    Holdings   The library contains the Glynne-Gladstone manuscripts which include extensive and important groups of family correspondence and papers of W. E. Gladstone and members of his family, including his father, Sir John Gladstone and son, Herbert, Viscount Gladstone. Also found are the personal papers of C. A. H. Green, Archbishop of Wales, 19th-century studies, and a large pamphlet collection. There are works in theology, history, philosophy, literature, and a strong collection in medieval, Tudor, and Stuart Studies. The library also holds Royal Historical and Camden Society material, Rolls and Manuscripts Commission series, HMSO publications, and the Loeb Classical Library (Greek and Latin).

    Conditions of   This is a residential library and has accommoda-
    admission and   tions for forty-six guests. It is for the use of
    access   students and scholars who reside there while conducting research, but scholars working in any field are welcome to use the facilities. A letter of introduction or testimonial is required for

residential readers and others must make application to use the collection. The County Archivist of the Clwyd Record Office acts as Hon. Archivist and as such deals with the listing and production of the manuscripts collection. Access to documents can be made through him with two days prior notice. Otherwise inquiries should be directed to the Warden and Chief Librarian.

Hours

The library is open all year, including Sundays, 9:00 AM - 10:00 PM, except for two weeks at Christmas.

Duplicating facilities

Full-size copying facilities are available.

Other services

Brief inquiries by telephone and post will be answered. The library has facilities for scholars to remain in residence while conducting research. A descriptive brochure is available.

Publications

Bibliographies of Books Printed Before 1800, Vol. 1- . Vol. 1, Biblical Study and Patristics, by G. C. Careless and P. Morris; Vol. 2, Philosophy and Christian Doctrine, by G. C. Careless; Vol. 3, Life in the Church: Spirituality, Morality, Homiletics, by G. C. Careless; Vol. 4, Liturgical Studies, by G. C. Careless; Vol. 5, Church History: Part One: The Beginnings to the Reformation: Roman Catholicism in Britain and Elsewhere; Continental Protestantism, by G. C. Careless; Vol. 6, Church History, Part Two, The Anglican and Protestant Churches in Great Britain and Ireland, by P. Morris; Vol. 7, European History, by G. C. Careless and P. Morris; Vol. 8, Language and Literature, by G. C. Careless; Vol. 9, Miscellaneous, by G. C. Careless; Ireland: A Bibliography of Material Held at St. Deiniol's Library, by H. C. Price.

HEBRIDES

See: STORNOWAY

HENDON

See: LONDON, London Borough of Barnet

HEREFORD (map)

118   Institution Address

Hereford and Worcester County Libraries
Hereford Library
Broad Street
Hereford HR4 9AU

Telephone

0432 272456

Holdings

The library maintains a collection of local studies material that includes maps, local newspapers from

1770 to the present, photographs relating to the history of Herefordshire, prints, cuttings, illustrations and directories. Census returns on microfilm are also held. A small manuscript collection is maintained.

Conditions of admission and access

The library is open to the public and no appointment in advance is necessary. Inquiries should be directed to the Librarian. The reference collection must be used on the premises. A lending collection of books relating to Herefordshire is kept in the Reference Library and issued from the Reference Library Enquiry Desk.

Hours

9:30 AM - 6:00 PM, Tuesday-Wednesday; 9:30 AM - 5:00 PM, Thursday; 9:30 AM - 8:00 PM, Friday; 9:30 AM - 4:00 PM, Saturday. (Closed Monday).

Duplicating facilities

There is a coin-operated copying machine available for public use.

Other services

Reference help is available for visiting scholars and brief questions by post or telephone will be answered. A detailed analytical index to the Herefordshire material, with references by person and place names, is available to aid researchers.

Publications

Introducing Hereford Library (1984).

HEREFORD (map)

119 Institution
Address

Hereford and Worcester County Record Office
The Old Barracks
Harold Street
Hereford HR1 2QX

Telephone

0432 265441

See also: WORCESTER, Hereford and Worcester County Record Office

Holdings

The collection contains records of Herefordshire Quarter Sessions and Hereford Diocese including probate material, 1540-1858, bishop's transcripts and tithe records, registers, the Mormon International Genealogical Index and other ecclesiastical records. Also found are Herefordshire County Council, Hereford City and Leominster Borough, District and Parish Councils originating in Herefordshire, and records of persons associated with Herefordshire. The office is a recognized repository for manorial and tithe documents, for certain public records, and for ecclesiastical records (Hereford). It continues to receive all classes of records created within the Old County, including census returns, records of businesses and trade, non-conformist church archives, maps, plans and photographs, schools, unions, and hospital papers. There are family records, among which are those relating to the Arkwrights of Hampton, Cotterells of Garnons, Dunnes of Gatley, Foleys of Stoke Edith, Herefords of Sufton, Hoptons of Canon Frome, and Traffords of Hill Court. The researcher will find manuscript material on the diocesan, political, economic, and social history of Herefordshire, resources on the Midlands Iron Works (16th to 18th centuries), and high farming in the 19th century.

Conditions of admission and access	The office is open to the public and no appointment is necessary, but because of heavy demand, it is advised to book microfilm equipment in advance. Also, some records require advance ordering. Inquiries should be directed to the Assistant Head of Record Services. All material must be used on the premises.
Hours	10:00 AM - 1:00 PM, 2:00 PM - 4:45 PM, Monday; 9:15 AM - 1:00 PM, 2:00 PM - 4:45 PM, Tuesday-Thursday; 9:15 AM - 1:00 PM, 2:00 PM - 4:00 PM, Friday.
Duplicating facilities	Full-size and microcopying facilities are available.
Other services	Only brief questions by post or telephone are answered. Reference help is available in the search room as well as works on local history. There are also indexes and guides to further aid the researcher. An explanation of how to use the indexes is provided. The staff will undertake to give lectures and arrange exhibits for interested groups either at the record office or elsewhere whenever possible.
Publications	The record office issues catalogues and guides which are available for consultation in the office. These are not at present published in a form which could be widely available. An exception is the guide, All (or Some) of What You Need to Know About the Hereford and Worcester County Record Office, which is provided for distribution.

HEREFORD (map)

120 Institution Address	Hereford Cathedral Library The Cathedral Hereford HR1 2NG
Telephone	0432 3537 (Mss.); 0432 58403
Holdings	The main emphasis of the collection is on religion

and ecclesiastical history. The special collections
include manuscripts from the 8th to the 15th century, early printed books (many of which are
chained), incunabula, 18th and 19th century manuscript and printed music. The archives of the
Dean and Chapter are housed in the muniment
room of the Cathedral. They range in date from
the 12th century to the present time. Also found
are administrative records of the Dean and Chapter
(medieval onward), Act Books, 1512 onward, accounts and records of Cathedral maintenance,
manorial records, records of peculiar jurisdictions
and of charities administered by the Cathedral
(e.g., hospitals).

Conditions of admission and access	The lower cloister library is open to the public, but research may be conducted only during certain hours without an appointment in advance (see hours below). The same is true for the chained library in the upper transept room and for subscribers in the diocese who have the use of a lending library of modern books. Inquiries should be directed to the Hon. Librarian. The collection may be used only on the premises.
Hours	The lower cloister library and the lending library are open 10:30 AM - 12:30 PM, Tuesday-Thursday (at other times, by prior appointment). The chained library in the upper transept room is open as a place of interest, 10:30 AM - 12:30 PM, 2:00 PM - 4:00 PM, Monday-Saturday, from April to October; 11:00 AM - 11:30 AM and 3:00 PM - 3:30 PM, Monday-Saturday from November to March (unless the Cathedral is closed for services). An appointment in advance is required for all other times.
Duplicating facilities	Some photocopying can be arranged. Positive microfilm copies of manuscript volumes can be supplied on request. Photographic prints can be made from negatives.
Other services	Only brief questions by post or telephone will be answered. There is some reference guidance provided at the library.
Publications	Hereford Cathedral: A Short Account of the Chained Library, rev. 3rd ed., by F. C. and P. E. Morgan; Hereford Cathedral Libraries (Including the Chained Library and the Vicars Choral Library and Muniments, by F. C. and P. E. Morgan, 2nd ed., rev. Both are illustrated pamphlets.

HERTFORD

121 Institution	Hertfordshire Record Office

Address	County Hall Hertford SG13 8DE
Telephone	0992 555105
Holdings	The collection includes official and semiofficial records, including records of the County Council, from 1888; Quarter Sessions, 1588-1971; Sheriffs, 1742-1932; Turnpike Trusts, 1725-1877; Highway Boards, 1868-1899; School Boards, 1876-1903; individual and grouped schools, 19th and 20th centuries; Boards of Guardians, 1834-1929; Local Boards of Health, 1849-1898; records of water, gas, and electricity undertakings; non-medical and administrative records of hospitals and Joint Hospital Boards, 1826-1948; records of the Borough of Hertford, from 1226; records of former Urban and Rural District Councils, 19th and 20th centuries, and of former Development Corporations of Hatfield, Hemel Hempstead, Stevenage, and Welwyn Garden City, 20th century. The collection contains ecclesiastical records, including records of the Diocese of St. Albans, 19th and 20th centuries, Archdeaconry of St. Albans, including probate records, 15th-19th centuries; Archdeaconry of Hunts, Hitchin division, including probate records, 16th to 19th century; rural deaneries, 19th to 20th century; parish records, including registers of baptisms, marriages, and burials from 1538, vestry minutes, churchwardens', overseers', constables', and surveyors' records; some non-conformist records, including Quaker records, 1658-1879. The record office holds deposited non-official records, including manorial records, title deeds, estate papers, personal correspondence and diaries, farm and business records. It also contains printed and manuscript maps, including estate, tithe and enclosure maps, and Ordnance Survey maps; books, pamphlets, and periodicals relating to local people and the history of the county and individual parishes; County Directories, 1826-1937; and appropriate works of reference.
Conditions of admission and access	The office is open to the public. A letter of introduction is unnecessary, but it is appreciated if an appointment is made in advance. All material must be used on the premises. Inquiries should be made to the County Archivist.
Hours	9:15 AM - 5:15 PM, Monday-Thursday; 9:15 AM - 4:30 PM, Friday.
Duplicating facilities	Full-size photocopies can be made and photographic reproduction can also be provided. Microcopies can be done upon request.
Other services	Reference aid is given on the premises. Inquiries

involving limited research by the staff may be answered by mail or by telephone and a fee is charged. Detailed research cannot be undertaken.

Publications

Guide to the Hertfordshire Record Office, Pt. I, Quarter Sessions and Other Records in the Custody of the Official of the County, by W. Le Hardy (1961); Catalogue of Manuscript Maps, ed. by Peter Walne (1969); Genealogical Sources, rev. ed. (1981); Hertfordshire County Records--Calendars to Sessions Rolls, Books, etc., Vol. IV, VI-IX, X, ed. by William Le Hardy; Industrial Monuments in Hertfordshire, by W. Branch Johnson (1967); Archive Teaching Units.

HEYWOOD

122 Institution
    Address

Rochdale Libraries
Heywood Area Central Library
Local Studies Collection
Church Street
Heywood OL10 1LL

Telephone

0706 60947

See also: MIDDLETON, Rochdale Libraries, Middleton Area Central Library; and ROCHDALE, Rochdale Libraries, Rochdale Area Central Library

Holdings

Records for the Borough Council (minutes and accounts), health reports, electoral registers, and documents from the Heywood and Middleton Water Board are found here. Local newspapers, maps, plans and photographs form part of the collection. Theatre posters and political handbills are also held.

Conditions of
admission and
access

The library is open to the public and appointments in advance are not required. Inquiries should be directed to the Assistant Librarian at the address above or to the Local Studies Librarian, Rochdale Libraries (Rochdale Area Central Library, Esplanade, Rochdale OL16 1AQ; telephone: 0706 47474, ext. 423). The archives and reference works must be used in the library.

Hours

9:30 AM - 8:00 PM, Monday, Thursday; 9:30 AM - 5:30 PM, Tuesday, Friday; 9:30 AM - 1:00 PM, Wednesday; 9:30 AM - 1:00 PM, 2:00 PM - 4:00 PM, Saturday.

Duplicating
facilities

Full-size copies can be provided.

Other services

Questions by telephone or post are answered if extensive research is not required. Reference aid is provided in the library.

Publications	<u>Introduction to the Local Studies Collection</u> (1981).

HUDDERSFIELD (map)

123 Institution	West Yorkshire Archive Service
Address	Kirklees Libraries and Museums Service
	Princess Alexandra Walk
	Huddersfield HD1 2SU
Telephone	0483 513808, ext. 207

The West Yorkshire Archive Service was formed from several separate agencies. <u>See also</u>: BRADFORD, HALIFAX, LEEDS, and WAKEFIELD

Holdings	The official records held include those from Kirklees Metropolitan Council and its eleven predecessor authorities, the County Boroughs of Dewsbury and Huddersfield, the Borough of Batley and Spenborough and the Urban Districts of Colne Valley, Denby Dale, Heckmondwike, Holmfirth, Kirkburton, Meltham and Mirfield. Many of these had also received material from predecessors, for example, Dewsbury Local Board of Health (1851-1862), Huddersfield Lighting and Watching Commissioners (1820-1848), and Improvement Commissioners (1848-1868). Family and estate records include deposits from the Ramsdens of Byram and Longley, Beaumonts of Whitley, Thornhills of Fixby and Saviles of Thornhill. The Ramsden Collection includes family and estate papers, deeds, rentals, surveys and valuations for Huddersfield and Almondbury, 1200-1921, and the Almondbury Court rolls, 1627-1934. The Beaumont family of Whitley Collection pertains to Kirkheaton, Lepton, Mirfield, South Grosland and Whitley. The Clarke-Thornhill family of Fixby Collection includes accounts, deeds and leases, mostly for the Calverley, Fixby, Lindley, Longwood and Rastrick areas and valuations (1429-1924). This material supplements that held by the Yorkshire Archaeological Society. Business records cover the textile industry in Huddersfield, Dewsbury and Batley areas. The papers of Joseph Kilner of Honley contain records of the production of healds and stays for looms (1868-1926). Correspondence, bills and accounts which relate to John Kay, a clothier at Almondbury (late 18th and early 19th century), give details of prices and terms of trade with London and Hamburg. Other firms' records are also found and include accountants, shovel makers, valve makers, shoe makers, land surveyors, auctioneers, tinsmiths, maltsters, iron and lead workers, the Huddersfield Canal Company, College Company and

Theatre Royal. Ecclesiastical records include the parish registers of Kirkheaton and Kirkburton, and the tithe awards for the Almondbury parish. Non-conformist records include Baptist, Christian Brethren, Congregational, Independent, Methodist, and Unitarian. Methodist Circuit records include Clayton West and Denby Dale and Huddersfield South and West. Marsden Congregational Chapel archives are found and have accounts of the building of the first chapel (1806-1813). Records of Highfield Independent Chapel contain material relating to Highfield Schools and the Huddersfield Girls College Company. Other records include those of societies, trade unions, and bodies established for special purposes.

Conditions of admission and access	The archives are open to the public, but advance notice of a visit should be given. Some collections are kept away from the premises and are not immediately available. Inquiries should be made to the District Archivist.
Hours	9:00 AM - 8:00 PM, Monday-Friday; 9:00 AM - 4:00 PM, Saturday.
Duplicating facilities	Photocopying facilities are available.
Other services	Brief questions are answered by post or telephone and reference help is provided.
Publications	Guides, brochures, and lists are produced by the West Yorkshire Archive Service and also the following publications: The West Riding County Council, 1889-1974: Historical Studies, by B. J. Barber and M. W. Beresford (1978); Search Guide to the English Land Tax, by R. W. Unwin (1982); Guide to the West Yorkshire Archive Service for Family Historians (1984); Guide to the Quarter Sessions of the West Riding of Yorkshire, 1637-1971 and other Official Records, by B. J. Barber (1984); Guide to Archive Collections of the Yorkshire Archaeological Society 1931-1983 and the Collections Deposited with the Society, by S. Thomas (1985).

HUNTINGDON

124 Institution Address	Cambridgeshire Record Office Grammar School Walk Huntingdon PE18 6LF
Telephone	0480 57734
	See also: CAMBRIDGE, County Record Office, Cambridge

Holdings

The office holds Parish registers and transcripts within Huntingdon Archdeaconry from 1538 to the 20th century. Bishops' transcripts (1604-1858), marriage allegations and bonds (1663-1883), nonconformist registers and other records from the 17th to the 20th century are also held. Probate records for the Commissory Court in the Archdeaconry of Huntingdon and peculiar courts (1479-1857), land tax (1767-1832), poll books and registers of electors (1768 to date), Parish Poor Law and Poor Law Union records from the 17th to the 20th century are found. Other records include Quarter Sessions from 1734, County Council from 1889, and District Council from 1894. Records from Huntingdon Borough from 1205, and Godmanchester Borough from 1212, School Log Books and Registers, 19th-20th century, maps from 1591, including Ordnance Survey maps from 1806, inclosure awards and maps, 1763-1884, tithe apportionments and maps, 1837-1936, manorial and estate, and family collections are available. Microfilm of records held elsewhere include census returns for the County of Huntingdon and the Soke of Peterborough, 1841-1881, Hunts lay subsidies, 1327-1664, Hearth Tax, 1664, 1666, and 1674, Hunts non-conformist registers found in the Public Record Office (RG4 series, 1742-1837). Microfiche of the Mormon International Genealogical Index for Hunts and the surrounding counties is kept as well as the British Record Society Index Library indexes to the P. C. C. Wills, 1383-1629, 1653-1660, 1671-1700, and Admons 1581-1596, and 1649-1660.

Conditions of admission and access

The record office is open to the public and no prior appointment is required except for Saturday mornings. It is, however, advisable to book microfilm readers in advance should their use be required. Inquiries should be made to the Senior Archivist. All material must be used in the search room.

Hours

9:00 AM - 5:00 PM, Monday-Friday; 9:00 AM - 12:00 noon, first Saturday morning in the month, by appointment.

Duplicating facilities

Full-size and microcopying facilities are provided. Photographs can be obtained by arrangement.

Other services

A small library of reference books is available for searchers' use and reference help is provided. Short inquiries by mail or telephone are answered. There are a number of indexes which are of use to the searcher as well as catalogs and other aids available.

Publications

Guide to the Huntingdon Record Office (out-of-print, 1958); Maps in the County Record Office, Huntingdon (1968); List of Inclosure Awards and Plans in the Custody of the Huntingdon and Peterborough County Council (1971). Genealogical Sources in Cambridgeshire, written in 1979 by J. M. Farrar, includes information on the Huntingdon Record Office. This publication is presently out-of-print, but a new edition is planned.

HUYTON   See: LIVERPOOL

HYTHE

125	Institution Address	Hythe Borough Archives Town Council Offices Oaklands Stade Street Hythe CT1 6BG
	Telephone	0303 66152/66153
	Holdings	The collection includes Borough of Hythe records from ca. 1300-1974; Churchwarden's accounts from the 17th century, charters from the 12th to the 16th century; ancient court books from the 15th century, including sessions books, sessions rolls, Jurants' accounts, Chamberlains' accounts, Town Clerks' bill books, and Treasurers accounts, deeds from the 17th to the 20th century, Hythe Session warrants and assembly books, appointments of Bailiff (by archbishops and others), various legal documents including writs, grants, deeds, petitions, depositions, leases, conveyances, book of fines and book of offences. Also found are overseers' accounts, parish accounts, proclamations, letters, political correspondence, and papers relating to elections.
	Conditions of admission and access	An appointment is required to use the collection. Inquiries should be made to the Archivist either at the Hythe address or at the Kent County Archives, South East Kent Area Office (Folkestone Central Library, Grace Hill, Folkestone CT20 1HD; telephone: 0303 57583). The collection may be used only on the premises.
	Hours	9:30 AM - 1:00 PM, 2:00 PM - 4:30 PM, Wednesday. Other arrangements can sometimes be made at the discretion of the Archivist.
	Duplicating facilities	There are very limited facilities for photocopying.
	Other services	The Archivist can offer guidance to the researcher and answer very brief queries by post or telephone.

Administrative assistance is given to Dover, Hythe, Lydd, and New Romney Town Councils, and to Shepway District Council, but control is not exercised over records held by other Councils. (See: MAIDSTONE, Kent County Archives Office, entry no. 204 for details.)

Publications   Catalogue of Documents Belonging to the Corporation of Hythe, 11th to 20th Century, comp. by Rev. H. D. Dale, and Dr. C. Chidell; A Revised Catalogue of Documents, by Mrs. M. P. Shaw (1985).

INVERNESS

126 Institution   Highland Regional Archive
     Address   The Library
                     Farraline Park
                     Inverness IV1 1LS

     Telephone   0463 36463

     Holdings   The collection includes Old Parish Registers, 1841 and 1851, census (on microfilm), and indexes to Old Parish Registers. There are long runs of local newspapers, many printed family and highland clan histories and collections of tombstone inscriptions. There is a very limited collection of wills, conveyances, etc., mainly restricted to the Burgh of Inverness. The Old Parish Register and the census material are available in the library because of the cooperation of the Highland Family History Society, whose property they are.

     Conditions of   The material is available to the public without a
     admission and   letter of introduction or appointment. Inquiries
     access   should be directed to the Records Officer, who is available part-time only. The records must be used on the premises.

     Hours   9: 30 AM - 5: 30 PM, Monday. The library hours are 9: 30 AM - 5: 30 PM, Monday-Friday; 9: 30 AM - 5: 00 PM, Saturday.

     Duplicating   Prints from microfilm can be made and full-size
     facilities   copying facilities are available. All copying is subject to copyright and condition of the document.

     Other services Reference help is provided and brief inquiries by post or telephone are answered. Microfilm readers are available.

     Publications   The Regional Archive produces catalogues.

IPSWICH (map)

127	Institution Address	Suffolk Record Office County Hall St. Helens Street Ipswich IP4 2JS
	Telephone	0473 55801, ext. 4235

See also: BURY ST. EDMUNDS, Suffolk Record Office

Holdings	Records of the County Council and those of official bodies, churches and chapels, businesses, societies, families and estates of the eastern area of the county are found in this branch of the record office. It is a repository for manorial and tithe documents and for ecclesiastical records of the St. Edmundsbury and Ipswich Archdeaconries of Ipswich and Suffolk. Collections date from the 12th century to the present day.
Conditions of admission and access	The record office is open to the public but because of limited space, visitors are asked to telephone or write for an appointment in advance. During busy periods it may be necessary to restrict visitors to half a day's use of a seat or microfilm reader. Inquiries should be directed to the County Archivist. Records for use on Saturday must be requested by 1:00 PM on Friday. All material must be used on the premises.
Hours	9:00 AM - 5:00 PM, Monday-Thursday; 9:00 AM - 4:00 PM, Friday; 9:00 AM - 1:00 PM, 2:00 PM - 5:00 PM, Saturday.
Duplicating facilities	Full-size and microcopies can be provided. Photographic reproductions can also be made.
Other services	Inquiries by telephone and by mail will be answered if they are brief. An education service is provided for students from schools and colleges to work under the guidance of an archive education officer and exhibitions and talks are given to local groups. There are facilities for the repair of manuscripts and ultra-violet lamps are provided.
Publications	There are guides for the record office user and other publications based on the record office's holdings, and a Guide to Genealogical Sources in Suffolk (2nd ed., 1985).

IRLAM	See: MANCHESTER
ISLE OF LEWIS	See: STORNOWAY

ISLE OF MAN   See: DOUGLAS

ISLE OF WIGHT   See: NEWPORT

JERSEY, CHANNEL   See: ST. HELIER
    ISLANDS

JOHNSTONE

128 Institution   Renfrew District Libraries Archives Service
      Address   Old Library
                    Collier Street
                    Johnstone PA5 8AR

      Telephone   0505 20804

      Holdings   Records of Town Councils, Burg records
                    (Renfrew from 1655, Johnstone from 1857,
                    Barrhead from 1894, and Paisley from 1594) and
                    papers of the cooperative movement in Paisley
                    are held. Plans from the Dean of Guild Courts
                    are also found.

      Conditions of   The user does not ordinarily need to make an
      admission and   appointment in advance unless he wishes to use
      access   the collection outside library hours. Inquiries
                    should be addressed to the Archivist or to the
                    Local History Librarian (Central Library, High
                    Street, Paisley PA1 2BB; telephone: 041 889
                    2360).

      Hours   9:30 AM - 4:30 PM, Tuesday, Thursday.

      Duplicating   Photocopies can be provided.
      facilities

      Other services   Questions by telephone or post are answered only
                    if they are brief. Some reference help is provided.

      Publications   None.

KENDAL (map)

129 Institution   Cumbria Record Office (Kendal)
      Address   County Offices
                    Kendal LA9 4RQ

      Telephone   0539 21000, ext. 329

                    See also: BARROW-IN-FURNESS, Cumbria Record
                    Office; CARLISLE, Cumbria Record Office

      Holdings   The records held relate mainly to the former County

of Westmorland, including Westmorland Quarter
Sessions records with order, indictment and minute
books from the year 1656, and sessions rolls from
1729; population returns for the East and West
Wards of the County and Stricklandgate, Kendal
(1787); Westmorland County Council records from
1889 are also available. The records of the District Councils from 1894 and the Borough records
of Kendal and Appleby are located at this office.
Also found are records of Turnpike Trusts, Boards
of Guardians, including minute and account books,
and other records, 1768-1913, as well as some
School Boards. The records of many Church of
England and Civil Parishes have been deposited
(some of which date from the 16th century), together with the records of some non-conformist
churches. Family and estate papers include Le
Fleming of Rydal, which have family, political, and
estate correspondence from 1654; personal and estate accounts (including records of the Dudley
family of Yanwath) from the early 16th century;
17th- and 18th-century records of the Coniston
Copper Mines and Iron Forge; and papers relating to the Office of Justice of the Peace, including
Hearth Tax and Poll Tax returns, 1674 and 1695.
Browne of Troutbeck papers have sixteen volumes
of manuscripts relating to the office of High
Constable, principally in the 18th century, and
many other 18th-century records which illustrate
the social and economic life of a statesman family
for a period of nearly 250 years. Hothfield of
Appleby, which have records relating to the Westmorland portion of the Clifford and Tufton estates,
are here. Also found are deeds, rentals accounts
and legal accounts, and other legal papers from the
early 16th century, including three volumes of
copy documents relating to the Veteripont and
Clifford families compiled about 1675, and lead and
coal mining records from the mid-18th century.
There is an incomplete series of family letters,
1584-ca. 1760 which includes letters to and from
Lady Anne Clifford, Countess of Dorset and Pembroke, 1617-1668. And finally, one will find many
solicitors' and business records.

Conditions of admission and access	The office is open to the public and no prior ap-pointment is necessary, but visitors requiring large numbers of records or special help should notify the record office in advance. Also, notice must be given for records from Levens Hall to be made available. All material must be used in the search room. Inquiries should be addressed to the Deputy County Archivist.
Hours	9:00 AM - 5:00 PM, Monday-Friday, except for public holidays.

Duplicating facilities	Full-size and microcopying facilities are available. Photographs can be provided.
Other services	The Curwen Library, found at the record office, contains valuable printed material for the local history of Lancashire, Yorkshire, Cumberland, and Westmorland, as well as works useful for the study of legal history, heraldry, and genealogy. Reference help is available and short questions are answered by post or telephone. Lengthy searches are not undertaken. Leaflets on copying facilities and educational use of records are provided.
Publications	Bibliography of the History and Topography of Cumberland and Westmorland, by W. H. Hodgson (1969); Fleming-Senhouse Papers, by E. Hughes (1961); Records at a Glance (1979); Subject Guides for enclosure, genealogy, hospitals, health and medicine, Leconfield and Lonsdale estate; Sources for Family History, Sources for School Records, Sources on World Wars I and II, Inclosure Awards List, Tithe Awards List, Guide to the Records of Lord Egremont at Cockermouth Castle. The following articles are about the record office: "Local Archives of Gt. Britain XXVIII. Cumberland, Westmorland, and Carlisle Record Office, 1960-1965," by B. C. Jones, Archives Vol. VIII, no. 34; "Cumberland and Westmorland Record Offices," 1968, The School of History, University of Leeds. Reprinted in Archives, Vol. VII, no. 34; Church of England Parishes in Cumbria, 1829, map, 1985.

KENSINGTON	See: LONDON, Kensington Central Reference Library

KIDDERMINSTER

130 Institution Address	Kidderminster Library Market Street Kidderminster DY10 1AD
Telephone	0562 752832
Holdings	Borough records in the collection include minutes, rate books, and valuation lists of the 19th century. Corporation yearbooks, 19th-20th century are also found. Church, school, and charity organizations' records are held, as are private papers and business archives. The Maiden Bradley Priory registers are found as are the Knight, Talbot, and Baxter Church manuscripts.
Conditions of admission and access	An appointment in advance is necessary to use the archives. Inquiries should be addressed to the

Assistant County Librarian. Archives must be used in the library.

Hours   9:30 AM - 5:30 PM, Monday, Friday; 9:30 AM - 7:00 PM, Tuesday, Thursday; 9:30 AM - 4:00 PM, Saturday. Closed Wednesday.

Duplicating facilities   Photocopying can be provided.

Other services   Brief questions by mail or telephone are answered and reference help is provided.

Publications   None.

KILKENNY (map)

131 Institution   Kilkenny County Library
    Address   6 John's Quay
                         Kilkenny, Co. Kilkenny

    Telephone   056 22021/22606

    Holdings   The collection includes histories of prominent families, books, pamphlets and periodicals relating to the local history of the area. There are Board of Guardian records, 1839-1923, Rural District Council records, 1894-1926, Grand Jury records, 1838-1898, and registers of Electors, 1940-1978. These are mostly in manuscript form and there are many gaps. Newspapers include Kilkenny People, 1896-1904, 1970 to date, Kilkenny Journal, 1832-1893, 1895-1900, and Kilkenny Moderator, 1828-1840, 1900-1902. Most of these holdings are on microfilm. There is also a large collection of maps, prints, photographs, and drawings.

    Conditions of   There are no conditions placed on use of the Local
    admission and   History Reference Room. Local history records,
    access   manuscripts and reference works must be used on the premises. A registration fee is required to borrow those books available for circulation. Inquiries should be addressed to the Librarian.

    Hours   10:30 AM - 1:00 PM, 2:00 PM - 5:00 PM, 7:00 PM - 9:00 PM, Monday, Wednesday; 10:30 AM - 1:00 PM, 2:00 PM - 5:00 PM, Tuesday, Thursday-Friday; 10:30 AM - 1:30 PM, Saturday.

    Duplicating   Photocopying facilities are available and full-size
    facilities   copies from microform can be provided.

    Other services   All inquiries are answered either by telephone, correspondence, or personally. Reference help and guidance are available in the library. There are lists and indexes available to aid the research-er.

Publications	<u>Lists of Books, Pamphlets, Maps, Prints in the Local History Collection</u> (typescript); indexes, guides.

KINGSTON-UPON-HULL
   (map)

132 Institution Address	Kingston-upon-Hull Record Office 79 Lowgate Kingston-upon-Hull HU1 2AA
Telephone	0482 222051/6
Holdings	The office holds registers of baptisms and marriages in non-conformist churches, 19th-20th century, and of deaths and burials. Also found are property deeds, census returns, and school admissions registers. The collection contains records of the City Council and all previous local authorities within the City from 1299, Quarter Session records from ca. 1693, deposited records of local businesses, churches, organizations, and individuals from ca. 1800, all aspects of local government, the administration of justice, manufacturing, commerce, transport, religion, genealogy and biography, topography, agriculture, architecture, and warfare. There are records of various corporation departments (clerks, treasurers, architects, education, etc.) and of various bodies whose functions have been taken over (School Boards, Poor Law Unions, Petty Sessions, Court of Record and Court for the Relief of Insolvent Debtors), and records deposited by companies, churches, public bodies and private individuals. Subjects covered include transportation by road, rail, air, sea and inland navigation; docks, harbors, shipping and the fishing industry; agriculture and estate management; trade and industry; demography, biography and genealogy; topography, architecture and the urban environment; public utilities and engineering; education, housing and the social services; crime and the penal system; and military history and warfare. There is a small library dealing with archival matters, local history, and a general background to the holdings.
Conditions of admission and access	The office is open to the public but researchers are requested to make an appointment before their first visit. Inquiries should be addressed to the City Archivist. The collection may be consulted only in the public search room of the record office.
Hours	8:30 AM - 5:00 PM, Monday-Thursday; 8:30 AM - 4:30 PM, Friday.

Duplicating facilities	Full-size copying facilities are available and dye-line prints and photographs can be supplied in appropriate cases.
Other services	Brief questions are answered by telephone and by mail. Reference help is available in the search room. There are a number of guides, lists and catalogues provided to aid the researcher. Also a Guide to the System of Finding Aids is provided.
Publications	Calendar of the Ancient Records, Letters, Miscellaneous Old Documents in the Archives of the Corporation of Kingston-upon-Hull, Deeds, Letters and Administrative Records, 1300-1800, by L. M. Stanewell; An Introduction to the History of Local Government in Kingston-upon-Hull, by G. W. Oxley; The Old Hull Borough Asylum, by J. A. R. Bickford; De La Pole Hospital (1883-1983), by J. A. R. Bickford; The Changing Plan of Hull, 1290-1650, by R. Horrox; Early Hull Printers and Booksellers, An Account of the Printing, Bookselling and Allied Trades from Their Beginnings to 1840, by C. W. Chilton; The Medical Profession in Hull, 1400-1900, by J. A. R. and M. E. Bickford; The City and School, Commemorating the 500th Anniversary of the Endowment of the Hull Grammar School; Guide to the Kingston-upon-Hull Record Office, Pt. I, Records of Local Authorities Whose Areas of Functions were Taken Over by the Former County Borough of Kingston-upon-Hull, by G. W. Oxley; Subject Guides: 1. World War II, 2. Transport by Sea, Rail and Inland Navigation; Teaching and Facsimile Sets: No. 1, Agriculture, 1750-1850, No. 2, Bridging the Humber, 1315-1935.

KINGSTON-UPON-THAMES
   (map)

133 Institution Address	Royal Borough of Kingston Archives c/o Surrey Record Office County Hall Penryhn Road Kingston-Upon-Thames KT1 2DN
Telephone	01 541 9057
Holdings	The collection includes records of the Borough and those of solicitors, businesses, and families in the Borough area. These are made available at the Surrey Record Office. Local directories, microfilm of census records and other printed sources are in the care of the Local History Librarian at the Heritage Centre (Fairfield West, Kingston-upon-Thames KT1 2PS; telephone: 01 546 5386).

Conditions of admission and access	An appointment in advance is required for the records to be made available at the Surrey Record Office at County Hall.
Hours	9:30 AM - 4:45 PM, Monday-Wednesday, Friday; 9:30 AM - 12:30 PM, second and fourth Saturday in the month by appointment only. Closed Thursday.
Duplicating facilities	Full-size copying facilities are available and will be provided if it is assured that no damage to the document will result. It should be noted that owners of privately deposited papers may forbid or restrict copying of their records. Photographic and microfilm services can also be provided.
Other services	Telephone and postal inquiries of a specific nature will be answered. The Heritage Centre staff (including the Archivist) will visit local groups to give talks, and exhibitions can be arranged on occasion.
Publications	Royal Borough of Kingston-upon-Thames; Guide to the Borough Archives (1971); postcards; portfolios; archive teaching units; "As It Was" series; Shire publications, and miscellaneous monographs.

KINGSTON-UPON-THAMES
(map)

134	Institution Address	Surrey Record Office County Hall Penrhyn Road Kingston-upon-Thames KT1 2DN
	Telephone	01 541 9065
	Holdings	In general, records relating to southwestern Surrey are held at Guildford, and those relating to other parts of the county (including the parts of Greater London which were in Surrey until 1965) are at Kingston-upon-Thames. The collection includes records of the Surrey Court of Quarter Sessions and of the County Council, Petty Sessions and some hospital records, and records of local authorities (including Parish Councils), as well as family and estate records, solicitors' records and records of local businesses. These include manorial records, deeds and Turnpike Trust records, and records of a number of charities, notably Smith's Charity. Anglican Parish records are deposited from those parishes in the Diocese of Southwark which are in Surrey or in those parts of London which were in Surrey until 1965 (including the Archdeaconry of Croydon, previously in Canterbury Diocese), and from parishes in the Deaneries of Emly and Epsom in the Diocese of Guildford.

Conditions of admission and access	A prior appointment is not required, except for Saturday visits, but is preferable and usually saves time on arrival. Inquiries should be addressed to the County Archivist. The collection may be used only on the premises.
Hours	9:30 AM - 4:45 PM, Monday-Wednesday, Friday; 9:30 AM - 12:30 PM, 2nd and 4th Saturday in the month, by appointment only.
Duplicating facilities	Full-size copying facilities are available and photocopies will be provided if this can be done without damage to the documents. Owners of privately deposited records may forbid or restrict copying of their records. Photographic and microfilm services can also be provided.
Other services	Telephone and postal inquiries of a specific nature will be answered. A reference library in the search room for the use of researchers includes large-scale Ordnance Survey maps. The staff will visit local groups to give talks and exhibits can be arranged on occasion.
Publications	Leaflets, brief guides, brochures, etc., which facilitate the use of the records are produced.

KINROSS See: PERTH

KINROSS County Council See: DUNDEE

KIRKLEES See: HUDDERSFIELD

KIRKWALL

135 Institution Address	The Orkney Library Orkney Archives Laing Street Kirkwall KW15 1NW
Telephone	0856 3166, ext. 5
Holdings	The holdings include local authority records such as minutes, education records, Parish Councils' papers and those relating to harbors. There are microfilm copies of census records, 1841-1881. Sheriff Court records, 1561-1953 are held and include some Justice of the Peace Court records, and some of the Admiralty Court are also found. Also held are family, business and estate collections relating to Orkney and papers of notable Orcadians. There are microfilm copies of newspapers, The Orcadian (1854 to date) and The

Orkney Herald (1860-1961), a sound archive, a photographic archive, and customs and excise records, 19th-20th century. The Mormon Microfiche Index to the Old Parish Registers is also available.

Conditions of admission and access	The archives are open to the public, but an appointment in advance is advisable, especially for the use of microfilm readers. Inquiries should be made to the Archivist. The collection must be consulted on the premises.
Hours	9:00 AM - 1:00 PM, 2:00 PM - 5:00 PM, Monday-Friday, except public holidays.
Duplicating facilities	Photocopies can be provided and prints can be made from microfilm.
Other services	Reference help is available and very brief questions can be answered by telephone or post.
Publications	Survey lists are available.

KNOWSLEY   See: LIVERPOOL

LAMBETH   See: LONDON, Lambeth Archives Department
Lambeth Palace Library

LANCASTER

136	Institution Address	Lancaster District Library Local Studies Department Market Square Lancaster LA1 1HY
	Telephone	0524 63266/63267
	Holdings	The collection includes local history material relating to Cumbria, Lancashire, and Yorkshire. There are maps and local newspapers dating from 1801. Methodist Circuit records, Port Commissioners' documents and apprentice registers are held.
	Conditions of admission and access	An appointment in advance is not required, but is recommended. Inquiries should be addressed to the District Librarian. Non-circulating material may not be removed from the premises.
	Hours	9:30 AM - 6:30 PM, Monday, Thursday; 9:30 AM - 5:00 PM, Tuesday; 9:30 AM - 1:00 PM, Wednesday; 9:30 AM - 7:00 PM, Friday; 9:30 AM - 4:00 PM, Saturday.

| Duplicating facilities | Photocopying and photography are available, except for some material, and full-size copies from microform can be provided. |

| Other services | Questions not requiring extensive research are answered by post or telephone. Reference help is available. |

| Publications | None. |

LEEDS

| 137 | Institution Address | University of Leeds
Brotherton Library
Department of Special Collections
Leeds LS2 9JT |

| Telephone | 0532 3175, ext. 7278 |

| Holdings | Papers relating to the wool textile industry are found in this collection, along with other business and trade records, Chamber of Commerce and society papers. Archives of the Dean and Chapter of Ripon are held, as are Quaker meeting documents. Estate papers (Woolley Hall), correspondence, diaries, and personal papers of prominent individuals and professors of the University are found. |

| Conditions of admission and access | Researchers who are not members of the University may use the collection, but are required to furnish identification and a letter of recommendation, and to make an appointment in advance. Inquiries should be directed to the University Librarian. The collection must be used in the library. |

| Hours | 9:00 AM - 5:00 PM, Monday-Friday. The library is subject to closure depending on University holidays. |

| Duplicating facilities | Full-size copies and microfilming can be provided, but there is usually a delay for this service. Photographs can also be arranged. |

| Other services | Brief questions by post or telephone are answered, and reference service is available in the library. |

| Publications | Handlists, catalogs, and brochures are produced. |

LEEDS (map)

| 138 | Institution Address | West Yorkshire Archive Service
Leeds District Archives
Chapeltown Road |

Sheepscar
Leeds LS7 3AP

The West Yorkshire Archive Service was formed
from several separate agencies. See also:
BRADFORD, HALIFAX, HUDDERSFIELD, and
WAKEFIELD

Holdings

The collection contains the records of Leeds Corporation and includes minutes from 1662, Quarter
Sessions records from 1698, Overseers' minutes
from 1726, and representative classes from the
modern departments of the City Council. Also
found are the records of the Boroughs of Morley
and Pudsey, the Urban Districts of Aireborough,
Garforth, Horsforth, Otley, and Rothwell, and the
Rural Districts of Wetherby and Wharfedale. All
of these were incorporated into Leeds Metropolitan
District in 1974. Other records held are Leeds
Board of Guardians and Public Assistance Commit-
tee (1844-1948), the Leeds School Board (1870-
1903), records received from the National Coal
Board, the health authorities and the Territorial
Army Association. The office also holds the
Archives of the Diocese of Ripon and of most
Anglican parishes in the vicinity of Leeds and
including some in the Diocese of Bradford. (The
Diocese of Ripon, formed in 1836, includes the
archives of the Archdeaconry of Richmond.)
There are also wills and records of the associated
probate jurisdiction dating from the 15th century.
There are Bishop's Transcripts of parish registers from the late 17th century, faculty papers
and tithe awards. Non-conformist records include
Yorkshire Congregational Union (1813-1968),
several United Reformed churches, and many
Methodist Circuits and organizations. Family and
estate records date from medieval times. One
finds records of Fountains Abbey, Studley Royal
and Ripley Castle. Also available are manorial
court rolls of Hatfield (1324-1818), Methley (1339-
1935), Pollington (1333-1935), Thorner (1345-1879),
and Sherburn-in-Elmet (1346-1922). There are
plans and accounts for building and furnishing
several houses, including Temple Newsom, Newby
Hall, and Harewood. Also found are political and
administrative papers such as the correspondence
of Sir John Reresby (1639-1688), George Canning
(1780-1827), Lord Canning's Indian papers (1856-
1862), and records relating to the Council of the
North (1585-1636), English and Irish Customs
Accounts (1604-1645), London Port books (1717-
1720), and the administration of Minorca (1735-
1755). Business records relate to textiles,
clothing, engineering, and mining. The archives
of Kirkstall Forge, Middleton Colliery and Tetley's
Brewery date from the 18th century. Also

deposited are papers of local solicitors and estate agents, and medieval court rolls, the records of local charities, title deeds, estate papers, plans, surveys, and rentals. The collection also includes deposits from voluntary, political, social, cultural, philanthropic, convivial, and educational bodies. Among these are the records of the local constituency organizations of the major political parties, the minutes of the Leeds Trades Council from 1882, the Archives of the Arthington Trust for supporting Christian missions abroad (1900-1937), the Leeds Babies' Welcome (1914-1974), the Conchological Society of Great Britain and Ireland (from 1876), the Yorkshire Naturalists' Union from 1849, the Leeds Rifles, the Yorkshire Ladies' Council for Education from 1871, and records of the temperance movement, sports clubs, change ringers, and boy scouts.

Conditions of admission and access	The office is open to the public, but an appointment in advance should be arranged by visitors. Some collections are kept away from the office and notice must be given for their production and use in the search room. Inquiries should be directed to the District Archivist. The collection must be used on the premises.
Hours	9:30 AM - 5:00 PM, Monday-Friday.
Duplicating facilities	Photocopies, photographs, and microfilm can be provided.
Other services	Brief questions by mail or telephone will be answered. The staff is happy to help visitors with advice on specific problems, but does not undertake extended research. There are various indexes, catalogs, and finding aids to further aid the researcher.
Publications	Guide to the West Yorkshire Archive Service for Family Historians; Guide to Sources of Business and Industrial History (1977); The West Riding Council 1889-1974: Historical Studies, by B. J. Barber and M. W. Beresford (1978); Search Guide to the English Land Tax, by R. W. Unwin (1982); Guide to the Quarter Sessions of the West Riding of Yorkshire 1637-1971 and Other Official Records, by B. J. Barber (1984); Guide to the Collections of the Yorkshire Archaeological Society 1931-1983 and to Collections Deposited With the Society, by S. Thomas (1985).

LEEDS (map)

139 Institution	Yorkshire Archaeological Society
Address	Claremont

23 Clarendon Road
Leeds LS2 9NZ

Telephone	0532 456362 (Archives); 0532 457910 (Library)

Holdings

The library houses a collection of historical material on the ancient County of Yorkshire. Information on architecture, archaeology and collections of photographs, prints, slides, and maps are available. An aerial photography archive and inventory of archaeological sites in North Yorkshire and Humberside is being developed. The archives, administered by the West Yorkshire Archive Service, contain family, manorial, estate and antiquarian papers, maps and drawings, and unpublished transcripts of some Yorkshire Parish registers and monumental inscriptions. The antiquarian papers include those of Roger Dodsworth and Ralph Thoresby. Manorial records include the series of Wakefield Court Rolls beginning in 1274. Family and estate records include Osbourne, Duke of Leeds, Clifford of Skipton Castle, Slingsby of Scriven, Fawkes of Farnley near Otley, Lister, Lord Rebblesdale, Middleton of Stockeld near Wetherby, Beaumont, Viscount Allendale of Bretton, and Clarke-Thornhill of Fixby.

Conditions of admission and access

The library is open to members of the Yorkshire Archaeological Society and to full members of its sections. Others are admitted at the discretion of the Librarian. The archives are open to the public. Inquiries should be addressed to the Librarian or to the Archivist in Charge. The collection must be used on the premises.

Hours

9:30 AM - 5:00 PM, Monday, Thursday-Friday (with exceptions, see below); 2:00 PM - 8:30 PM, Tuesday-Wednesday; 9:30 AM - 5:00 PM, first and third Saturday of the month and closed the following Monday.

Duplicating facilities

Photocopies can be provided.

Other services

Brief inquiries by post or telephone are answered and reference help is available. An ultra-violet lamp and a microfiche reader are available. Lists, catalogues, and indexes are provided.

Publications

The Yorkshire Archaeological Society has a very active publishing program and provides a list of those available. The library and archives have published Catalogue of Manuscripts and Deeds in the Library, by E. W. Crossley (2nd ed., 1931); Y A S List of Portraits in the Y A S Library, by C. E. Kirk (1959); Periodicals Catalogue (1977);

Parish Registers in the Y A S Library and Archives
(1986); Y A S Library and Archives Newsletter
(Vol. 1, 1983-   ).

LEICESTER (map)

140	Institution	Leicestershire Record Office
	Address	57 New Walk
		Leicester LE1 7JB

Telephone

0533 554566

Holdings

The record office holds works on the history of Leicestershire and Rutland, and contains official records of the two counties and the city of Leicester. Parish records are kept here as are records of the Leicester Archdeaconry, family and estate papers, and maps. The office is appointed by the Lord Chancellor as a repository for individually specified classes of public records, recognized by the Master of the Rolls as a repository for manorial and tithe documents and designated to receive ecclesiastical records (Leicester, Peterborough: Rutland parish records).

Conditions of admission and access

The office is open to the public and no advance appointment is required. Inquiries should be addressed to the County Archivist. Some records (less than thirty years old) are not available for consultation. Also those in process of arrangement or repair may be withheld until the work has been finished, and those in fragile condition will be produced at the discretion of the Archivist. No documents are produced after 4:45 PM on Monday to Thursday, 4:30 PM on Friday, or 12:00 noon on Saturday, and ordinarily only three items are produced at a time. Some collections are kept in storage outside the record office and must be requested in advance for use in the office. The delay may be as long as a week. The material must be used in the search room.

Hours

9:15 AM - 5:00 PM, Monday-Thursday; 9:15 AM - 4:45 PM, Friday; 9:15 AM - 12:15 PM, Saturday.

Duplicating facilities

Photocopies, microfilm, and photographs can be provided.

Other services

Brief questions are answered by telephone or post. Reference help is available in the search room and an ultra-violet lamp is provided.

Publications

Various handlists, e.g., to parish records, are available; Sectional Lists to family collections, Quarter Sessions records, etc., are in preparation.

LEIGH

141	Institution Address	Wigan Record Office Town Hall Leigh WN7 2DY

Telephone   0942 672421, ext. 266

Holdings   The collection includes public records, such as Quarter Sessions, hospital records, Hearth Tax records (on microfilm) and census records (also on microfilm). Local authority records include Wigan Borough records from the 14th century; for example, Wigan Courts from 1626, including Leet and other areas of the present Wigan Metropolitan Borough from the 17th century. Church registers and records include both Church of England and non-conformist for the Metropolitan Borough area. There are records of businesses and solicitors and transactions of societies and large family and estate collections. There is also the Edward Hall International Collection of Diaries, 1658-1945, and a very large collection of photographs.

Conditions of admission and access   The office is open to the public, but document production is limited; an appointment in advance is strongly advised. No borrowing is permitted and the collection must be used on the premises.

Hours   10:00 AM - 4:00 PM, Monday-Friday.

Duplicating facilities   Photocopies and photographs can be provided.

Other services   Only brief inquiries are answered by telephone or post, but reference help is available in the office. There is a reference library available to further aid the researcher. An ultraviolet lamp is provided.

Publications   Guide to the Record Office (out-of-print); Guide to Genealogical Sources; Those Dark Satanic Mills; Annual Reports; Accessions Lists; general handouts, leaflets, and catalogs of specific collections, for example, the Edward Hall Diary Collection.

LERWICK

142	Institution Address	Shetland Archives 44 King Harald Street Lerwick ZE1 0EQ

Telephone   0595 3535, ext. 269

Holdings	The collection contains Crown records including those of the Sheriff Court and wills, records of the local authorities, family and estate papers, and archives deposited by individuals and organizations.
Conditions of admission and access	The archives are open to the public, but an appointment in advance is preferred. The collection must be consulted on the premises. Inquiries should be directed to the Archivist.
Hours	9:00 AM - 1:00 PM, 2:00 PM - 5:00 PM, Monday-Thursday; 9:00 AM - 1:00 PM, 2:00 PM - 4:00 PM, Friday.
Duplicating facilities	Photocopying facilities are provided.
Other services	Brief questions are answered by telephone or by mail and reference help is available in the search room. There is a small reference library and an ultra-violet lamp is provided.
Publications	Finding-aids, lists, indexes, and brochures are produced.

LETTERKENNY

143	Institution Address	Donegal County Library Central Library High Road Letterkenny, Co. Donegal
	Telephone	074 21968
	Holdings	The library contains a 1630 Muster Roll printed in the Donegal Annual, Vol. X, no. 2, 1972, and 1778-1790 Catholic Qualification Rolls, also printed in the Donegal Annual, Vol. I, no. 3, 1949. There is a Civil Survey, Vol. III (1654), the Census of Ireland (1659), and a Register of Freeholders (1769). Griffith's Valuation (1857-1858) is also found.
	Conditions of admission and access	The library is open to the public for reference and an appointment in advance is not required. Inquiries should be directed to the County Librarian. The collection must be used on the premises.
	Hours	11:00 AM - 4:30 PM, Monday-Friday.
	Duplicating facilities	Photocopying facilities are available.
	Other services	Postal inquiries are answered and reference help is available.

| Publications | "Index to the <u>Donegal Annuals</u>, 1947-1967," (not formally published). |

LEWES

144	Institution	East Sussex Record Office
	Address	The Maltings
		Castle Precincts
		Lewes BN7 1YT
	Telephone	0273 475400, ext. 12/359
	Holdings	The record office collection contains Quarter Sessions records for the County (Judicial: sessions rolls, indictment books, minute books, appeals and traverses entry books and other records; Administrative: finance, bridges, buildings, constabulary, militia, store house, committees and functions and other records; Enrolment, registration, and deposit: deeds, awards and agreements, land tax and electoral registers, societies, deposited plans, poor law, public utilities and other records; Clerk of the Peace; and Justices of the Peace, and non-County Courts. Petty Sessions records are also held as are those for Lieutenancy, Coroners, probate, tithe records, school building grants, hospitals, registry of shipping and seamen, inland revenue, Insurance Committees, and motor taxation. Local authority records include County Council (Architect's Department, Clerk's Department, Education Department, School Records, Fire Brigade, Health Department, Estates Department, Planning Department, Engineer's and Surveyor's Departments, Social Services Department, Treasurer's Department, Weights and Measures Department). Boroughs, County Boroughs and Urban District Councils' records are held for Battle Urban District Council, Bexhill Borough Council, Brighton County Borough Council, Eastbourne County Borough Council, Hastings County Borough Council, Hove Borough Council, Lewes Borough Council, Newhaven Urban District Council, Pevensey Borough Council, Portslade Urban District Council, Rye Borough Council, Seaford Urban District Council, Uckfield Urban District Council, Winchelsea Borough Council. Rural District Councils' records include those for Battle, Chailey, Eastbourne, West Firle, East Grinstead, Hailsham, Hastings, Lewes, Newhaven, Rye, Ticehurst, and Uckfield. Other records include Boards of Guardians, Parish Councils, School Boards, Burial Boards, Gas Boards, River Boards, and Harbour Commissioners, and Turnpike Trusts. An extensive collection of parish records dates from the 16th century and includes non-conformist records for Society of Friends, United Reformed Church

(Congregational and Presbyterian), Countess of Huntingdon's Connexion, Unitarian, Methodist, and Baptist. Family and estate archives include Asburnham, Battle Abbey, Chichester, Gage, Glynde, Danny, Frewen Gilbert, Monk Bretton, Shiffner, Sheffield Park. There are also solicitors' records, business archives, papers for organizations, records formerly deposited with the Sussex Archaeological Society (at Barbican House), prints, handbills, and maps.

Conditions of admission and access

The record office is open to the public and no advance appointment is required. Inquiries should be directed to the County Records Officer. The collection must be used on the premises.

Hours

8: 45 AM - 4: 45 PM, Monday-Thursday; 8: 45 AM - 4: 15 PM, Friday.

Duplicating facilities

Full-size copying facilities are available.

Other services

Limited telephone and mail inquiries are answered for a small search fee. An ultraviolet lamp is provided. There is a reference library for the use of staff and searchers, and reference help is available.

Publications

East Sussex Record Office: A Short Guide, by J. A. Brent (1983); A Descriptive Report on the Quarter Sessions, Other Official and Ecclesiastical Records in the Custody of the County Councils of East and West Sussex (1954); A Catalogue of the Battle Abbey Estate Archives, by J. A. Brent (1973); The Hickstead Place Archives, A Catalogue, by J. A. Brent (1975); Sussex Poor Law Records, A Catalogue, by J. M. Coleman (out-of-print, 1960); The Records of Rye Corporation, by R. F. Dell (out-of-print, 1962); Winchelsea Corporation Records, by R. F. Dell (1963); The Glynde Place Archives, by R. F. Dell (1964); Rails Across the Weald, by S. C. Newton (out-of-print, 1972); Records of the Corporation of Seaford, by F. W. Steer (out-of-print, 1959); A Catalogue of the Shiffner Archives, by F. W. Steer (out-of-print, 1959); The Ashburnham Archives, A Catalogue, by F. W. Steer (out-of-print, 1958); John Philipot's Roll of the Constables of Dover Castle and Lord Wardens of the Cinque Ports, 1627, by F. W. Steer (out-of-print, 1956); A Catalogue of Sussex Estate and Tithe Award Maps, by F. W. Steer (1962); A Catalogue of Sussex Maps, by F. W. Steer (1968); A Handlist of Sussex Inclosure Acts and Awards, by W. E. Tate (out-of-print, 1950); A Catalogue of the Frewen Archives, by H. M. Warne (1972); The Danny Archives, A Catalogue, by J. A. Wooldridge (1966); How to

Trace the History of Your Family, by J. A. Berry
(1971); A Short Economic and Social History of
Brighton, Lewes and the Downland Between the
Adur and the Ouse 1500-1900, by C. E. Brent
(out-of-print, 1979); The History of a Parish or
Locality, by J. A. Brent (1970); Searchers Guide,
by S. C. Newton (out-of-print, 1972); The Arms
of the County Councils of East and West Sussex
and the Diocese of Chichester, by F. W. Steer
(1959); The First East Sussex Record Office,
by K. J. Wallace (1974); How to Trace the History
of Your House, by D. C. Williams (1971). In addition, the record office publishes a number of
local history research units. The following are
in-print: Sussex Election 1807 (1968); Brighton
Election 1832 (1968); Lewes: The Historical Development of a County Town, by C. E. Brent
(1974); The Rural Economy of Eastern Sussex
1500-1700, by C. E. Brent (1978); The Maritime
Economy of Eastern Sussex 1550-1700), by C. E.
Brent (1980).

LEWIS, ISLE OF

See: STORNOWAY

LEWISHAM

Institution   See: LONDON, Lewisham Local History Centre

LICHFIELD (map)

145 Institution   Lichfield Joint Record Office
     Address   Lichfield Library
                 Bird Street
                 Lichfield WS13 6PN

     Telephone   0543 256787

                       See also: STAFFORD, Staffordshire Record Of-
fice

     Holdings   The collection includes probate records of the
Diocese of Lichfield (250,000 documents from ca.
1520-1858) and other historical documents of the
diocese, Bishops Registers (which date from 1298),
and the records of the Dean and Chapter of
Lichfield from the 13th to the 20th century. Administrative records of the diocese include presen-
tation deeds, subscription books, institution
papers, licences for curates, schoolmasters, parish
clerks, surgeons and mid-wives, returns of Roman
Catholics and registration of protestant meeting
houses. There are also Clergy livings: (i) Dilapi-
dation Papers; (ii) Queen Anne's Bounty, consecration deeds; (iii) returns and mortgage papers;

(iv) glebe exchanges. Consecration deeds are still in the custody of the Diocesan Registrar, but found here are orders in council, tithe awards, papers relating to convocation, miscellaneous parliamentary returns, including clerical taxation, financial records of the registrars and the courts, registrars' correspondence, precedent books, temporalities, miscellaneous statutory deposits, official but non-diocesan activities of the Bishop, Acts of Parliament, charity commissioners' orders, etc., rural deans and deaneries, diocesan councils and committees. The Ecclesiastical Court records contain court books, cause papers, marriage allegations and bonds, surrogates' bonds, probate records, faculties, special courts and commissions, caveats. Visitation records include visitation and excommunication books, citations, presentments and primary visitation returns, glebe terriers and parish register transcripts. The diocese included Staffordshire, Derbyshire and half of Warwickshire and Shropshire. Also held are archdeaconry records, diocesan records from Lichfield Cathedral Library, Lichfield city records, 14th-20th century and other deposits relating to Lichfield.

Conditions of admission and access

The record office is open to the public and visiting scholars are welcome to use the records. An appointment in advance is strongly advised as space is limited. General inquiries should be directed to the Librarian; historical inquiries should be addressed to the Archivist. The collection must be used in the record office search room. Documents required for use on Saturday must be ordered in advance. The Archivist in consultation with the Librarian shall determine the number of documents which may be issued to a reader at any one time. This will not be more than five, with a total maximum of twenty per day.

Hours

10:00 AM - 5:15 PM, Monday, Tuesday, Thursday, and Friday; 10:00 AM - 4:30 PM, Wednesday.

Duplicating facilities

Photocopying facilities are available. Arrangements can be made for microcopies.

Other services

Brief questions are answered by post or telephone and reference help is provided in the search room. An ultra-violet lamp is available. Information concerning the records is provided, but in-depth searches must be undertaken by the inquirer.

Publications

Staffordshire Record Office Cumulative Handlist, Pt. I: Litchfield Joint Record Office; Diocesan, Probate, and Church Commissioners Records (1970).

LIMERICK

146	Institution	The City of Limerick Public Library
	Address	Limerick, Co. Limerick
	Telephone	061 314668
	Holdings	The library holds microfilm copies of the Limerick Chronical newspaper, 1832-1975; the Munster News, 1850-1900; and the Limerick Leader, 1893-1904. Microfilms of church registers of births and marriages up to 1880 are held by the Archivist at 104 Henry Street, Limerick.
	Conditions of admission and access	The facilities are available to all and no advance appointment or letter of introduction is necessary. Inquiries should be directed to the Librarian.
	Hours	10:00 AM - 1:00 PM, 2:30 PM - 6:00 PM, Monday-Wednesday; 10:00 AM - 1:00 PM, 2:30 PM - 5:30 PM, Thursday-Friday; 10:00 AM - 1:00 PM, Saturday.
	Duplicating facilities	Photocopying facilities are available.
	Other services	Reference advice is provided and questions are answered by mail and by telephone if necessary, but by mail is preferred.
	Publications	There is a good catalog and the library produces a brochure giving a brief resumé of what is available.

LINCOLN (map)

147	Institution	Lincolnshire Archives Office
	Address	The Castle
		Lincoln LN1 3AB
	Telephone	0522 25158
	Holdings	The record office collection provides sources for studying most aspects of the lives of the inhabitants of the County and Diocese from the 12th century onwards. The holdings include parish registers from the mid-16th century, Bishop's Transcripts and non-conformist registers. Among these are Methodist, Baptist, some former Congregational Chapels, and Quaker records. The Mormon Computer File Index (IGI) is available. Also found are probate records, Civil Parish records (particularly Poor Law, marriage bonds, full transcription of the licence bonds, 1574-1846) and registers of licences (1837-1954). Further, the collection includes land tax records, freeholders lists,

registers of electors, ale-house licence recognizances and enclosure awards. Family and estate records, manorial documents, business and solicitors' records have also been deposited. Title deeds and maps are available as are Quarter Sessions (for Lindsey, Kesteven and Holland) and County Council records for Lindsey, Kesteven and Holland (1889-1974) and for Lincolnshire from 1974; Lincoln Diocesan Records from the 13th century, Dean and Chapter records from the 12th century, and wills and administrations from 1320. The office is a recognized repository for certain classes of public records, for manorial and tithe documents and for ecclesiastical records (Lincoln).

Conditions of admission and access

The record office is open to the public, but at least twenty-four hours' advance notice of intended visits is required. Inquiries should be directed to the Principal Archivist. Young children are not normally allowed in the search room. Documents may not be ordered after 3:45 PM for use on the same day and the Archivist reserves the right to impose restrictions on the use of any document. No documents or books may be removed from the search room without permission.

Hours

9:15 AM - 4:45 PM, Monday-Friday.

Duplicating facilities

Photocopies, photographs, microfilm and printouts from microforms can be supplied.

Other services

Brief telephone and postal inquiries are answered. Lectures, classes, group visits, exhibitions, and displays can be arranged, if sufficient notice is given. Reference help and an extensive reference library of printed sources, including directories, handlists, indexes, calendars, journals, and finding aids are available to further aid the searcher. Microform equipment and an ultraviolet lamp are also provided.

Publications

None.

LIVERPOOL

148 Institution
Address

Knowsley Library Information Services
Knowsley Central Library
Local Studies and Archives Collection
Derby Road, Huyton
Liverpool L36 9UJ

Telephone

051 480 6126, ext. 28

Holdings

The collection contains newspaper cuttings, the Knowsley Photograph Collection, and a sound archive is being developed. There are also parish registers and Bishop's Transcripts, and tithe awards. Council minutes for Huyton-with-Roby, Kirkby and Prescot Urban District and Whiston Rural District, census returns and directories are found. Documents concerning land in Huyton in the 18th and 20th centuries (Molyneux-Steel papers), school records, records of the mine-workers union, and political and education material are held.

Conditions of admission and access	Visiting scholars may use the collection. Inquiries should be addressed to the Principal Librarian. Archives and special collections must be used in the library.
Hours	10:00 AM - 7:00 PM, Monday-Wednesday, Friday; 10:00 AM - 1:00 PM, Thursday; 10:00 AM - 5:00 PM, Saturday.
Duplicating facilities	Photocopying, photography and full-size copies from microform can be provided.
Other services	Brief postal and telephone inquiries are answered and reference help is available.
Publications	Registers of Kirkby St. Chad's Chapelry, ed. by W. L. French; Baptisms, 1610-1839 (1977); Marriages and Burials, 1610-1839 (1979); Prescot Records: The Court Rolls, 1602-1648, ed. by J. Knowles (1980/81); Inns of Prescot and Whiston, ed. by J. Knowles (1981).

LIVERPOOL (map)

149	Institution Address	Liverpool City Libraries Central Libraries William Brown Street Liverpool L3 8EW
	Telephone	051 207 2147
	Holdings	The library holds extensive collections of monographs and serials on all aspects of the social sciences as well as other disciplines. These include newspapers, directories, encyclopedias, British government publications, publications of international organizations, law reports, and statistical series. The Record Office and Local History Department is a multi-media local history resource center which contains over half a million manuscripts, over 100,000 printed books and pamphlets, and over 50,000 audio-visual records. Here are found the archives of Liverpool Corporation, private papers of prominent local families, archives of local industrial, commercial, and shipping companies, and extensive

collections of photographs and registers, the
International Genealogical Index for Great Britain,
transcripts and indexes of wills, probate registers,
local directories, trade directories, indexes of the
peerage and landed gentry, army and navy lists,
and biographical dictionaries. Church records held
include Anglican parish registers, nonconformist
(Quaker, Jewish and Roman Catholic) registers,
and records of Liverpool Cemeteries and Liverpool
Diocesan Registry. The Corporation archives include City Charters from 1207, minute books from
1550, records of townships subsequently incorporated in the city, records of School Boards,
Boards of Guardians, and school logbooks. Also
found are family papers including the Moore deeds
and letters, the Plumbe-Tempest deeds and papers,
the Norris deeds and papers and the manorial and
estate records of the Marquess of Salisbury. The
Library is a recognized repository for public
records, for manorial and tithe documents and for
ecclesiastical records.

Conditions of admission and access	The library is open to the public and no special arrangements need be made to use the collection. Inquiries should be addressed to the City Librarian. Research material must be used on the library premises. Proof of identity may be required for certain items. Closed access material will usually be made available within a short time.
Hours	9:00 AM - 9:00 PM, Monday-Friday; 9:00 AM - 5:00 PM, Saturday.
Duplicating facilities	There are facilities for photocopying, photostating, full-scale reproductions of microforms, microfilming, and reproduction of photographs. In some cases notice may be required.
Other services	There are subject specialists available in all depart- ments of the library to aid the visiting scholar. On-line information retrieval service is available, as is a facsimile transmission service.
Publications	Catalogue of the Liverpool Free Public Library 1850-1891 (3 vols.); Catalogue of Non-Fiction 1925- 1971 (10 vols.); Liverpool Print and Documents Catalogue; Catalogue of the Art Library of H. F. Hornby; Catalogue of the Music Library (2 vols.); Introducing the Liverpool City Libraries; Record Office and Local History Department--General Information; Record Office and Local History De- partment--Brief Guide for Genealogists; Liverpool 1207-1257; Liverpool under James I; Liverpool Under Charles I; William Roscoe; Liverpool Town Books; Liverpool, a Brief History; Liverpool Directories 1766-1824 (microfilm); Events and Exhibitions (monthly); Local Government Information

Bulletin (monthly); Ladsirlac Newsletter (ir-
reg.).

LIVERPOOL (map)

150	Institution Address	National Museums and Art Galleries on Merseyside Archives Department 64-66 Islington Liverpool L3 8LG
	Telephone	051 207 3697

See also: National Museums and Art Galleries
on Merseyside. Maritime Records Centre (entry
no. 151)

Holdings — Records of the port authority are held as well as shipping registers and other shipping records. Dock Company papers are from 1793 to date and registers of shipping (ship ownership mainly) are from 1730 to 1802. Pilotage records date from 1766 to ca. 1970, and papers of the Royal Liverpool Seamen's Orphan Institution are from 1869 to date. Also found are Brocklebank, Ocean, PSNC, Shipping Company records and the Bryson and Danson Miscellaneous collections. Emigration records are held, but original ships' passenger lists are not available.

Conditions of admission and access — Some collections require a week's notice and some must be arranged for a month in advance. An appointment is essential for every day except Wednesday. Inquiries should be directed to the Keeper of Archives. There are plans to transfer the Maritime records to the Maritime Records Centre.

Hours — 10:00 AM - 5:00 PM, Monday-Friday. For use on Monday-Tuesday and Thursday-Friday, an appointment is required; Wednesday, the collection may be used without an appointment.

Duplicating facilities — Photocopying facilities are available and photographs can be arranged.

Other services — Services are limited at present, but brief inquiries by post or telephone are answered.

Publications — Several monographs, articles and contributions to other works concerning the museum are available. There are also archive teaching units on a number of subjects.

LIVERPOOL (map)

151	Institution	National Museums and Art Galleries on Merseyside

Address	Merseyside Maritime Museum Maritime Records Centre Pier Head Liverpool L3 1DN
Telephone	051 7091551
	See also: National Museums and Art Galleries on Merseyside. Archives Department (entry no. 150)
Holdings	The Record Centre is presently under development. When complete it will hold original plans of the dock system, photographs, ships' plans and logs, records of dock administration and the papers of local businesses related to shipping and port in- dustries. Also a film collection, a sound archive, and books, articles and periodicals are planned or are already available. Original archive material will be installed when the correct environmental conditions have been established.
Conditions of admission and access	Searchers must obtain a day pass to enter the Records Centre. A small fee is charged and proof of identity is required. Individuals under eighteen years of age must be accompanied by an adult (with some exceptions if advance arrangements have been made). Immediate access to the search room may not be possible on busy days, in which case a queueing system is employed. Reference material is available on open shelves and request forms are provided for documents not on open ac- cess. Records are not issued between 1:00 PM and 2:00 PM or after 4:00 PM.
Hours	10:30 AM - 4:30 PM, Monday-Friday.
Duplicating facilities	Photocopying can be provided.
Other services	Brief questions by post or telephone are answered and reference help is available in the search room. Information sheets are provided to further aid the researcher.
Publications	Brochures, leaflets, and guides are produced.

LIVERPOOL

Institution	Liverpool Record Office See: LIVERPOOL, Liverpool City Libraries

LLANDRINDOD WELLS

152	Institution Address	Powys County Council

Libraries and Museums Department
Cefnllys Road
Llandrindod Wells LD1 5LD

Telephone

0597 2212

Holdings

Deposits include the records of Brecon Borough,
deposited by Brecknock Borough Council (Borough
minutes from 1667 and deeds dating from the 16th
century), records relating to Pen-y-bont Hall
(Radnor) and Abercamlais (Llansbyddyd) estates,
the latter including deeds dating from the 1550s
and correspondence belonging to Archdeacon
Richard Davies of Brecon for the late 18th and
early 19th centuries. Also held are records of
solicitors such as Messrs. Humphreys and Parsons
(Machynlleth), J. W. Griffiths (Hay and Aber-
gavenny), Jeffreys and Powell (Brecon), and
Gilbert Davies and Roberts (Welshpool). Deposits
from all three District Borough Councils, Dyfed-
Powys Police and the Welsh Water Authority are
found.

Conditions of
admission and
access

A full county archives service does not at present
exist for Powys, but the Archivist has a small
strong room and an office in the Library Headquarters in Llandrindod and offices in the present
County Hall. These circumstances may change for
the better in the future. It is also possible that
certain official records, for example, Quarter
Sessions, Petty Sessions, the Coroners, the old
County Councils and District Borough authorities
may be transferred back to Powys from the
National Library of Wales of Aberystwyth. Ecclesiastical Parish records (Church in Wales),
many non-conformist chapel records, and private
deposits and donations are likely to remain at the
National Library. All visits by searchers must
be by appointment only, at least two weeks in
advance. Inquiries should be addressed to the
Archivist. The collection may be consulted only
on the premises. The Local History Room of the
Library serves as a search room.

Hours

9:00 AM - 5:00 PM, Monday-Thursday; 9:00 AM -
4:00 PM, Friday.

Duplicating
facilities

Photocopies can be provided.

Other services

Limited inquiries can be answered by telephone or
post. Questions requiring lengthy research are
referred to professional searchers. Reference
help is provided as far as possible. The Archivist
will give lectures to local groups.

Publications

Lists are provided for searchers. Indexing of
the collection is underway.

LLANGEFNI

<table>
<tr><td>153</td><td>Institution
Address</td><td>Gwynedd Archives Service
Llangefni Area Record Office
Shire Hall
Llangefni LL77 7TW</td></tr>
<tr><td></td><td>Telephone</td><td>0248 723262, ext. 26</td></tr>
</table>

The Llangefni Area Record Office is part of the Gwynedd Archive Service (which comprises the former Anglesey, Caernarfon, and Merionethshire Record Offices). See also: CAERNARFON (Caernarfon Area Record Office) and DOLGELLAU (Dolgellau Area Record Office)

Holdings — The office holds the official records of the County, shipping records, private papers, tithe maps, Anglesey Calvinistic Methodists Chapel records, and Eisteddfodau Papers. It is a depository for manorial and tithe documents.

Conditions of admission and access — The office is open to the public and no advance appointment is necessary except for evening hours. Inquiries should be directed to the Area Archivist. All material must be used on the premises.

Hours — 9:00 AM - 1:00 PM, 2:00 PM - 5:00 PM, Monday-Friday. Late opening by appointment only.

Duplicating facilities — Full-size and microcopying facilities are available. Photographs can be provided.

Other services — Brief questions by mail or telephone are answered. Reference help is provided in the search room.

Publications — Gwynedd Archives Service Bulletin (annual); and miscellaneous guides, calendars, and books on local history.

LOCHGILPHEAD

<table>
<tr><td>154</td><td>Institution
Address</td><td>Argyll and Bute District Archives
Department of Administration
Argyll and Bute District Council
Kilmory
Lochgilphead PA31 8RT</td></tr>
<tr><td></td><td>Telephone</td><td>0546 2127, ext. 120</td></tr>
</table>

Holdings — The collection is composed mainly of records of defunct local authorities in the former counties of Argyll and Bute. These include County Councils, Town Councils, parochial boards, school boards, road trustees, and others. The records date from the 17th to the 20th century. There are also a few estate records. No records of births, marriages, or deaths, and no wills or census returns are kept.

Conditions of admission and access	There are no conditions placed on admission, but an appointment in advance can be helpful. Inquiries should be addressed to the Archivist. The collection must be used on the premises.
Hours	9: 00 AM - 1: 00 PM, 2: 00 PM - 5: 00 PM, Monday-Friday.
Duplicating facilities	Full-size photocopying can be provided.
Other services	There is a small library of reference works and very limited reference help is provided. Very brief inquiries by telephone or post can be answered.
Publications	Typescript lists are produced.

LONDON

155	Institution Address	Barnet Public Libraries Local History Library Hendon Catholic Social Centre Egerton Gardens, Hendon London NW4 4BE
	Telephone	01 202 5625, ext. 27, 28, 55
	Holdings	The library contains material relating to the London Borough of Barnet and the former Borough of Hendon and Finchley, including local records and collected archives. Newspaper cuttings, photographs, and maps are also held. The library is recognized as a repository for manorial and tithe documents.
	Conditions of admission and access	Scholars may use the collection, but should make an appointment in advance. Inquiries should be addressed to the Archivist (at City Library, Ravensfield House, The Burroughs, Hendon, London NW4 4BE). The collection must be used on the premises.
	Hours	9: 30 AM - 5: 30 PM, Monday-Friday; 9: 00 AM - 4: 00 PM, every other Saturday. All hours are preferably by appointment.
	Duplicating facilities	Photocopying can be arranged.
	Other services	Brief questions by post or telephone are answered and reference help is provided.

Publications	None.

LONDON (map)

156 Institution   British Library
     Address   Great Russell Street
                 London WC1B 3DG

     Telephone   01 636 1544 (Reader Admissions Office, ext. 325;
Information and Admissions Service, ext. 749;
Main Reading Room, North Library, North Library
Gallery, ext. 209; Official Publications Library,
ext. 234/235; Music Reading Area, ext. 668; Map
Library, ext. 461/609; Manuscripts Students'
Room, ext. 371)

     Underground   Russell Square, Tottenham Court Road, Goodge
Road, Holborn

Also part of the British Library:

     Newspaper Library
     130 Colindale Avenue
     London NW9 5HE
     Tel. 01 200 5515

     Oriental Reading Room
     Store Street
     London WC1E 7DG
     Tel. 01 636 1544, ext. 259/581

     Science Reference Library
     25 Southampton Buildings
     Chancery Lane
     London WC2A 1AW
     Tel. 01 405 8721, ext. 3344/3345

     and

     9 Kean Street
     London WC2B 1AT
     Tel. 01 636 1544, ext. 229

     India Office Library and Records
     (See entry no. 157)
     197 Blackfriars Road
     London SE1 8NG
     Tel. 01 928 9531

     India Office Library and Records Newspaper
         Reading Room
     Bush House, Aldwych
     London WC2B 4PH

     Library Association Library
     Ridgemount Street

London WC1E 7AE
Tel. 01 636 1544, ext. 200; 01 636 7543

Holdings

The British Library is the national library for
the United Kingdom and was established in 1973
under Act of Parliament as a center for reference,
lending, bibliographic, and other information
services based on its collections. These include
books in all subjects and all languages. The institutions which came together to form the British
Library are the library departments of the
British Museum, the National Central Library,
the National Lending Library for Science and
Technology, the British National Bibliography,
the functions of the office for Scientific and
Technical Information (in 1974), and in 1982, the
India Office Library and Records (entry no. 157)
were deposited on trust with the British Library,
and the library assumed responsibility for the
National Sound Archive in 1983. The main operat-
ing divisions of the British Library are Reference,
Lending, and Bibliographic Service; in addition,
there are Research and Development, the National
Sound Archive, and Central Administration. The
library is located in a number of buildings in
London (see addresses above) except for the
Lending Division which is at Boston Spa in West
Yorkshire. The Reference Division constitutes
one of the world's greatest libraries with more
than eleven million volumes which include hundreds
of thousands of Western and oriental manuscripts,
maps, periodicals, newspapers, and philatelic collections. The Department of Printed Books is
the most comprehensive copyright deposit library
in the United Kingdom. It is the largest department in the Reference Division and holds large
collections of early books and periodicals and
houses the Division's main collections of current
and historical printed material in Western and
Slavonic languages covering the humanities and
related disciplines. Here are found family histories, parish registers, biographical records,
educational and professional records, passenger
lists, poll books and electoral registers, and
wills. An excellent guide to this material is British
Family History: Printed Sources in the Department
of Printed Books, compiled by Mary S. Hurworth
(1981), Department of Printed Books, Reader
Guide No. 10. Also found here are works on
place names and topography including the Victoria
History of the Counties of England, directories,
gazetteers and books of travel, regional surveys,
and details of buildings. A guide to this information is English Places: Sources of Information
(1979), Department of Printed Books, Reader
Guide No. 6. Those seeking information on family
and personal names would be well advised to

consult Family and Personal Names: A Brief Guide
to Sources of Information (1979), Department of
Printed Books, Reader Guide No. 8. Within this
Department, the Map Library, Music Library and
Newspaper Library are responsible for the collections of printed works in their own areas. The
Department of Manuscripts covers western history,
art, and literature, including illuminated manuscripts and manuscript maps and music from the
earliest times to the present day in the form of
books and other documents. There are many
records of interest to genealogists and family
historians here, including manorial records dating
from the 13th century and covering all of the
United Kingdom. There are also North American
Colonial records. The Department of Oriental
Manuscripts and Printed Books covers the languages and literature of Asia and northern Africa.
The collection is important for the comprehensive-
ness of the coverage of religious, literary and
historical works of the countries concerned. The
India Office Library and Records is covered in
entry number 157.

Conditions of
admission and
access

The Reference Division is open to those who need
to use material not readily available to them elsewhere or who can show need of regular or frequent access to a large research library. Admission to the reading rooms (except for those of
the Science Reference Library and the Library
Association Library) is by a Reader's Pass which
may be applied for at the Reader Admissions
Office. The issuing of a pass is not guaranteed.
If it appears that an applicant can be better
served in another kind of library, the admissions
office reserves the right to refuse admission.
Passes are not normally given to those under
twenty-one years of age nor to those studying
at first-degree level or below (exceptions will be
considered). Application must be made in person,
as a photograph of the holder is taken for each
pass. Proof of identity is required for all applicants. There are short-term passes, valid for
not more than fourteen days, and long-term passes
valid for between one and five years. Long-term
pass applicants must submit a written statement of
the nature of their research. Long-term passes
can be renewed up to one month before they are
due to expire (or after expiration). The photographic pass is needed for the Reading Room, the
North Library, North Library Gallery, Official
Publications Library, Music Reading Area, and the
Department of Manuscripts. A supplementary pass
is needed for this last-named department as well
as the photographic pass. Applications should be
taken directly to the Department of Manuscripts.
A written statement of the purpose and subject of

research and a letter of recommendation from a
person of recognized position (not a close relative), based on personal knowledge of the applicant, must be submitted. Renewal applications
should be accompanied by the previous supplementary pass. Admission for one day may be
granted at the Students' Room without the
photographic pass, at the discretion of the Officer
in Charge. The greater part of the library's
collection is in closed stacks and material must
be identified in reference books and catalogs and
ordered. There is usually a delay of about one
hour for books housed in the Great Russell
Street building and of twenty-four hours for those
kept in other facilities. The photographic pass
will also admit to the Map Library, the Newspaper
Library, Oriental Reading Room and the India Office Library and Records. However, one may
apply directly to these departments without the
photographic pass if the research requires the use
of only these reading rooms. The lower age
limit for the Oriental Reading Room and the India
Office Library and Records is 18 rather than 21.
Further, for borrowing facilities in the India
Office Library and Records, an additional form
must be completed. This can be obtained from
the Reader Admissions Office or by post from the
India Office Library and Records. When completed it should be stamped with the official stamp
of the applicant's institution or accompanied by a
letter of recommendation. These passes are valid
for three years and must be renewed within three
months of expiration. Normally material must be
used in the room in which it is housed, or in a
specified reading room. Inquiries should be
addressed to the Admissions Officer, the Director
General, or the Directors or Keepers of the Departments in which the searcher is interested.

Hours

Reader Admissions Office, 9:00 AM - 4:30 PM,
Monday, Friday-Saturday; 9:00 AM - 8:00 PM,
Tuesday-Thursday.
Main Reading Room, North Library, North Library
Gallery, 9:00 AM - 5:00 PM, Monday, Friday-
Saturday; 9:00 AM - 9:00 PM, Tuesday-Thursday.
Official Publications Library, 9:30 AM - 4:30 PM,
Monday, Friday-Saturday; 9:30 AM - 8:45 PM,
Tuesday-Thursday.
Music Reading Area, 9:30 AM - 4:45 PM, Monday,
Friday-Saturday; 9:30 AM - 8:45 PM, Tuesday-
Thursday.
Map Library, 9:30 AM - 4:30 PM, Monday-Saturday.
These areas are closed the week following the last
full week in October.
Manuscripts Student's Room, 10:00 AM - 4:45 PM,
Monday-Saturday. Closed the week following the
Main Reading Room closed week.

Newspaper Library, 10:00 AM - 5:00 PM, Monday-
Saturday. Closed the week following the last full
week in October.
Oriental Reading Room, 9:30 AM - 4:45 PM,
Monday-Friday; 9:30 AM - 12:45 PM, Saturday.
Closed the week preceding the last full week in
October.
Science Reference Library (25 Southampton Build-
ing), 9:30 AM - 9:00 PM, Monday-Friday; 10:00 AM
- 1:00 PM, Saturday.
Science Reference Library (9 Kean Street), 9:30
AM - 5:30 PM, Monday-Friday.
India Office Library and Records, 9:30 AM - 5:00
PM, Monday-Friday; 9:30 AM - 1:00 PM, Saturday.
India Office Library and Records Newspaper Room,
10:00 AM - 5:30 PM, Tuesday, Thursday.
Library Association Library, 9:00 AM - 6:00 PM,
Monday, Wednesday, Friday; 9:00 AM - 8:00 PM,
Tuesday, Thursday.
These areas have no annual closed week. All
services are closed on Sunday, New Year's Day,
Good Friday, the first Monday in May, Christmas
Eve, Christmas Day, and Boxing Day (December
26). Public announcements are made in advance
of any additional closures.

Duplicating   Facilities are available for photographs, photo-
facilities   copies, electrostatic prints, microfilm, microfiche,
                 and transparencies. Copies of one kind or an-
                 other can be supplied of material in the library's
                 collection except in cases where to do so is likely
                 to cause damage to the work. The restrictions
                 placed on photocopying books include (but are not
                 limited to): printed in 1701 or before, ten pounds
                 or more in weight, over sixteen by eleven inches
                 in size, bound in vellum, and too tightly bound to
                 open flat. The proper form must be completed
                 for copying orders to be filled. A "Photographic
                 Service Guide and Price List" is provided to aid the
                 researcher in the proper procedure.

Other services   The Reference Division provides a wide range of
                 information and other services to researchers in
                 the library and to remote users. There are many
                 specialist catalogues, scholarly monographs, and
                 illustrated books based on the collections. The
                 reprographic services also help make the collec-
                 tions more widely available. Research is not under-
                 taken by staff in behalf of visiting scholars, but
                 reference help is provided to readers and every
                 effort is made to accommodate the user's needs.
                 A computer search service is offered through
                 various systems, including Dialog, Blaise-Line,
                 and Télésystèmes-Questel. A brochure is provided
                 which describes this service and its cost. The
                 library's exhibition galleries, located in the
                 British Museum building, have some of the

outstanding items in the collections on permanent
display and temporary exhibitions on special
topics are regularly mounted. (The Library's
galleries are open without charge to the public
10:00 AM - 5:00 PM, Monday-Saturday, 2:30 PM -
6:00 PM, Sunday.)

Publications

The library has a very active publishing program
for which a catalog is issued annually. In addition, there are numerous guides, brochures, and
leaflets produced to aid the scholar in the use of
the library's collections and facilities. There
are also catalogs, indexes, finding aids, and lists
which help in the identification and location of
library material.

LONDON (map)

157 Institution
    Address

The British Library
India Office Library and Records
Orbit House
197 Blackfriars Road
London SE1 8NG

Telephone

01 928 9531

Underground

Waterloo, Blackfriars

See also: LONDON, The British Library (entry
no. 156)

Holdings

The collections of the Library and the Records
reflect the interests and activities of the East
India Company and the India Office, and include
literature and documents on the states of South
Asia and the neighboring countries, St. Helena,
the Persian Gulf States, South Africa, Malaysia,
Singapore, Indonesia, China, and Japan. The
library houses books in European and Asian
languages and represents a major international
specialist collection in Indological and South Asian
studies, especially for the history of India during
the British period. The archives of the India
Office Records form an invaluable source of information on the history of British trade and government in South Asia and neighboring areas. The
Library contains oriental printed books and manuscripts, prints and drawings, and photographs.
The Records include the registers of baptism,
marriage, and burial relating mainly to European
and Eurasian Christians in India, Burma and other
areas administered by the East India Company and
the Government of India. The India Office Records
are an accumulation of archival material relating to
the responsibilities of the India Office (1858-1947),
the Burma Office (1937-1948), the East India

Company (1600-1858), the Board of Control (1784-
1858), and a number of other British agencies
which were connected with one or more of the
four main bodies. The collections include official
publications, and also British government publications relating to Indian affairs. The collection of
European manuscripts is comprised mainly of private papers, mostly in English, but some in other
European languages. Correspondence, minutes,
memoranda, diaries, and memoirs are included.
There are also microfilm copies or photocopies of
manuscripts where the originals are in private
hands or in other repositories. A collection of
oral archives, consisting of tape-recorded interviews with persons who lived and worked in
British India in the first half of this century, is
being developed. The large map collections form
part of the India Office Records and consist of
manuscript and printed maps, atlases, journals,
and reports. Most are housed in the map room,
but there are also maps in files and volumes elsewhere and in the European manuscripts collection.

Conditions of admission and access	The Library and the Record Office are open to the public, but full facilities are available only to members. Application for membership may be made by completing a form supplied by Public Services. Readers passes are normally granted to those recommended by persons of recognized posi- tion who have known the researcher for at least two years, and members of the Diplomatic Service. All applicants must produce proof of identity. A limited number of volumes or records may be con- sulted at any one time and all material must be used in the proper place. Subject to certain provisos, some printed books may be borrowed by members. A list of Rules and Regulations is available to further aid the researcher in gaining access to the collections. Inquiries should be made to the Director or to the Archivists in charge of the various collections.
Hours	9:30 AM - 5:45 PM, Monday-Friday; 9:30 AM - 12:45 PM, Saturday. Closed on Sunday, bank holidays, the Saturday preceding bank holidays, or immediately following the Christmas and New Year holidays.
Duplicating facilities	Photocopies, full-size copies from microfilm and microfilm copies can be provided. A brochure ex- plaining these services, how to acquire copies, and the charges, is provided.
Other services	Brief questions by post or telephone are answered and reference help is available in all the various departments of the Library and Records. Indexes, guides, finding aids, and lists are provided to further aid the scholar.

Publications	The India Office Library and Records publishes catalogs and guides to the printed books, records, manuscripts, and prints and drawings. Color postcards and prints in folders are also produced. Brochures which give information on the use of the facilities and the collections are supplied. A list of all publications still in print can be obtained on request and is included in the main British Library <u>Catalog of Publications</u>.

LONDON (map)

158 Institution Address	Chelsea Library Old Town Hall King's Road London SW 3 5EZ
Telephone	01 352 2004/6056
Underground	South Kensington, Sloane Square
	<u>See also:</u> LONDON, Kensington Central Reference Library
Holdings	The collection contains illustrations, microfilm of early newspapers and census returns (1841-1881), photographs, drawings and paintings, and prints and engravings. A collection of cuttings compiled between 1887 and 1939 is available and has been indexed. Albums of special subjects include Cremorne Gardens and early library history. Maps and plans are also available. Directories are held, particularly those for Chelsea and the London Post Office Directory (scattered holdings, 1953-1970, and from 1971 to date). Electoral registers are held for 1863, 1885/86, 1887, 1889, 1891 to date and also the original census book of 1801 for the parish of St. Luke, Chelsea. Microfilm copies of baptisms, marriages, and burials for St. Luke's, Chelsea are available as well as Church Wardens' vestry records, documents relating to charities, poor law records, council and committee minutes and rate and valuation records. Session records are held for Chelsea Petty Sessions (minute book of proceedings, 1792-1802) and records of schools and other institutions, and papers of families and estates, and the Chelsea Arts Club (1890-1974) are kept.
Conditions of admission and access	The collection is open to the public but advance notice should be given for the use of archival material. Inquiries should be directed to the Reference Librarian. The collection must be used on the premises.
Hours	10: 00 AM - 8: 00 PM, Monday-Tuesday, Thursday;

10:00 AM - 1:00 PM, Wednesday; 10:00 AM - 5:00 PM, Friday-Saturday.

Duplicating facilities	A photocopying and photographic service is available.
Other services	Brief questions by post or telephone are answered and reference help is available. Many finding aids, catalogs, and indexes are provided to further aid the researcher.
Publications	Leaflets, pamphlets, sets of historical maps and postcards are produced.

LONDON

159		
	Institution Address	The College of Arms Queen Victoria Street London EC4V 4BT
	Telephone	01 248 2762
	Underground	Blackfriars or Mansion House; St. Paul's
	Holdings	The collections include official records, pedigrees, royal (and other) ceremonials, records of visitations, Garter King of Arms, those of the Court of Chivalry, enrolments of royal warrants, grants of arms, and the administrative records of the College (founded in 1484). Semi-official and unofficial records include papers relating to orders of chivalry, rolls of arms and armorials, and painters' work books. Miscellaneous family and estate papers and some fifty collections of individual heralds are held. The College holds the Arundel Manuscripts, the Combwell Priory and other charters. Also found are collections of bookplates and seals.
	Conditions of admission and access	The archives are not directly open to genealogical and heraldic researchers, but are examined for them by the Officer in Waiting. An appointment in advance is necessary and a fee is usually charged.
	Hours	10:00 AM - 4:00 PM, Monday-Friday.
	Duplicating facilities	Facilities are available for photocopying and arrangements can be made for photography and microfilming. Permission must be obtained for the reproduction of documents and official records may not be copied by mechanical means. The Officer in Waiting will advise on the copying of any material.
	Other services	Brief questions by post or telephone will be answered and should be directed to the Officer in Waiting.

Publications	Catalogue of the Arundel Manuscripts in the ... College of Arms, by W. H. Black (1829); The Records and Collections of the College of Arms, by A. R. Wagner (1952); Report on the Welsh Manuscripts Contained in the Muniments of the College of Arms, by F. Jones (typescript, 1957); Report on Miscellaneous Deeds, Including Charters Relating to Combwell Priory ... in the Collections of the College of Arms, by L. M. Midgley (typescript, 1980). There are a number of specialized and unpublished works available. It is hoped that the first volume of a major catalog of the College of Arms will be published soon.

LONDON

160 Institution
   Address

Corporation of London Records Office
P.O. Box 270
Guildhall
London EC2P 2EJ

Telephone

01 601 3030, ext. 2251

Underground

St. Paul's, Bank, Moorgate

Search Room: Guildhall
North Office Block
Room 221
(entrance via Basinghall Street)

Holdings

This is one of the most extensive collections of municipal archives in England; it ranges in date from the 11th to the 20th century and includes material of national as well as local interest. The office contains the official records of the Corporation of the City of London and also royal charters, records of rentals and deeds, both in London and outside the City, judicial records from the Civic Courts and the Sessions of Gaol Delivery and Peace as well as financial records comprised of ledgers, accounts, assessments for the levying of taxes, and records of admissions to the freedom of the City (1681-1915). Medieval compilations of City Law and Custom and administrative records such as the proceedings of the Courts Aldermen and Common Council and their numerous committees are also found.

Conditions of
admission and
access

The search room is open to the public and appointments are not generally necessary in order to consult the records, but in some cases, advance warning of a proposed visit may help both readers and staff. Inquiries should be directed to the Deputy Keeper of the Records. The records must be used on the premises. Records may not be ordered after 4:30 PM, but they may be reserved

in advance. A separate order slip is usually
needed for each item required. Ordinarily up to
six items may be ordered at one time, but this
may be limited under some circumstances.

Hours   9: 30 AM - 4: 45 PM, Monday-Friday. The office
                     is closed for bank holidays.

Duplicating   The record office has no separate copying facili-
facilities   ties, but uses the services of the Guildhall Library.
                     Many of the records are not suitable for photo-
                     copying, but arrangements can be made to photo-
                     graph items on a commercial basis.

Other services   Brief questions are answered by post or telephone,
                     and reference help is available in the search room.
                     An ultra-violet lamp is also available on request.

Publications   The Corporation of London Records Office has
                     published A Guide to the Records at Guildhall,
                     London, by P. E. Jones and R. Smith (1951);
                     Calendars of Letter Books A-L, 1275-1498, by
                     R. R. Sharpe, 11 vols. (1899-1912); Calendar of
                     Wills, Court of Husting, London, 1258-1688, by
                     R. R. Sharpe, 2 vols. (1889); Calendar of Letters,
                     City of London, 1350-1370, by R. R. Sharpe
                     (1885); Calendar of Coroners' Rolls of the City
                     of London, 1300-1378, by R. R. Sharpe (1913);
                     Munimenta Gildhallae Londoniensis, Liber Albus,
                     Liber Custumarum et Liber Horn (Liber Horn not
                     covered), by H. T. Riley, 3 vols. in 4 (1859-
                     1862); Liber Albus (translation), by H. T. Riley
                     (1861); Memorials of London and London Life,
                     1276-1419, by H. T. Riley (1868); Liber de
                     Antiquis Legibus, by T. Stapleton (London:
                     Camden Society, 1846); Chronicles of Old London,
                     by H. T. Riley (1863); The Historical Charters
                     and Constitutional Documents of the City of London,
                     by W. de G. Birch (1884) and 1887); Calendar
                     of Early Mayors Court Rolls, 1298-1307, by A. H.
                     Thomas (Cambridge, 1924); Calendars of Plea
                     and Memoranda Rolls, 1323-1437, by A. H. Thomas,
                     4 vols. (Cambridge, 1926, 1929, 1932, 1943);
                     Calendars of Plea and Memoranda Rolls, 1437-
                     1482, by P. E. Jones, 2 vols. (Cambridge, 1954,
                     1961); The Fire Court, Calendars to the Degrees,
                     1667-1668, by P. E. Jones, 2 vols. (1966, 1970);
                     Analytical Index to the Remembrancia 1579-1664, by
                     W. H. and H. C. Overall (1878).
                          The London Record Society has published
                     London Possessory Assizes: A Calendar (Calen-
                     dar Rolls AA-FF, 1340-1451), by H. M. Chew,
                     Vol. 1 (1965); London Inhabitants Within the
                     Walls, 1695, by D. V. Glass, LRS Vol. 2 (1966);
                     The London Eyre of 1244, by H. M. Chew and
                     M. Weinbaum, LRS Vol. 6 (1970); The London
                     Eyre of 1276, by M. Weinbaum, LRS Vol. 12

(1976); London Assize of Nuisance, 1301-1431, by H. M. Chew and W. Kellaway, LRS Vol. 10 (1973); The Church in London 1375-1392, by A. K. McHardy, LRS Vol. 13 (1977); London Politics 1713-1717, by H. Horwitz, LRS Vol. 17 (1981); Chamber Accounts of the Sixteenth Century, by B. R. Masters, LRS Vol. 20 (1984); A Survey of Documentary Sources for Property Holding in London Before the Great Fire, by D. Keene and V. Harding, LRS Vol. 22 (1985).

The London Topographical Society has published The Public Markets of the City of London Surveyed by William Leybourn in 1677, by B. R. Masters, LTS Publication No. 117 (1974); The Artillery Ground and Fields in Finsbury; Two Maps of 1641 and 1705, by J. R. Sewell, LTS Publication No. 120 (1977).

The Catholic Record Society has published London Sessions Records, 1605-1685, by Dom. H. Bowler (1934).

The Magna Carta Book Company, located in Baltimore, Maryland, has published A List of Emigrants from England to America, 1682-1692, by M. Ghirelli (1968); A List of Emigrants from England to America, 1718-1759, by J. and M. Kaminkow (1964). There is also Emigrants to America, Indentured Servants Recruited in London, 1718-1733, by J. Wareing.

Publications of particular interest to genealogists are: "Some Genealogical Sources in the Corporation of London Records Office," by B. R. Masters, in: Genealogists' Magazine, Vol. 20, nos. 10 and 11 (June and September, 1982); English Convicts in Colonial America, Vol. II, London 1656-1775, by P. W. Coldham (New Orleans, Polyzanthos, 1976); Lord Mayor's Court of London Depositions Relating to Americans 1641-1736, by P. W. Coldham (National Genealogical Society, Washington, 1980).

LONDON

161	Institution	Greater London Record Office and History Library
	Address	40 Northampton Road
		London EC1R 0HB
	Telephone	01 633 6851

Requests for information from this record office failed to elicit a response; therefore some details are lacking.

Holdings   The office holds records of many predecessors of the London County Council, the Greater London Council, and from Middlesex County Council and

their predecessors. The collection includes ecclesiastical, manorial, family, estate, business,
and other private records. Among the archives
preserved in the record office are those of
Commissioners of Sewers (1570-1847), Metropolitan
Commission of Sewers (1847-1855), Metropolitan
Buildings Office (1845-1855), Metropolitan Board
of Works (1855-1889), London County Council
(1889-1965), School Board for London (1870-1904),
Technical Education Board (1893-1904), Board
of Guardians (1834-1930), and Metropolitan Asylums
Board (1867-1930). Among deposits under the
Public Records Act, 1958, are the records of
Westminster Hospital and St. Thomas' Hospital
Group (13th to 20th century), including those of
the Nightingale Training School and the Nightingale Collection. Other official records include
those of the Middlesex Deeds Registry (registers,
1709-1938). The records of the Middlesex Sessions,
1549-1971, and the Gaol Delivery of Newgate for
Middlesex, 1549-1834 are also found. The record
office is the Diocesan Record Office for parish
records of the Dioceses of London, Southwark,
and Guildford. Diocesan archives include
Bishop's Transcripts, records of the Consistory
Court of London (1467-1858), and records dealing
with judicial, testamentary and matrimonial
business. Some tithe awards and plans for the
Diocese of London are also held. Congregational
Church records include registers, minutes of
church meetings, and trust deeds from the
seventeenth century for more than sixty churches,
as well as records of the London Congregational
Union. Among Methodist archives received are
circuit, the mission minutes, chapel, deeds, and
registers. The manorial family, estate, business,
and other private records relating primarily to the
area of the former London County Council have
been accepted as gifts or on deposit since at
least 1946. They include those of the manors of
Stepney, Barnsbury, and Rotherhithe and the
three Hackney manors. Court rolls of the manor
of Tooting Bec (1394-1843) were inherited from
the Metropolitan Board of Works. Among records
of important estates are those of St. Pancras
estates of Lord Camden and Lord Southampton,
the Islington and Clerkenwell estates of the
Marquess of Northampton, the Bedford estates
in Convent Garden and south London, the
Maryon-Wilson estates in Hampstead and Charlton,
and the De Beauvoir property, chiefly in Hackney
and Shoreditch. The office contains strong
archival collections of charities, societies, and
schools, such as the Foundling Hospital, the
Surrey Dispensary, the Corporation of the Sons
of the Clergy, the Royal Standard Benefit Society,
the Liberation Society, and the Bacon Free School,

Bermondsey. Business records include those of
gas companies (predecessors of the North Thames
Gas Board), breweries, makers of chemicals,
sweets, boots, hats, baskets, eye ointment and
gin. The records of the Northwick Park estate
of the late Lord Northwick, the Osterley estate
of the Earl of Jersey (with much family material),
the Middlesex and other estates of the Marquess
of Anglesey, the Harefield estate of F. H. M.
Fitzroy Newdegate, the Middlesex and other widely
scattered estates of the Hawtrey Dean family and
the Littleton Park estate are housed here. There
are also printed maps, prints, drawings, watercolors, and photographs.

Conditions of admission and access	The Record Office is open to the public and so far as is known, appointments in advance of a visit are not required to use the search room. Inquiries should be directed to the Head Archivist and should be accompanied by postage, which may or may not elicit a response.
Hours	Unknown. At one time the hours were 9:45 AM - 4:45 PM, Monday, Wednesday-Friday; 9:45 AM - 7:45 PM, Tuesday. Those wishing to use the search room after 4:45 PM on Tuesday must give prior notice of their requirements.
Duplicating facilities	Copying facilities are available.
Other services	Telephone and postal inquiries are not usually answered if they concern the holdings. Questions concerning hours or search room rules would probably receive a reply.
Publications	Guide to the Records in the London County Record Office, Pt. I: Records of the Predecessors of the London County Council, Except the Boards of Guardians (1962); A Survey of the Parish Registers of the Diocese of London, Inner London (1968); A Survey of the Parish Registers of the Diocese of the Southwark, Inner London Area (1970); Court Minutes of the Surrey and Kent Sewer Commission, 1569/70-1579 (1909); Court Rolls of Tooting Bec Manor, 1394-1422 (1909); Guide to the Middlesex Sessions Records, 1549-1889 (1965); Middlesex County Records 1549-1688 (old series), ed. by J. Cordy Jeaffreson, Vols. 1-4 (1886-1892); Middlesex County Records: Calendar of the Sessions Books, 1689-1709, ed. by W. J. Hardy (1905); Middlesex County Records: Reports, 1902-1928 (being reports by W. J. Hardy and W. Le Hardy on the contents of unpublished Calendars of the Sessions Records) (1928); Middlesex Sessions Records, 1612-1618 (new series), ed. by W. Le Hardy, Vols. 1-4 (1935-1941).

LONDON

162	Institution Address	Guildhall Library Aldermanbury London EC2P 2EJ

Telephone

01 606 3030

Underground

Bank, Moorgate, St. Paul's, Mansion House

Holdings

This library holds considerable resources for English genealogy, particularly relating to the City of London. It also holds some material for the rest of the British Isles and overseas, and a major collection on all aspects of London history. Among the manuscripts one finds Parish registers of nearly all the City of London parishes and of St. Leonard, Shoreditch; Registers of some Anglican churches overseas; rate books and (pre-1834) poor law records for City parishes; marriage licence records for the Diocese of London, Dean and Chapter of St. Paul's Cathedral and Royal Peculiar of St. Katherine by the Tower; probate records (pre-1858) for the Archdeaconry and Commissary Courts of London, apprenticeship and membership records of most of the City livery companies and related organizations; ordination and other records of clergy in the Diocese of London; registers of children attending Christ's Hospital and some other schools in or connected with the City; Lloyd's "Captains Registers" relating to the careers of Master Mariners since 1851. Printed material includes family and local histories; journals, etc., of national and local historical, genealogical and record societies; directories of London from the 1730s, many English towns from the 1800s; poll books of many English towns and counties; electoral registers of the City of London from 1832; census returns for the City of London, 1841-1881; published and unpublished register transcripts of many English parishes; Boyd's marriage index for Middlesex and London, and Shropshire; Boyd's Burial Index for Middlesex and London; the Apprentices of Great Britain, 1710-1774 (compiled from Inland Revenue records); clerical, medical, legal and armed services directories; registers of schools, colleges and universities; The International Genealogical Index, compiled by the Mormon Church, of baptisms and some marriages in the British Isles.

Conditions of admission and access

The Guildhall Library is a reference library open to the public. No letter of introduction or appointment in advance is required. Inquiries should be directed to the Principal Reference Librarian or to the Keeper of Manuscripts. The collection must be used on the premises.

Hours	9:30 AM - 4:45 PM, Monday-Saturday.
Duplicating facilities	Photocopying facilities are available, but special arrangements must be made for microcopying.
Other services	Reference help is provided to the visiting scholar.
Publications	The Guildhall Library Sales Office issues a Catalog of Publications. Among the categories included in the "Contents" are Journals, Bibliographies, Catalogues, Atlases, Books and Leaflets about Guildhall, Books Relating to Genealogy, Facsimiles, Guildhall Art Gallery Handbooks, and Greeting Cards.

LONDON

163	Institution Address	Hackney Archives Department Rose Lipman Library De Beauvoir Road London N1 5SQ
	Telephone	01 241 2886
	Holdings	The department holds the records of Hackney Borough and its predecessors, those of Bryant and May, matchmakers, and subsidiaries from ca. 1850 to ca. 1965, and other business firms. Non-conformists' records from the 19th and 20th centuries are also found. The Tyssen Collection of manuscripts contains mid-19th century transcripts of records formerly in the Tower of London. These include Close and Patent Rolls, 1291-1597, fines, 1189-1730, Commissary Court wills, 1374-1692, and manorial records, 1327-1857. There are also books, maps and plans, drawings and paintings. The John Dawson Collection of six hundred books printed before 1767 (believed to be the only surviving Parochial Library in London), manuscript notebooks, and a diary is available here. There is a theatre collection of a thousand playbills of four Shoreditch theaters (ca. 1831-1890), cuttings, illustrations and some manuscripts. Also found are maps and plans, paintings and drawings, pamphlets and several thousand (mainly topographical) photographs.
	Conditions of admission and access	The department is open to the public, but an appointment in advance should be made. Official records have a thirty-year closure and access to the Bryant and May archive is restricted.
	Hours	10:00 AM - 8:00 PM, Monday; 10:00 AM - 5:30 PM, Tuesday, Thursday-Friday; 10:00 AM - 1:00 PM, 2:00 PM - 5:30 PM, Wednesday; 10:00 AM - 1:00 PM, 2:00 PM - 5:00 PM, Saturday.

Duplicating facilities	Photocopying facilities are available and arrangements can be made for photographs.
Other services	Brief questions by post and telephone are answered and reference help is available. Lists and indexes are provided to aid the researcher.
Publications	Leaflets, brochures, and postcards are produced. Also available are Hackney Society publications and the East London Record.

LONDON (map)

164 Institution Address	The Honourable Society of Lincoln's Inn Holborn London WC2A 3TN
Telephone	01 242 4371
Underground	Chancery Lane
Holdings	The library contains information on law books, the Inns of Court and a comprehensive collection of the laws and law reports of the British Commonwealth. There are works on history, Parliamentary Papers, and biographical details of members. Special collections include the Sir Matthew Hale collection of Manuscripts and House of Lords Appeals and Privy Council cases.
Conditions of admission and access	Visiting scholars must obtain permission to use the library's resources. Inquiries should be directed to the Librarian by letter. The collection must be used on the premises.
Hours	9:30 AM - 7:00 PM, Monday-Friday except from August to mid-September, when the hours are 10:00 AM - 4:00 PM, Monday-Friday.
Duplicating facilities	Photocopying facilities are available and arrangements can be made for microfilming.
Other services	Reference help is available in the library, but only limited inquiries are answered by telephone or post.
Publications	Catalogue of the Library, 1859 (1890); Catalogue of Pamphlets, 1506-1700; Records of the Society, 1422-1914; Guide to Commonwealth Collection in Lincoln's Inn (1974).

LONDON

165 Institution Address	Honourable Society of the Inner Temple The Inner Temple Library The Inner Temple London EC4Y 7DA

Telephone	01 353 2959
Underground	Temple
Holdings	This is a private library which primarily serves the professional lawyer in the United Kingdom. The library resources include legislation, law reports, journals, treatises relating to English, Commonwealth, and international law, heraldry, and London topography. The manuscript collection includes Inner Temple records (a selection of miscellaneous domestic records), Mitford Legal Manuscripts and Petyt and Barrington Manuscripts. Membership (of the Inner Temple) records are not held nor are birth, marriage, death or wills records. The printed collection does include biographies of legal figures, county history, ecclesiastical law and history, records of parliament and loyal learned society publications.
Conditions of admission and access	Visiting scholars can use the manuscript collection only with the permission of the Librarian. A letter of introduction is required and use is by appointment only. Inquiries should be directed to the Librarian and Keeper of Manuscripts. The collection may be used only on the premises. Manuscript material is not available in August and September. Inquiries concerning membership in the Inn should be directed to the Inner Temple Treasurer's Office at the address above.
Hours	10:00 AM - 6:00 PM, Monday-Friday, October-July; 10:00 AM - 4:00 PM, August-September.
Duplicating facilities	Self-operated photocopying facilities are available for use by the reader for selected printed material only. No postal photocopying service is available. Manuscript material may be duplicated only by overhead camera supplied by an outside agency and upon special application.
Other services	Legal bibliographical information is provided only to lawyers or librarians working at other libraries. A fee is charged for services to the general public.
Publications	Catalogue of Manuscripts in the Library of the Inner Temple, ed. by J. Conway Davies, 3 vols., (1972).

LONDON

166	Institution	The Honourable Society of the Middle Temple
	Address	Middle Temple Lane
		London EC4Y 9BT
	Telephone	01 353 4303

Underground	Temple
Holdings	The collection includes legal resources covering all parts of the world. The special collections include books from Donne's Library (works on religious controversy, apologetics, philosophy, and magic), the Phillimore Collection (international law), Lord Chancellor Eldon (law books), and the Ashly Collection (geography, astronomy, and history). Records of the Inn and of the members in their relationship with the Inn are kept.
Conditions of admission and access	The library is available to non-members on written application to the Librarian and Keeper of the Records. The material must be used on the premises, under supervision.
Hours	9:30 AM - 7:00 PM, Monday-Friday.
Duplicating facilities	Full-size copying facilities are available. Permission must be granted to copy documents.
Other services	Very brief questions by post or telephone will be answered. Limited reference help is provided.
Publications	A list of publications is available on request. These include Middle Temple Admission Register, 1501-1944, 3 vols.; and Middle Temple Library Catalogue, 1914-1925, 4 vols.

LONDON

167	Institution Address	House of Lords Record Office House of Lords London SW1A 0PW
	Telephone	01 219 3074
	Underground	Westminster
	Holdings	Over three million records are held by the office and date from 1497. They include archives of the House of Commons (some from 1547 but mainly from 1835 on) as well as those of the House of Lords. Other groups of records which have accumulated within the Palace of Westminster, such as those of the Lord Great Chamberlain, are also found. The Private Bill Records contain information about local history such as railways, roads, canals, gas and water works. Special collections include the papers of First Viscount Samuel, Lord Beaverbrook, Lloyd George, and Bonar Law, Brand Papers (1855-1892), Braye Manuscripts (1572-1748), Nalson Manuscripts (1628-1660), the Onslow Manuscripts (1547-1801), Tickell Manuscripts (1709-1733), Walker papers (1643-1649),

and the Willcocks collection. Committee proceedings, original Public and Private Acts of Parliament (1497 to date), records of debates of both Lords and Commons, the records of the Lord Great Chamberlain and judicial records are held.

Conditions of admission and access

The record office is open to the public, but searchers are asked to notify the Clerk of the Records of those needed ahead of time. A description of the research to be conducted should be given, and if possible the documents to be consulted. A letter of introduction is not required. If the documents to be used are for business or legal purposes, a fee is charged for each one produced. No fee is charged for those to be used for historical research. The collection must be used in the search room. Approach to the office is via the Chancellor's Gate, Old Palace Yard.

Hours

9: 30 AM - 5: 00 PM, Monday-Friday.

Duplicating facilities

Photocopies, microfilm, full-size copies from microfilm, and photographs can be supplied. Copying is undertaken at the discretion of the Clerk of the Records. Those at risk of damage cannot be copied.

Other services

Brief inquiries by post or telephone are answered and reference help is provided in the search room. A variety of finding aids, lists, calendars, and indexes are available to further aid the researcher.

Publications

House of Lords Record Office Occasional Publications (HMSO); Calendars of House of Lords Manuscripts, Vols. I-XII (new series) 1693-1718 (HMSO); Annual Reports; Handlists; Records of Parliament: A Guide for Genealogists and Local Historians; Memoranda; Guide to the Records of Parliament, by M. F. Bond (HMSO, 1971, is now available only from the House of Lords Record Office).

LONDON (map)

167a Institution Address

Imperial War Museum Libraries and Archives
Lambeth Road
London SE1 6HZ

Telephone

01 735 8922

Underground

Lambeth North, Elephant and Castle

Holdings

The library contains materials relating to all aspects of the two world wars and other military,

political, and economic activities of Britain and the
Commonwealth since 1914. Specifically included are
histories of service units, technical literature, and
wartime periodicals of both British and foreign
origin. The Department of Documents collects and
disseminates information on the documentary holdings of European and American archives and research institutes. It has two main groups of
works, namely British private papers and captured
German material. For the period of the First World
War, one finds the diaries and correspondence of
Sir John French (Commander-in-Chief of the British
Expeditionary Force in 1914 and 1915) and Sir
Henry Wilson (Chief of the Imperial General Staff
from 1918 to 1922) and the papers of other military
figures. For the study of the Second World War,
the diaries, letters and other writings of Field
Marshal Viscount Montgomery are available. Other
officers' records and those of lower ranking ser-
vicemen from all branches of military service as
well as the memoirs of civilians are also preserved.
Foreign records of German and Italian origin are
held, mostly photocopies or microfilm, which show
invasion plans, intelligence data on allied armies,
information relating to war economy, technical
development and personnel. The collection contains campaign files for the Western, Norwegian,
and Eastern campaigns in World War II, the plans
for the Austrian and Czechoslovakian invasions,
and a number of high-level military intelligence
documents. The collection of High Command files
contains material on the organization of the German armed forces in the pre-war period. The two
largest microfilm collections of German official files
contain material from the Reich Ministry of Arma-
ments and War Production (the Speer Ministry)
and from the Reich Air Ministry. The Speer
Ministry records include the ministerial papers of
Speer himself, the minutes of the Central Planning
Committee, and the records of the Planungsamt
and the Rofstoffamt. The German collections also
contain material from the Reich Ministry of Eco-
nomics, the records of major German industrial
firms, and the various War Crimes Trials. The
Italian material held by the museum includes
largely the records of the Italian Ministry of War
Production from 1940 to 1943. Private papers include the letters and diaries of Field Marshal Sir
Henry Wilson (see above) and the papers of
Marshal of the Royal Air Force, Lord Douglas
of Kirtleside, Major-General G. P. Dawnay, Admiral Sir Dudley de Chair, Major-General L. O.
Lyne, General Sir Ivor Maxse, Admiral Sir Edward Parry, and Air Commodore C. R. Samson.
The Department of Printed Books contains detailed coverage of the two world wars, but also
includes works on other 20th-century wars. The

library has strong holdings of British, French, German, and American unit histories. There is an important collection of technical manuals and handbooks, examples of wartime propaganda, ration books, enlistment cards, and army forms, news cuttings, trench maps and situation and order of battle maps.

The Department of Sound Records is engaged in an oral history program which is designed to collect interviews with individuals from all walks of life whose experience falls within the museum's field of study. There are also recordings of commentaries, war reports, speeches, and other broadcasts.

The Department of Photographs contains over five million photographs and negatives concerning war in the twentieth century. The two world wars are covered and material on other conflicts involving Britain and the Commonwealth are also kept. Official photographs taken by well known individuals such as James Jarché, Sir Cecil Beaton, and Bert Hardy are held and photographs of professional (but not official) and amateur photographers in both world wars are being acquired. Collections donated from private sources are becoming increasingly important and include photographs relating to the career of Colonel T. E. Lawrence in Egypt and Palestine in 1917 and 1918.

The museum also owns paintings, drawings, and sculptures, consisting mostly of works commissioned by the Ministry of Information during both World Wars. A selection is on display in the galleries. The Department of Art has an archive of papers and correspondence from the War Artist schemes. Works of art not on display may be viewed by special arrangement.

Conditions of admission and access

The collections are available to scholars for research on the premises. An appointment at least 24 hours in advance is required for all departments except Art, which requires 48 hours. Inquiries should be made to the individual in charge of each section (Film Librarian, Keeper of Art, Keeper of the Document Department, etc.). The researcher should have means of identification on first appearing at the museum. Material is not issued after 4:45 PM in the Department of Printed Books and visitors are not admitted after 4:30 PM. Access to some collections is governed by special conditions.

Hours

The research departments of the museum are open 10:00 AM - 5:00 PM, Monday-Friday except for the Art Reference Room which is open, 10:00 AM - 4:30 PM, Tuesday-Wednesday, Friday. The Public Galleries are open 10:00 AM - 5:50 PM, Monday-

Saturday, 2:00 PM - 5:50 PM, Sunday. The Department of Printed Books does not admit visitors after 4:30 PM. The museum is closed on New Year's Day, Good Friday, Spring Bank Holiday, Christmas Eve, Christmas Day, and Boxing Day. The Department of Printed Books is closed the last two full weeks in October.

Duplicating facilities

Full-size copying and other photographic reproduction processes are available. Copies of the museum's photographs and photographs of the paintings and posters are available to order. In some cases, there may be long delays before a copying order is completed. Application forms and a scale of fees are available on request.

Other services

Reference service is available, but extensive research is not undertaken for scholars either on a personal visit or by post or telephone. In some departments, there are facilities for tape recorders and typewriters.

Publications

A Concise Catalogue of Paintings, Drawings and Sculpture of the First World War, 1914-1918, 2nd ed.; A Concise Catalogue of Paintings, Drawings and Sculpture of the Second World War, 1939-1945, 2nd ed.; Provisional Reports on archives which include repositories in the United Kingdom, the German Federal Republic, Italy, the German Democratic Republic, and Poland are available, as are accessions lists, book lists, and bibliographies on over five hundred topics. A guide to these is also available for purchase. Catalogues of oral history recordings and broadcast recordings are provided.

LONDON

Institution

India Office Library and Records
See: LONDON, The British Library, India Office Library and Records

LONDON (map)

168 Institution
Address

Kensington Central Reference Library
Hornton Street
London W8 7RR

Postal address

Phillimore Walk
London W8 7RX

Telephone

01 937 2542

Underground

High Street Kensington
See also: LONDON, Chelsea Library

Holdings	The collection contains illustrations, microfilm of early newspapers and census returns (1841-1881); photographs, drawings and paintings, and prints and engravings. Also available is the Brough- shane Collection of cuttings, which is comprised of twenty albums spanning the period 1899-1949. Maps and plans are also available. Many direc- tories are held and include several from London and also local directories for Kensington. Elec- toral registers are held from 1890 to date and there is a microfilm of the ecclesiastical census of 1851 for Kensington and Chelsea Parishes. Contemporary copies of burial and baptism records for St. Mary Abbot Church for the 18th and early 19th century are found as well as Church Wardens' vestry records, documents re- lating to charities, poor law records, Council and committee minutes and rate and valuation records. Also held are records of schools, institutions, the Kensington Turnpike Trust, 1726-1826, manorial records, family and estate records and business papers.
Conditions of admission and access	The collection is open to the public. Inquiries should be directed to the Librarian. The collec- tion must be used on the premises.
Hours	10:00 AM - 8:00 PM, Monday-Tuesday, Thursday- Friday; 10:00 AM - 1:00 PM, Wednesday; 10:00 AM - 5:00 PM, Saturday.
Duplicating facilities	A photocopying and photographic service is avail- able.
Other services	Brief questions by post or telephone are answered and reference help is available. Many finding aids, catalogs and indexes are provided to further aid the researcher.
Publications	Leaflets, pamphlets, sets of historical maps and postcards are produced.

LONDON (map)

169 Institution Address	Lambeth Archives Department Minet Library 52 Knatchbull Road London SE5 9QY
Telephone	01 733 3279
Underground	Briston (Victoria Line); Oval (Northern Line)
Holdings	The Surrey Collection is the local history collec- tion of Lambeth Public Libraries. It covers the pre-1888 county of Surrey which included the then

parishes of Battersea, Wandsworth, Lambeth, Camberwell, Southwark, Bermondsey, Rotherhithe, as
well as the areas covered in 1964. The collection
includes Lambeth parish records, Church Wardens' accounts, vestry minutes, other vestry
papers, and other parish records. Overseers'
accounts, workhouse records, collectors of the
poor accounts, and rate books are also kept. The
Surrey Collection is recognized as a manorial repository and contains court rolls, court books,
estreat rolls, court minute books, and rentals for
the manors of Bermondsey and Deptford Strand;
Camberwell Friern; Camberwell Duckingham;
Dunsford (Wandsworth); Ewell, Cuddington,
East and West Cheam; Farncomb; West Horsley;
Leigham Court (Streatham); Norbury, Beddington,
Ravensbury, Walton-on-the-Hill, and Banstead;
Paris Garden (Southwark); Reigate; Tadworth
(in Long Ditton); Sanderstead with Langhurst;
Kingston-upon-Thames. Deeds and copies of
wills are kept, as are letters and family papers,
estate surveys, accounts and rentals, tellers'
bills, apprenticeship indentures, and welfare
records. Maps and plans, photographs, works
relating to the Crystal Palace and Vauxhall Gardens are also available. There are parish register transcripts, newspapers, cuttings, prints,
sale catalogs, and brass rubbings. Copies of
census returns for Lambeth are also kept.

Conditions of admission and access	The collection is open to the public, but visitors should make an appointment in advance. Inquiries should be directed to the Archivist. The material must be used in the Archives Department.
Hours	9: 30 AM - 1: 00 PM, 2: 00 PM - 5: 00 PM, Monday-Tuesday, Thursday-Friday; 9: 30 AM - 1: 00 PM, 2: 00 PM - 4: 45 PM, on alternate Saturdays.
Duplicating facilities	Photocopies can be provided and arrangements can be made for photographs.
Other services	Brief questions by post or telephone are answered and reference help is available. Finding aids, catalogs, and indexes are provided to aid the researcher.
Publications	A Short Guide to the Surrey Collection, by M. Y. Williams (1965); postcards. A printed catalog of the Surrey Collection was published in 1901 and supplements were compiled in 1910 and 1912. A cumulated supplement was produced in 1923, with additions since 1912. Although the collection has greatly increased since that time, these early catalogs are still useful.

LONDON

170	Institution Address	Lambeth Palace Library Lambeth Palace Road London SE1 7JU
	Telephone	01 928 6222
	Underground	Lambeth North, Westminster, Waterloo
	Holdings	Lambeth Palace Library is the historic library of the Archbishops of Canterbury, dating back to 1610. It is the principal library of the Church of England and holds extensive collections of books, archives, and manuscripts dating from the Norman Conquest to the present day. It covers a very broad field and contains material on almost every aspect of medieval civilization including art, history, poetry, medicine, philosophy, liturgy, the Bible, and Greek and Latin classical literature. The primary focus of the collections is on ecclesiastical history and the contents include several thousand volumes of manuscripts dating from the 9th century. The records of use to genealogists are mainly confined to the 17th, 18th and 19th centuries, and in some instances the material may only be consulted on microform. The collections include the allegations for marriage licences issued by the Faculty Office, the Vicar General of the Archbishop of Canterbury and the Archbishop's surrogates for the Peculiars of the Arches (London), Croydon (Surrey), and Shorham (Surrey and Middlesex). Apart from the wills recorded in the medieval registers of the Archbishops of Canterbury, the library has the testamentary records of the three Peculiars of the Arches, Croydon and Shorham. The records of the Court of Arches, the Court of Appeal for the province of Canterbury, include much material on matrimonial and testamentary matters, principally from the 17th to the mid-19th century. The Library's extensive ecclesiastical collections provide information on the clergy of the dioceses of Canterbury and of London and on those of other dioceses who held in plurality.
	Conditions of admission and access	The library is open to bona fide students on production of a letter of introduction from a person of recognized standing. Inquiries should be directed to the Librarian. An appointment in advance is recommended.
	Hours	10:00 AM - 5:00 PM, Monday-Friday. The library is closed on public holidays, for ten days at Christmas beginning on Christmas Eve, and for ten days at Easter beginning on Good Friday.

Duplicating facilities	Photocopying and microfilm facilities are available. Much of the material is not suitable for photocopying.
Other services	Microform equipment, ultra-violet lamp and reference help are provided in the library.
Publications	Calendar of Marriage Licences issued by the Faculty Office, 1632-1714, ed. by G. E. Cokayne and E. A. Fry (1905) (Index Library, Vol. 33); Allegations for Marriage Licences issued by the Dean and Chapter of Westminster, 1558 to 1699; also, for those issued by the Vicar-General of the Archbishop of Canterbury, 1660 to 1679, extracted by J. L. Chester and ed. by G. J. Armytage (1886) (Harleian Society, Vol. 23); Allegations for Marriage Licences issued by the Vicar-General of the Archbishop of Canterbury, 1660 to 1668, ed. by G. J. Armytage (1892) (Harleian Society, Vol. 33); Allegations for Marriage Licences Issued by the Vicar-General of the Archbishop of Canterbury, 1669-1679, ed. by G. J. Armytage (1892) (Harleian Society, Vol. 34); Allegations for Marriage Licences issued by the Vicar-General of the Archbishop of Canterbury, July 1679 to June 1687, ed. by G. J. Armytage (1890) (Harleian Society, Vol. 30); Allegations for Marriage Licences Issued by the Vicar-General of the Archbishop of Canterbury, July 1687 to June 1694, ed. by G. J. Armytage (1890) (Harleian Society, Vol. 31). Index of Wills Recorded in the Archiepiscopal Registers at Lambeth Palace, by J. C. Smith (1919) (Reprinted from Genealogists, new series, Vols. 34-35); Index to the Testamentary Records of the Deanery of the Arches in Lambeth Palace Library, by J. Foster (1985) (Index Library, Vol. 98). Index of Cases in the Records of the Court of the Arches at Lambeth Palace Library 1660-1913, ed. by J. Houston (1972) (Index Library, Vol. 85). Index to the Act Books of the Archbishops of Canterbury, 1663-1859, by E. H. W. Dunkin, ed. by C. Jenkins and E. A. Fry, 1929, 1938 (Index Library, Vols. 55, 63). The medieval registers, act books, and Fulham Papers are available on microfilm from World Microfilm Publications (62 Queen's Grove, London NW8 6ER). The film of the Fulham papers may also be consulted in a number of American libraries. Many of the Court of Arches records are available on microform from Charles Chadwyck Healey Limited (Cambridge Place, Cambridge CB2 1NR) and copies are in the Center for Research Libraries, Chicago. The Calendars of the Vicar General and Faculty Office marriage allegations are available from Harvester Press Microform Publications Ltd. (17 Ship Street, Brighton BN1 1AD).

LONDON (map)

171 Institution	Lewisham Local History Centre
Address	The Manor House
	Old Road, Lee
	London SE13 5SY

Telephone — 01 852 5050

Holdings — The collection includes general historical books on Lewisham and the surrounding area and there are biographies of important local persons and works of local authors. Directories and pollbooks are available and files of local newspapers from the 19th century onward are held on microfilm. There are also newspaper cuttings from the 18th century to the present including a series of 19th-century Deptford cuttings. The illustrations collections contain photographs, postcards, prints, slides, paintings, and drawings, mainly relating to Lewisham. A photographic survey of the Borough was begun in the early 1960s and negatives are kept from which prints can be supplied for a fee. Maps date from the 18th century and include copies of tithe and enclosure maps and Ordnance Survey maps in various scales. Also held are the official records of the Council and its predecessors, the parochial vestries, Boards of Works, etc. Family and estate papers, records of local businesses, and of organizations and societies, and a large number of local deeds are held. Anglican Parish Registers and those of some nonconformist churches have been deposited. The census returns, 1841-1881 are held on microfilm. The centre is an approved repository for parish, manorial, tithe and local public records.

Conditions of admission and access — The collection is open to the public and no appointment in advance is required. The collection must be used on the premises. Inquiries should be addressed to the Archivist.

Hours — 9:30 AM - 5:00 PM, Monday, Friday-Saturday; 9:30 AM - 8:00 PM, Tuesday, Thursday. Closed Wednesday, and Saturdays preceding bank holidays.

Duplicating facilities — Facilities for photocopying and photography are available.

Other services — Brief questions by post or telephone are answered and reference help is available. Lectures and slide shows can be arranged for schools and local groups. Exhibitions are arranged on the premises.

Publications — Leaflets and brochures are produced.

LONDON

172 Institution   Library of the Religious Society of Friends
     Address   Friends House
                        Euston Road
                        London NW1 2BJ

     Telephone   01 387 3601

     Holdings   Digests of registers of births, marriages, and
                        burials dating from the 17th century are kept
                        (originals are in the Public Record Office) and
                        correspondence, papers, printed works, and
                        Quaker periodicals are found. Families whose
                        papers are held include the Gurney family of
                        Norfolk, the Lloyd family of Dolobran,
                        Montgomeryshire and Birmingham; the Barclay
                        family, and the Wilkinson family of Yanwath and
                        Westmorland. There are also photographs,
                        paintings, drawings, lithographs and engravings
                        kept as part of the collection.

     Conditions of   Researchers wishing to use the collection must
     admission and   make an appointment in advance and provide a
     access   letter of recommendation. Fees are required for
                        genealogical research and some records are re-
                        stricted. Inquiries should be directed to the
                        Librarian. The collection may be consulted only
                        in the library.

     Hours   10:00 AM - 5:00 PM, Monday-Friday. The li-
                        brary is closed the week preceding the Spring
                        bank holiday and for a week in August.

     Duplicating   Photocopying facilities are available.
     facilities

     Other services   Reference help is available in the library and
                        questions by post or telephone are answered if
                        they are not extensive.

     Publications   Journal of the Friends Historical Society (1903-);
                        lists, indexes, guides.

LONDON

173 Institution   London Borough of Barking and Dagenham Public
     Address   Library
                        Valence Reference Library
                        Becontree Avenue
                        Dagenham RM8 3HT

     Telephone   01 592 2211, ext. 5

     Holdings   The collection contains records of the Borough of
                        Barking and Dagenham and its predecessors,

which date from 1666 for Barking and 1838 for Dagenham. There are papers of local businesses, notably those of the Lawes Chemical Company. The papers of the Fanshawe family form an important part of the collection and include correspondence, family history, pedigrees, and genealogical material. There are also maps, plans, drawings, prints, illustrations, paintings and photographs.

Conditions of admission and access	Visiting scholars must obtain permission to use the collection and an appointment in advance is needed. A written application is required. Part of the collection is housed at the Valence House Museum (Fanshawe papers, visual material such as paintings and photographs). Inquiries should be directed to the Archivist/Curator. The archives must be used on the premises.
Hours	9:30 AM - 7:00 PM, Monday-Tuesday, Thursday-Friday; 9:30 AM - 1:00 PM, Wednesday, Saturday.
Duplicating facilities	Full-size copying facilities are provided.
Other services	There is staff available to give reference advice, brief questions by telephone are answered and those by post will receive a response.
Publications	Dagenham Place Names, by J. G. O'Leary; Essex and Dagenham; The Book of Dagenham; guides, lists, catalogs.

LONDON

174 Institution Address	London Borough of Bexley Bexley Library Service Local Studies Section Hall Place Bourne Road London Borough of Bexley DA5 1PQ
Telephone	0322 526574
Holdings	The collection includes the surviving rate books and local authority minutes from 1790. Ordnance Survey maps and tithe maps are found as well as an important collection of photographs and prints. The archives of Danson and Hall Place estates are held and a strong collection relating to the County of Kent.
Conditions of admission and access	The library is open to the public and a prior appointment is not required. Inquiries should be addressed to the Local Studies Officer.

Hours	9:00 AM - 5:00 PM, Monday-Saturday. Note: During the winter months, the library may have an earlier closing.
Duplicating facilities	Photocopying and full-size copies from microforms can be provided.
Other services	Questions by telephone or post are answered if they are not too extensive. Reference help is provided, as are catalogs and indexes which further aid the scholar.
Publications	Papers on local matters of interest such as houses, individuals, industries and transportation are available for duplication.

LONDON

175	Institution Address	London Borough of Bromley Public Libraries Central Library Archive Section Tweedy Road London Borough of Bromley BR1 1EX
	Telephone	01 460 9955
	Holdings	The local history collection includes information on Bromley, Kent, and the Crystal Palace. Also found are the records of local authorities and Councils and the archives of private individuals.
	Conditions of admission and access	The library is open to the public for reference. Inquiries should be directed to the Borough Librarian. Appointments in advance are not necessary except for Saturday use.
	Hours	9:30 AM - 8:00 PM, Tuesday, Thursday; 9:30 AM - 6:00 PM, Wednesday, Friday; 9:30 AM - 5:00 PM, Saturday by appointment.
	Duplicating facilities	Photocopying facilities, photography and full-size copies from microforms are available.
	Other services	Brief questions by post or telephone are answered and reference help is provided.
	Publications	A Bibliography of Printed Materials Relating to Bromley, Heyes and Keston, in the County of Kent, by B. Burch (1964); The Catalogue of the H. G. Wells Collection in the Bromley Public Libraries, ed. by A. H. Watkins (1974); The Manor and Town of Bromley AD862-1934, by A. H. Watkins (1972); Portfolio of Views of the London Borough of Bromley (in the 18th and 19th Centuries) (1972); Introduction to the History of Orpington, comp. by Peter Heinecke (1975); History of Bromley, by A. H. Watkins (n.d.).

LONDON

| 176 | Institution Address | London Borough of Camden |
| | | Local History Library |

176 Institution   London Borough of Camden
    Address   Local History Library
                   Holborn Library
                   32-38 Theobalds Road
                   London   WC1X 8PA
                   and
                   Swiss Cottage Library
                   88 Avenue Road
                   London   NW3 3HA

    Telephone   01 405 2706 (Holborn Library)
                   01 278 4444, ext. 3001/3007 (Swiss Cottage Library)

    Holdings   The collection contains rate books (from 1726 to
                   1958), registers of burials (Highgate Cemetery,
                   1839-1968), transcriptions of tombstone inscrip-
                   tions, census returns (1841-1881) and the original
                   census returns for Hampstead (1801 and 1881).
                   Also found are maps, prints, drawings, and
                   photographs. There are Borough minutes (from
                   1617) and other archives of the Borough and
                   papers relating to Hampstead Manor (1742-1843).

    Conditions of The libraries are open to the public and research-
    admission and ers may use the records, except for those with
    access   restrictions. Inquiries should be addressed to the
                   Librarian in Charge (Holborn Library) or the
                   Local History Librarian (Swiss Cottage Library).
                   The collections may not be removed from the
                   premises.

    Hours   9:30 AM - 8:00 PM, Monday-Thursday; 9:30 AM -
                   6:00 PM, Friday; 9:30 AM - 5:00 PM, Saturday.

    Duplicating   Photocopying and full-size copies from microforms
    facilities   can be provided and arrangements can be made
                   for photography.

    Other services Reference help is available and questions by post
                   or telephone are answered if they are brief.

    Publications   Beginning in Local History, by C. Lavell (1972).
                   Guides, lists, brochures.

LONDON

177 Institution   London Borough of Croydon Public Libraries
    Address   Central Library
                   Local Studies Library
                   Katharine Street
                   Croydon   CR9 1ET

    Telephone   01 688 3627, ext. 48

Holdings	The collection contains pamphlets, cuttings, prints, photographs, maps, paintings, and postcards. Local newspapers are held from 1855 and the census returns, 1841-1881 are kept. The Croydon Collection, consisting of both printed and manuscript records, includes manorial documents, parochial archives, deeds, rate books, workhouse records and records of local government. There is the Mills Collection of notebooks, plans and drawings, and the Paget Collection of notebooks on the history of Croydon. There are also items concerning Addiscombe College. Council minutes are found as are papers relating to the sale of land and property.
Conditions of admission and access	The library is open to the public, but advance notice of a visit by those intending to consult this collection is appreciated. Inquiries should be directed to the Local Studies Librarian. Archives and reference material must be used in the Library.
Hours	9:30 AM - 7:00 PM, Monday; 9:30 AM - 6:00 PM, Tuesday-Friday; 9:00 AM - 5:00 PM, Saturday.
Duplicating facilities	Photocopying facilities are available.
Other services	Brief questions by telephone or post are answered and reference help is available. There are indexes and catalogs provided to aid the researcher.
Publications	Handlist of the Archive Holdings.

LONDON

178 Institution Address	London Borough of Enfield Libraries Department Local History Section Southgate Town Hall Green Lanes Palmers Green London N13 4E4
Telephone	01 886 6555, ext. 15
Holdings	The records of the Borough and material concerning Edmonton and Southgate as well as Enfield are held. Documents from former authorities are also found. There are School Board and Boards of Health papers for Enfield and Edmonton, and maps, prints, paintings, drawings and photographs in the collection.
Conditions of admission and access	Scholars are advised to make an appointment in advance of a visit. Inquiries should be directed to the Local History and Museum Officer. The collection must be used in the library.

Hours	9:00 AM - 5:00 PM, Monday-Saturday.
Duplicating facilities	Photocopying facilities are available.
Other services	Reference help is provided and brief questions by telephone or by post will be answered.
Publications	None.

LONDON (map)

179 Institution Address	London Borough of Greenwich Local History Library Woodlands 90 Mycenae Road Blackheath London SE3 7SE
Telephone	01 858 4631
Holdings	There are four constituent parts of the collection: the Local Collection (books, pamphlets, prints, drawings, maps, photographs, etc., relating to the history of the towns and villages within the London Borough of Greenwich); the Kent Collection (concerned with the history and topography of the County of Kent); the Martin Collection (a very extensive private bequest of documents on the history of Blackheath, Greenwich, Lewisham, and Kidbrooke); and the Archive Collection (the official records of the Borough and the former Civil Parishes, and other deposited records). Specifically the holdings include watercolors, drawings, prints, photographs and an indexed collection of transparencies. There are bound volumes of cuttings dating from 1895 and a comprehensive collection of maps. Several newspapers are held, dating from 1834, and a large group of directories, the earliest of which is 1792. The library has been appointed a Diocesan Record Office and is the official repository for records generated by the present Borough and former Metropolitan Borough. Several Parish registers are kept and include St. Luke's Charlton (baptisms, 1653-1864, marriages, 1653-1913, burials, 1653-1933), Holy Trinity Charlton (baptisms, 1886-1924, marriages, 1894-1939), St. Paul's, Charlton (baptisms, 1862-1901, marriages, 1867-1898), St. George's, Westcombe Park (baptisms, 1892-1950, marriages, 1892-1971), St. James', Kidbrooke (baptisms, 1867-1947, marriages, 1867-1967). Transcripts of other registers are also held. The records of the Roman Catholic, Our Lady Star of the Sea, have been deposited as well as Church Wardens' and vestry records from several parishes. Also parish rates, tithe maps

(photostat), charity records, overseers' accounts, workhouse minutes, Council and Committee minutes, electoral registers, sessions licencing records, schools', hospitals' records and manorial records are found. Microfilm copies of the census, 1841-1881, business records, deeds, family and estate records, organizations and societies' records and political party records are held.

Conditions of admission and access	The library is open to the public and visiting scholars are welcome to use the collection. The material must be used on the premises. Inquiries should be addressed to the Local History Librarian.
Hours	9:00 AM - 8:00 PM, Monday-Tuesday, Thursday; 9:00 AM - 5:00 PM, Saturday. Closed Wednesday and Friday.
Duplicating facilities	There are facilities available for photocopying, photography, and to make prints from microfilm.
Other services	Reference help is available in the library and brief questions can be answered by post or telephone. An educational service is available for local schools and colleges, and local history exhibitions are regularly held in the library.
Publications	The Buildings of Greenwich, by Alan Glencross (1974); Riverside Walk, by Alan Glencross and Julian Watson (1975); Around Greenwich Park, by Alan Glencross and Julian Watson (1976); John Julius Angerstein and Woodlands, by J. C. Bunston (1974).

LONDON

180 Institution Address	London Borough of Hammersmith Public Libraries Archives Department Shepherd's Bush Library 7 Uxbridge Road London W12 8LJ
Telephone	01 743 0910
Holdings	The library holds records from the Metropolitan Borough of Hammersmith and from Fulham. The Fulham Pottery records (1865-1968) and the Hammersmith Bridge Company records (1824-1880) are found here. There are also papers of individuals, including William Morris, Burne-Jones, and Sir William Bull. In addition one finds drawings, prints, and photographs, newspapers (West London Observer, from 1856) and newspaper cuttings. The census returns, 1841-1881 are held on microfilm.

Conditions of admission and access	Visiting scholars must have an appointment to use the collection. Inquiries should be addressed to the Borough Archivist. The collection must be used on the premises.
Hours	9:15 AM - 5:00 PM, Monday, Thursday-Friday; 9:15 AM - 8:00 PM, Tuesday; closed Wednesday. All hours are by appointment.
Duplicating facilities	Arrangements can be made for photocopying and photographs.
Other services	Brief questions by post or telephone are answered and reference help is provided.
Publications	Catalogs, lists, indexes.

LONDON

181	Institution Address	London Borough of Haringey Libraries Museum and Arts Service Bruce Castle Museum Lordship Lane London N17 8NU
	Telephone	01 808 8772
	Holdings	The library contains material relating to Haringey, Hornsey, Wood Green and Tottenham. The collection includes court rolls of the Manor of Tottenham, 1318-1732, parish records from Tottenham and Hornsey from the 15th century, Borough records and papers concerning Alexandra Park and Place. Census returns are kept, as are maps, plans, photographs, prints and news-papers. The library is a recommended depository for manorial and tithe documents.
	Conditions of admission and access	Researchers should give advance notice of a visit. Inquiries should be directed to the Archivist. The collection may be consulted only on the premises.
	Hours	10:00 AM - 5:00 PM, Tuesday-Friday; 10:00 AM - 12:30 PM, 1:30 PM - 5:00 PM, Saturday.
	Duplicating facilities	Photocopying and photography can be provided.
	Other services	There are indexes by person and place to the archives and reference aid is available. Brief questions by telephone or mail are answered.
	Publications	Court Rolls of the Manor Tottenham; handlists, indexes, translations, guides.

LONDON

182	Institution Address	London Borough of Havering Central Library St. Edward's Way Romford RM1 3AR
	Telephone	07 46040, ext. 355 during daytime hours; 07 44297, after five and on Saturday
	Holdings	Council minute books are held for Romford Urban District Council, Hornchurch Urban District Council, and Romford Borough. There are also parish rate books, Board of Health records and Liberty of Havering Treasurer's book (1835-1843). Newspaper cuttings, maps, plans, postcards, posters, and microfilm of items held in the Essex Record Office are found here.
	Conditions of admission and access	The library is open to the public. Inquiries should be addressed to the Reference and Information Librarian. Archives and reference books must be used in the library.
	Hours	9:30 AM - 8:00 PM, Monday-Friday; 9:30 AM - 5:00 PM, Saturday.
	Duplicating facilities	There are facilities for photocopying material.
	Other services	Reference help is provided and questions by post or telephone are answered.
	Publications	Romford Record, 1-14 (1969-1982); Subject Index to Romford Record; Subject Index to Havering Review, 1-10; guides, lists, indexes, and brochures.

LONDON

183	Institution Address	London Borough of Hounslow Reference Library Local History Collection Treaty Road Hounslow TW3 1DR
	Telephone	01 570 0622
	Holdings	The collection contains maps, plans and newspapers of the area and paintings, prints, and photographs. Church records include parish records from All Saints Church, Isleworth (1564-ca. 1900) and St. Lawrence's Church, Brentford (18th century), and St. Mary the Virgin, East Bedfont (dating from the 17th century). Local archives include minutes, rate books, and electoral registers.

Conditions of admission and access	The library is open to the public and appointments in advance are not required. Inquiries should be directed to the Local Studies Librarian. Reference works and archives must be used on the premises.
Hours	9:00 AM - 8:00 PM, Monday-Tuesday, Thursday; 9:00 AM - 1:00 PM, Wednesday; 9:00 AM - 5:00 PM, Friday-Saturday.
Duplicating facilities	Photocopies and full-size copies from microforms can be provided.
Other services	Brief questions are answered by telephone and by mail and reference help is available.
Publications	None.

LONDON

184 Institution Address	London Borough of Newham Local Studies Library Stratford Reference Library Water Lane London E15 4NJ
Telephone	01 534 4545, ext. 309/334
Holdings	Included in the collection are the archives of Newham Borough, Quarter Sessions Rolls from West Ham (1894-1965), and manorial documents. There are parochial records from East Ham, West Ham, Little Ilford, and Newham. Non-conformist records are also kept. Family and estate papers include those of Rawstorne of Plaidstow, Henniker of Stratford and East Ham and Stratford Abbey Landowners.
Conditions of admission and access	Researchers should make an appointment in advance of an intended visit. Inquiries should be addressed to the Assistant Borough Librarian of the Local Studies Library. The collection must be used on the premises.
Hours	9:30 AM - 7:00 PM, Monday-Tuesday, Thursday-Friday; 9:30 AM - 5:00 PM, Wednesday, Saturday.
Duplicating facilities	Photocopies and full-size copies from microforms can be provided.
Other services	Brief questions by mail or telephone are answered and reference help is available.
Publications	Brochures, indexes, guides.

LONDON

185	Institution Address	London Borough of Richmond-upon-Thames Libraries Department Central Library Reference and Information Service Little Green Richmond TW9 1QL

Telephone   010 940 9125

Holdings   The collection includes rate books, workhouse
                       records and Richmond vestry minutes for the 19th
                       and 20th century, and Council records and other
                       papers concerning Richmond, East Sheen, Peter-
                       sham, Kew, Ham, and Mortlake. Burial records
                       from Richmond Cemetery are also held. School
                       records, deeds, press cuttings, newspapers, and
                       playbills are found. The collection of Douglas
                       Sladen, which contains correspondence and cut-
                       tings, is held by the library. The census returns,
                       1841-1881 are on microfilm and there are postcards,
                       prints, drawings, engravings, and photographs.

Conditions of   It is advisable for researchers to make an appoint-
admission and   ment in advance of a visit. Inquiries should be
access   directed to the Reference Librarian. The collec-
                       tion must be used on the premises.

Hours   10:00 AM - 6:00 PM, Monday-Friday; 9:00 AM -
                       5:00 PM, Saturday.

Duplicating   Photocopies and full-size copies from microfilm
facilities   can be provided.

Other services   Reference help is available and those questions by
                       telephone or post that do not require extensive
                       research are answered.

Publications   Indexes, guides, and brochures are produced.

LONDON

186	Institution Address	London Borough of Tower Hamlets Local History Library Tower Hamlets Central Library 277 Bancroft Road London E1 4DB

Telephone   01 980 4366, ext. 47

Underground   Mile End, Stepney Green

Holdings   The library contains photographs, prints, cuttings,
                       directories, and local newspapers. The census
                       returns, 1841-1881 are held on microfilm. A large

collection of title deeds is found and also records relating to World War II. Material concerning Tower Hamlets and the former Metropolitan Boroughs of Stepney, Poplar, and Bethnal Green are also found. Papers about merchant shipping include the Bolt Collection of notes, cuttings, and photographs of ships.

Conditions of admission and access	The library is open to the public and advance notice of a visit is not required.
Hours	9:00 AM - 8:00 PM, Monday-Tuesday, Thursday-Friday; 9:00 AM - 5:00 PM, Wednesday, Saturday.
Duplicating facilities	Photocopying facilities are available and full-size copies from microforms can be provided.
Other services	Reference help is available, questions by telephone are answered, and those by mail that require brief responses are answered.
Publications	Bygone Tower Hamlets (portfolio of prints); History of Tower Hamlets, by C. Kerrigan.

LONDON

Institution	Mocatta Library See: LONDON, University College London, Mocatta Library

LONDON

Institution	National Monuments Record See: LONDON, Royal Commission on Historical Monuments

LONDON (map)

187 Institution Address	Office of Population Censuses and Surveys St. Catherines House 10 Kingsway London WC2B 6JP
Underground	Holborn
Telephone	01 242 0262
Holdings	The Office of Population Censuses and Surveys was created in 1970 by the merger of the General Register Office for England and Wales and the Government Social Survey. The General Register Office was established in 1837 to coordinate local registrations of births, deaths, and marriages, to

organize the decennial census of population, and
to collect demographic, social, and medical data
(e.g., population estimates and projections, cancer registrations, statistics on abortions and infectious diseases, etc.). There is still a Social
Survey Division of the Population Censuses and
Surveys which carries out continuous and ad hoc
surveys, e.g., Family Expenditure and Labor
Force (continuous) and Access to Primary Health
Care and Smoking Attitudes and Behavior (ad
hoc).

The major subject areas in the library are
demography, vital registration, epidemiology, survey methodology, computing, and both social and
health sciences. Special collections include Censuses of the United Kingdom from 1801 onwards,
Census Small Area Statistics for 1971 and 1981
(in microform), a complete set of population and
health statistics (which, since 1974, has been
divided into nineteen annual topic volumes), and
a complete set of Social Survey reports from 1941.
Foreign censuses and statistical series are also
kept and include the United States Census from
1830 (the fifth), Belgian material from 1846, and
material from international organizations. There
are also a number of older books and manuscripts
which illustrate the role played by vital statistics
in the public health movement in the 17th, 18th
and 19th centuries. These include works by John
Graunt, John Snow, William Farr, and Florence
Nightingale. Other resources include social survey
reports, material relating to law, demography,
statistical methods, and administration of births,
deaths, and marriage registration. The Office
contains a central record of all births, deaths,
and marriages registered in England and Wales
since 1837. An index to these records, arranged
in alphabetical order within each quarter of each
year, gives in all cases the surname, forename,
place, year, and quarter for each event. In the
case of births, the mother's maiden name is given,
and in the case of marriage, the name of both
persons being married is given. Specific information in the Census of Population (held every ten
years) is kept secret for one hundred years, then
deposited in the Public Record Office. Published
census statistics are available in the library as
noted. Unpublished statistics may be acquired
from Office of Population Censuses and Surveys
Customer Service (Segensworth Road, Titchfield,
Fareham, Hampshire PO15 5RR; telephone: 0329
442511).

Conditions of
admission and
access

Visiting scholars are welcome to use the library.
Because space is limited, an appointment in advance is recommended and is essential when research requires use of the Census Small Area

Statistics. The collection must be used on the premises. The indexes held by the office are available to the public, but the records themselves are not. Copies of records can be acquired, however, by anyone who wishes to see them, on payment of a fee. Copies may be acquired either in person or by post. For copies of certificates, inquiries should be addressed to the Registrar General. Because of the arrangement of the indexes, specific dates are needed and genealogical research is difficult.

Hours

The hours for the Public Search Room are: 8:30 AM - 4:30 PM, Monday-Friday; the hours for the Library are 9:00 AM - 4:00 PM, Monday-Friday.

Duplicating facilities

A copying service is available from within the office, but not from within the library. A twenty-four-hour delay should be expected.

Other services

Inquiries for specific records are handled for a fee. No extensive searches are undertaken, so a reasonable amount of information is necessary. The library will lend material to other libraries.

Publications

Statistics of population, births, deaths, marriages, divorces, migration, infectious diseases, and morbidity are published. Some of these are weekly publications, some quarterly, and some annual. A complete list of publications is found in Her Majesty's Stationery Office Sectional List No. 56. In addition, library staff produces a number of publications which are available free upon request. A monthly accessions bulletin is issued, as are, periodically, bibliographies and lists on topics of special interest to the Office, comprising items held in library stock. These topics include The 1981 Census of Population; Cancer Statistics: Some Works ...; William Farr: Some Works by and About Him ...; Migration and the UK ...; Population Projections ...; Tracing Your Family History; Ethnic Minorities .... (A complete list of these is available.)

LONDON (map)

188 Institution
    Address

Principal Registry of the Family Division
Somerset House
Strand
London   WC2R 1LP

Telephone

01 936 7000

Underground

The Temple

Holdings	The collection consists of a copy of every will proved in England and Wales since January 12, 1858. Index books (Calendar Books), which detail all grants of representation issued, are available for inspection. A number of other documents relating to cases not more than fifty years old are kept, but access to these may be restricted.
Conditions of admission and access	The collection is open to the public and the Calendar Books may be consulted without a fee. When a specific entry has been located, a copy of the grant or of the will may be inspected on payment of a fee. Copies may be obtained, and in this case a per page fee is charged. A Literary Permit (sometimes called a Search Permit) will allow viewing of documents (including original and copies of wills) more than one hundred years old without payment of the fee. These are normally issued to persons engaged in regular genealogical research. This permit does not exempt one from paying a fee for viewing a document less than one hundred years old. Inquiries should be directed to the Record Keeper. The material must be used on the premises.
Hours	10:00 AM - 4:30 PM, Monday-Friday.
Duplicating facilities	Facilities for copying documents are available.
Other services	Brief questions by telephone or post are answered and reference help is available.
Publications	Information concerning the location of documents is provided in leaflets and pamphlets. Forms are provided for ordering documents or copies of documents.

LONDON (map)

189 Institution Address	Public Record Office Chancery Lane London WC2A 1LR
Telephone	01 405 0741
Underground	Chancery Lane; Temple
	and Ruskin Avenue Kew, Richmond Surrey TW9 4DU
Telephone	01 876 3444
Underground	Kew Gardens

Holdings

The Public Record Office is the repository for
those records of the government of the United
Kingdom and of the Courts of Law of England and
Wales selected for permanent preservation. They
date from 1086, the Domesday Book, to the
present. The history of the British Isles is represented and all those parts of the world with
which Great Britain has been involved. Records
of government activity or government-sponsored
activity including scientific research, exploration,
medical and artistic administration, and political,
social, economic, and administrative history are
found in the collection. Records from the Norman
Conquest onwards of the King's Court and the
branches through which administrative, financial,
and judicial functions are discharged are held.
Archives of the Chancery, the Exchequer and the
various Courts of Common Law, the Palatinates
and other special jurisdictions are kept. Also
found are state papers from the accession of
Henry VIII onward, and also the records of the
Admiralty and all central government departments
of later origin. In one year, 3,960 linear feet
were added to the holdings, which occupy over
85 miles of shelving.

Conditions of
admission and
access

The Record Office is open to the public, but a
reader's ticket must be obtained for admission.
These are available at either address. No prior
formality is involved, but positive proof of identification must be produced. Records are normally
available for public inspection when they are
thirty years old. Records of the Courts of Law
from the earliest times until the present day, and
of the central government until approximately
1800, are held in Chancery Lane. Records of
modern departments of state are held at Kew.
The division of the records between the two addresses is shown in "Information for Readers,"
which is available from the record office. There
is a census reading room at Chancery Lane where
the population census returns, 1841-1881 may be
seen on microfilm. In general, documents must
be requested before 3:30 PM for use on the same
day, and only three documents may be ordered at
one time without special arrangements. Written
communication should be addressed to the Enquiries Desk (Requisitions). Records which are
open to inspection are seen only in the building
in which they are stored. Not all official records
are located at the Public Record Office as some
have been placed in local repositories. In addition, some government departments keep their
own records. The Principal Probate Registry contains registrations of wills (see entry no. 188)
and the Foreign and Commonwealth Office holds
the records of the former India Office, including

those of the East India Company and those relating
to the Indian Army (see India Office Library and
Records, entry no. 157). Other official deposi-
tories outside the Public Record Office include the
House of Lords Record Office (entry no. 167), the
Scottish Record Office (entry no. 97), the Public
Record Office of Northern Ireland (entry no. 27),
The General Registrar's Office for Northern Ire-
land (entry no. 25).

Hours	9: 30 AM - 5: 00 PM, Monday-Friday.

Duplicating
facilities

The Photographic Section of the Public Record
Office furnishes copies of documents by microfilm,
photocopy, electro-static prints from microfilm,
and photographic processes. There is usually a
delay in receiving copies and this may be up to a
week for photocopying (depending on demand).
For microfilm, three months or more should be allowed for documents which have already been
filmed, and six months or more for those which
have not.

Other services

Visiting scholars should go first to the Enquiries
Desk where they will be directed to the appro-
priate search room. The staff will assist them in
a procedure for ordering documents for which
requisition forms are provided. Only brief
queries by post or telephone can be answered,
but reference help is available in the search rooms.
Ultra-violet lights are provided.

Publications

Guide to Contents of the Public Record Office,
Vol. 1- ; brochures and information leaflets on
areas of frequent study, "Information for Readers"
and "Notes for New Readers" are provided to aid
the researcher. A list and description of other
publications can be found in Her Majesty's Stationery Office Sectional List No. 24, British National
Archives. The Current Guide to the Public
Records is available in loose-leaf form in the
reference and reading room at Kew and Chancery
Lane.

LONDON (map)

190 Institution
Address

The Royal Commission on Historical Manuscripts
Quality House, Quality Court
Chancery Lane
London WC2A 1HP

Underground

Chancery Lane

Telephone

01 242 1198

Holdings

The commission maintains the National Register of

Archives, in which are filed some 30,000 unpublished lists of the manuscript holdings of record offices, libraries, private organizations and individuals, with details of location and conditions of access. There are indexes of prominent personages, of companies and of subjects. A leaflet is available on request which describes this scope. The search room also holds many published finding aids. Records of central government departments and courts are not included.

Conditions of admission and access	Visiting scholars are welcome to consult the National Register of Archives. Inquiries should be directed to the Secretary. No appointment in advance is required. The Register may be consulted only in the Commission's search room.
Hours	9:30 AM - 5:00 PM, Monday-Friday, except public holidays.
Duplicating facilities	Copying facilities are not available.
Other services	The commission advises scholars on the location of primary sources. Limited and specific inquiries can be answered by post.
Publications	Secretary's Report to the Commissioners (annual); Accessions to Repositories (annual); Record Repositories in Great Britain (8th ed., 1987); Occasional Commissioners' Reports to the Crown-- Twenty-Sixth Report 1968-1981 (HMSO 1983). For a complete list see HMSO's Sectional List no. 17.

LONDON

191 Institution Address	Royal Commission on the Historical Monuments of England National Monuments Record Fortress House 23 Savile Row London W1X 1AB
Telephone	01 734 6010
Underground	Oxford Circus; Piccadilly Circus
	See also: ABERYSTWYTH, Royal Commission on Ancient and Historical Monuments in Wales; EDINBURGH, Royal Commission on the Ancient and Historical Monuments of Scotland
Holdings	The collection includes periodicals, books on English architectural history, and works on architecture of all styles. A copy of the Council for British Archaeology, Industrial Archaeology

<u>Index</u>, Goodhart Rendel's Index of <u>19th Century</u>
<u>Churches</u>, and lists of English buildings of ar-
chitectural or historic interest are found. The
Architectural Records Section contains about a
million photographs of over 100,000 buildings and
measured drawings of buildings. Other archaeological material, including the <u>Ordnance Survey Ar-</u>
<u>chaeological Index</u>, is kept as well as air photo-
graphs and other material on historic buildings.
Excavation records are held on microfiche.

Conditions of admission and access	The collection is open to the public and no ap-pointment in advance is required. Computeriza-tion of the archives and automated accession and retrieval is an on-going project. Inquiries should be directed to the Secretary. The collection must be used on the premises.
Hours	10:00 AM - 5:30 PM, Monday-Friday, except pub-lic holidays.
Duplicating facilities	Photography and photocopies can be supplied for a fee.
Other services	Brief questions by post or telephone are answered and reference help is available.
Publications	The Royal Commission on Historical Monuments is-sues many publications through HMSO. These in-clude inventories, monographs, brochures, reports, and lists.

LONDON

192 Institution Address	Society of Antiquaries of London Library Burlington House Piccadilly London W1V 0HS
Telephone	01 734 0193; 01 437 9954
Underground	Piccadilly Circus
Holdings	The library contains works on archaeology, both British and foreign. There are resources in his-tory, genealogy, bibliography, topography, pre-history, classical archaeology, architecture, and heraldry, a small collection on Celtic art, and some liturgical works. British and foreign periodicals and the publications of other societies are held. There are special collections of manuscripts, early printed books, broadsides, seal casts, brass rubbings, proclamations, and prints and drawings. An extensive collection of works by and about William Morris is held, but prior arrangements must be made to gain access.

Conditions of admission and access	The library is open to those with a valid reason for studying the material it contains, but a letter of introduction, preferably by a Fellow, is required to use the collection. Inquiries should be directed to the Librarian. Visiting scholars must use the collection on the premises.
Hours	10:00 AM - 5:00 PM, Monday-Friday.
Duplicating facilities	Photocopying, microfilming, and photographic facilities are available.
Other services	Brief questions by telephone or post are answered. Reference help is provided in the library as are catalogs, indexes, and other finding aids.
Publications	History of the Society of Antiquaries, by Joan Evans (1956); Catalogue of the Manuscripts in the Library of the Society of Antiquaries, by H. Ellis (1816).

LONDON

193 Institution Address	Society of Genealogists 14 Charterhouse Buildings Goswell Road London EC1M 7BA
Telephone	01 251 8799
Underground	Barbican
Holdings	The Library of the Society of Genealogists has one of the best collections, including printed books and manuscripts, on the subject in the United Kingdom. The country's largest collection of Parish Register copies is found here and includes an almost complete series of all that have ever been printed and many in manuscript and typescript. There are also poll books, directories, publications of County Records and archaeological societies, and topographical material. The published matriculation registers of Oxford, Cambridge, and other universities are found here, as are army and navy lists dating from the mid-eighteenth century, a collection of regimental histories, and naval biographies. Monumental inscriptions and county histories are also held. Records of City livery companies, and papers of Inns of Court, wills, marriage licences, individual pedigrees, information on families, and family histories form an important part of the collection. The International Genealogical Index (IGI) (world-wide coverage), the Australian General Register Office Indexes (except Tasmania), the Scottish General Register Office Indexes to 1920, and Irish Will Abstracts and

Marriage Licences, 1599-1800 are available here.
There are also sections dealing with professions,
religious denominations, the peerage and heraldry,
and collections of material on English persons
living abroad--in the Commonwealth and in the
United States. A large collection of genealogical
periodicals constitutes an essential part of the
library and the finding aids, indexes, catalogues,
lists, and calendars, both printed and manuscript,
contribute in large part to making this one of the
finest libraries of its kind to be found.

Conditions of admission and access

The library is open to members of the Society and
to others on payment of a fee. One can become
a member on being proposed and seconded by
members or through a letter of recommendation
from a responsible party to the Executive Committee.
Inquiries concerning the collection should be directed to the Librarian. Those concerning the Society
should be addressed to the Director and Secretary.
The collection must be used on the premises by
non-members. Members may borrow printed books
with certain exceptions.

Hours

10:00 AM - 6:00 PM, Tuesday, Friday and Saturday; 10:00 AM - 8:00 PM, Wednesday and Thursday.
Closed on Monday and for one week in February
and in October.

Duplicating facilities

Photocopying facilities are available.

Other services

Brief questions by telephone and by post are
answered and reference help is provided in the
library. The Society will undertake research for
non-members in the Society's rooms and elsewhere
for a fee. The many indexes, catalogues and
other finding aids further aid the researcher in
his work.

Publications

Genealogists' Magazine (quarterly); Genealogists'
Handbook (1969); National Index of Parish
Registers, Vol. 1- ; A Catalogue of Parish Regis-
ter Copies in the Possession of the Society of
Genealogists (1985); A Catalogue of Directories and
Poll Books in the Possession of the Society of
Genealogists (1984); A Key to Boyd's Marriage In-
dex (1984); My Ancestor Was a Merchant Seaman
(1986); My Ancestors Were Jewish (1983); My
Ancestor Was a Methodist (reprint); Using the
Library of the Society of Genealogists (1985);
Marriage Licences: Abstracts and Indexes in the
Society of Genealogists (1983); Monumental In-
scriptions in the ... Society of Genealogists: Pt.
1: Southern England (1984); My Ancestors Were
Quakers (1983); Lancashire Association Oath Rolls
1696 (1985); Society of Genealogists Leaflets Nos.
1-15; "Introduction to" ... various topics.

LONDON

194 Institution   Southwark Local Studies Library
Address   211 Borough High Street
                   London SE1 1JA

Telephone   01 403 3507

Holdings   The library contains poor law records, family and estate papers, churchwardens' accounts, rate books, highway records and parish records for St. Saviour, St. Olave, St. Giles (Camberwell), St. George, Christ Church, St. Thomas, St. Mary Magdalen (Bermondsey), St. Mary (Newington) and St. Mary (Rotherhithe), and St. John Harsleydown. These date from 1546. Methodist records are kept, deeds are found and there are maps, prints, and photographs. Press cuttings, newspapers, and directories are also found. Census returns are held on microfilm.

Conditions of   The library is open to the public, but there are
admission and   restrictions on some records. Advance notice is
access   appreciated and is necessary for Saturday visits. Inquiries should be directed to the Local Studies Librarian. The collection must be consulted in the library.

Hours   9:30 AM - 12:30 PM, 1:30 PM - 8:00 PM, Monday, Thursday; 9:30 AM - 12:30 PM, 1:30 PM - 5:00 PM, Tuesday, Friday; 9:30 AM - 1:00 PM, Saturday, by appointment.

Duplicating   Photocopies and full-size copies from microforms
facilities   can be provided.

Other services   Name and place indexes and a calendar of the deeds are available. Short questions are answered by telephone or by mail and reference service is provided.

Publications   Calendars, indexes, guides.

LONDON (map)

195 Institution   University College London
Address   Manuscripts Room, The Library
                   Gower Street
                   London WC1E 6BT

Telephone   01 387 7050, ext. 249

Underground   Goodge Street, Euston Square, Russell Square

Holdings   The correspondence and papers of political, literary, and scientific figures are held, including that

of Lord Brougham (1778-1868), Jeremy Bentham
(1748-1832), Sir Edwin Chadwick (1800-1890),
Karl Pearson (1857-1936), Sir Francis Galton
(1822-1911), Lionel Penrose (1878-1972), and
George Orwell (1911-1950). The publishing archives of Routledge and Kegan Paul, Ltd. (ledgers, authors' agreements, correspondence, printed
catalogs, and other papers, 1853-1973; correspondence files are at the University of Reading
Library) are found and the papers of the Society
for the Diffusion of Useful Knowledge. Papers of
U.C.L. professors and college archives are also
kept. (Some records are held by the College
Records Office.) The Latin American Business
Archives form a very important collection. Photographs are also kept. Medieval manuscripts and
collections of Celtic, English, French, Icelandic,
Italian and Spanish manuscripts are also found.

Conditions of admission and access	Visiting scholars should have a letter of introduc-tion and an appointment in advance is essential. Proof of identity is also required. Users must sign a statement that they will abide by the rules governing access to archives and manuscripts, and that they will indemnify the college and the owners of deposited collections against claims for libel, infringement of copyright or breach of confidence. Inquiries should be addressed to the Archivist. The collection may be consulted only on the premises. In general, manuscript collections are closed to access for thirty years. At the discre-tion of the Archivist or at the request of the owner, some are closed for longer periods, and collections are closed until they have been cataloged. A list is available which indicates restrictions.
Hours	10:00 AM - 5:30 PM, Monday-Friday during the term (by appointment); 10:00 AM - 5:00 PM, Monday-Friday during vacation (also by appoint-ment). The college is closed for a week at Christmas and Easter. The Manuscripts Room closes for part of the summer vacation and may be closed at short notice at other times.
Duplicating facilities	Photocopies, microfilms and photographs can be provided. The originals must be in sound condi-tion and there may be no infringement of copy-right.
Other services	Brief postal and telephone inquiries are answered and reference help is available. The staff does not undertake research inquiries, but will advise users about resources for their work. Many lists, indexes, and finding aids are provided, and an ultra-violet lamp is available.
Publications	The University College London has a very active

publishing program. Publications relating to the
Manuscripts Collection include <u>Descriptive Cata-</u>
<u>logue of Manuscripts in the Library of University</u>
<u>College</u>, by D. K. Coveney (1935); <u>Catalogue of</u>
<u>the Manuscripts of Jeremy Bentham in the Library</u>
<u>of U.C.L.</u>, by A. Taylor Milne (1937); <u>Medieval</u>
<u>Manuscripts in British Libraries, London</u>, by
N. R. Ker (1969); <u>Manuscript Collections in the</u>
<u>University College London</u>, by J. Percival;
(Occasional Publications of U.C.L. Library, No. 1,
London, 2/1978; Nos. 3-7, handlists to the Chad-
wick Champers and Society for the Diffusion of
Useful Knowledge papers and to the Archives of
Routledge and Kegan Paul and of the Peruvian
Corporation); <u>A List of the Papers and Corres-</u>
<u>pondence of Sir Francis Galton, 1822-1911</u>, by M.
Merrington and J. Golden (1978); <u>A List of the</u>
<u>Papers and Correspondence of Lionel Sharples</u>
<u>Penrose, 1898-1972</u>, by M. Merrington, and
others (1979); <u>A List of the Papers and the Cor-</u>
<u>respondence of George Bellas Greenough, 1778-</u>
<u>1855</u>, by J. Golden (1981); <u>A List of the Papers</u>
<u>and Correspondence of Karl Pearson</u> (in prepara-
tion).

LONDON (map)

196	Institution Address	University College London Mocatta Library Gower Street London WC1E 6BT
	Telephone	01 387 7050, ext. 778
	Underground	Goodge Street, Euston Square, Russell Square
	Holdings	Papers of Jewish persons, including those of Lucien Wolff (manuscripts of Anglo-Jewish inter- est); the Lowy family papers from the early 18th century, which include a history of the Jews in Moravia (1722); and the diaries, account books, and letters of Sir Moses Montefiore (1827-ca. 1874) are kept here. Also found are the letters of George and Henry Gawler, which relate to ag- ricultural and industrial training, and the corres- pondence, manuscripts, photographs, and ephemera of Dr. Moses Gaster (1870-1939). The Collyer- Ferguson collection (genealogy) is held on micro- film and portraits and caricatures of Anglo-Jewish people and newspaper cuttings are also found. Located next to the Mocatta Library is the Anglo- Jewish Archive (a branch of the Jewish Historical Society), a collection which began about 1968. Prior to that time, deposits were made in the Mo- catta Library. The Archive consists of material relating to Anglo-Jewish individuals and institutions,

mostly from the 19th century, including the records of the Anglo-Jewish Association and the papers of the historian, Cecil Roth.

Conditions of admission and access

The collection is open to members of the Jewish Historical Society of England and of the University College London. The public may use the material, but if the research is extensive, permission is required of the Librarian of University College. The collection may be used on the premises. Inquiries should be made to the Librarian (of the Mocatta Library or of the University College).

Hours

2:00 PM - 4:00 PM, Monday-Friday. The collection may be consulted on Monday and Friday morning by prior appointment and the Gaster papers may be used in the mornings, but arrangements must be made in advance.

Duplicating facilities

Photocopying facilities are available.

Other services

Brief questions by post or telephone are answered and reference help is provided. A card index of the collection is available and a microfilm reader is provided, by arrangement.

Publications

The University College London engages in a very active publishing program. Publications relating to the Mocatta Library collection include Guide to the Gaster Papers (1973); The Gaster Papers, Occasional Paper, No. 2 (1976).

LONDON (map)

197 Institution
Address

University of London Library
Senate House
Malet Street
London WC1E 7HU

Telephone

01 636 4514

Underground

Russell Square

Holdings

The library contains over a million volumes with material covering a wide range of subjects. There are many special collections which render the library a valuable resource, including Goldsmiths' Library, the United States Library, and the Family Welfare Association Library. The Palaeography Room houses many interesting manuscripts and includes works on English social and economic history, papers of individuals formerly connected with the university, and some medieval, palaeographical, topographical, and literary material. Among the papers held are those of Colonel

Alfred Claude Bromhead, August De Morgan, Sir
Banister Flight Fletcher, Colonel Thomas Herbert
Lewin, Malcolm Morley, Thomas Newton, Harry
Price, Herbert Spencer, and Cyril Ernest Wright.
A collection of eighty charters dating from ca.
1162 to 1659 is also found. Archives of the Committee on Adult Education, the Institute of Historical Research manuscripts, the Scarman Inquiry,
and the Stourbridge Ironworks are available.
The Newton Estate (Barbados) papers and a microfilm copy of the Blathwayt Papers are found.

Conditions of
admission and
access

Visiting scholars should provide a letter of introduction and make an appointment in advance of
their first visit. Inquiries should be directed to
the Archivist (Palaeography Room) or to the
Director of Central Library Services and Goldsmiths' Librarian. In order to use the library,
the visitor must apply in writing to the Director
and must show a particular need to use the collection (such as the presence in the Library of material which is unavailable elsewhere). If one is
issued a Library Ticket it will normally be for
reference use only. Some collections are subject
to restrictions and most material in the archives
is subject to the thirty year rule.

Hours

9:30 AM - 9:00 PM, Monday-Thursday; 9:30 AM -
6:30 PM, Friday; 9:30 AM - 5:30 PM, Saturday
during term and Easter vacation. 9:30 AM -
5:30 PM, Monday-Saturday, Christmas and summer vacation. Book-stack service is not available
through the full range of opening hours. The
Palaeography Room is open 9:30 AM - 5:30 PM,
Monday-Friday.

Duplicating
facilities

Photocopying facilities are available, and microfilm,
enlargements, and slides can be provided. Details are available in the leaflet, "Photocopying."

Other services

Brief questions by post or telephone will be
answered and reference help is provided. The
staff does not undertake research for the scholar.
Many finding aids, lists, catalogs, and indexes
are available to further aid the scholar.

Publications

The University of London Library engages in an
active publication program and has produced many
valuable guides, bibliographies, descriptions, and
lists which facilitate the researcher's use of the
collection. Other institutions have also published
works relating to this material.

LONDON

198 Institution   Upper Norwood Public Library
     Address

Westow Hill
Upper Norwood
London SE19 1TJ

Telephone	01 670 2551
Holdings	Newspapers and press cuttings are found here and maps, handbills, and pamphlets are kept. The collection includes works on the local history of Southwark, Camberwell, Dulwich, Sydenham, Penge, Croydon and Anerley, and material relating to the Crystal Palace.
Conditions of admission and access	The library is open to the public and arrangements do not have to be made in advance of a visit. Inquiries should be addressed to the Librarian. The archives must be used in the library.
Hours	10:00 AM - 7:00 PM, Monday; 9:00 AM - 7:00 PM, Tuesday-Friday; 9:00 AM - 5:00 PM, Saturday.
Duplicating facilities	Facilities for photocopying are available.
Other services	Questions by telephone or mail will be answered if they are short. Reference help is available in the library.
Publications	Lists, guides, fact-sheets, brochures.

LONDON

199	Institution Address	Westminster Abbey Muniment Room and Library Westminster Abbey London SW1 3PA
	Telephone	01 222 5152, ext. 28
	Underground	Westminster, St. James's Park
	Holdings	The holdings include Westminster Abbey registers for baptisms, 1608-1876, for marriages, 1655-1876, and for burials, 1604 to date. St. Margaret's Westminster Parish Registers include baptisms, 1538-1944, marriages, 1538-1973, and burials, 1538-1853. Coroners inquests for Westminster, 1760-1878 are also found, as are lease books for abbey property, 1485-1846 and local history records of some abbey parishes for varying dates, including some maps, plans, and deeds. There are works in the library on the history and building of Westminster Abbey and its estates from AD 784.
	Conditions of admission and access	Bona fide scholars are allowed to use the collection. An appointment in advance is necessary and

students should provide a letter of introduction. The collection must be used on the premises. Inquiries should be made to the Keeper of the Muniments.

Hours	10:00 AM - 1:00 PM, 2:00 PM - 4:45 PM, Monday-Friday.
Duplicating facilities	Photocopying is available if the document is suitable, and photography can be provided.
Other services	Reference help is available and very brief questions by post or telephone are answered. An ultra-violet lamp is provided.
Publications	There are no recent publications. The <u>Transactions of the Royal Historical Society</u>, 4th series, Vol. 19 (1936) gives a description of the muniments.

LONDON (map)

200 Institution Address	Westminster City Libraries Marylebone Library Westminster Archives and Local History Department Marylebone Road London NW1 5PS
Telephone	01 798 1030
Underground	Baker Street
	<u>See also</u>: LONDON, Westminster City Libraries, Victoria Library
Holdings	Material relating to the former St. Marylebone and Paddington is found here. The St. Marylebone Archives include the Ashbridge Collection, which is a comprehensive private collection of books, maps, prints, watercolors, and drawings relating to St. Marylebone. The Paddington Archives include official papers, vouchers and miscellaneous papers relating to the parish from ca. 1750-1850. Among the illustrations are prints, watercolors, drawings, and photographs pertaining to St. Marylebone and Paddington and dating from the 17th century. Portraits of celebrities who lived in St. Marylebone are also found. A cutting collection is maintained and also maps and plans, newspapers, and directories. Parochial and other religious records include church wardens and vestry records, parish rates, tithe, charity and poor relief. Local government archives include council and committee minutes, accounts and financial papers, ratebooks, and electoral registers. Sessions records, licensing records, schools, hospitals and

other institutions' papers, and manorial records
are also found. Census returns are available on
microfilm. Business records, deeds, family and
estate records, the papers of societies and a miscellaneous collection of mainly nineteenth-century
letters from well-known residents of Paddington
and St. Marylebone are also available.

Conditions of admission and access	The Library and the Archives Department are open to the public. An appointment in advance is not required, but notification of a visit is preferred. The collection must be used on the premises. Inquiries should be directed to the Chief Archivist (Westminster City Libraries Victoria Library, Westminster Archives and Local History Department, 160 Buckingham Palace Road, London SW1W 9UD; telephone 01 798 2180) or to the Archivist at the address above.
Hours	9:30 AM - 7:00 PM, Monday-Friday; 9:30 AM - 1:00 PM, 2:00 PM - 5:00 PM, Saturday.
Duplicating facilities	Photocopies can be supplied and arrangements can be made for photographs of material. Full-size copies of microfilm can be provided.
Other services	Brief postal or telephone inquiries are answered and reference help is available. Exhibitions are organized and lectures and slide-talks are given.
Publications	Guides, brochures, lists, and a folder of black and white reproductions of eighteenth- and nine-teenth-century engravings and postcards of prints have been produced.

LONDON (map)

201	Institution Address	Westminster City Libraries Victoria Library Westminster Archives and Local History Department 160 Buckingham Palace Road London SW1W 9UD
	Telephone	01 798 2180
	Underground	Victoria
		See also: LONDON, Westminster City Libraries, Marylebone Library
	Holdings	The department holds the records of the ten parishes which formed the City of Westminster in 1900. The collection includes prints, watercolors, engravings, and photographs. A cuttings collection is maintained and includes items from 19th-century editions of the Illustrated London News.

Maps and plans are kept and there is a large collection of theater material including programs, playbills, newscuttings and portraits dating from the early 19th century. Directories are also found. Parochial and other religious records include parish registers, churchwardens' and vestry records, parish rates, tithe records, charity and poor relief papers, and the records of non-conformist churches (St. Mary, Lutheran Church of the Savoy, Chelsea Methodist Church). Local government archives include council and committee minutes, Westminster Court of Burgesses, Strand Board of Works, and Westminster City Council accounts and financial papers, rate books, and electoral registers. Sessions records, licencing records, legal and judicial papers, schools, hospitals and other institutions' papers are also kept. Manorial records, wills proved in the Commissary Court of the Dean and Chapter of Westminster and census returns are found. Business records, deeds, family and estate records and papers of societies are available.

Conditions of admission and access	The collection is open to the public and no appointment in advance is required. Inquiries should be addressed to the Chief Archivist. The collection must be used on the premises.
Hours	9:30 AM - 7:00 PM, Monday-Friday; 9:30 AM - 1:00 PM, 2:00 PM - 5:00 PM, Saturday.
Duplicating facilities	Photocopies and full-size copies from microforms can be provided and arrangements can be made for photographs of material.
Other services	Brief postal and telephone inquiries are answered and reference help is provided. Exhibits are organized and lectures and slide talks are given, and an ultra-violet lamp is available.

LONDONDERRY (map)

202		
	Institution Address	University of Ulster Magee College Northland Road Londonderry BT 48 7JL
	Telephone	0504 265621
	Holdings	Some sources indicate this is a rich source of genealogical material concerning the families of the county of Derry and City of Londonderry and that the collection contains the "Adair Narrative," 1622-1670, transcripts of minutes of meetings and typed copies of documents formerly found in the Public Record Office (Dublin) concerning protestant emigrations. There is also an extensive

collection of old newspapers. A reply received from the University, however, indicated that only secondary sources are available. The scholar may wish to send a letter of inquiry before a visit.

Conditions of admission and access	The collection may be used by students and faculty of the university and such external readers as are authorized by the Librarian. The material must be used on the premises. Inquiries should be directed to the Librarian.
Hours	9:30 AM - 9:00 PM, Monday-Thursday; 9:30 AM - 5:30 PM, Friday; 9:30 AM - 12:30 PM, Saturday during term. 9:30 AM - 12:45 PM, 2:00 PM - 5:00 PM, Monday-Friday, during vacation.
Duplicating facilities	Facilities are available for duplicating material.
Other services	Brief questions by post or telephone are answered and reference aid is available.
Publications	Reader's Guides are available in the library.

LYDD

203	Institution	Lydd Borough Archives
	Address	Corporate Member of the Confederation of the Cinque Ports
		The Town Clerk
		The Guild Hall
		High Street
		Lydd, Romney Marsh TN29 9AF
	Telephone	0679 20999
		See also: MAIDSTONE, Kent Archives Office
	Holdings	The collection includes the Borough of Lydd records from ca. 1400-1974 and some parish, charity and drainage records. Charters from the 14th to the 17th century, court books from the 16th century, including sessions books and Borough Court of Record, and plea books are held. Legal documents, including grants, deeds, petitions and depositions, are found, as are militia lists, oath rolls, burgess rolls and freeman records, jurats' and chamberlains' accounts (from 1422), minute books, rentals, rate books and scot lists, some 16th-century drainage records, church wardens' and overseers' accounts, the tithe map and apportionment and Ordnance Survey maps from 1871.
	Conditions of admission and access	The collections can only be used by appointment and on the premises. The majority of the 19th-

and 20th-century documents are as yet uncata-
loged, although most are briefly listed. Uncata-
loged archives will only be made available in ex-
ceptional circumstances. A letter of introduction
is normally required from a professional referee
with personal knowledge of the applicant. No
access to casual callers is permitted and persons
without appointments or credentials will be refused
access. Inquiries should be directed to the Town
Clerk.

Hours 9: 00 AM - 12: 30 PM, 1: 30 PM - 4: 30 PM, Monday,
Wednesday-Thursday by appointment and at the
Town Clerk's discretion.

Duplicating Photocopying facilities are very limited.
facilities

Other services The Honorary Historian to the Town Council will
offer guidance to researchers, but can only answer
very brief inquiries by post. International postage
coupons would be appreciated for overseas inquiries.

Publications Catalogue of Lydd Borough Records 1412-1941,
comp. by J. M. Farrar and H. A. Hanley; The
Records of Lydd, ed. by A. Finn (1911) (a trans-
cription of the Chamberlains' or Jurats' Accounts
1422-1484 and the Churchwardens' Accounts 1519-
1559 [the text of the Chamberlains' Accounts is
largely accurate, that of the Churchwardens' Accounts has many omissions]).

MAIDSTONE

204 Institution Kent Archives Office
Address County Hall
Maidstone ME14 1XQ

Telephone 0622 671411

Holdings The office holds probate records for Canterbury
and Rochester Dioceses, parish records for
Rochester Diocese and Maidstone Archdeaconry
of Canterbury Diocese. There are official records
of the County Council, Quarter Sessions (some
covering late 16th and early 17th centuries), some
boroughs, and Boards of Guardians. Also a large
number of school records, and a collection of ecclesiastical archives belonging to the Dean and
Chapter of Rochester are found here. There are
many private collections of business, family, and
estate muniments, tithe maps, Quaker records, and
land drainage records. The office is a recognized
repository for certain public records, for manorial
and tithe documents, and for ecclesiastical records

(Rochester. Canterbury: archdeaconry of Maidstone). The date span of the collection is 699 to the present. (See also "Other services" below.)

Conditions of admission and access	It is essential that the scholar make an appointment in advance of his visit. Inquiries should be addressed to the County Archivist. The collection may be used only on the premises.
Hours	9:00 AM - 4:30 PM, Tuesday-Friday.
Duplicating facilities	The office has a full range of photocopying, photographic and microfilm facilities.
Other services	Brief questions are answered by telephone and post, and reference help is available in the search room. Ultra-violet lamps are provided. Administrative assistance is given to Dover, Hythe, Lydd, and New Romney Town Councils, and to Shepway District Council, but control is not exercised over records held by other Councils. Records for the former Borough of Dover, which date from ca. 1312 to 1971 are found in the Kent County Archives Office. Some material is held by the New Romney Town Council, but the older records of the New Romney Borough are deposited here. The Shepway District Council did not retain the records of Councils it superseded (Boroughs of Folkestone, New Romney, Hythe, Lydd and the Rural District Councils of Elham and Romney Marsh). Inquiries are usually referred to the Kent Archives Office. The Lydd Town Council holds a good archival collection at its offices (see entry no. 203).
Publications	Some Roads and Bridges, ed. by Elizabeth Melling (1959); Kent and the Civil War, ed. by Elizabeth Melling (1960); Aspects of Agriculture and Industry, ed. by Elizabeth Melling (1962); The Poor, ed. by Elizabeth Melling (1964); Some Kentish Houses, ed. by Elizabeth Melling, illustrated by Anne M. Oakley (1965); Crime and Punishment, ed. by Elizabeth Melling (1969); Handlist of Kent County Council Record, 1889-1945, prepared by Felix Hull; Guide to the Kent County Archives Office, ed. by Felix Hull (1958) and First Supplement 1957-1968, ed. by Felix Hull and Second Supplement 1969-1980, ed. by Elizabeth Melling; Catalogue of Estate Maps, 1590-1840, ed. by Felix Hull; Kentish Maps and Map-Makers, 1590-1840, prepared by Felix Hull.

MAN, ISLE OF	See: DOUGLAS

MANCHESTER

204a Institution	Chetham's Library

Address	Long Millgate Manchester M3 1SB
Telephone	061 834 7961
Holdings	The library was established in accordance with the wishes of Humphrey Chetham who died in 1653. His will, proved the following year, provided for the endowment of a school and a library and furnished a considerable fortune for this purpose. The history and topography of northwestern England is emphasized in the collection and there are works on local history, the arts, and examples of fine printing and binding. Manuscript material includes deeds and letters in the Chetham archives and deeds collected by others which relate mainly to Lancashire, Cheshire, and Yorkshire. There are manorial court rolls, accounts of overseers of highways and of the poor, and local societies' minute books. The transcripts of Richard Kuerden and Christopher Towneley concerning history and archaeology are held and those of William Asheton Tonge, whose work comprises volumes of extracts from parish registers. Other famous manuscripts include the Flores Historiarum of Matthew Paris, a copy of Gower's Confessio Amantis, service books, medical works, account books (among them, Horace Walpole's) and works of poetry. There are many of the publications of the Record Commission, the Public Record Office, and the Historical Manuscripts Commission found. Early local newspapers are kept, including an almost complete file of the Manchester Mercury, 1752-1825, and local directories, publications of local societies, newspaper cuttings, prints, maps, pamphlets, and photographs are held. One finds histories of the county, and of towns and villages, ecclesiastical history, and works on genealogy and heraldry.
Conditions of admission and access	Works from the collection are made available on request and may be used only on the premises. (Originally the books were chained.) The library is open to all over the age of eighteen, but visiting scholars are asked to provide references. Inquiries should be directed to the Librarian.
Hours	9:30 AM - 12:30 PM, 1:30 PM - 4:30 PM, Monday-Friday.
Duplicating facilities	Photocopies can be provided if the material is suitable, and arrangements can be made for photographs.
Other services	Brief questions by post or telephone are answered and reference help is available. There is a printed catalog of the collection up to 1883, a

card catalog of printed books added since then
and a typescript list of the manuscripts available
in the library. There is no guidebook at present,
but it is hoped one will be produced in the future.

Publications   Bibliothecae Chethamensis Catalogus, Manchester,
1701-1883, 6 vols.; A Catalogue of the Library
of ... John Byrom ..., by James O. Halliwell
(-Phillipps), London, 1851; A Catalogue of the
Collection of Tracts for and Against Popery
(published in or about the Reign of James II) in
the Manchester Library Founded by Humphrey
Chetham, ed. by Thomas Jones, Manchester, 1859-
65 (2 vols.), (Chetham Society, Original Series,
48, 64); Catalogue of the John Radcliffe Collec-
tion, comp. by C. T. E. Phillips, Manchester,
1937; "A Selection from the list of Historical
Manuscripts in the Chetham Library," comp. by
G. H. Tupling (in Bulletin of the Institute of
Historical Research, Vol. X, 1932-33, pp. 69-72).
The following articles give information about
Chetham's Library: Hilda Lofthouse, "Unfamiliar
Libraries 1: Chetham's Library," The Book Col-
lector, vol. 5 (1956), 323-330; Hilda Lofthouse,
"Chetham's Library," in Rich Inheritance: a
Guide to the History of Manchester, ed. by N. J.
Frangopulo, Manchester, 1963, pp. 246-54; Moelwyn
Williams, ed., Directory of Rare Book and Special
Collections in the United Kingdom and the Repub-
lic of Ireland, London, 1985, pp. 398-401; A. F.
Maclure "The Minute Books of Chetham's Hospital
and Library, Manchester," Transactions of the
Lancashire and Cheshire Antiquarian Society,
Vol. 40 (for 1922-23), 1925, pp. 16-42; C. T. E.
Phillips, "Humphrey Chetham and His Library,"
Manchester Review, 3, 1944, pp. 280-92; A. C.
Snape, "Seventeenth-Century Book Purchasing in
Chetham's Library, Manchester," Bulletin of the
John Rylands University Library of Manchester,
67, 1985, pp. 783-796; A. C. Snape, "Chetham's
Hospital and Library, Manchester," (reprinted
from Country Life, August 25th and September 1,
1934).

MANCHESTER (map)

205 Institution   Greater Manchester County Record Office
     Address   56 Marshall
                   New Cross, Ancoats
                   Manchester M4 5FU

     Telephone   061 247 3383

     Holdings   Public records found in the collection include those
                   for coroners, hospitals, probate (indexes to the

Grants of Wills and letters of Administration made in the principal probate registry and in the several district registries of Her Majesty's Court of Probate, 1858-1934), motor vehicle registration, Quarter Sessions, Charity Commissioners, and customs and excise. Business and commercial papers include records relating to canals, railways, textiles, engineering firms, and architects. Among the family and estate papers are found records of the Egerton family, Earls of Wilton, Assheton family, Baronets of Middleton (1200-1837), Ackers family of Manchester (1712-1881), Bagot family of Bolton, Buckley family of Saddleworth (1758-1852), King, Wadkin, Barrow and other Quaker families in Lancashire (1682-1909), Stott family of Rochdale (1619-1849), Royds family of Falinge (1792-1845), Hassall family, Manchester and Ballarat, Australia (late 19th and early 20th centuries), Jones family of Doncaster, Charles William Blacklock (18th-20th century), Daniel Adamson, the Dearden and Wild families, and the Haworths of Tottington. Maps and plans include historical maps, tithe maps, and Ordnance Survey maps. The records of trade unions, societies and organizations are held as are directories, and files of newspapers, both national and local. Deeds, letters, and sale particulars are also found.

Conditions of admission and access	The office is open to the public and advance notice of a visit is not necessary. The collection must be used on the premises. Inquiries should be addressed to the County Archivist.
Hours	9:30 AM - 4:30 PM, Monday-Thursday; 9:30 AM - 4:00 PM, Friday; 9:00 AM - 12:00 noon, second and fourth Saturday in the month.
Duplicating facilities	Photocopies, full-size copies from microfilm, microfilm copies and photographs can be supplied. Specially commissioned microfilm and photographic copies are quoted on request.
Other services	Brief questions are answered by post or telephone and reference help is available in the search room. A reference library is also available to further aid the researcher. An ultraviolet lamp is provided.
Publications	Summary of Collections in the Greater Manchester Record Office; leaflets, brochures.

MANCHESTER

205a Institution Address	John Rylands University Library of Manchester University of Manchester Deansgate

Manchester   M3 3EH

and
Oxford Road
Manchester   M13 9PL

Telephone

061 834 5343 (Deansgate)
061 273 3333 (Oxford Road)

Holdings

The library is a merger between the John Rylands
Library and the University of Manchester Library.
The manuscript collections are kept in the former
John Rylands Library at Deansgate except for the
archives of the university and the Manchester
Guardian, which are found at the University Library in Oxford Road. Genealogical material re-
lates principally to Cheshire, Derbyshire, Lancashire, Lincolnshire, Suffolk, Warwickshire, and
Yorkshire and contains deeds, family records, and
papers of individuals. There are charters, estate
papers, and manorial records of twenty-five prominent north-western families such as Bagshawe,
Bromley-Davenport, Cornwall-Legh, Mainwaring,
Roundell, Stamford, Tabley and Warburton of Arley.
The dates of these extend from the twelfth to the
twentieth century. The papers of Sir John
Bowring, John Fielden and Sir James Kay-Shuttleworth and correspondence and dispatches to and
from the Manchester Guardian are found. The
University archives include the papers of profes-
sors and others connected with academic pursuits.
Business records are found, especially for the
textile and cotton industry, and there are diaries,
correspondence, and memoirs of prominent in-
dividuals. Among these are the archives of
Samuel Oldknow, Thomas Botfield and Company,
McConnel and Kennedy, Hodgson and Robinson,
Owen Owens and Sons, and Textile Associations.
Records of military interest include those of
Colonel Samuel Bagshawe, Alexander, 6th Earl of
Balcarres, and Field Marshal Sir Claude Auchin-
leck. Nonconformists' records include Baptists,
Congregationalists, Unitarians, Moravians, and
Methodists. The Methodist Archives, which in-
clude diaries and notebooks of John Wesley, are
housed here in a special collection, and remain
the property of the Methodist Church.

Conditions of
admission and
access

Researchers should make an application in writing
to use the collection. Inquiries should be made
to the Librarian or to the Keeper of Manuscripts.
The material must be used on the premises.
Some of the material is unavailable because of its
fragile condition and some cannot be retrieved
because it has not been sorted, listed or cataloged
in any way.

Hours	9:30 AM - 5:30 PM, Monday-Friday; 9:30 AM - 1:00 PM, Saturday, by appointment.
Duplicating facilities	Full-size copies and microcopies can be provided but there may be long delays before the work can be completed.
Other services	Reference help is provided and brief questions are answered by telephone or post.
Publications	Catalogue of the Christie Collection (1915); Bulletin of the John Rylands Library (semi-annual); Annual Report; Accessions Lists; Latin Manuscripts, by M. R. James (1921); Arabic Manuscripts, by A. Mingana (1934); Catalogues, Printed Books and Manuscripts, 3 vols. (1899); English Incunabula (1930); English Books to 1650 (1895); English Bible, by R. Lovett (1899); Arabic Papyri, by D. S. Margoliouth (1933); and Domotio Papyri, 3 vols., by F. L. Griffiths (1909). There are also brochures, slides, postcards, Christmas cards, and other products of a popular nature available.

MANCHESTER (map)

206 Institution Address	Manchester City Archives Department Central Library St. Peter's Square Manchester M2 5PD
Telephone	061 2369422, ext. 269
Holdings	This collection contains the parish records for Manchester Diocese, Methodist records for Manchester and Stockport District (excluding the Borough of Stockport) and other non-conformist records for the City of Manchester. Also found are Society of Friends records, Hardshaw and Hardshaw East, Jewish records, City of Manchester local government records and various family, business, society, and trade union archives. The department acquires and preserves the official records of the City of Manchester and has among its most important documents the minute books of the Chamber of Commerce. The earliest document is a 12th-century deed. For the most part, post-1837 parish registers are available for consultation in the Archives Department. Earlier ones are held on microfilm in the Local History Library. The Local History Library also has census returns, 1841-1881, directories, 1772-1969, the Mormon indexes (on microfiche) of Lancashire and Cheshire parish registers (of which it has copies). The Archives Department is recognized as a manorial repository by the Master of the Rolls,

and by the Lord Chancellor as a repository for various categories of local public records, and by the Bishop of Manchester as the Diocesan Record Office.

Conditions of admission and access	The department is open to the public and scholars are welcome to use the collection. It is advisable, however, to make an appointment in advance because of limited seating. Documents may be ordered in advance, thus avoiding delay. Inquiries should be directed to the archivist. The collection must be used on the premises.
Hours	9:00 AM - 12:00 noon, 1:00 PM - 9:00 PM, Monday; 9:00 AM - 12:00 noon, 1:00 PM - 5:00 PM, Tuesday-Friday.
Duplicating facilities	Full-size and microcopies can be supplied. Some material (e.g., Anglican registers) cannot be copied.
Other services	Reference help is available in the Archives Department and brief questions by post or telephone will be answered. Calendars of collections are available in the department and the Local History Library (and are also sent to the National Register of Archives in London). Card indexes of each calendar by person, place, and subject are available in the department.
Publications	The library and its many departments issue many publications including guides, brochures, and leaflets. Among these is The Local History Library: A Guide to its Resources.

MANCHESTER (map)

207 Institution Address

Salford Archives Centre
658/662 Liverpool Road, Irlam
Manchester M30 5AD

Telephone	061 775 5643
Holdings	The holdings include Salford City Council, Poor Law Union, Quarter Sessions, Coroner, hospital and other local authorities, and the Borough of Eccles records. Borough of Swinton and Pendlebury (and its predecessors) are also held. Non-conformist records, school papers, family and estate archives and those of businesses and local organizations, societies, and charities are found. Local rate books for the 19th and 20th centuries are available.
Conditions of admission and access	The collection is open to the public, but a prior appointment is advisable. Inquiries should be

	addressed to the Cultural Services Manager, or to the City Archivist. The collection must be used on the premises.
Hours	9:00 AM - 4:00 PM, Monday-Friday.
Duplicating facilities	Photocopying facilities are available.
Other services	Brief postal and telephone inquiries are answered and reference help is available. Indexes of persons, places and subjects are maintained.
Publications	Genealogical Sources for the City of Salford (typescript); brochures and lists are produced.

MAN, ISLE OF   See: DOUGLAS

MARGATE

208	Institution Address	Margate Central Library Local History Collection Cecil Square Margate CT9 1RE
	Telephone	0843 23626/22895
	Holdings	The collection includes the papers and archives of Dr. Arthur Rowe which contain material concerning the local history of the area. Family and private papers are those of the Thanet families (pedigrees), Reverend John Predden, John Anderson, Edward White, and W. J. Mercer. Found among the collections are letters, descriptions, post cards, scrapbooks, press cuttings and illustrations. There are also minute books, accounts, gravestone inscriptions, and photographs, maps, plans, and newspapers.
	Conditions of admission and access	The collection is open to the public without prior arrangement. Inquiries should be directed to the Librarian. The collection must be used in the library.
	Hours	9:30 AM - 6:00 PM, Monday-Friday; 9:30 AM - 5:00 PM, Saturday.
	Duplicating facilities	Photocopying facilities are available and arrangements can be made for photography.
	Other services	Reference aid is available and questions by post or telephone are answered if they are brief.
	Publications	None.

MATLOCK (map)

209	Institution Address	Derbyshire Library Services Local Studies Department County Offices Matlock DE4 3AG
	Telephone	0629 3411, ext. 6840
	Holdings	The Barmasters Library here includes account books, ledgers and other material relating to lead-mining in Derbyshire. The census returns are kept on microfilm (1841-1881). The papers and scripts of L. du Garde Peach are here and also newspapers and maps.
	Conditions of admission and access	The library is open to the public and advance arrangements are not necessary except for Saturday visits. Inquiries should be directed to the Librarian. The collection must be used on the premises.
	Hours	9:00 AM - 5:00 PM, Monday-Friday; 9:30 AM - 1:00 PM, Saturday, by appointment.
	Duplicating facilities	Facilities for photocopying and full-size copies from microfilm can be provided.
	Other services	Reference advice is given and questions by telephone or through the mail are answered.
	Publications	Derbyshire Local Studies Collection: A Guide to Resources (1982); Catalogue and Indexes of the British Museum Additional MSS 6676-6686 (1977); other guides, indexes, and lists are also available.

MATLOCK (map)

210	Institution Address	Derbyshire Record Office County Offices Matlock DE4 3AG
	Telephone	0629 3411, ext. 7347
	Holdings	The office holds records of Quarter Sessions, County Council and District Councils, schools, charities, hospitals, Parish Councils, manufacturing and industry, retail trade, trades unions, private clubs and societies, Anglican Parish records, including baptism, marriage and burial registers, records of non-conformist churches, also including baptism, marriage, and burial registers. Bishop's transcripts of the parish registers survive in broken series from the mid-seventeenth to the early nineteenth century and

will be found at the Lichfield Joint Record Office (see entry no. 145). Registers of wills proved at the Derby Probate Registry, together with Derby administrations, 1858-1928, are held by the office and there is an index of wills found in family and solicitors' deposits. Also there are electoral registers, 1832 to the present. There are Boards of Guardians papers, family and estate collections and the Dakeyne Collection, compiled about 1800, which contains pedigrees of many of the more notable Derbyshire families. There is also an index to this material. Land tax assessments for 1780-1832, lists of jurors from the late 18th century, and title deeds are kept here. In addition there are maps, including tithe, railway, inclosure, canal, turnpike and Ordnance Survey maps, and manorial records. The office is a recognized repository for certain public records, for manorial and tithe documents, and for ecclesiastical records (Derby).

Conditions of admission and access

The office is open to the public and while no prior appointment is required it is helpful to give notice of a visit ahead of time. It is necessary to book microfilm readers before a visit and some records require advance notice to be produced. Unless otherwise provided by statute, public records less than thirty years old, most County Council records less than thirty years old, and some deposited records less than one hundred years are not usually open to inspection. Applications for examining such documents must be made in writing and the reason for wishing to see them stated. Letters of introduction or reference may be required in these instances. Inquiries should be directed to the County Archivist. Only three records will be produced at any one time except with special permission and those in poor condition may be denied until they can be rendered fit for handling or are microfilmed. If original material has been microfilmed, only the microfilm will be produced for study, not the original. All material must be used on the premises.

Hours

9:30 AM - 1:00 PM, 2:00 PM - 4:45 PM, Monday-Friday.

Duplicating facilities

Photocopying facilities are available, but the photocopying of volumes, including parish registers is not permitted. Photography of records may be allowed with the permission of the county Archivist. Maps are usually too large for the photocopying facilities available.

Other services

Brief questions by post or telephone can be answered, but the staff cannot undertake extensive research. Advice on sources is given and a

list of record agents for genealogical research is
available. Reference help will be given visiting
scholars and an extensive search room library is
maintained. Ultra-violet lamps are provided and
all necessary microform equipment is available.

| Publications | List of Anglican and Non-conformist Registers in Derbyshire Record Office (currently being revised); Report of the Archivist, 1962-1973 (1974); Annual reports are found in the Derbyshire Archaeological Journal (1962-   ). |

MIDDLESBROUGH

211 Institution Address	Cleveland County Libraries Archives Department Exchange House 6 Marton Road Middlesbrough TS1 1DB
Telephone	0642 248321
Holdings	The collection contains the records of local authorities, Boards of Guardians, Turnpike Trusts, Parish Councils, Motor Taxation, Burial Boards, schools and School Boards. Church records are of Church of England parishes and non-conformist churches (Methodist Circuit, United Reformed Church, Roman Catholic, Society of Friends, and Baptist). The areas covered are listed in the Department's "Brief Guide." Churchwardens' accounts, when found among the parish records, may include lists of rate payers. Many business records are found, as well as family and estate archives, manorial records, electoral registers, workhouse registers, and papers of societies, clubs, political organizations, and trade unions. Tithe maps and apportionments, enclosure maps and awards, and a large collection of Ordnance Survey maps are also available. Census returns for the whole of Cleveland County for 1841 through 1881 are available on microfilm.
Conditions of admission and access	An appointment is necessary to consult the collection. It is advisable, if possible, to note the class of records required, because some records are stored away from the library and a week's notice is required to make them available. Inquiries should be directed to the Archivist. The collection must be used on the premises.
Hours	9:00 AM - 1:00 PM, 2:00 PM - 4:30 PM, Monday-Thursday; 9:00 AM - 1:00 PM, 2:00 PM - 4:00 PM, Friday.
Duplicating facilities	Photocopies and full-size copies from microfilm can be provided.

Other services	Brief questions by telephone or post are answered. Short specific searches will be undertaken if sufficient information concerning names, dates, and addresses is supplied. Reference help is available in the department. An ultra-violet lamp is provided.
Publications	Brief Guide (1982); Genealogical Sources (updated regularly).

MIDDLETON

212 Institution Address	Rochdale Libraries Middleton Area Central Library Local Studies Collection Long Street Middleton M24 3DU
Telephone	061 643 5228
	See also: HEYWOOD, Rochdale Libraries, Heywood Area Central Library; ROCHDALE, Rochdale Libraries, Rochdale Area Central Library
Holdings	The collection includes newspapers, photographs, maps (including tithe maps) and plans. Also found are highway rates, poor law records and other Borough papers. Some church records are held.
Conditions of admission and access	The library is open to the public and it is not necessary to make arrangements beforehand to use the collection. Inquiries should be directed to the Assistant Librarian or to the Local Studies Librarian at Rochdale Libraries, Rochdale Area Central Library (Esplanade, Rochdale OL16 1AQ; Telephone: 0706 474747, ext. 423). Archives and reference works must be used on the premises.
Hours	9:30 AM - 8:00 PM, Monday, Thursday; 9:30 AM - 5:30 PM, Tuesday, Friday; 9:30 AM - 1:00 PM, 2:00 PM - 5:00 PM, Wednesday; 9:30 AM - 1:00 PM, 2:00 PM - 4:00 PM, Saturday.
Duplicating facilities	Photocopying facilities are available.
Other services	Questions are answered by telephone and by mail and reference help is provided.
Publications	Introduction to Local Studies Collections (1981).
MORAY	See: FORRES

MONTROSE

213	Institution Address	Angus District Libraries and Museums Montrose Public Library Pell Place Montrose

Telephone   0674 3256

Holdings   The genealogical records of the Mudy, Scott,
                   Straton and Walker families are found here. These
                   date from the 12th to the 19th century. There
                   are also papers from local associations, societies,
                   charities, businesses and trades. Early library
                   records and papers of the Montrose Royal Lunatic
                   Asylum and Dispensary are kept.

Conditions of   The collection is open to the public, but applica-
admission and   tion must be made in advance and in writing.
access   The collection may be used only on the premises.
                   Inquiries should be addressed to the Librarian.

Hours   10:00 AM - 6:00 PM, Monday-Saturday.

Duplicating   Arrangements can be made for photocopying.
facilities

Other services   Brief questions by post or telephone will be
                   answered and reference help is provided.

Publications   None.

NEW ROMNEY   <u>See</u>: MAIDSTONE, Kent Archives Office

NEWCASTLE-UPON-TYNE (map)

214	Institution Address	Newcastle-upon-Tyne City Libraries Local Studies Collection Central Library Princess Square Newcastle-upon-Tyne NE99 1DX

Telephone   091 261 0691

Holdings   The geographical area covered by this collection
                   includes the counties of Tyne and Wear, Northum-
                   berland, and Durham. There are press cuttings
                   and a very extensive newspaper collection. There
                   are also town and county maps, manuscript maps
                   and plans, and Ordnance Survey maps and plans.
                   Census records are kept on microfilm from 1841-
                   1881. There are transcripts of parish registers
                   and indexes to aid in their use. Wills, family
                   papers, individual pedigrees and evidences are
                   found. There are monumental inscriptions,

estate papers, deeds, and correspondence available here.

Conditions of admission and access	The collection is open to the public and formal arrangements ahead of time are not necessary in order to consult the material. The records must be used on the premises. Inquiries should be directed to the Local Studies Librarian.
Hours	9:30 AM - 8:00 PM, Monday-Thursday; 9:30 AM - 5:00 PM, Friday; 9:00 AM - 5:00 PM, Saturday.
Duplicating facilities	Photocopying facilities are available and full-size copies from microforms can be provided. Rare material, that in poor condition, and that of unsuitable format may not be copied.
Other services	Brief questions by post or telephone are answered and the staff is always on duty during open hours to give reference help.
Publications	A series of User's Guides is produced to aid the scholar in the use of the collection.

NEWCASTLE-UPON-TYNE (map)

215 Institution Address	Northumberland Record Office Melton Park North Gosforth Newcastle-upon-Tyne NE3 5QX
Telephone	091 236280
Holdings	The office houses the official archives of the County and extensive collections of records deposited by local authorities, parishes, corporate bodies, families, estates, industrial and commercial firms, and individuals. The collection includes such subjects as administration of local government at county, district, and parish levels; roads, railways, transport, and public works; education, schools, charities, and societies; industries, especially coal and lead mining; urban growth and village change; estate management and farming; social, domestic, and working conditions; population and occupations; elections and local politics; architecture and building; biographies of prominent Northumbrians; and family history. The office is a recognized repository for certain public records, for manorial and tithe documents, and for ecclesiastical records (Newcastle). There are extensive Quarter Sessions and County Council archives and the family records include those of Ridley of Blagdon, Middleton of Belsay, Swinburne of Capheaton, Blackett of Matfen, Allgood of Nunwick, the Delaval Manuscripts and the Allendale

Manuscripts. Also found are the papers of the
Reverend John Hodgson, the Woodman Collection
relating to Morpeth, the Bell family papers, and
the Wilson collection relating to Gateshead. The
census returns are held on microfilm and there
is an extensive collection of photographs and
Ordnance Survey maps.

Conditions of
admission and
access

The office is open to the public and no prior
appointment is necessary. There are facilities
for group visits. Inquiries should be addressed
to the County Archivist. The collection must
be used on the premises and no archives or books
may be borrowed.

Hours

9:00 AM - 9:00 PM, Monday; 9:00 AM - 5:00 PM,
Tuesday-Thursday; 9:00 AM - 4:30 PM, Friday.

Duplicating
facilities

Full-size and microcopying facilities are available.

Other services

Brief questions by telephone or post will be
answered, and reference help is available in the
search rooms. Guidance is offered on sources
of information elsewhere. Services to schools are
described in "Teachers Guide." Exhibits are arranged and talks to societies either at the office
or elsewhere can be negotiated.

Publications

Northumberland Record Office, 1958-1974; Annual
Reports, 1975- ; Teachers Guide; Brief Guides
(leaflets) to records: Northumberland Quarter
Sessions, Berwick Borough Records, Education
Records, Coal Mining Records, Transport and
Communication, Genealogical Source List. Joint
publications with the Durham Record Office and
the Tyne and Wear Archives Office: North East
Ancestors, North East Archives (annual news-
letter). Publications of the Association of North-
umberland Local History Societies: Tyne and
Tweed (annual periodical); Northumberland History: Handlist of Sources: Pt. 1, General; Pt. 2,
Topography.

NEWCASTLE-UPON-TYNE (map)

216 Institution
Address

Tyne and Wear Archives Service
Blandford House, West Blandford Street
Newcastle-upon-Tyne NE1 4JA

Telephone

091 2326789

See also: NORTH SHIELDS, Tyne and Wear
Archives Service, Branch Office

Holdings

The department holdings include both official and

non-official records relating to the entire Tyne and Wear County area. Genealogical material includes census and-parish registers on microfilm, non-conformist registers, electoral rolls, and other valuable material. Non-conformist registers available are Methodist, Quaker, Presbyterian, Roman Catholic, Unitarian, and United Reform. Cemetery records for eight cemeteries are located here and guild and freemen records are also found. These date from 1696 to 1830 for apprenticeships and from 1409 to 1974 for guild and freemen's rolls.

Conditions of admission and access	No prior appointment is required unless the visitor intends to consult microfilm, where a booking system is employed. Last requests for documents from Monday to Thursday must be made by 4:45 PM; Friday by 4:15 PM. A self-service system for the use of microforms enables researchers to locate microfilm or microfiche and operate readers. A descriptive leaflet is provided. Records embargoed by statute, owners, or because of fragile conditions, will not be produced. All inquiries should be directed to the County Archivist in the first instance. Papers may be consulted only under supervision in the public search rooms, and in accordance with search room rules.
Hours	8:45 AM - 5:15 PM, Monday, Wednesday-Friday; 8:45 AM - 8:30 PM, Tuesday.
Duplicating facilities	Photocopying, photographic and microfilming facilities are available.
Other services	Only brief, specific inquiries, by post or by telephone, can be considered. A list of local record agents is, however, available. Group visits can be arranged, but prior notice is required. There are catalogs and indexes available to aid the searcher and microfilm readers, and an ultra-violet lamp is provided.
Publications	User guides, leaflets, and brochures are produced to help readers use the collection and the facilities.

NEWPORT

217	Institution Address	Isle of Wight County Record Office 26 Hillside Newport PO3C 2EB
	Telephone	0983 524031, ext. 132/133
	Holdings	The usual holdings of a county record office are found, but no ancient county records as such are kept here. The office is a repository for public records and is recognized by the Master of the

Rolls to receive manorial and tithe documents. It has been designated as a repository for Anglican records also (Portsmouth Diocese: parish records of the Archdeaconry of the Isle of Wight).

Conditions of admission and access	The office is open to the public and no advance arrangements are necessary to use the collections. Inquiries should be directed to the County Archivist. The material may be used only on the premises.
Hours	9:30 AM - 5:00 PM, Monday-Tuesday, Thursday-Friday; 9:30 AM - 8:30 PM, Wednesday.
Duplicating facilities	Copying facilities are available.
Other services	Brief postal or telephone questions are answered, and reference help is available. An ultra-violet lamp is provided.
Publications	None.

NITHSDALE District Archives	See: DUMFRIES, Dumfries Archive Centre (entry no. 84)
NITHSDALE District Council	See: DUMFRIES (entry no. 83)

NORTH SHIELDS

218 Institution Address	Tyne and Wear Archives Service, Branch Office Local Studies Centre Howard Street North Shields NE30 1LY
Telephone	091 2582811
	See also: NEWCASTLE-UPON-TYNE, Tyne and Wear Archives Service
Holdings	Census records and some parish records for North Tyneside are held here.
Conditions of admission and access	An appointment in advance is not required. Inquiries should be directed to the Chief Archivist at Tyne and Wear Archives Service, Blandford House, West Blandford Street, Newcastle-upon-Tyne NE1 4JA; telephone: 091 2326789. The collection must be used on the premises.
Hours	9:00 AM - 1:00 PM, 2:00 PM - 5:00 PM, Monday, Thursday-Friday; 9:00 AM - 1:00 PM, 2:00 PM - 7:00 PM, Tuesday; 9:00 AM - 1:00 PM, Wednesday.

Duplicating facilities	Photocopying, photographic and microfilming facilities are available.
Other services	Only brief, specific inquiries by post or telephone are answered. Group visits can be arranged, but prior notice is required. Microform equipment and an ultra-violet lamp are provided.
Publications	User guides, leaflets, and brochures are produced by the Tyne and Wear Archives Service to help readers use the collection and the facilities.

NORTHALLERTON

219	Institution Address	North Yorkshire County Record Office County Hall Northallerton DL7 8AD
	Telephone	0609 3123, ext. 455
	Holdings	This office was formerly the North Riding County Record Office and includes in the collection the official records of the County (Quarter Sessions, County, District, and Parish Councils), family and estate papers, and parish records. Local history and historical geography of the North Riding (or North Yorkshire) and manuscript sources are available. The office is a recognized repository for certain public records, for manorial and tithe documents and for ecclesiastical records (Bradford, Ripon, York: parish records).
	Conditions of admission and access	The office is open to the public, but an appointment in advance is requested. Inquiries should be directed to the County Archivist. The collection must be used on the premises. Most records are made available for consultation in the form of microfilms, facsimiles, typed transcripts and typed abstracts.
	Hours	9:00 AM - 4:50 PM, Monday-Tuesday, Thursday; 9:00 AM - 8:50 PM, Wednesday; 9:00 AM - 4:20 PM, Friday.
	Duplicating facilities	Full-size and microcopying facilities are available.
	Other services	Brief questions by post or by telephone will be answered. Reference help is available in the search room and there are lists, guides, and catalogs available to aid the researcher.
	Publications	Hird's Annals of Bedale; Copper-Mining in Middleton; History of the North Riding County Council; Journal, No. 1- ; Craven Muster Roll, 1803; Richmond Burgages, ed. by L. P. Wenham;

North Riding Naval Recruits; Richmond Municipal
Reform Association, 1841-1859, ed. by L. P.
Wenham; A Richmond Miscellany; Malton in the
Early Nineteenth Century; North Yorkshire Essays,
1780-1850, by R. P. Hastings. Histories of places,
people, families, and organizations within North
Yorkshire are also produced. The Annual Report
lists records deposited each year and describes
some of the collections. There are also leaflets,
guides, and brochures.

NORTHAMPTON (map)

220	Institution Address	Northamptonshire Record Office Delapre Abbey Northampton NN4 9AW
	Telephone	0604 762129

Holdings

The record office collection contains information
about individuals, local government, parish
government, landed estates, businesses, societies,
diocesan and other matters connected with Northamptonshire and the Soke of Peterborough. There
are parish registers, census returns, charters,
court rolls, deeds, maps, letters, diaries, accounts, minute books, wills, and photographs.
The holdings include official, judicial, and administrative records of the county and smaller
local government units, records of the Diocese of
Peterborough covering Northamptonshire, the Soke
of Peterborough and Rutland, probate records of
the same area, records of ecclesiastical parishes
in Northamptonshire and the Soke, records of local
families and estates, business and professional
firms, societies, non-conformist churches and
charities. Documents date from the 12th century
to the present day. The office is a recognized
repository for certain public records, for manorial
and tithe documents and for ecclesiastical records
(Peterborough).

Conditions of
admission and
access

The office is open to the public and visitors are
welcome to consult the documents and reference
works. In certain circumstances, however,
searchers may be required to provide a letter of
introduction and groups wishing to visit should
make an appointment in advance. Inquiries
should be directed to the Chief Archivist. The
collection may be used only on the premises.
Documents required on Saturday, Thursday
evening, or between 12:00 noon and 2:00 PM on
weekdays should be requested in advance.

Hours

9:00 AM - 4:45 PM, Monday-Wednesday; 9:00 AM -
7:45 PM, Thursday; 9:00 AM - 4:30 PM, Friday;

9:00 AM - 12:15 PM, first and third Saturdays in each month, unless the Saturday precedes a Monday holiday, in which case the office will be open the next Saturday. In the event of staff shortages, the office may close between 1:00 PM and 2:00 PM without prior notice.

Duplicating facilities

Full-size photocopies of documents within a given size can usually be made on the same day as requested. Microfilming and photography will be done once a month, but prints from microfilms are not undertaken at the record office and when supplied from council premises elsewhere, may be subject to long delays.

Other services

Only brief inquiries by telephone or post will be answered. Reference help is available in the search rooms and there are reference works, lists, guides and catalogues to aid the researcher. There is a large collection of pamphlets (to which there are separate indexes) and card indexes of personal names, place names, subjects, maps and pictorial material. Certain large collections have their own indexes. Arrangements can be made for small groups to visit the record office and lectures on local history and the work of the record office can be planned if sufficient notice is given. Exhibitions can also be provided. The Northamptonshire Record Society has its headquarters at Delapre Abbey and its excellent historical library is housed here. The staff of the record office have permission to borrow books for the use of readers in the search rooms, but access to the Society's rooms is restricted to members. A list of the Society's publications is found below.

Publications

Summary Guide to the Northamptonshire Record Office, by P. I. King (1954, out-of-print); List of Parish and Non-Conformist Registers in the Office; Northamptonshire Record Office. The following are publications of the Northamptonshire Record Society and are available through the Society's Secretary at Delapre Abbey: Northamptonshire Past and Present (the Society's Journal, Vol. 1- ; and the Society's main series of volumes: Quarter Sessions Records of the County of Northampton, 1630, 1657, 1657-8; Henry of Pytchley's Book of Fees; Musters, Beacons, Subsidies, etc., in the County of Northampton, 1568-1623; Facsimiles of Early Charters from Northamptonshire Collections; The Earliest Northamptonshire Assize Rolls, 1202 and 1203; Kettering Vestry Minutes, 1797-1853; Luffield Priory Charters, Pt. I, II; The Royal Forest of Northamptonshire in the Sixteenth and Seventeenth Centuries; The Letters of Daniel Eaton to the Third Earl of Cardigan, 1725-1732; Northamptonshire Militia Lists, 1777; Northampton-

shire Lieutenancy Papers and Other Documents,
1580-1614; The Montagu Musters Book, 1602-1623;
Wellingborough Manorial Accounts, 1258-1323;
Peterborough Churchwardens' Accounts, 1467-1573;
Peterborough Feoffees' Accounts, 1614-1764; Rolls
of Northamptonshire Sessions of the Peace, 1314-
1316, 1320; The Last Days of Peterborough
Monastery; The Foundation of Peterborough
Cathedral, 1541; A Descriptive List of the Printed
Maps of Northamptonshire, AD 1576-1900; Sir
Christopher Hatton's Book of Seals, 11th-15th
Century; The Book of William Morton, Almoner of
Peterborough Monastery, 1448-1467; The Corres-
pondence of Bishop Brian Duppa and Sir Justinian
Isham, 1650-1660; Elizabethan Peterborough; The
Wealth of Five Northamptonshire Families, 1540-
1640; Carte Nativorum; John Isham, Mercer and
Merchant Adventurer; Northamptonshire and Rut-
land Clergy, AD 1500-1900.

NORWICH (map)

221 Institution
Address

Norfolk Record Office
Central Library
Norwich NR2 1NJ

Telephone

0603 611277, ext. 261/262

Holdings

The office holds the records of the Norfolk County
Council and its predecessors, District and Parish
Councils in Norfolk, and the City of Norwich.
Also found are those of the Borough of Great
Yarmouth and the Diocese of Norwich. Local
probate court records are also held. Ecclesiastical
parishes in the Diocese of Norwich and the
Deaneries of Feltwell and Fincham in Ely Diocese
records are found here. The collection also includes business, societies, estate, family and other
privately deposited records relating wholly or
principally to Norfolk. The office is a recognized
repository for certain public records, for manorial
and tithe documents and for ecclesiastical records
(Norwich). Records in the office date from the
11th to the 20th century.

Conditions of
admission and
access

The office is open to the public and whereas no
advance appointment is required, space can be
reserved in advance if one intends to arrive before 9:30 AM. Also, advance application for
documents can be made and is necessary for items
to be available at 9:00 AM and at 1:00 PM for use
between 1:00 PM and 2:00 PM. Items required for
use at 9:00 AM on Monday must be requested by
4:30 PM the previous Friday, for Tuesday to
Saturday, by 4:30 PM the previous day, and for
1:00 PM, by 12:30 PM that day. Requests for

documents are taken from the search room at
9:05 AM and at half-hourly intervals from 9:30
AM to 12:30 PM, and from 2:00 PM to 4:30 PM
Monday through Friday and at 9:05 AM, 9:30 AM
to 11:30 AM on Saturday. Access to certain
classes of records--mainly recent records of a
confidential nature--is restricted. All the material
must be used on the premises. Inquiries should
be addressed to the County Archivist.

Hours	9:00 AM - 5:00 PM, Monday-Friday; 9:00 AM - 12:00 noon, Saturday.
Duplicating facilities	Full-size and microcopying facilities are available. Photography can also be supplied.
Other services	Only brief questions by mail or telephone will be answered. Reference help is available in the search room. Limited searches will be carried out by the record office staff for a fee.
Publications	Guide to the Great Yarmouth Borough Records, by P. Rutledge (1973); A Revised Catalogue of the Records of the City of Norwich, 1898, by W. Hudson and J. C. Tingey; Norfolk Parish Map; Recipes on Record; Guide to Genealogical Sources (1985). Not published at the record office, but for sale there, are How to Record Your Family Tree, by Patrick Palgrave-Moore; and Beginning Your Family History, by George Pelling.

NORWOOD, UPPER   See: LONDON, Upper Norwood Public Library

NOTTINGHAM (map)

222 Institution	Nottingham University Library
Address	Manuscripts Department
	University Park
	Nottingham NG7 2RD
Telephone	0602 506101, ext. 3440
Holdings	The collection includes large holdings in family papers and estate records. Among these are found the personal papers of the Bentinck, Earls and Dukes of Portland and their predecessors at Welbeck Abbey, the Cavendish and Holles Dukes of Newcastle and the papers and estate records of the Pelham-Clinton Dukes of Newcastle. A comprehensive collection of records of the estates of the Pierrepont family, Dukes of Kingston and Earls Manvers from the late 17th century to the 20th century is held. The Middleton Collection contains estate records, including medieval deeds (from the 12th century), manorial records, and

16th and 17th century industrial records, notably those relating to the coal mining interests of the Willoughby family. Also contained in this group is the Ray Willoughby Collection on natural history. The estate records and some personal papers of the Monckton and Arundel families, who became Viscounts Galway, with estates in Nottinghamshire and South Yorkshire, are found, as well as the estate records and some personal papers of the Clifton family and the Mellish family of Hodsock. Literary manuscripts include those of Henry Kirke White, D. H. Lawrence, and Coventry Patmore. Among the ecclesiastical material are records of the Archdeaconry of Nottingham which stem from the Archdeacon's twice-yearly visitations and cases pursued in his court, from the 16th to the 20th century, and High Pavement Chapel, Nottingham papers, the earliest being a 1656-1660 minute book. Generally these records date from 1689 to the 20th century. Other church records include St. Andrew's with Castle Gate United Reformed Church, Nottingham, Mansfield Road Baptist Church, Nottingham and Old Meeting House, Mansfield. Also found are records of the Severn-Trent Water Authority and its forerunners, the Cotton Research Corporation, hospital records, business and trade union records, and university records.

Conditions of admission and access	Visiting scholars may use the collection but must provide proof of identity and a letter of recommendation. It is also essential to notify the department in advance of an intended visit. Some collections are subject to special conditions or are very fragile, and access may be refused, and many public and modern records are open for inspection after varying periods of time, namely thirty to one hundred years. The collection must be used in the Manuscript Department. Inquiries should be directed to the Keeper of the Manuscripts.
Hours	9:00 AM - 5:00 PM, Monday-Friday, except on public holidays and the days each year when the university is closed.
Duplicating facilities	A full range of services is available in the Library Photographic Unit and coin-operated photocopiers are available. A leaflet is provided describing these facilities. A minimum charge is imposed for telephone requests. To copy a manuscript, a photographic request form must be completed and submitted through a member of the department's staff. They may not be copied on a coin-operated machine.
Other services	Brief questions are answered by post and telephone and reference help is available in the department. If a lengthy search is undertaken, a

fee is charged, dependent upon the length of time involved. Various finding aids are available as well as detailed calendars and indexes to further help the reader. Ultra-violet lamps and microform equipment are provided and accommodations can be arranged for readers to use their own electric typewriters or tape cassettes.

Publications

The library produces a variety of guides and brochures concerning the services available. The Manuscripts Department produces the following: Archive Teaching Units: 1. The Invasion of England in 1688; 2. Working Class Unrest in Nottingham 1800-1850; 3. Public Health and Housing in Early Victorian Nottingham; 4. Laxton: Life in an Open Field Village; 5. The 1745 Rebellion; 6. Sir Henry Clinton and the War for America 1774-1783; and Illustrated Collection Catalogues: D. H. Lawrence, Vols. 1-2.

NOTTINGHAM (map)

223 Institution
    Address

Nottinghamshire Record Office
County House
High Pavement
Nottingham NG1 1HR

Telephone

0602 504524

Holdings

The collection includes copies of all parish registers prior to 1900 on microfiche, Quarter Sessions records for City and County, most pre-1940 Nottinghamshire probate records (some are at Borthwick Institute of Historical Research, St. Anthony's Hall, York and some at the Public Record Office, Chancery Lane, London). Also held are transcripts of bishops registers, hearth tax, and forest records, enclosure awards, and tithe awards. Ninety percent of the parish registers in the Diocese of Southwell are deposited in the Nottinghamshire Record Office. Personal name indexes exist for Nottingham Burgess Enrolments (1683-1919), Nottingham Borough Apprenticeship Registers (1724-1882), Charity Apprenticeship Registers (1691-1813), Watch and Ward Registers (1812-1816), Corporation archives lists, transportation, bastardy and removal orders (1723-1858), Quaker records, 17th-19th century. Private deposits include papers of landed families, estates, solicitors, industrial firms, societies, and individuals. The office is a recognized repository for certain public records, for manorial and tithe documents, and for ecclesiastical records (Southwell).

Conditions of

The record office is open to the public and no

admission and access	prior appointment is required. Microforms are readily available at any time, but original documents are produced for readers only at hourly intervals (at fifteen minutes past each hour as follows: 9:15 AM - 3:15 PM, Monday, Wednesday-Friday; 9:15 AM - 6:15 PM, Tuesday; 9:15 AM - 11:15 PM, Saturday). Certain classes of archives stored at Shire Hall (chiefly those relating to the County Council, Nottingham City Council [from the 12th century], district councils [including building plans], courts, collieries and non-conformist sects) require one day's notice to be produced in the office and one week's notice is needed for those stored at Shakespeare Street (chiefly modern Nottingham City Council, and Inland Valuation records). Normally a maximum of three archives may be requested at any one time. The collections may be used only in the search rooms. Inquiries should be directed to the Principal Archivist.
Hours	9:00 AM - 4:45 PM, Monday, Wednesday-Friday; 9:00 AM - 7:15 PM, Tuesday; 9:00 AM - 12:15 PM, Saturday.
Duplicating facilities	Full-size and microcopies can be supplied and microfilm of long series of records can be obtained through facilities at the University of Nottingham. Photographs can usually be furnished through local firms. Parish registers, documents which could be damaged by the process, or material still in copyright may not be copied.
Other services	Only brief inquiries by telephone or post will be answered, but reference help is available in the search rooms. There are a number of lists, indexes, catalogs, and guides to help the researcher use the material as well as a collection of reference books which also aid the reader. In addition there are general card indexes of subjects, places, and persons which relate mostly to privately deposited records. There are facilities for group visits and exhibitions of archives can be arranged. Ultra-violet lamps and microform equipment are provided.
Publications	Guide to the Nottinghamshire County Record Office, ed. by P. A. Kennedy (1960, out-of-print); The Nottinghamshire Records Office: a Users' Guide.

OLDHAM

224 Institution Address	Oldham Library Service Local Studies Library 84 Union Street Oldham OL1 1DN

Telephone	061 678 4654
Holdings	County Borough records are held, as are those of Crompton, Lees, Failsworth, Saddleworth, Chadderton, and Royton Urban Districts. Also maps, photographs, and pamphlets, and microforms concerning the history of Oldham. Of special interest are the Rowbottom Diaries and the Butterworth manuscripts. Business records include those of Trade Unions.
Conditions of admission and access	Visiting scholars are welcome to use the collection. Inquiries should be addressed to the Local Studies Officer. The collection must be consulted on the premises.
Hours	10:00 AM - 7:00 PM, Monday, Wednesday-Friday; 10:00 AM - 1:00 PM, Tuesday; 10:00 AM - 4:00 PM, Saturday.
Duplicating facilities	Copying facilities are not provided.
Other services	Brief questions are answered either by mail or by telephone. Reference help is available.
Publications	Calendars, catalogs, and special indexes.

ORKNEY ISLANDS   <u>See</u>: KIRKWALL

OXFORD (map)

225 Institution
     Address

Bodleian Library
Broad Street
Oxford OX1 3BG

Telephone	0865 244675
Holdings	The Bodleian Library, the principal library of the University of Oxford, dates effectively from 1598, when Sir Thomas Bodley began to refurbish and restock an earlier University Library which had fallen into decay. From its opening in 1602, Bodley's new library rapidly attained universally recognized importance throughout the world of scholarship, and with the successful conclusion of an agreement with the Stationers' Company in 1610 whereby a copy of every book registered with the Company was to be made available free to the Library, the Bodleian became pre-eminent in the United Kingdom. It is now exceeded in its resources only by the British Library, and it is not only the University Library, but also a national and international research and reference library admitting some 9,000 new readers per year,

with over 4.5 million volumes (of which some
800,000 are on open access), a staff of nearly
four hundred and some twenty-two reading rooms.
For the genealogist and local historian the Library's
substantial collections of printed poll books, pedigrees, family histories, printed parish registers
(many published privately) and early English
newspapers will be of special interest. However,
the most important collections are, without doubt,
the unique collections of manuscripts in the Department of Western Manuscripts, covering all aspects of English history, particularly local history
(e.g., MSS. Ashmole, Dodsworth, Dugdale, Gough,
Hearne, Phillips-Robinson, Rawlinson, Tanner,
Willis and Wood). The library also holds a large
collection of deeds and charters, relating to all
parts of the country, but especially for Oxfordshire, Berkshire and Buckinghamshire, such
counties being further represented by the deposited
collections of deeds and papers of notable local
families, such as the Dashwoods of West Wycombe
(Bucks), the Berties, Earls of Abingdon (Berks),
the Barbers and Risleys of Adderbury, the Har-
courts of Stanton Harcourt and Nuneham Courte-
nay, the Simeons and Welds of Britwell Prior and
the Wykeham-Musgraves of Thame. It should be
noted, however, that many deposited collections of
family papers (other than those listed above) have
been transferred to the Oxfordshire County Record
Office which is now also the recognized repository
for the deposit of Church of England records for
the historic (i.e., pre-1974) County of Oxford
(see entry no. 226).

Most Oxford colleges and halls (see list at the
end of this section) maintain their own archives
and are entirely separate from the Bodleian.
Access to these records must therefore be sought
from the relevant college Archivist or Librarian.
However, All Souls College has deposited most of
its archives in the Bodleian; Christ Church and
Queen's College have deposited their medieval
deeds, and Jesus College its records of internal
college administration. (Permission is required
from the respective Librarian and Keeper of the
Archives to consult All Souls and Queen's College
material).

The Bodleian buildings also house the University
Archives, although not formally part of the library.
To consult such material, application should be
made to the Keeper of the University Archives.

Conditions of
admission and
access

Anyone wishing to apply for reading privileges in
the Bodleian Library and its dependent libraries
(i.e., Law Library, Indian Institute Library,
Radcliff Science Library and Rhodes House Li-
brary--all situated elsewhere in the City center)
should write to the Admissions Office for an

application form for a reader's ticket, stating
clearly the nature of the intended research.
A charge is made for use of the library.

Hours

9:00 AM - 7:00 PM (10:00 PM in Oxford University
full term), Monday-Friday; 9:00 AM - 1:00
PM, Saturday. In addition to normal bank
holidays, the library is closed for the week beginning the late summer bank holiday and December 24 to January 1.

Duplicating
facilities

There is an extensive range of photographic processes and photocopying. All copying is subject
to British copyright law.

Other services

A specialist staff and reference librarians are
available for helping visiting researchers. There
is no general subject catalog, although there are
many useful finding aids, indexes and calendars.

Publications

Bodleian Quarterly Record 1914-1938; Bodleian
Library Record, 1938- ; Annals of the Bodleian
Library, by W. D. Macray (2nd ed., 1890);
History of the Bodleian Library 1845-1945, by E.
Craster (1952); Summary Catalogue of Western
Manuscripts in the Bodleian Library, 7 volumes
(1895-1953, reprinted, 1980). There are also
separate "Quarto Catalogues" for MSS Ashmole,
Rawlinson and Tanner. Calendar of Charters
and Rolls, by W. H. Turner and H. O. Coxe;
Index of Persons in Oxfordshire Deeds in the
Bodleian Library, by W. O. Hassall (Oxfordshire
Record Society, 45, 1966); Summary Catalogue of
Manuscripts in the Bodleian Library Relating to
the City, County, and University of Oxford, 1915-
1962, by P. S. Spokes (Oxford Historical Society,
new series XVII, 1964); A Bibliography of Printed
Works Relating to Oxfordshire, by E. H. Cor-
deaux (1955, with supplement, 1981); Oxford City
(1976); Oxford University (1968); Oxford Libraries
Outside the Bodleian: A Guide, by Paul Morgan
(2nd ed., 1980); A Guide to Microform Holdings in
the Bodleian Library (1982); Manuscript Collections
in Rhodes House Library, by Louis B. Frewer and
W. S. Byrne (4 volumes, 1968-1978).

List of Oxford Colleges and Halls:

All Souls College	New College
Balliol College	Nuffield College
Blackfriars	Oriel College
Brasenose College	Pembroke College
Campion Hall	The Queen's College
Christ Church College	Regent's Park College
Corpus Christi College	St. Anne's College
Exeter College	St. Antony's College
Greyfriars	St. Edmund Hall

Hertford College
Jesus College
Keble College
Lady Margaret Hall
Lincoln College
Magdalen College
Manchester College
Mansfield College
Merton College

St. Hilda's College
St. John's College
Somerville College
Trinity College
University College
Wadham College
Wolfson College
Worcester College

(Courtesy of D. G. Vaisey, Keeper of Western Manuscripts.)

OXFORD (map)

226 Institution
    Address

Oxfordshire County Record Office
County Hall
Oxford OX1 1ND

Telephone

0865 815203

Holdings

The manuscript records held by this office include those of the Oxfordshire County Council and the Oxfordshire Court of Quarter Sessions from 1687. There is also a very large collection of privately deposited papers. These are comprised of deeds, family and estate papers, maps, sale catalogs, business records, political papers, solicitors' records, probate records, papers relating to charities, and manorial documents (A Summary Catalogue is available; see "Publications" below). The Quarter Sessions papers contain records of crimes and of the administrative business of the court and include about two hundred enclosure awards, ca. 1750-1850, and land tax assessments (1782-1832), gamekeepers' deputations (1784-1925 for Lords of the Manor), victuallers' recognisances (1753-1822 for inns), and registers of electors of the County (1832 to the present). Quarter Sessions rolls have been calendared for 1687-1830 and are indexed. In 1984 a number of records (Church of England) were transferred from the Bodleian Library, Oxford to this office and include probate records for Oxford Diocese and Oxford Archdeaconry, 1516-1858, Diocese of Oxford records, 1542 to the present, parish records for Oxford Archdeaconry, Oxford Archdeaconry records, 1560 to the present, and records of areas of peculiar jurisdictions for Oxfordshire from the 16th century to the mid-19th century. Found among these are wills, parish registers, court records, deeds, maps, Church Wardens' accounts and Church Wardens' presentments. The record office is a recognized repository for certain classes of public records and for manorial and tithe documents and for ecclesiastical documents.

Conditions of admission and access	The record office is open to the public but it is necessary to make an appointment in advance. Some collections are not housed at County Hall and require approximately a week's notice to be brought for use in the record office search room. Inquiries should be addressed to the County Archivist. The collection must be used on the premises.
Hours	9:00 AM - 1:00 PM, 2:00 PM - 5:00 PM, Monday-Thursday; 9:00 AM - 1:00 PM, 2:00 PM - 4:00 PM, Friday.
Duplicating facilities	Full-size copying facilities are available.
Other services	Only brief inquiries can be answered by post or telephone, but reference help is available in the search room. There are also catalogs, lists, and indexes provided to further aid the visiting scholar. These include personal names, subjects, and places for Quarter Sessions (1687-1830). For privately deposited records, indexes are to personal names, places, subjects, trades and professions, maps, sale catalogs, and surveyors. There is also an ultra-violet lamp available. The record office does undertake searches of material on payment of an hourly fee. Details of this service are available on request.
Publications	The Oxfordshire County Record Office and its Records (1938 out-of-print); A Handlist of Inclosure Acts and Awards Relating to the County of Oxford (rev. ed., 1975); A Handlist of Plans, Sections and Books of Reference for the Proposed Railways in Oxfordshire (1964); Summary Catalogue of the Privately Deposited Records in the Oxfordshire County Record Office (2nd ed., 1984); Catalogue of an Exhibition of Heraldic Seals (1967); The Oxfordshire Election of 1754 (an Archive Teaching Unit).

PERTH

227	Institution Address	Perth and Kinross District Council Archive Sandeman Library 16 Kinnoull Street Perth PH1 5ET
	Telephone	0738 23329
	Holdings	The archive holds the official archives of the City and Royal Burgh of Perth and the Burghs of Aberfeldy, Abernethy, Alyth, Auchterarder, Blaergowrn and Rattray, Coupar Angus, Crieff, Kinross, and Pitlochry. It also holds, on loan

from the Tayside Regional Council, the records of
the former County Councils of Perth, Kinross,
and Perth and Kinross. There are also several
series of records that have been re-transmitted
by the Keeper of the Records of Scotland and
private records relating to the district. These
include business archives, association and society
records, and the papers of individuals. In the
Local History Department one finds Perth Directories, 1837-1939, a collection of histories of local
families and clans, and background histories of
Perthshire towns and parishes. The census returns, 1841-1881 for the City of Perth and Old
Parochial Registers for the Parish of Perth (pre-
1855) are held on microfilm.

Conditions of admission and access	The archives are open to the public, but an appointment in advance is preferred. Inquiries should be directed to the Archivist. The records must be consulted on the premises.
Hours	9:30 AM - 5:00 PM, Monday-Friday. The Local History Department is open until 8:00 PM, Thursday and Friday.
Duplicating facilities	Photocopying facilities are available.
Other services	Reference help is available and brief questions by telephone or post are answered.
Publications	A Local History booklet is produced.

PERTH County Council	See: DUNDEE
PITLOCHRY	See: PERTH

PLYMOUTH (map)

228 Institution Address	Devon Library Services West Area Library (Plymouth) Central Library Drake Circus Plymouth PL4 8AL
Telephone	0752 21312, ext. 4675/4676
Holdings	The collection includes Plymouth and district census returns, 1841-1881 inclusive. All have street indexes and some have surname indexes as well. Also found are directories, 1812-1955, for Plymouth, and Devon and Cornwall County directories. Published genealogies of local families, and published parish records (mainly

issued by Devon and Cornwall Record Society)
are also held. The International Genealogical
Index for Devon and Cornwall is available on microfiche, as well as microfilms of local newspapers
from the nineteenth century to date.

Conditions of admission and access	The library is open to the public for reference use only. Microfilm and microfiche readers may be reserved in advance at no charge. Some newspapers not on microfilm must be ordered at least two days ahead of time. Inquiries should be directed to the Area Librarian.
Hours	9:00 AM - 9:00 PM, Monday-Friday; 9:00 AM - 4:00 PM, Saturday.
Duplicating facilities	Coin-operated photocopiers are available for the public. Microcopying is undertaken by the staff upon request.
Other services	Brief questions by telephone or mail will be answered. Advice is freely given on genealogical queries and staff will undertake a small amount of research using library sources.
Publications	Nineteenth- and twentieth-century street maps of Plymouth, postcards, and prints of old Plymouth are produced here.

PLYMOUTH (map)

229 Institution Address	West Devon Record Office Unit 3, Clare Place Coxside Plymouth PL4 0JW
Telephone	0752 264685
	See also: EXETER, Devon Record Office
Holdings	The office contains records of the City of Plymouth which include a collection of Charters from 1554 onwards, the Black Book or town ledger begun 1535-36, receivers' accounts from 1486 to 1807 (which trace the financial history of the Borough). It holds the County and District Councils' records for the West Devon area and Parish registers for Plymouth and West Devon. Among the records of parishes are found Buckland Monachorum, whose registers date from 1538 and whose Church Wardens' accounts include way and tin wardens' accounts for the 17th century; Wembury, which includes a register of church briefs, 1690-1743; Plympton St. Mary, which has workhouse accounts from 1775-1799; and Thrushelton, which has records of the Clothing Club, 1828-1832

and Sheaf tithe valuations, 1809-1836. There are records of other religious denominations and pre-1812 Bishops' transcripts available on microfilm. Business records include the Bayly Timber Company, with timber account books from 1771-1834, and journals, ledgers, and minute books of the Octagon Brewery (on microfilm). There are many solicitors' records which have local significance (where necessary, the records are closed or have restricted access). Small private collections include the letters of John Ginnys (sent to his family at Buckland Monachorum while he was with the East India Company), 1797-1816. Among the large family and estate deposits are records of the Bastards of Kitley, Parkers of Saltram, Yonges of Puslinch and Woollcombes of Hemerdon. The office is a repository for manorial and tithe documents and for ecclesiastical records (Exeter).

Conditions of admission and access	The record office is open to the public and prior appointments are not required. Inquiries should be directed to the Area Archivist. The collection may be used only on the premises.
Hours	9:30 AM - 5:00 PM, Monday-Thursday; 9:30 AM - 4:20 PM, Friday. The office is also open on the first Wednesday of the month until 7:00 PM. A list of these dates is available from the record office.
Duplicating facilities	Full-size photocopying facilities are available.
Other services	Very brief questions will be answered by telephone or mail. A list of genealogists known to be working in the area can be provided by the office. There are lists, indexes and catalogs available for researchers to use and reference aid is provided.
Publications	A Guide to the Archives Department of Plymouth City Libraries, Pt. I (Official Records, 1962); Plymouth City Charters, 1439-1935 (1962).

PORTADOWN

230 Institution Address	Southern Education and Library Board Library Services Local History Department Old Technical School 113 Church Street Portadown, Co. Armagh also: Portadown Library Headquarters 1 Markethill Road Armagh, Co. Armagh

Telephone	Portadown 335247 or 335296
Holdings	The library contains the Crossle Collection (fourteen volumes) which includes twelve volumes containing miscellaneous information relating to Newry and District (some of which is press cuttings). The remaining two volumes are copies of valuation books giving names of occupiers, annual rates, etc., in Newry. There are family histories which are a collection of notebooks giving information about Newry families which has been extracted from various sources. The library also holds General Valuation of Rateable Property in Ireland (Griffith) for the following unions in the Board's area: Armagh, Banbridge, Castleblayney, Clougher, Cookstown, Dundalk, Dungannon, Kilkeel, Lurgan, Newry and Omagh. There are copies of miscellaneous maps relating to estates in counties Armagh, Down and Tyrone, many of which give names of tenants, and a small collection of local and provincial directories.
Conditions of admission and access	The library is open to the public and no advance appointment or letter of introduction is necessary. Inquiries should be made to the Local History Librarian. The material must be used on the premises.
Hours	9:00 AM - 8:00 PM, Monday, Wednesday; 9:00 AM - 5:15 PM, Tuesday, Thursday-Friday; 10:00 AM - 1:00 PM, Saturday, except for July and August when the hours are: 9:00 AM - 5:15 PM, Monday-Friday.
Duplicating facilities	Photocopying facilities are available in the library.
Other services	Reference help is available and brief inquiries will be answered by mail or telephone. Microform equipment is provided.
Publications	None.

PORTSMOUTH (map)

231	Institution Address	City Records Office 3 Museum Road Portsmouth PO1 2LE
	Telephone	0705 829765
	Holdings	The collection includes the official records of the City of Portsmouth and large collections of public and private records relating to Portsmouth and its hinterland. Among the official records are charters and letters patent from 1313, election

and sessions material from 1531, manorial material from 1380, records of Poor Law administration from the 18th century, Improvement Commissioners records from 1764 and the records of local Burial Boards. Family and estate material includes the records of the Hewetts and Andersons of Titch-field from 1719, the Hulberts of Waterlooville from 1764, and the Wiltshires of Hayling Island from the 13th century. The Portsmouth City Records Office is also the Diocesan Record Office for three rural deaneries: Portsmouth, Alverstoke and Havant, and church holdings include the records of most of the parishes in those rural deaneries, some of which survive from 1538. There are also noncon-formist records: Roman Catholic from 1794, Uni-tarian from 1697, Methodist from 1798, Congrega-tional from 1769, Presbyterian from 1856, and Baptist from 1775. Nineteenth-century business papers include the records of the Portsmouth Water Company, Portsmouth United Breweries, the Port-sea Island Gaslight Company and the Port of Ports-mouth Floating Bridge Company.

Conditions of admission and access	The office is open to the public and visiting scholars are welcome to use the collection without advance appointment. The material is readily available in the search room and must be consulted there. Inquiries should be addressed to the City Records Officer.
Hours	9:30 AM - 12:30 PM, 2:00 PM - 5:00 PM, Monday-Wednesday; 9:30 AM - 12:30 PM, 2:00 PM - 7:00 PM, Thursday; 9:30 AM - 12:30 PM, 2:00 PM - 4:00 PM, Friday.
Duplicating facilities	Full-size and microcopying facilities are available. Photographic services can be provided. There is a reprographic fee for other than personal or private use.
Other services	Brief questions by telephone or post will be answered. Staff will advise on availability and suitability of material for research but cannot undertake research themselves. Microfilm equip-ment and an ultra-violet lamp are provided. There is a small reference library and a good selection of printed journals.
Publications	Guide to the Collection, Pt. I: Church Records (1977), Pt. II: Private Deposits (1985); Ports-mouth Archives Review, Vols. 1- , 1976- (con-tains annual reports, short articles on archival topics, transcripts of documents, notes, queries, and reviews of books).

PORTSMOUTH (map)

232 Institution Address	Hampshire County Library Portsmouth Division Portsmouth Central Library Guildhall Square Portsmouth PO1 2DX
Telephone	0705 819311-7
Holdings	The genealogical collection contains printed material including guides to genealogy, periodicals, histories of families, an incomplete collection of printed parish registers, lists of wills and probate records, lists of marriage licences, books on place names, finding aids for parish registers, wills, etc., epitaphs and brasses, heraldry and visitation, crests, coats of arms, and mottoes, flags, seals, and collections of Burke's, Debrett's and other peerages. The Local Collection contains nearly 10,000 printed books on the history of Hampshire, West Sussex, and the Isle of Wight, with emphasis on the history of Portsmouth. Maps of Portsmouth from the mid-sixteenth century are available, with some covering other parts of Hampshire. There are pamphlets, printed ephemera, photographs and other illustrations. Also available are newspapers, local census returns, 1841-1881, the Mormon International Genealogical Index for Hampshire and Sussex, Register of Electors, directories and lists (Army List, Air Force List, Navy List, etc.).
Conditions of admission and access	The library is open to anyone who can produce proof of identification. An appointment in advance is not required except for the use of microfilm of newspapers and census returns. Inquiries should be directed to the Divisional Librarian. Most books are for reference use on the premises only, but each collection has a section from which books can be borrowed for use elsewhere.
Hours	10:00 AM - 7:00 PM, Monday-Friday; 10:00 AM - 4:00 PM, Saturday.
Duplicating facilities	Photocopying and photography are available by several different processes, texts and films. Copying is at the discretion of the Librarian, and may be refused because of the condition of the material, its size or other restrictions.
Other services	Reference help is available and brief questions are answered by telephone or post. Tours can be arranged and talks by staff will be given to local groups when there is sufficient notice.
Publications	Brochures, lists, finding aids, and leaflets such

as "Beginners' Guide to Genealogy," "Sources for Local Studies and Their Location," and "Guide to Local and Genealogical Collections" (in preparation).

PRESTON

233	Institution Address	Lancashire Record Office Bow Lane Preston PR1 8ND
	Telephone	0772 54868

Holdings

The office contains manuscript sources relating to pre- and post-1974 Lancashire and elsewhere. Public records include those of Quarter Sessions, Petty Sessions, Coroners and District Valuation Officers. Manorial holdings contain those of the Honor of Clitheroe. Probate materials include wills and some inventories from the 15th century to 1858 and copies of wills from the Probate Registries of Lancashire and Liverpool, 1858-1940. Official classes of records include County Council, Borough, Urban and Rural District Council, Poor Law Union and School Board collections. Ecclesiastical archives contain diocesan material (mostly originating from the Diocese of Chester), Archdeaconry, most significantly that of Richmond (including deaneries of Amounderness, Copeland, Furness, Kendal and Lonsdale), and parish collections which include registers of baptisms, marriages and burials and records of the overseers of the poor. There are extensive deposits made by denominations such as the Methodists, as well as the Roman Catholic Church. There are many family and estate collections, notably those of the Earls of Derby and the Scarisbrick of Scarisbrick, Clifton of Lytham, Cavendish of Holker, Hesketh of Rufford, Molyneux of Sefton and Kay-Shuttleworth of Gawthorpe families. In addition there are business records which include those of solicitors and textile manufacturers. Certain records are made available in microform. Records date from the 12th century to the present. The office is a recognized repository for certain public records, for manorial and tithe documents, and for ecclesiastical records (the dioceses of Blackburn, Bradford, Carlisle, Liverpool and Manchester).

Conditions of admission and access

The office is open to all bona fide searchers who are of secondary school age or older. An advance appointment is not necessary. The collections must be consulted on the premises and access to certain records is restricted. Inquiries should be addressed to the County Archivist.

Hours	10:00 AM - 8:30 PM, Tuesday; 10:00 AM - 5:00 PM, Wednesday-Friday; Closed Monday.
Duplicating facilities	Full-size and microcopying facilities are available. Photographic services can also be arranged.
Other services	Brief questions by post will be answered and reference help is available in the search room. There is an ultra-violet lamp for reading faded documents. There is a lecture room available for group visits, and exhibitions and talks can be provided on written request with sufficient notice.
Publications	Guide to the Lancashire Record Office, ed. by R. Sharpe France (3rd ed., 1985); Handlist of Genealogical Sources (1983).

RAMSGATE

234	Institution Address	Kent Archives Office North East Kent Branch Ramsgate Library Guildford Lawn Ramsgate CT11 9AY
	Telephone	0843 53532
	Holdings	The collection includes records of local government and material concerning Thanet (transferred from other locations). Papers accumulated from private hands or organizations are also found. The library holds a Kent and Ramsgate local collection.
	Conditions of admission and access	Users should make an appointment in advance of an intended visit. Inquiries should be directed to the Archivist-in-Charge. The collection must be used on the premises.
	Hours	To use the Archives Office Collection it is necessary to make an appointment. The library is open 10:00 AM - 7:00 PM, Monday-Friday; 10:00 AM - 1:00 PM, Saturday.
	Duplicating facilities	Photocopies can be provided.
	Other services	Brief questions by post or telephone are answered and reference help is provided.
	Publications	None.

READING (map)

235	Institution Address	Berkshire Record Office Shire Hall

Shinfield Park
Reading RG2 9XD

Telephone	0734 875444, ext. 3182

Holdings

The office is a repository for historic records of the Royal County of Berkshire, which include Quarter Sessions (from 1703), records of some Boroughs and small towns within the County, and records of other official and semi-official bodies. Archives of the Thames Navigation Commission, companies owning the old toll bridges, records of the Society of Friends and many other public and private organizations are found. Parish registers of baptisms, marriages, and burials for a large proportion of the ancient parishes in the county are in the record office, with other parish records, mainly of the 18th and 19th centuries. These include records of poor relief, which are followed, after 1834, by the series of Poor Law Guardians records for each Union in the County. Records of private families or of individuals form one of the largest classes of papers and may be very varied material, such as title deeds (medieval and modern), records of manorial courts, maps of farms and family estates with accounts, bills (personal and household), letters and diaries. These family records are of varying sizes, from one item to several hundred. The record office is a recognized repository for certain public records and for ecclesiastical documents (Oxford: Archdeaconry of Berkshire).

Conditions of admission and access

The office is open to the public. A prior appointment is recommended, but not required. Many records are subject to the thirty-year rule restricting access to them and some personal records are closed for longer periods. The collection must be used in the search room. Inquiries should be made to the County Archivist.

Hours

2:00 PM - 5:00 PM, Monday; 9:00 AM - 5:00 PM, Tuesday-Wednesday; 9:00 AM - 9:00 PM, Thursday; 9:00 AM - 4:00 PM, Friday.

Duplicating facilities

Full-size and microcopying facilities are available.

Other services

Brief questions by telephone or mail will be answered and reference help is available in the office. There is a reference library of local and county histories, family histories, pamphlets and general reference books available and also lists, indexes and catalogs are provided to aid the researcher. Arrangements can be made for group visits and advice is given to owners of documents on the better preservation of their records.

Publications   <u>Guide to the Berkshire Record Office</u>, by F. Hull (1952, out-of-print); <u>Finding Your Family: A Genealogist's Guide to the Berkshire Record Office</u> (1982); descriptive leaflets on various types of records are issued and sets of photocopies of records for teaching or personal use are available for sale.

READING (map)

236 Institution
    Address

Institute of Agricultural History and Museum of
    English Rural Life
University of Reading
Whiteknights
P.O. Box 229
Reading RG6 2AG

Telephone   0734 875123, ext. 475

<u>See also</u>: READING, University of Reading Library

Holdings   The collections date from 1750 and cover all aspects of agricultural history and rural life, with emphasis on historical development of agricultural equipment, agricultural processing and servicing industries. The archival collections include 18th- to 20th-century records kept by English farmers. Each English county is represented. Also represented are trade collections comprising the business records of agricultural machinery manufacturers, dealers and contractors, and material from other agricultural service concerns such as seedsmen, agrochemical companies and animal foodstuffs producers. These include Beeby Brothers, Bomford and Evershed, Ltd., Clayton and Suttleworth, Ltd., John Fowler and Co., Guinness, International Harvester Co. of Great Britain, Massey-Ferguson (U.K.), H. Plowright and Sons, Ltd., Sutton Seeds, Ltd., and The Wantage Engineering Co., Ltd. National agricultural societies and organizations are held along with publicity material and social and personal accumulations. Records of the Royal Agricultural Society of England are held and include the archives of the Board of Agricultural and Internal Improvement, 1793-1822. Also found are the records of the National Union of Agricultural and Allied Workers Union and the National Farmers Union. The Country Landowners Association, Royal Agricultural Benevolent Institution, Council for the Protection of Rural England, Agricultural Apprenticeship Council, and the Agricultural Cooperative Society Records are found. There are also other collections relating to agriculture and the countryside containing papers of agricultural scientists and writers, and material concerning rural crafts and industries and auction of stock.

Conditions of admission and access	The collection is open to the public by appointment. Some records require a week's notice for consulting. Inquiries should be directed to the Librarian. The material must be used on the premises. In certain cases, depositors have placed restrictions on their collections.
Hours	9:30 AM - 1:00 PM, 2:00 PM - 5:00 PM, Monday-Thursday; 9:30 AM - 1:00 PM, 2:00 PM - 4:30 PM, Friday. Saturday hours by prior arrangement.
Duplicating facilities	Photocopying, microfilm, slides, dielines, and photographs can be supplied.
Other services	Brief telephone and postal inquiries are answered and reference service is available. There are many indexes and other finding aids provided. Classes and visits by students can be arranged. Some indexes are held by the University of Reading Library.
Publications	Lists, guides and brochures are produced, and some publications of the University of Reading Library refer to this collection.

READING (map)

237 Institution Address	University of Reading Library Department of Archives, Manuscripts, and Rare Books Whiteknights Reading RG6 2AE
Telephone	0734 874331, ext. 137
	See also: READING, Institute of Agricultural History and Museum of English Rural Life, University of Reading
Holdings	The collection includes historical and literary manuscripts and the records of British publishing and printing firms. These include correspondence, books of accounts, photographs, prints, drawings, agreements with authors, leases, deeds, and other papers. Among the firms represented are Baillière, Tindall and Cox Limited, George Bell and Sons Limited, The Bodley Head Limited, Jonathan Cape Limited, Chatto and Windus Limited, De La Rue and Company Limited, Hogarth Press Limited, London Typographical Designers Limited, the Longman Group Limited, Macmillan and Company Limited, Charles Elkin Mathews, Phoenix House Limited, Routledge and Kegan Paul Limited (correspondence files, 1935-1970; ledgers, authors'

agreements, printed catalogs, and other papers, 1853-1973 are found at the University College London), and Secker and Warburg, Limited. Historical farm records are held and include correspondence, books of account, farm diaries, maps and plans, reports, sale catalogs, cropping books, leases and other deeds, registers and valuation, and printed material, from the 16th century to date. (See also: University of Reading, Museum of English Rural Life, entry no. 236.) Records of contemporary writing (since about 1880) are also found. Modern political papers include those of Nancy, Viscountess Astor, Waldorf, 2nd Viscount Astor, the Reading branch of the "Britain in Europe" movement, Cecil Jackson, Squire Sprigge, the Italian Refugees Relief Committee and the Salo (fascist) Republic of Northern Italy. The University archives and records are held, as well as other historical and literary collections such as the Agricultural Education Association, Henley Parochial Church Council, Huntley and Palmers, Limited, Peek Frean and Company, Limited, and papers of Aubrey Beardsley, Henry Curtis Cherry, Lewis Mumford, and Kingsley Read.

Conditions of admission and access	The department is open to staff and students of the University with no conditions, and to the general public by appointment. The material may be used only in the Special Collections Reading Room. Inquiries should be directed to the Keeper of Archives and Manuscripts.
Hours	9: 00 AM - 1: 00 PM, 2: 00 PM - 5: 00 PM, Tuesday-Friday.
Duplicating facilities	Photocopying can be done by the archives staff and photographs can be supplied by the University photographer.
Other services	Brief questions by post or telephone are answered and reference help is available.
Publications	A Brief Guide to Archives and Manuscripts (1983); Exhibition Catalogues; Historical Farm Records: A Summary Guide (1973) are among the publications by the University which relate to the Department.
RICHMOND-UPON-THAMES	See: LONDON, London Borough of Richmond-upon-Thames Library Department

ROCHDALE

238 Institution	Rochdale Libraries
Address	Rochdale Area Central Library

Local Studies Collection
The Esplanade
Rochdale OL16 1AQ

Telephone   0706 474747, ext. 423

                              See also: HEYWOOD, Rochdale Libraries, Heywood
                              Area Central Library; MIDDLETON, Rochdale
                              Libraries, Middleton Area Central Library

Holdings   Highway rates, Turnpike Trust (Rochdale to
                              Burnley), poor law records, Gas Commissioners
                              papers, and other records from the Metropolitan
                              Borough are held. Local newspapers are also in-
                              cluded in the collection. There are manorial,
                              family and estate papers, deeds and other archives
                              concerning families of the area. These include
                              Dearden, and Stott of Bent House, Littleborough.
                              Maps (including tithe maps) and plans are also
                              found. Church records (including Methodist
                              archives) and documents concerning the construc-
                              tion of Rochdale Canal are held. Business papers,
                              trade union records, papers of the Temperance
                              Society and the Literary and Philosophical Society
                              are found.

Conditions of   The library is open to the public and formal ar-
admission and   rangements to use the collection are not required.
access   Inquiries should be directed to the Local Studies
                              Librarian. Archives and reference works must be
                              used in the library.

Hours   9:30 AM - 7:30 PM, Monday-Tuesday, Thursday;
                              9:30 AM - 5:00 PM, Wednesday; 9:30 AM - 5:30
                              PM, Friday; 9:30 AM - 4:00 PM, Saturday.

Duplicating   Photocopying can be provided.
facilities

Other services   Brief questions by post or telephone are
                              answered and reference help is provided.

Publications   Introduction to the Local Studies Collection
                              (1981).

ROMFORD   See: LONDON, London Borough of Havering

ROTHERHAM

239 Institution   Rotherham Libraries, Museums, and Arts
    Address   The Brian O'Malley Central Library and Arts
                                  Centre
                              Walker Place
                              Rotherham S65 1JH

    Telephone   0709 2121, ext. 3119

Holdings	Records of the Metropolitan Borough Council and the predecessor authorities, County Borough, Rural District Council, and Urban District Council are held. There are also non-conformist church records, photographs, press cuttings, newspapers, maps, and illustrations.
Conditions of admission and access	The library is open to the public. Inquiries should be directed to the Principal Librarian. Archives and reference works must be used on the premises.
Hours	10:00 AM - 4:45 PM, Monday-Tuesday, Thursday-Friday; 9:00 AM - 12:30 PM, Saturday. Closed Wednesday.
Duplicating facilities	There are facilities for photocopying available.
Other services	Questions by post or telephone will be answered if they are short. Reference help is provided.
Publications	None.

RUTHIN

240 Institution Address	Clwyd Record Office 46 Clwyd Street Ruthin LL15 1HP
Telephone	08242 3077
	See also: HAWARDEN, Clwyd Record Office
Holdings	The Clwyd Record Office has custody of the public and official records of Flintshire and Denbighshire from the 16th century. The collection contains commercial directories which give a description of towns and parishes and list principal inhabitants for the following years and districts: 1818-1820, 1829 (Wrexham only), 1830, 1835, 1840 (all North Wales), 1844, 1850, 1856, 1868, 1874, 1876, 1883, 1886 (Flintshire and Denbighshire), 1889-1890, 1895 (Denbighshire). Microfilm copies of the census of Denbighshire for 1841, 1851, 1861, 1871, and 1881 are held. These are arranged by parishes and list the members of each household and give age, relation to head of household, occupation and, from 1851, place of birth. Non-conformists' records for Denbighshire, 1713-1837 are found and include Wesleyan and Primitive Methodist Chapels in the Wrexham Circuit (Wrexham, Ruabon and neighborhood, 1843-1966), Electoral registers for Denbighshire from 1832 (with occasional gaps); tithe maps for Denbighshire (dated mainly between

1839-1849), Poor Law records of Llanrwst, Ruthin, and Wrexham Unions, school records for Denbighshire, taxation records of Denbighshire, hearth tax returns, 1663-1671, the Quarter Sessions records for Denbighshire from 1649 are found and include land tax assessments for Denbighshire, 1778-1830 (incomplete). Also highway records, Borough and District Council records are found. The office holds archives of local families and estates and business and industrial records. The office is recognized as a repository for manorial and tithe documents and designated to receive ecclesiastical records (St. Asaph parish records).

Conditions of admission and access

Researchers with limited research time or long-term projects are advised to make an appointment in advance of their visit. Most documents can be produced with no prior notice, but documents are not produced between 12:00 noon and 1:30 PM unless ordered in advance. All material must be used on the premises. Inquiries should be addressed to the County Archivist.

Hours

9:00 AM - 4:45 PM, Monday-Thursday; 9:00 AM - 4:15 PM, Friday.

Duplicating facilities

Full-size and microcopying facilities are available, and photographs can be provided.

Other services

Questions by mail or telephone are answered if they are brief. Reference help is available for visiting scholars as well as lists, indexes and an extensive library of printed sources on local history and topography. The staff are available for illustrated talks and will arrange exhibits. The County Archivist acts as Hon. Archivist to St. Deiniol's Library, Hawarden.

Publications

Guide to the Flintshire Records (1974 out-of-print); Hand List of the County Records (1955); Calendar of the Flintshire Quarter Sessions Rolls 1747-1752 (1983); Clwyd in Old Photographs (1975); Historic Ruthin (1979); Clwyd Archives Cookbook (1980); Plas Newydd and the Ladies of Llangollen (1980); Wrexham Directory (1981); Mr. Gladstone and Hawarden (1982); Parish Map (1982); Hand List of the Denbigh Borough Records (1975); Handlist of the Topographical Prints of Clwyd (1977); Archive Teaching Units (collection of about fifteen facsimilies of documents with introduction and explanatory notes), which include The River Dee (1981), Coal Mining (1975), Daniel Owen (1975), illustrated booklets as follows: Ruthin Gaol (1977), The Mold Riots (1977), The Tithe War (1978), Rhyfel Y Degwm (1978), facsimilies of maps and prints; and postcards.

ST. ANNE'S (map)

241	Institution Address	Alderney Society Museum The Old School High Street St. Anne's Alderney, Channel Islands

Telephone   Alderney 3222

Holdings
The collection includes some land registers and documents concerning the church and the government of the island. Cemetery registers and census of property (1940) are also held. There are papers of Alderney families, the militia, and local history. Material concerning preservation of island customs and traditions, genealogy, folk life, the German occupation, archaeology, geology, and natural history are also found.

Conditions of admission and access
The museum is open to the public. Inquiries concerning use of the collection should be directed to the Curator. Material may be removed only with permission.

Hours
10:00 AM - 12:30 PM, Monday-Saturday; on hydrofoil and steamer days, the museum will remain open until 3:30 PM at the discretion of the custodians and other opening times may be arranged with the curator.

Duplicating facilities
Copying facilities are available.

Other services
Brief telephone or postal inquiries will be answered.

Publications
Afoot in Alderney; Alderney, Fortress Island; Alderney Scrap Book; The Alderney Story; Geology of Alderney; Flowers and Plants of Alderney; Birds of Alderney.

ST. HELENS

242	Institution Address	St. Helens Local History Library Central Library Gamble Institute Victoria Square St. Helens WA10 1DY

Telephone   0744 24061, ext. 2234

Holdings
Records of the Borough Council and its predecessors are kept along with family and estate records and business papers. Poor Law documents for the Township of Parr (1688-1828), Grundy's

Ironmongers papers (1913-1970), and the Sherdley estate papers (1477-1900) are found here. In addition there are maps, newspapers, and pamphlets.

Conditions of admission and access	The library is open to the public and advance arrangements are not necessary. Inquiries should be directed to the Local History Librarian and Archivist. The collection must be used on the premises.
Hours	9:00 AM - 6:00 PM, Monday-Friday; 9:00 AM - 1:00 PM, Saturday.
Duplicating facilities	Photocopying facilities are available.
Other services	Questions are answered by mail or telephone if they are short. Reference advice is offered.
Publications	Genealogical Sources; and indexes, guides and brochures are issued.

ST. HELIER (map)

243	Institution Address	Judicial Greffe Royal Court Chambers 10, Hill Street St. Helier, Jersey
	Telephone	0534 75472
	Holdings	The only records held by this department, which in theory are accessible for research by the public, are those of the Public Registry, comprising land transactions in Jersey from 1602 to the present day. These documents are in French and are in chronological order and indexed under the names of the persons transacting.
	Conditions of admission and access	As these records are maintained primarily for business purposes, their use for genealogical research is not encouraged. There is also a limitation of working space. Inquiries should be directed to the Judicial Greffier or Registrar of Deeds.
	Hours	10:00 AM - 1:00 PM, 2:00 PM - 5:00 PM, Monday-Friday.
	Duplicating facilities	Photocopying facilities can be provided.
	Other services	The staff cannot undertake searches on a regular basis, but will endeavor to cooperate in response to an occasional inquiry.

Publications   None.

ST. HELIER (map)

244 Institution   La Société Jersiaise
     Address   Lord Coutanche Library
                    7 Pier Road
                    St. Helier
                    Jersey, Channel Islands

Telephone   0534 30538

Holdings   Family trees and records of the relevant research are kept here and are arranged by family name. These date from the fifteenth century. There is also a collection of works on local history.

Conditions of admission and access   The visiting scholar is welcome to use the collection but an advance appointment is advised. Inquiries should be directed to the Librarian. The material must be used on the premises.

Hours   10:00 AM - 4:30 PM, Monday-Friday, 10:00 AM - 12:30 PM, 2:00 PM - 4:30 PM, Saturday.

Duplicating facilities   Photocopying facilities are available.

Other services   Inquiries by telephone or post will be answered and reference help is provided in the library. Genealogical research will be carried out for a fee.

Publications   The Société Jersiaise publishes an annual Bulletin.

ST. PETER PORT

245 Institution   The Greffe
     Address   Royal Court House
                    St. Peter Port
                    Guernsey, Channel Islands

Telephone   0481 25277

Holdings   The Greffe is a working archive in daily use by members of the Guernsey bar and other authorized persons. It contains contemporary copies of charters granted to the Bailiwick from 1394 and judicial records of the Royal Court of Guernsey from 1527. Also found here are legislative records from 1553 and records of the States of Guernsey from 1605. Records of land conveyances are held from 1576 and registers of births, marriages, and deaths from 1840. The Bailiwick census returns for 1841-1881 are on microfilm and are part of the collection. Wills of real property from 1841, when it first became possible to make wills of realty, are part of this collection. Wills of personalty, from 1664, are held at the Greffe, but form part of the archive of the Ecclesiastical Court which exercises probate jurisdiction in respect of Guernsey, Alderney and Sark. Permission to consult this class of records must be obtained from the Registrar of the Ecclesiastical Court (12 New Street, St. Peter Port; telephone: 0481 21732). Surviving records of the German Feldkommandantur (1940-1945) may be consulted here, but it should be noted that these records (some three hundred files) are all in German. Identity Card records from the period of the German Occupation (1940-1945) are found, including passport-type photographs of civilian residents fourteen years of age and over. Access to this class is restricted and prior permission must be obtained from H. M. Greffier for inspection. In addition, there are private collections deposited by local families, notably the de Sausmariz papers. Virtually all records prior to 1948 are in French and a command of that language is essential for all serious scholars researching at the Greffe.

Conditions of admission and access	Written application to use the records should be made to Her Majesty's Greffier. A letter of introduction is recommended. None of the material is loaned, and all must be used on the premises.
Hours	9:00 AM - 1:00 PM, 2:00 PM - 4:00 PM, Monday-Friday.
Duplicating facilities	Photocopying can be accomplished at the Greffe.
Other services	Telephone or written inquiries will be answered as resources permit. Reference help is available and indexes and other finding aids are provided to further aid the researcher.
Publications	A list of bound volumes at the Greffe was published by the List and Index Society (Volume 2 in the Society's Special Series). A brief calendar of single documents under the Bailiwick Seal, primarily from the period 1350-1600, was published in 1978 as Volume 11 in the same series. A calendar of all single documents exists in typescript and may be consulted at the Greffe. Also a general introduction is found in "The Records of the Royal Court," by J. Conway Davies, La Société Guernesiaise, Transactions XVI (1956-60), pp. 404-414.

ST. PETER PORT

246	Institution	Prialux Library
	Address	Candie Road
		St. Peter Port
		Guernsey, Channel Islands

Telephone 0481 21998

Holdings The collection includes the pedigree rolls of certain local families, files of documents, deeds, and livres de perchages (feudal records). Also copies of entries from some church records are found. Pamphlets, trade directories, scrapbooks, photographs, and transactions of local history societies are also held. Some militia records, army lists, 1661-1714 and 1756-1920, and some privateering crew lists and accounts are available. Local newspapers, 1812-1850, and press cuttings are housed here and there is a collection of local history books and local heraldry.

Conditions of admission and access The library is open to the public and no advance notice of a visit is required. Most items must be used on the premises, although certain works may be borrowed by members. Membership is limited to Guernsey residents. Inquiries should be directed to the Chief Librarian.

Hours 9:30 AM - 5:00 PM, Monday-Saturday.

Duplicating facilities Facilities for photocopying are available.

Other services Postal inquiries and questions by telephone are answered. Reference help is provided in the library. The staff will undertake research.

Publications None.

SALFORD See: MANCHESTER

SALISBURY

Institution Diocesan Record Office
See: TROWBRIDGE, Wiltshire County Record Office

SCARBOROUGH

247	Institution	North Yorkshire County Library, Eastern Division
	Address	Central Library
		Vernon Road
		Scarborough YO11 2NN

Telephone	0732 64285
Holdings	The library holds Scarborough town rate books, Harbour Commissioners' minutes and accounts (1752-1904), the Cliff Bridge Company papers, and records of societies and associations. There are some family papers which include deeds, ship logs, and indentures. There are also prints and photographs.
Conditions of admission and access	Researchers are allowed to use the collection but must have a means of identification. Arrangements in advance are advised. Inquiries should be addressed to the Assistant County Librarian. The collection must be used on the premises.
Hours	10:00 AM - 5:30 PM, Monday-Thursday; 10:00 AM - 7:00 PM, Friday; 10:00 AM - 4:00 PM, Saturday.
Duplicating facilities	Facilities for photocopying are available.
Other services	Postal inquiries and those by telephone are answered if they are brief. Reference service is available.
Publications	Catalogs and guides are issued.

SELKIRK

248	Institution Address	Borders Regional Library St. Mary's Mill Selkirk TD7 5EU
	Telephone	092 20842
	Holdings	County and all the predecessor authorities' records are held here and include burial records for Berwickshire and Peeblesshire, poor relief records for Berwickshire and Selkirkshire, and School Boards, Police and Turnpike Trustees documents. Peebles Town Council and Burgh Court papers, Roxburghshire Heritors' records and Valuation Rolls, and Lieutenancy and Valuation Rolls for Selkirkshire are also found.
	Conditions of admission and access	Searchers must make an appointment to use the collection. Inquiries should be directed to the Regional Librarian. The collection may be consulted only on the premises.
	Hours	8:30 AM - 5:00 PM, Monday-Thursday; 8:30 AM - 4:30 PM, Friday.
	Duplicating facilities	Photocopying facilities are available.

Other services	Brief questions by post or telephone are considered. Reference help is given.
Publications	None.

SHEFFIELD

249 Institution Address	Sheffield City Libraries, Archives Division Central Library Surrey Street Sheffield SI1 1XZ
Telephone	0742 734756
Holdings	The collection includes Church of England parish registers for parishes in the Archdeaconry of Sheffield from the 16th to the 20th century and manorial records, deeds, and estate records from the 12th to the 20th century. There is also miscellaneous probate material (16th to the 20th century) and miscellaneous pedigrees. Rate books, 18th to the 20th century, burial registers of public and private cemeteries, 19th and 20th centuries, and other similar records are also found. The South Yorkshire County Record Office has been subsumed within this institution. Point of contact is Sheffield City Libraries, Sheffield Record Office at the same address and telephone number as above. This material contains microfilm of the census for 1841-1881 of all places in the County of South Yorkshire and for several adjacent places in Derbyshire, Humberside, Nottinghamshire, and West Yorkshire. Microfilm copies of the Bishops' transcripts of those parish registers of South Yorkshire, of which the originals are held by the Borthwick Institute in York, are included. Lists of monumental inscriptions and burial registers (on microfilm) of municipally controlled cemeteries in Barnsley, Doncaster, Rotherham, and Sheffield are found. A few original wills and photocopies of wills and inventories for parishes formerly in Derbyshire, including Beighton, Dore and Totley, Mosborough and Norton (ca. 1530-1750), are also part of this material. Some baptismal registers for central Barnsley Methodist churches and registers of baptisms, marriages and burials are found for various Congregational churches including Mount Zion in Sheffield, Netherfield in Thurlstone, Maltby and Swinton. Poll books, local histories, family histories and some pedigrees are found along with records of business firms, schools and institutions.
Conditions of admission and access	The archives are open to the public and a prior appointment is not required except for Saturday and Monday evening openings, but advance notice

of a visit is still advisable. Manuscripts are issued at set times, i.e. 10:00 AM, 11:00 AM,
12:00 noon, 2:00 PM, 3:00 PM, and 4:00 PM.
Users wanting material before 10:00 AM must request it the previous day. All material for use
on Saturday must be ordered in advance. It
should also be noted that many of the documents
are stored outside the central premises. Manuscripts must be returned by 5:00 PM on weekdays
and by 4:00 PM on Saturdays. All material must
be used on the premises. Inquiries should be
directed to the Archivist.

Hours

9:30 AM - 5:30 PM, Monday-Friday; 9:00 AM -
4:30 PM, Saturday by appointment only, which
must be made in advance; on the second Monday
of the month, the Division is open to 8:30 PM
by appointment only, which must be made by the
preceding Thursday. The office closes for lunch,
1:00 PM - 2:00 PM.

Duplicating
facilities

Photocopies can be provided if the material is suitable. Facilities are available to produce microfilm,
prints from microfilm, and photographs.

Other services

Brief questions will be answered by post and by
telephone and reference help is available. There
is also a reference collection to aid the user and
an ultra-violet lamp and microform equipment are
available.

Publications

Guide to the Manuscript Collection (1956);
Supplement, 1956-1976 (1976).

SHEFFIELD

Institution

South Yorkshire Record Office
See: SHEFFIELD City Libraries

SHEPWAY District
Council

See: MAIDSTONE, Kent Archives Office

SHETLAND ISLANDS

See: LERWICK

SHREWSBURY (map)

250 Institution
Address

Local Studies Library
Shropshire Libraries
Castle Gates
Shrewsbury SY1 2AS

Telephone

0743 61058

Holdings	The collection contains books, pamphlets, news-papers, magazines, photographs, prints, maps, plans, parish registers (before 1812), census records for Shropshire, 1841-1881, directories, pedigrees, and family histories relating to the County of Shropshire. There are also archaeological and local history journals and reference books about the area surrounding the County. The Local Studies Library is a recognized repository for manorial and tithe documents and for ecclesiastical records (Hereford: parish records of Archdeaconry of Ludlow; Lichfield: parish records of Archdeaconry of Salop). The Local Studies Library is located in the Old Shrewsbury School Building.
Conditions of admission and access	The library is open to the public and no advance appointment is required. However, researchers wishing to use microfilms (such as census records) are advised to book a microfilm reader in advance. Inquiries should be directed to the Local Studies Librarian. The collection must be used on the premises.
Hours	9:30 AM - 12:30 PM, 1:30 PM - 5:30 PM, Monday, Wednesday; 9:30 AM - 12:30 PM, 1:30 PM - 7:30 PM, Tuesday, Friday. 9:30 AM - 12:30 PM, 1:30 PM - 5:00 PM, Saturday. Closed Thursday.
Duplicating facilities	Photocopying facilities are available.
Other services	Only brief questions can be answered by post or telephone, but reference help is provided at the library.
Publications	None.

SHREWSBURY (map)

251	Institution Address	Shropshire Record Office Shirehall Abbey Foregate Shrewsbury SY2 6ND
	Telephone	0743 252851/3
	Holdings	The office contains County and some Borough records of Quarter Sessions, Town Court for Shrewsbury and Ludlow, Manor Court, Overseers of the Poor, the Police (from the mid-19th century), the civil parishes and businesses. It also holds the records of former local authorities such as Urban and Rural District Councils and ad hoc authorities such as poor law unions. Also found are Coroners' records from the 17th century for

Ludlow Borough, from the mid-16th century for Shrewsbury Borough and from the 18th century for the County. In addition, the record office is a recognized repository for certain public records, for manorial and tithe documents and for ecclesiastical parish records from the Archdeaconry of Ludlow in Hereford Diocese and the Archdeaconry of Salop in Lichfield Diocese. It also holds many non-conformist records. Copies of wills are held which were proved in the Shrewsbury Probate Register from 1858-1940.

Conditions of admission and access	The office is open to the public and researchers are permitted to use the records. Seats should be booked in advance. The collections may be used only in the search room. Inquiries should be directed to the County Archivist.
Hours	9:30 AM - 12:40 PM, 1:20 PM - 5:00 PM, Monday-Thursday; 9:30 AM - 12:40 PM, 1:20 PM - 4:00 PM, Friday.
Duplicating facilities	Full-size and microcopying facilities are available.
Other services	Only brief questions can be answered by post or telephone, but reference help is available in the record office. There is a reference library of works on local history. An ultra-violet lamp is provided and a card index of places and some subjects will be found.
Publications	Guide to Shropshire Records, by M. C. Hill (1952); List of Inclosure Awards; Gazetteer of Shropshire Place-Names, by H. D. G. Foxall, 2nd ed.; List of Original Parish Registers Held; Shropshire Parish Documents (out-of-print); List of Canals and Railways (out-of-print); List of Partial Abstracts of Contents of Quarter Sessions Rolls (three parts, out-of-print); Abstract of Quarter Sessions Orders (out-of-print); Abstract of the Quarter Sessions Rolls, 1820-1930 (1974, out-of-print); Shropshire Peace Roll, 1400-1414, ed. by E. G. Kimball (1959, out-of-print); Printed Maps of Shropshire, 1577-1900, by G. C. Cowling (1959, out-of-print); Catalogue of Estate Maps to 1850 for Shropshire.

SOUTHAMPTON (map)

252	Institution Address	Southampton City Record Office Civic Centre, Room 101 Southampton SO9 4XR
	Telephone	0703 223855, ext. 2251

Holdings   The most important records are the city's official
                        archives from 1199 including memoranda and
                        minute books from the 13th century, and other
                        classes from the 15th century. These include
                        accounts of treasurers, petty customs (port), and
                        brokerage (landgate tolls). The office also holds
                        parish, family, and business records for the
                        town, and an illustrations collection. The Parish
                        registers (indexed to the mid-nineteenth century)
                        include those for All Saints, Holy Rood, St.
                        Lawrence with St. John, St. Mary, St. Mary
                        Extra, St. Michael, South Stoneham, Millbrook,
                        Holy Trinity, St. Augustine (Northam), St. James
                        (Docks), St. Luke, St. Mark, St. Matthew, St.
                        Peter, Sholing, Freemantle, Shirley, Maybush,
                        Redbridge, Highfield, St. Denys (Portswood),
                        Bittern Park, Weston, and West End. There are
                        non-conformist church records for Above Bar
                        Congregational Church, Unitarian Church, St.
                        Andrew's Presbyterian Church, and Methodist
                        Chapels. Among the corporation records one
                        finds Burgesses' and Freemen's Admissions (1496-
                        1835), Nomination Books (1604-1836), Series of
                        Corporation Deeds from ca. 1275 and leases from
                        1378 (name-indexed to the early 19th century),
                        Registers of Apprentices (1609-1740), Rate and
                        Tax Assessments (1552 onwards), Defence Rate
                        Terrier (1454), Electoral registers (1832-1918,
                        1931 to date), School Admission Registers (from
                        1863 for a few schools). Deposited records in-
                        clude Moberly and Wharton, Solicitors (wills,
                        1659-1918, and marriage settlements, 1736-1912),
                        and Beeston, funeral directors (order books,
                        1922-1928).

Conditions of   The office is open to the public and no advance
admission and   appointment is necessary. The collection must be
access   used on the premises. Inquiries should be directed
                        to the City Archivist.

Hours   9:00 AM - 1:00 PM, 1:30 PM - 5:00 PM, Monday-
                        Friday. The office is open until 9:00 PM on two
                        evenings in each month. The dates are available
                        on request.

Duplicating   Full-size copying facilities are available and other
facilities   photographic services can be provided by special
                        arrangement.

Other services   Brief telephone and postal inquiries are answered
                        and reference help is available in the record of-
                        fice. There is a reference library which includes
                        publications of edited texts by the Southampton
                        Record Society and Records Series to further aid
                        the researcher. Also provided are various guides,
                        lists, indexes, and catalogs.

Publications	Crossing the Itchen, The Floating Bridge and Roads, 1834-1934, by B. C. Jones (1978, 3rd ed.); Visitors' Descriptions of Southampton, 1540-1956, comp. by R. Douch (1978, 3rd ed.); The Old Mills of Southampton, by R. A. Pelham (1978, 2nd ed.); Southampton City Charters, by E. Welch (1966); The Bankrupt Canal: Southampton and Salisbury, 1795-1808, by E. Welch (1978, 2nd ed.); Monuments and Memorials of Southampton, by R. Douch (1978, 2nd ed.); Minstrels and Players in Southampton, 1428-1635, by Clive Burch (1969); The Southampton Police Force, 1836-1856, by Anne Cookes (1972); The Southampton and Netley Railway, by E. Course (1985, 2nd ed.); Castleman's Corkscrew. The Southampton and Dorchester Railway, 1844-1848, by J. G. Cox (1985, 2nd ed.); Southampton Maps; Plan of Southampton, 1846; Southampton in 1620 and the Mayflower; A Survey of Southampton and its Region, ed. by Professor F. J. Monkhouse (1964, out-of-print); Collected Essays on Southampton, ed. by P. Peberdy and J. Morgan (1958, out-of-print); Tudor Merchants Hall (1975); The Population of Southampton (reprint 1978); Southampton's History. A Guide to the Printed Sources (1977, 2nd ed.); Southampton and the Sea--Horizons and Hazards (1979); Guides to Records: Southampton Records I (1964); The Southampton Record Office (1966).

SOUTHEND-ON-SEA (map)

253 Institution Address	Essex Record Office Central Library Victoria Avenue Southend-on-Sea SS2 6EX
Telephone	0702 612621, ext. 49
	See also: CHELMSFORD, Essex Record Office and COLCHESTER, Essex Record Office
Holdings	The archives in the collection relate to the area administered by the Southend-on-Sea Borough Council, Castle Point District Council, and Rochford District Council. Among the records found are parish registers, records of past and present local authorities, maps and plans, deeds of many properties within the area, photographs and engravings, sale catalogs of numerous properties, records of the old Poor Law Unions, and records of local societies and organizations. The branch office has access through microfilm, to catalogs and indexes to the collection at the headquarters office in Chelmsford.
Conditions of	The office is open to the public and an advance

admission and access	appointment is not strictly required, but is advisable. It is also appreciated if the type of material wanted is indicated so it may be prepared ahead of time. All material must be used on the premises. Inquiries should be directed to the County Archivist (County Hall, Chelmsford CM1 1LX; telephone, 0245 267222, ext. 2101) in the first instance, then to the Branch Archivist.
Hours	9:15 AM - 5:15 PM, Monday-Thursday; 9:15 AM - 4:15 PM, Friday.
Duplicating facilities	Facilities for reproduction of documents by photocopying are available. Arrangements can be made for microfilming, photography, and printouts from microfilm.
Other services	Brief questions by telephone or mail are answered and reference help is available in the office. There are indexes to the collection arranged by personal name, place, and subject, and for the Southend-on-Sea Urban Area there is an index by streets. Also available are a collection of books and pamphlets on local history, and a Local Studies Collection housed in the Central Library which should be used in conjunction with the record office.
Publications	The Essex Record Office has an extensive publication program and produces books on local themes. There is a catalog available and some publications are on sale at the branch office. Among these publications one finds Catalogue of Maps in E. R. O., 1566-1855 (reprint, 1969); First Supplement (1952 out-of-print); Second Supplement (1964); Third Supplement (1968); Guide to Essex Record Office, by F. G. Emmison (1969); Essex Parish Records, 1240-1894 (1966); Elizabethan Life (5 vols., 1970-1980, Vol. 3, out-of-print); Essex and the Industrial Revolution, by John Booker (1974 out-of-print); No. 1 Essex Quarter Session Order Book 1652-1661, ed. by D. H. Allen (1974); Guide to the Southend-on-Sea Branch of the Essex Record Office; Handlist of Parish and Non-Conformist Registers in the Essex Record Office (revised annually); Medieval Essex Community: Lay Subsidies of 1327, ed. by Jennifer C. Ward (Essex Historical Documents, Vol. 1, 1983).

SOUTHWARK	See: LONDON, Southwark Local Studies Library

SOUTHWELL

Institution	Diocesan Record Office See: NOTTINGHAM, Nottinghamshire Record Office

STAFFORD (map)

254	Institution	Staffordshire County Record Office
	Address	Eastgate Street
		Stafford ST16 2LZ

Telephone   0785 3121, ext. 8380

Holdings

The collection includes ecclesiastical parish records for most of Staffordshire, official records of the County, business and industrial records (especially mining) and solicitors' deposits, all from about the 16th to the 20th centuries. There are microfilm records of the census returns for Staffordshire, 1841-1881, and non-conformist church records, 18th-20th centuries. Family and estate records include Sutherland, Hatherton, Lichfield, Giffard, Anglesey, and Bagot. In addition there are police records which have registers of members of the county force, 1842-1894, school records, chiefly relating to those which were or became part of the state system, Ordnance Survey maps of Staffordshire (1879-1939) and a few tithe maps (a complete set of tithe maps and awards for Staffordshire is at the Lichfield Joint Record Office and some 19th-century copies are in the William Salt Library [see entry nos. 145 and 255]); poor law records, Quarter Sessions and Land Tax records, and Stafford Borough records, ca. 1528-1940. The record office is a recognized repository for certain classes of public records, manorial and tithe documents and for ecclesiastical records (Lichfield: parish records of the Archdeaconry of Stafford).

Conditions of admission and access

Appointments in advance are not necessary for individuals, but are essential for groups planning a visit. Young children are not usually admitted. The researcher is also advised to determine whether the record office holds the material in which he is interested. Inquiries should be directed to the County Archivist. Records will not be produced after 4:30 PM, Monday-Thursday, or after 4:00 PM on Friday. Access to certain classes of documents is restricted and the researcher may be asked to state why he wishes to consult them. It is possible to arrange for up to six items to be transferred to the William Salt Library (see entry no. 255) for use on Saturday between the hours of 9:30 AM and 1:00 PM. This service is by appointment only and a limit of five readers may book for each Saturday. Documents should be requested as early as possible for this transfer and at the latest by 1:00 PM on the preceding Friday. Otherwise the collection must be used on the premises.

Hours	9:00 AM - 1:00 PM, 2:00 PM - 5:00 PM, Monday-Thursday; 9:00 AM - 1:00 PM, 2:00 PM - 4:30 PM, Friday.
Duplicating facilities	Photocopying and photostat services are available.
Other services	Brief queries are answered by telephone or post. The staff cannot undertake genealogical research, but a list of record searchers is available. Reference help is available in the reading room, and there are lists, catalogs, finding aids and a card index available to further aid the user. An ultra-violet lamp is available.
Publications	List of Staffordshire Parish Registers, Transcripts and Copies in the County Record Office and William Salt Library; List of Staffordshire Non-Conformist Records in the County Record Office; List of Registers of Staffordshire Non-Conformist Churches in the County Record Office; County Record Office: Information for Readers; County Record Office: How to Use the Record Office; Outline Map of Ancient Staffordshire Parishes; Hand-list to Diocesan Probate and Church Commissioners' Records at Lichfield Joint Record Office; Summary List of Microfilms of Census Returns in the County Record Office; Place-Name Index to Townships in Staffordshire; Staffordshire Estate Maps Before 1840 and Supplement; Staffordshire Family Collections; Staffordshire Business Records; Staffordshire Farm Records; Staffordshire and the Great Rebellion; Summary List of Microfilms of Census Returns in the County Record Office (out-of-print); Staffordshire Tithe Maps and Inclosure Maps; Public Utilities in Staffordshire.

STAFFORD (map)

255	Institution Address	William Salt Library 19 Eastgate Street Stafford ST16 2LZ
	Telephone	0785 52276
	Holdings	The library is principally a local history reference library and was originally based on the collections of William Salt. The resources relate to the history of Staffordshire and other parts of England. Salt commissioned the copying of Staffordshire documents held in other repositories, and these manuscripts form an important part of the holdings. There are, in addition, several Anglo-Saxon charters, the earliest being 956, Staffordshire maps from the 16th century, a comprehensive set of royal proclamations, the Compton Census of 1676

(a religious census of the province of Canterbury), the Staffordshire Advertiser (a newspaper) from 1795, and many antiquarians' notes, such as those of Stebbing Shaw. The library is a repository for manorial and tithe documents.

Conditions of admission and access

The library, which is open to the public, is operated in close association with the Stafford-shire Record Office and the Lichfield Joint Record Office. Inquiries should be directed to the Librarian who is also the County Archivist. No appointment in advance is required. The collection must be used on the premises.

Hours

9:30 AM - 12:45 PM, 1:45 PM - 5:00 PM, Tuesday-Thursday; 9:30 AM - 12:45 PM, 1:45 PM - 4:30 PM, Friday; 9:30 AM - 1:00 PM, Saturday.

Duplicating facilities

Photocopying and photostating facilities are available through the County Record Office.

Other services

Only brief questions can be answered by post or telephone. Reference help is available at the library.

Publications

None.

STALYBRIDGE (map)

256 Institution
Address

Tameside Local Studies Library
Stalybridge Library
Trinity Street
Stalybridge SK15 2BN

Telephone

061 338 3831

Holdings

The library collects material relating to Ashton, Audenshaw, Denton, Droylsden, Dukinfield, Hyde, Longdendale, Mossley, and Stalybridge. One finds trade directories, 1814 to date, dialect works, geography, geology, transport, the cotton and other industries, and works on the history of the area. General works on other districts of Greater Manchester, Lancashire, Cheshire, and the Northwest as a whole are also found. Local newspapers from 1855 to date are available on microfilm, as well as the Manchester Guardian, 1821-1864 and the Cotton Factory Times, 1885-1937. Census records for all the towns in Tameside, 1841-1881 are also held. Parish registers of most local churches, including non-conformist, are also available on microfilm (before 1837). Ordnance Survey maps and plans from 1843 and small-scale county maps from 1577 are held, and a collection of photographs, engravings, posters, and broadsheets, is also found. Also included in the collection are records of the local authorities which preceded Tameside, trade unions, hospitals, businesses, local parishes, transport, organizations, and public undertakings. Indexes to wills at Cheshire (pre-1857 only), and the International Genealogical Index for Lancashire, Cheshire, Yorkshire, and Derbyshire are found.

Conditions of admission and access

The library is open to the public and no prior appointment is necessary. Inquiries should be made to the Local Studies Librarian. The collection must be used on the premises.

Hours

9:00 AM - 7:30 PM, Monday-Wednesday, Friday; 9:00 AM - 4:00 PM, Saturday; Closed Thursday.

Duplicating facilities

Photocopies, full-size copies from microfilm and photographs can be provided.

Other services

Brief questions by post or telephone are answered and reference help is available in the library. Exhibitions and slide packs on various topics are available.

Publications

Tameside, an Outline History, by C. Wilkins-James; Victorian Ashton, ed. by S. A. Harrop and E. A. Rose (1974); Guide to the Archive Collection (1984); history fact sheets, a series of books of old photographs of the towns in the area, postcards, greeting cards, and brochures are issued.

STIRLING

257 Institution
Address

Central Regional Council Archives Department
Old High School
Spittal Street
Stirling FK8 1DG

Telephone

0786 73111, ext. 466

Holdings

The collection includes all extant records of local government for Central Region from 1360. This includes Stirling Burgess entries, and Court and Council records and registers from 1519. Also found are Stirling and Clackmannanshire Valuation Rolls from 1855 and School Board and subsequent education material from 1872. Poor Law material dates from 1845 and the Stirling Guildry and Incorporated Trades records are from 1460-1900. The records of the Whinwell Children's Home, Stirling, date from 1884-1980. Also in the holdings are MacGregor of MacGregor papers, 1320-1921, burial records, "Stirling Observer" file, 1836-1974, Stirling and Dunblane and Falkirk Presbytery and Kirk Session records from 1581.

Conditions of admission and access	The archives are open to the public and an appointment in advance is not necessary. Inquiries should be directed to the Archivist. The collection must be used on the premises.
Hours	9:00 AM - 5:00 PM, Monday-Friday, except public holidays.
Duplicating facilities	Facilities for photocopying are available.
Other services	Reference help is available for the users and brief questions are answered by post or telephone.
Publications	A complete inventory of the collection is available.

STOCKPORT

258	Institution Address	Stockport Central Library Wellington Road South Stockport SK1 3RS
	Telephone	061 480 3038/7297
	Holdings	The library contains works about the history of Stockport Metropolitan Borough and Stockport in the context of the Greater Manchester County, Lancashire and Cheshire. A wide variety of subjects covered includes industrial archaeology, railway building, and the Stockport Market. Census records, 1841-1881 are held as well as directories, voter lists, maps and plans, the International Genealogical Index for Cheshire, and newspapers and newspaper cuttings. There are also copies of many local Church of England parish registers, either transcripts, photocopies, or microfilms. The Archive Service contains papers of businesses, trade unions, local government, nonconformist churches, societies and clubs, and private individuals. These documents date from 1274. The non-conformist archives include Methodist Church and circuit records (baptisms, marriages and burials), and some Congregational and Unitarian Church records. Business papers are of local firms such as Chaskip hat manufacturers. There are solicitors' papers and records of the Stockport Metropolitan Borough Council and its predecessor authorities, including rate books. Family and estate records include those of the Bradshaw-Isherwood estate.
	Conditions of admission and access	The library is open to the public. Advance notice by those intending to use archival material is appreciated. The Archivist is usually available from 9:00 AM to 5:00 PM, Monday to Friday. The Archive collection and all reference works must be

	used on the premises. Inquiries should be addressed to the Archivist or Head of Reference Services.
Hours	9:00 AM - 8:00 PM, Monday-Friday; 9:00 AM - 12:00 noon, Saturday.
Duplicating facilities	Facilities for photocopying and photography are available.
Other services	Reference help is available and brief questions by post or telephone are answered. A detailed list of manuscript records is contained in Archive Calendars, 1-14.
Publications	The Andrews and Comstall, their Village (1972); Bramall Hall (1977); Bygone Bramhall (1980); Cheadle in 1851 (1979); Cricketer Preferred (1979); Discovering Cheshire's Civil War (1983); From the Ground Upwards: Stockport Through its Building (1982); Half Timer: A Stockport Mill Boy Remembers (1983); The Hatting Industry in Stockport (1983); Hazel Grove: T'Other end O'Village (1985); Heaton Mersey, A Victorian Village, 1851-1881; A Hillgate Childhood (1981); History of the Stockport Court Leet (1974); Industrial Archaeology of Stockport (1975); The Macclesfield, Bollington and Marple Railway (1983); A Recording of Gravestones in the Churchyard of Chadkirk Old Chapel, 1981-1982 (1983); Reddish Remembered (1983); Remembering in Rhyme (1979); Stockport Corporation Tramways (1975); Stockport Viaduct (1983); Those Were the Days (1981); Tramways in Stockport (1985); Treasure on Earth (1981); Walking Around Marple, Lyme Park and Surrounds (1983); William Plant, Wood Block and Woodcraft Manufacturers (1977); Mary Ann's Girl: Memories of Newbridge Lane (1984); Poynton, A Coalmining Village (1983); also archive guides and local history handlists.

STORNOWAY

259 Institution Address	Western Isles Islands Council (Comhairle Nan Eilean) Sandwich Road Stornoway PA87 2BW (Isle of Lewis)
Telephone	0851 3773
Holdings	The collection includes Council records for the Western Isles Islands and its predecessors. Also Stornoway Road Trustees, parochial boards, and Parish councils, Education District Subcommittees, and housing registers are found.

Society and association papers and the Dean of Guild Court records and the D. L. Robertson Trust records are kept.

Conditions of admission and access	Written application must be made to use the collection. Inquiries should be addressed to the Director of Administration and Legal Services. The collection must be used on the premises.
Hours	9:00 AM - 5:30 PM, Monday-Thursday; 9:00 AM - 9:00 PM, Friday.
Duplicating facilities	Arrangements can be made for photocopying.
Other services	Short questions by telephone are answered and those by post are dealt with.
Publications	Indexes.

STORNOWAY

260 Institution
Address

Western Isles Libraries
2 Keith Street
Stornoway PA87 2QG

Telephone	0851 3064
Holdings	The library contains the Western Isles Island Council agendas and minutes and school log books and school board minutes, 1873-1919. Photographs and post cards, including the T. B. Macaulay Photographic Collection, are held and newspapers are kept.
Conditions of admission and access	Researchers should make an appointment in advance to use this collection. Inquiries should be directed to the Chief Librarian. The collection must be used on the premises.
Hours	10:00 AM - 5:00 PM, Monday, Wednesday-Thursday; 10:00 AM - 7:30 PM, Tuesday, Friday; 10:00 AM - 12:30 PM, Saturday.
Duplicating facilities	Arrangements can be made for photocopying.
Other services	Brief questions are dealt with whether they are by telephone or by post.
Publications	Catalogs, indexes, guides are issued.

STRATFORD-UPON-AVON
(map)

261 Institution   Shakespeare's Birthplace Trust Records Office

Address   The Shakespeare Centre
           Henley Street
           Stratford-upon-Avon CV 37 6QW

Telephone   0789 4016

Holdings   The original purpose of this collection was to
           preserve records relating to Shakespeare and his
           times, but a broader concept was adopted and
           historical records relating to Stratford and to
           large areas of Warwickshire and adjoining areas
           of Worcestershire and Gloucestershire are also
           preserved. Records of the Stratford-upon-Avon
           Corporation from the mid-16th century to 1974,
           records of the Guild of the Holy Cross (medieval
           period) are held here. There are also papers re-
           lating to local organizations and institutions, canals,
           railways and roads, manorial courts and other ju-
           dicial proceedings as well as records of Stratford
           firms and businesses. Stratford's parish registers
           have also been deposited and the church records
           include Church of England, Congregational,
           Methodist, Roman Catholic (some records are on
           temporary deposit or can be obtained for use),
           and Baptist. The earliest of these is 1558 and
           most include baptisms, marriages, and burials.
           Some of these records have been reprinted by
           the Parish Register Society and a few are on
           microfilm. Census records include photocopies of
           those of 1851, 1871 for the Borough of Stratford-
           upon-Avon and parish of Old Stratford. There
           is also a local census of 1765 which gives heads
           and size of households and place of legal settle-
           ment, and a local survival of the 1831 census which
           lists heads and size of household and occupation
           for the Borough of Stratford-upon-Avon and the
           parish of Old Stratford. Also found here are wills,
           directories, burgess' rolls (1835 onwards), rate
           books (1774-1913), and settlement certificates and
           registers (18th and early 19th centuries). Records
           of Warwickshire families are also held and include
           Leigh of Stoneleigh Abbey, Willoughby de Broke of
           Compton Verney, and Throckmorton of Coughton.
           Transcripts of parish registers for most villages
           of south Warwickshire and adjoining parishes in
           Worcestershire and Gloucestershire are kept. A
           list with dates and type of record (baptism, mar-
           riage, burial) is kept by the office. In addition
           to these is a collection of prints, drawings, photo-
           graphs, and other illustrative material relating to
           properties, buildings, personalities, and events
           in Stratford and Warwickshire. The office is a
           recognized repository for specified public records,
           for manorial and tithe documents (one of the first
           to be recognized by the Master of the Rolls), and
           for ecclesiastical records (Coventry: Stratford-
           upon-Avon parish records).

Conditions of admission and access	The record office is open to the public and with very few exceptions the records are available for use. No advance appointment is required. Inquiries should be addressed to the Senior Archivist or to the Director. The material may not be removed from the premises.
Hours	9:30 AM - 1:00 PM, 2:00 PM - 5:00 PM, Monday-Friday; 9:30 AM - 12:30 PM, Saturday.
Duplicating facilities	Photocopying facilities are available.
Other services	Only brief inquiries can be answered by post or telephone but reference help is available at the office. Exhibitions and lectures can be arranged for groups from schools, colleges, and societies. There are many finding aids, indexes and catalogs available to help the researcher. These include place names (divided by county), personal names, subjects, a list of photographic reproductions of records held elsewhere, an index of local photographs and of local prints and drawings, and an index to the Stratford-upon-Avon Herald which presently covers the first thirty-two years (1860-1892), as well as a local history and genealogy library.
Publications	None.

SUTTON

262 Institution Address	Sutton Central Library St. Nicholas Way Sutton SM1 1EA
Telephone	01 661 5050
Holdings	The library contains family and estate papers, church records and local government records. These include court rolls for the Manor of Sutton (1720-1905) and of Carsbolton (with transcripts dating from 1346), and the Phillips Collection concerning the Carew family of Beddington (15th-17th centuries). Rate books, vestry minutes, Church Wardens' accounts, valuation lists, school records and deeds are also found, as are transcripts of Beddington parish registers. There are also photographs, prints and drawings, newspapers, maps and census returns.
Conditions of admission and access	The collection is open to visiting scholars, preferably by appointment. Inquiries should be addressed to the Principal Librarian or the Local History Librarian. The material may not be removed from the library.

Hours	9:30 AM - 8:00 PM, Tuesday-Friday; 9:30 AM - 5:00 PM, Saturday. Closed Monday.
Duplicating facilities	Photocopies and full-sized copies from microform can be supplied.
Other services	Questions by telephone are answered and those by mail are dealt with if they are brief.
Publications	The library engages in an active publishing program and will provide details on request.

SWANSEA

263	Institution Address	Swansea Central Library Alexander Road Swansea SA1 5DX
	Telephone	0792 54065/54066 (Central Library) 0792 55521 (Reference Library)
	Holdings	The library holds material relating to the local history of the area. This includes business records, papers relating to education, individuals' archives and film copies of Welsh manuscripts concerning this area.
	Conditions of admission and access	The library is open to the public and researchers are not required to make an appointment in advance. Inquiries should be directed to the County Librarian or to the Local History Librarian.
	Hours	9:00 AM - 7:00 PM, Monday-Wednesday, Friday; 9:00 AM - 5:00 PM, Thursday, Saturday.
	Duplicating facilities	Photocopying facilities are available.
	Other services	Questions by telephone or post are answered if they are short. Reference help is available.
	Publications	Manuscript Collection at the Swansea Public Library, by A. F. Peplow; handlists, guides.

SWANSEA

264	Institution Address	Swansea City Council City Archives Guildhall Swansea SA1 4PE
	Telephone	0792 50821, ext. 2115/2122
	Holdings	The Archives consist of the records of the City Council, its predecessor authorities and its

departments. The collection contains photographs, cine films of local events and a sound archive is being developed.

Conditions of admission and access	Researchers should make an appointment in advance and must apply to use some material. Inquiries should be addressed to the City Archivist. The collection must be used on the premises.
Hours	9: 30 AM - 12: 45 PM, 2: 15 PM - 4: 30 PM, Tuesday-Wednesday.
Duplicating facilities	Photocopying is available and arrangements can be made for photography and full-size copies from microforms.
Other services	Telephone and postal inquiries are dealt with, but they must be brief.
Publications	Calendar of Swansea Freemen's Records, by J. R. Alban (1982); Air Raids on Swansea (1981); indexes, lists, and guides.

SWANSEA

265	Institution Address	West Glamorgan Area Record Office County Hall Oystermouth Road Swansea SA1 3SN
	Telephone	0792 471589
		See also: CARDIFF, Glamorgan Record Office
	Holdings	The collection includes records of the County Council, Petty Sessions, local Boards of Health and Boards of Guardians, for the area of West Glamorgan. Also found are estate papers, industrial records, maps, and manorial and tithe documents for this area. Ecclesiastical (parish) records are found and an index to pre-1858 wills of West Glamorgan area proved at St. David's Court (the originals are at the National Library of Wales, Aberystwyth). Glamorgan Quarter Sessions records remain in Cardiff.
	Conditions of admission and access	The office is open to the public and appointments are not necessary except for Monday evening. Brief questions should be directed to the Assistant Archivist. Correspondence should be addressed to the Archivist, Glamorgan Archive Service, Glamorgan Record Office, County Hall, Cathays Park, Cardiff CF1 3NE. The collection must be used in the search room.
	Hours	9: 00 AM - 12: 45 PM, 2: 00 PM - 4: 45 PM, Monday-

Wednesday; 5:30 PM - 7:30 PM, Monday by appointment.

Duplicating   Full-size copying facilities are available.
facilities

Other services   Reference help is available in the search room
                   and brief questions will be answered by telephone.
                   Postal inquiries should be sent to the Cardiff
                   address (see "Conditions of admission ..." above).

Publications   All publications are produced in Cardiff.

TAUNTON

266 Institution   Somerset Record Office
     Address   Obridge Road
                   Taunton TA2 7PU

     Telephone   0823 87600/78805

     Holdings   The holdings of the record office are comprised
                   of the official records of the County Council, in-
                   cluding those of the Court of Quarter Sessions,
                   the Diocesan records of Bath and Wells, and
                   parish records for over four hundred parishes.
                   There are also records of many former local coun-
                   cils and public local authorities, and a mass of
                   privately deposited material relating to Somerset
                   families, estates, and businesses. The parish
                   records include areas which in 1974 were removed
                   from Somerset to form the new county of Avon.
                   Records date from the 8th century. The office
                   is a recognized depository for manorial and tithe
                   documents and for ecclesiastical records (Bath
                   and Wells).

     Conditions of The office is freely open to all. No advance ap-
     admission and pointment is required, but two or three days'
     access   notice of an intended visit is appreciated and
                   will insure a place to work in the search room.
                   The resources may be consulted only on the
                   premises. Inquiries should be directed to the
                   County Archivist.

     Hours   9:00 AM - 4:50 PM, Monday-Thursday; 9:00 AM -
                   4:20 PM, Friday; 9:15 AM - 12:15 PM, Saturday
                   (by appointment only).

     Duplicating   Photocopying facilities are available at the
     facilities   record office.

     Other services Only brief questions are answered by post or
                   telephone. Reference help is available in the
                   office and a reference library is provided to fur-
                   ther aid the searcher. This includes HMSO's
                   Calendars of Public Records and a wide range of

local and national handbooks relating to history
and local history, genealogy, archives, Somerset,
and other works to be used in the interpretation
of the manuscript holdings. Microform equipment
and ultra-violet lamps are provided.

Publications	Interim Handlist of Somerset Quarter Sessions Documents and other Official Records (1947); Primary Genealogical Holdings in the Somerset Record Office (1983). "Annual List of Main Manuscript Accessions" is published in the Proceedings of the Somerset Archaeological Society. Off-prints are available.
TAYSIDE Regional Council	See: DUNDEE
TOWER HAMLETS	See: LONDON, London Borough of Tower Hamlets
TROWBRIDGE	See: Pages 305-06.

TRURO (map)

267 Institution Address	Cornwall Record Office County Hall Truro TR1 3AY
Telephone	0872 73698
Holdings	The records include the official records of the County from 1732 as well as records of Boroughs and District Councils. There are also parish registers, including registers from 1539, bishops' transcripts, and diocesan records, including tithe maps. Wills of the former Archdeaconry of Cornwall from 1600 to 1857 and family and estate papers from medieval times to the present day are held. The collection also contains mining records, business records, Methodist and other nonconformist records including registers. Microfilm copies of the census returns for Cornwall for 1841, 1851, 1861, 1871, and 1881 are found here.
Conditions of admission and access	The record office is open to the public, but it is essential to make an appointment four weeks in advance if by telephone, five weeks if by post. Inquiries should be directed to the County Archivist. The collection must be consulted on the premises. Some documents are stored in auxiliary facilities at some distance from County Hall and cannot be produced on demand. It may be helpful for the visiting scholar to know that the office is particularly busy from April to October and during school holidays.
Hours	9:30 AM - 1:00 PM, 2:00 PM - 5:00 PM, Tuesday-

Thursday; 9:30 AM - 1:00 PM, 2:00 PM - 4:30
PM, Friday; 9:00 AM - 12:00 noon, Saturday.
The office is closed on Monday. The office is
also closed on every bank holiday, the Saturday
preceding and the day following the bank holiday,
and the first two full weeks in December (for
stock-taking).

Duplicating
facilities

Photocopying, photostat and microfilming facilities
are provided.

Other services

Only limited inquiries by post or telephone can
be answered, but reference help is available at
the office. There are lists and indexes available
to aid the visiting scholar. Also provided are
microform equipment and an ultraviolet lamp.
Professional searches are carried out by the staff
for a fee.

Publications

List of Parish Registers (1981); List of Methodist
Registers (1983); Map of the Ecclesiastical
Parishes in Cornwall (1983); List of Accessions
1981-1982 (1982); List of Accessions 1982-1983
(1983); List of Accessions 1983-1984 (1984); List
of Accessions 1984-1985 (1985); List of Accessions
1985-1986 (1986); The United States of America,
Maps, Letters, Diaries (Handlist 1, 1981 out-of-
print); Records of Schools (Handlist 2, rev.
1984); Pedigrees and Heraldic Documents (Hand-
list 3, rev. 1985); Parish Poor Law Records
(Handlist 4, rev. 1984); Turnpikes, Canals and
Ferries (Handlist 5, 1983); A. K. Hamilton Jenkin:
Mines and Miners of Cornwall I to XVI; Wendron
Tin (1982); Family History Information Sheet;
History of a House Information Sheet; Guide to
Sources for Cornish Family History (1984); Guide
to Cornish Probate Records (1984).

TRURO (map)

268 Institution
Address

Royal Institution of Cornwall
The Courtney Library
County Museum
River Street
Truro TR1 2SJ

Telephone

0872 72205

Holdings

The holdings include a manuscript collection of
Cornish material, microfilms of parish registers,
conveyances and estate records and some maps.
The Ross marriage index, the Mormon International
Genealogical Index on microfiche and Henderson
Calendars of manuscripts are found. There are
also transcripts of parish registers and a good
genealogical section in the library. There is a

photograph collection and some newspapers and
works on Cornish history and the Cornish language.

Conditions of admission and access	There are no restrictions on admission to the Courtney Library; however, an appointment in advance is desirable for those wishing to use microfilm or microfiche. The collection must be used on the premises. Inquiries should be directed to the Curator.
Hours	9:00 AM - 1:00 PM, 2:00 PM - 5:00 PM, Monday-Saturday.
Duplicating facilities	Photocopying can be provided.
Other services	Reference help is available to the visiting scholar and brief questions by telephone or post are answered.
Publications	None.

TROWBRIDGE

269	Institution Address	Wiltshire County Record Office County Hall Trowbridge BA14 8JG
	Telephone	02214 3641
	Holdings	The record office is the official repository for Wiltshire records, both public and private. It contains Quarter Sessions records from 1563 which relate to such things as poor relief, the regulation of wages, upkeep of roads and bridges, taxation, prisons, lunatics, licensing of ale houses, the administration of oaths of loyalty, registration of Papists' property, licensing of non-conformist places of worship, as well as to matters of crime and police. The most important series of documents found in Quarter Sessions are the Great Rolls (bundles of all the different documents produced before the Justices at each Sessions), minute books of the proceedings and enclosure awards (mostly late 18th century and early 19th century). There is one for many of the parishes in the County and nearly all are accompanied by detailed maps. There are also plans of roads, railways, and other public undertakings. In addition, the record office contains records of private estates, families, businesses, solicitors, and local organizations. Among these are found the papers of the Marquess of Ailesbury, the Earl of Suffolk and Berkshire, Lord Heytesbury, Lord Radnor, the Benetts of Pyt House, the Penruddockes of Compton Chamberlayne, the Hoares of

Stourhead, the Awdrys of Melksham, the Ashes
of Langley Burrell, the Goldneys of Chippenham,
and the Temples of Bishopstrow. These accumulations nearly always include the deeds of land
(the earliest dates from ca. 1150) and often manorial court and account rolls, estate maps and plans
(some from the 17th century), estate and household accounts and private letters and journals.
Papers of families who engaged in trade include
the Cunningtons, who had a wine business in
Devizes, and the Wanseys, who were clothiers in
Warminster. Also found are probate records of
the local ecclesiastical courts covering Wiltshire
from the 16th century to 1857, tithe apportionments from ca. 1840, the records of parishes and
the central records of the Diocese of Salisbury.
(The Diocesan Record Office at Salisbury no longer
exists, the records having been transferred to
Trowbridge several years ago). The record office
is a recognized repository for certain classes of
public records, for manorial and tithe documents,
and for ecclesiastical records (Salisbury. Bristol:
parish records of Archdeaconry of Swindon).

Conditions of admission and access The record office is open to the public and no appointment is required, but researchers wishing to
use the collection for extensive research should
give advance notice. Inquiries should be directed
to the County Archivist. All records and books
must be consulted on the premises.

Hours 9:00 AM - 12:30 PM, 1:30 PM - 5:00 PM, Monday-
Friday; Wednesday opening hours extend to 8:30
PM.

Duplicating facilities Full-size copying facilities are available. Microfilming and photographic services can also be pro-
vided.

Other services Brief telephone and postal inquiries are answered.
Reference help is available and a small library of
reference books useful to those studying the documents is provided.

Publications Guide to the Records in the Custody of the Clerk
of the Peace for Wiltshire, by M. G. Rathbone,
(Guide to the County and Diocesan Record Offices,
Pt. I); Guide to the Records of the Diocese of
Salisbury (Record Office Guides, Pt. IV); Summary
Guide to Private Records in the Wiltshire County
Record Office (1969) (typescript).

UPPER NORWOOD See: LONDON, Upper Norwood Public Library

WAKEFIELD (Map)

270	Institution	Wakefield Department of Archives and Local Studies
	Address	Library Headquarters
		Balne Lane
		Wakefield WF2 0DQ

Telephone   0924 371231

Holdings

The holdings include the census for the whole West Riding, 1841-1881. Also found are manorial and family and estate papers, including the archives of the Pilkington of Chevet, and ecclesiastical records. Local government records and those concerning taxation, education, and business are held. Archives relating to the City of Wakefield and former local authorities, including the archives of Pontefract Corporation, with Charters dating from 1194, and minute books from the 17th century, are here. Local government and local history are well represented and maps, plans, the archives of societies and miscellaneous manuscripts are to be found. Trade directories and other similar works are kept for an area about ten miles around Wakefield. Detailed indexes to local newspapers and manuscripts from ca. 1800-1855, 1900-1913, 1950 to date are held.

Conditions of admission and access

The Department is open to the public and visiting scholars are welcome to use the collection. An appointment in advance is preferred and is required for the use of manuscripts. Inquiries should be directed to the Archivist. The collection must be used on the premises.

Hours

9:30 AM - 7:00 PM, Monday; 9:30 AM - 5:00 PM, Tuesday-Friday; 9:30 AM - 4:00 PM, second Saturday in each month.

Duplicating facilities

Photocopies can be provided if the material is suitable. Much of the manuscript material may not be copied.

Other services

There is an experienced local history advisory staff to aid the scholar and brief questions by post or telephone will be answered. Indexes and finding aids are available to further help the reader.

Publications

Guides to the archive collection and to particular parts of the printed book collection have been developed.

WAKEFIELD (map)

271	Institution	West Yorkshire Archive Service Headquarters
	Address	Registry of Deeds
		Newstead Road
		Wakefield WF1 2DE

Telephone	0924 367111, ext. 2352

The West Yorkshire Archive Service was formed from several separate Agencies. See also: BRADFORD, HALIFAX, HUDDERSFIELD, and LEEDS

Holdings

The collection includes West Riding Quarter Sessions records from the 17th century, including the Liberty of Ripon, land tax duplicates, records of Turnpike Trusts, plans of public undertakings and tithe enclosure awards. Also found are the archives of the West Riding County Council and its committees and departments. West Riding Registry of Deeds archives include copies and memorials of documents of title dating from 1704-1970. The Headquarters office is the record office for the Diocese of Wakefield and the majority of parishes (and virtually all the ancient parishes) have deposited their records. Nonconformist records include Methodist Circuits for the county. Business and solicitors' collections, records of British Waterways, West Yorkshire Passenger Transport Executive, and Health Authority archives are available, as are Conveyances (records of West Riding Registry of Deeds, 1704-1970). Volumes of wills proved in Wakefield (1858-1941) and probate calendars (1858-1928) are found. Land tax records (West Riding, 1781-1832), Electoral Registers (West Riding County Constituencies, 1840-1974; West Yorkshire, 1974 to date), and tithe, enclosure and Ordnance Survey Maps are also held.

Conditions of admission and access

The collection is open to the public and an appointment in advance is not required. Inquiries should be directed to the Archivist to the Joint Committee. The material must be used on the premises.

Hours

9:00 AM - 8:00 PM, Monday; 9:00 AM - 5:00 PM, Tuesday-Thursday; 9:00 AM - 1:00 PM, Friday.

Duplicating facilities

Photocopying facilities are available.

Other services

Brief inquiries by post or telephone are answered and reference help is provided. Ultra-violet lamps and microform readers are available. A local history library, lists of collections within the West Yorkshire Archive Service and computerized databases of holdings of the other offices (with index) are also available.

Publications

Guides, brochures, and lists are produced by the West Yorkshire Archive Service, and also the following publications: The West Riding County Council, 1889-1974: Historical Studies, by B. J. Barber and M. W. Beresford (1978); Search Guide

to the English Land Tax, by R. W. Unwin (1982);
Guide to the West Yorkshire Archive Service for
Family Historians (1984); Guide to the Quarter
Sessions of the West Riding of Yorkshire, 1637-
1971 and other Official Records, by B. J. Barber
(1984); Guide to the Archive Collections of the
Yorkshire Archaeological Society, 1931-1983 and
to Collections Deposited with the Society, by S.
Thomas (1985).

WALSALL (map)

272	Institution Address	Walsall Library and Museum Services Walsall Local History Centre Essex Street Walsall WS2 7AS
	Telephone	0922 37305/37306
	Holdings	The collection includes records of Walsall Quarter Sessions, Magistrates and Coroners Courts, nine- teenth and twentieth centuries, and many docu- ments concerning the history of the borough since the first charter was received during the reign of King John (1199-1216). Material dating from the seventeenth century and later is particularly plentiful. Many records concerning the history of Methodism in the borough and some Congregational, Presbyterian and Strict Baptist church records are also found. Papers relating to local businesses, trade unions, societies and clubs, and the papers of local historians and antiquarians are available.
	Conditions of admission and access	No conditions are placed on use of the archives. Inquiries should be directed to the Archivist. The collection must be used on the premises.
	Hours	9:30 AM - 5:30 PM, Tuesday; 9:30 AM - 7:00 PM, Wednesday; 9:30 AM - 5:30 PM, Thursday; 9:30 AM - 5:00 PM, Friday; 9:30 AM - 1:00 PM, Satur- day. Closed Monday.
	Duplicating facilities	Photocopies, microfilm prints, and photographic prints can be provided.
	Other services	Reference help is available and brief questions by telephone or post are answered. Exhibitions can be arranged and talks to local groups are undertaken. Microfilm equipment and ultraviolet lamps are available.
	Publications	Walsall Chronicle (No. 1, 1979- . Annual); Birchills: An Oral History; Aldride and District Yesterdays; Willenhall and Darlaston Yesterdays; Pleck: A History; Church Hill Trail; Handlist of Accessions; Genealogists' Guide; Brownhills

Local History Trail; A Short History of Rushall;
Streetly Local History Trail; Darlaston Town
Trail.

WARWICK (map)

273 Institution   Warwick County Record Office
     Address   Priory Park
                  Cape Road
                  Warwick CV34 4JS

     Telephone   0926 493431, ext. 2506, 2507, 2508

     Holdings   The record office contains records of the County
Council and its predecessors, Quarter Sessions
(from 1625), and Petty Sessions, Parish records
for the Dioceses of Birmingham (part), and
Coventry. There are also business records and
those of schools, public undertakings, local
landed estates and private individuals. In addition there are maps of Warwickshire and other
topographical sources, local newspaper files,
prints and views, and photographs. The office
is a recognized repository for certain classes of
public records and for manorial and tithe documents.

     Conditions of   The record office is open to the public and no
     admission and   advance appointment is required. Inquiries should
     access   be directed to the County Archivist. The mate-
rial must be used on the premises.

     Hours   9:00 AM - 1:00 PM, 2:00 PM - 5:30 PM, Monday-
Thursday; 9:00 AM - 1:00 PM, 2:00 PM - 5:00
PM, Friday; 9:00 AM - 12:30 PM, Saturday.

     Duplicating   There are facilities available for photocopying,
     facilities   photostat copying, and microfilm.

     Other services   Only brief queries can be answered by post or
telephone. Reference help is available in the
reading room and an ultra-violet lamp is provided.

     Publications   Quarter Sessions Order Book, Easter 1625 to
Trinity 1637, ed. by S. C. Ratcliff and H. C.
Johnson (Warwick County Records, Vol. I, 1935);
Quarter Sessions Order Book, Michaelmas 1637
to Epiphany 1650, ed. by S. C. Ratcliff and H.
C. Johnson (Warwick County Records, Vol. II,
1936); Quarter Sessions Order Book, Easter 1650
to Epiphany 1657, ed. by S. C. Ratcliff and
H. C. Johnson (Warwick County Records, Vol.
III, 1937); Quarter Sessions Order Book, Easter
1657 to Epiphany 1665, ed. by S. C. Ratcliff and
H. C. Johnson (Warwick County Records, Vol. IV,
1938); Orders Made at Quarter Sessions, Easter

1655 to Epiphany 1674, ed. by S. C. Ratcliff and
H. C. Johnson (Warwick County Records, Vol. V,
1939); Quarter Sessions Indictment Book, Easter
1631 to Epiphany 1674, ed. by S. C. Ratcliff and
H. C. Johnson (Warwick County Records, Vol. VI,
1946); Quarter Sessions Records, Easter 1674 to
Easter 1682, ed. by S. C. Ratcliff and H. C.
Johnson (Warwick County Records, Vol. VII,
1946); Quarter Sessions Records, Trinity 1682
to Epiphany 1690, ed. by H. C. Johnson, with a
supplement to the introduction, Warwickshire Non-
conformist and Quaker Meetings and Meeting-
Houses, 1660-1750, by J. H. Hodson (Warwick
County Records, Vol. VIII, 1953); Quarter Sessions
Records, Easter 1690 to Michaelmas 1696, ed. by H.
C. Johnson and N. J. Williams (Warwick County
Records, Vol. IX, 1964); Hemlingford Hundred:
Tamworth and Atherstone Divisions, ed. by Mar-
garet Walker with an introduction by Philip
Sytles (Warwick County Records, Hearth Tax Re-
turns, Vol. I, 1957); The Printed Maps of
Warwickshire 1576 to 1900, by P. D. A. Harvey
and Harry Thorpe (1959, out-of-print); Sir William Dugdale, 1605-1686: A List of His Printed
Works and of His Portraits, with Notes on His Life
and the Manuscript Sources, by Francis Maddison,
Dorothy Styles and Anthony Wood (1953); The
Manor of Thurlaston Before and After Inclosure
1717-1720; A Portfolio of Maps and Schedules,
with a Booklet Containing Manorial Bylaws and
the Text of the Inclosure Award (Archive teaching unit, out-of-print); The Town Maps of Warwick, 1610-1851, a ring-binder of maps of the
historic town center with schedules of inhabitants
street by street, ending with the 1851 census and
local Board of Health map (Archive teaching unit).

WEST BROMWICH

274	Institution	Sandwell Public Libraries
	Address	Central Library
		Archives and Local History Department
		High Street
		West Bromwich B70 8DZ
	Telephone	021 569 2416
	Holdings	The library is the Diocesan Record office for

The library is the Diocesan Record office for
Birmingham Rural Deanery of Warley, parish
records of West Bromwich. The collection includes
parish registers, Methodist records, records of
local government and local history and archival
material. The Jesson Deeds, 1589-1784 are found
here. Photographs and maps, including mining
maps are also here.

Conditions of admission and access	The library is open to the public, but visiting researchers should make an appointment in advance of a visit. Inquiries should be directed to the Reference Librarian. Archives and references may not be removed from the library.
Duplicating facilities	Photocopying, microfilming, and photography can be provided.
Other services	Telephone and postal questions are answered if they are brief. Reference help is available in the library.
Publications	Indexes, catalogs, and guides are issued.

WESTERN ISLES   See: STORNOWAY

WIGAN   See: LEIGH, Wigan Record Office

WIGHT, ISLE OF   See: NEWPORT

WINCHESTER (map)

275 Institution Address	Hampshire County Record Office 20 Southgate Street Winchester SO 93 9EF
Telephone	0962 63153
Holdings	The record office holds records on the history of Hampshire since the 12th century in all its aspects, including administrative, legal, financial, and ecclesiastical. The office holds parish and non-conformist records for Hampshire in the original, on microfilm, or has a photocopy. These include registers of baptism, marriage, burial and documents concerning poor relief. The non-conformist records include Baptist, Congregational, Methodist, Presbyterian, Society of Friends, Roman Catholic (microfilm) and Unitarian. Microfiche copies of Hampshire Parish registers held by Southampton City Record Office and the Guildford Muniment Room, Surrey Record Office are available. Records of local government include Quarter and Petty Sessions, the Lieutenancy, the County Council, Rural and Urban District Councils, Parish Councils, Boroughs, manors and statutory authorities. The Hampshire Record Office is also the Winchester Diocesan Record Office. Records held include the bishops' registers, wills and inventories to 1858 (copies of wills proved in the Winchester Probate Registry from 1858 are also held), records of the Consistory Court, and records of the

Bishops' estates, school records, and private
records, including family, estate, business, and
society archives are also kept. Copies of the
census returns for the whole of Hampshire, 1841,
1851, 1861, 1871, and 1881 are available. The
map collection contains Ordnance Survey maps,
tithe and enclosure maps which are accompanied
by awards, estate maps, county maps, and maps
and plans relating to the city of Winchester.
There are also building plans, and plans of
churches, parsonages, and other church property.
A miscellaneous group of maps include road maps
dating from Ogilby's strip maps of 1698 to modern
Automobile Association maps, railway maps, and
maps of natural features. In addition, plans of
individual houses and housing development are
kept. The record office also holds the Winchester
City Archives (from 1155). The office is a
recognized repository for certain classes of public
records, for manorial and tithe documents, and for
ecclesiastical documents (Winchester).

Conditions of   The record office is open to the public and no
admission and   prior appointment is required, but notice of a
access   visit is appreciated, particularly if the visitor's
                    search is likely to be time consuming or to require
                    a large number of documents. It is advisable to
                    book microfilm readers in advance. Inquiries
                    should be directed to the County Archivist. Docu-
                    ments are not produced between 10:00 AM and
                    10:20 AM, 12:50 PM and 2:10 PM, 3:00 PM and
                    3:20 PM, and one half-hour before closing.
                    Documents for use on Saturday must be requested
                    by 3:00 PM on the previous Friday. No documents
                    may be borrowed and some are subject to special
                    restriction. In the event both the original and
                    microfilm of a document are held, the searcher is
                    expected to use the film copy.

Hours   9:00 AM - 4:45 PM, Monday-Thursday; 9:00 AM -
                    4:15 PM, Friday. Saturday opening is by appoint-
                    ment only as follows: from October to March, it is
                    possible to make arrangements to use the record
                    office every Saturday. From April to September,
                    the office will open on the second and fourth
                    Saturday by prior appointment. The office will
                    not open on Saturday before a bank holiday.

Duplicating   Facilities for photocopying, microfilm and photog-
facilities   raphy are available. Parish registers, most manu-
                    script books, and large documents are not copied.
                    All copying is subject to the physical condition
                    and other special restrictions on a document.

Other services   Brief questions can be answered by post or tele-
                    phone and staff is available to help with inquiries,
                    but they cannot undertake extensive research.

A list of professional searchers will be supplied
on request. There is a reference library available
to further aid the researcher and other printed
sources which include newspapers, trade directories, electoral rolls and pictorial material. Lectures and exhibitions can be arranged with sufficient notice. Lectures outside the office require
traveling expenses; lectures at the office include
a tour. An education service is also offered and
there is a leaflet available which gives details.

Publications

Poor Law in Hampshire Through the Centuries
(1970, out-of-print); Transport in Hampshire and
the Isle of Wight (1973, out-of-print); Education
in Hampshire and the Isle of Wight (1977); Notes
on the History of the Former Church of St.
Thomas and St. Clement, Winchester (1972).
There are also informational leaflets available, e.g.,
"The Hampshire Record Office," and the record
office participates in the publication programs of
the Hampshire Archivists' Group, the Hampshire
Record Series, and the Hampshire Field Club. A
series of "Guides to Records" is also being produced.

WIRRAL

See: BIRKENHEAD

WOLVERHAMPTON

276 Institution
Address

Wolverhampton Borough Archives
Central Library
Snow Hill
Wolverhampton WV1 3AX

Telephone

0902 773624

See also: BILSTON, Wolverhampton Borough
Archives

Holdings

The records held are chiefly those of the Wolverhampton Borough Council and its predecessor
authorities, and other papers donated or deposited
by private organizations, businesses, or individuals. These archives include records of Quarter
Sessions Court of Wolverhampton County Borough,
1864-1971, and records of the Wolverhampton
Coroners, 1864-1972. Local Government papers
are also found. Nonconformist records of Methodist, Baptist, Unitarian and Congregationalist
Churches are held. Business records include
Bailey and Sons, Chemical Manufacturers, Chilling-
ton Ironworks (visitors book, 1838-1874), Forders
Carriage Works, Russell Brewery Co., and Victoria Hotel Co. Local organizations' papers, family
and estate records, manorial documents, historians

manuscripts and transcripts are found along with
miscellaneous collections such as Wolverhampton
Charity School, South Staffordshire Mines Drainage
Commission (1873-1976), Grant Theatre Records
(19th-20th century), and Wolverhampton Orphan
Asylum, maps and photographs.

Conditions of admission and access	The library is open to the public and no advance appointment is required. Inquiries should be made to the Archivist. The collection must be used on the premises. Documents for use on Saturday should be requested in advance.
Hours	10:00 AM - 1:00 PM, 2:00 PM - 5:00 PM, Monday-Saturday.
Duplicating facilities	Photocopies and photographs can be provided.
Other services	Brief questions by post or telephone are answered and reference help is available.
Publications	Wolverhampton Archives: Summary of the Collection; "Selections," leaflets on various topics, and brochures are produced.

WORCESTER (map)

277	Institution Address	Hereford and Worcester County Record Office County Buildings (Headquarters) Spetchley Road Worcester WR5 2NP and St. Helen's Fish Street Worcester WR1 2NN
	Telephone	0905 353366, ext. 3612/3613 (Headquarters) 0905 353366, ext. 3616 (St. Helen's)

See also: HEREFORD, Hereford and Worcester
County Record Office

Holdings	At Headquarters are found the modern administrative archives of the present County Council, the old Worcestershire County Council and some District Councils. Also here, are the records of the courts of Petty Sessions and Quarter Sessions. The latter date back to 1590 and contain legal information and records of the Justices of the Peace in Quarter Sessions who administered the day-to-day affairs of the County prior to 1889. These include such topics as land inclosure, registration, the militia, lunatic asylums, gaols, turnpike roads, railways, and canals. The extensive Worcestershire Photographic Survey is

available at Headquarters. Parish registers, bishops' transcripts, wills, marriage bonds and allegations, census returns, newspapers, electoral registers, genealogical publications and the Mormon International Genealogical Index (for the entire county) are also kept at Headquarters. The office is a recognized repository for certain public records, and for manorial and tithe documents.

At St. Helen's the collection contains historic Worcestershire archives and the Diocesan records dating from the 12th century. These include probate and tithe records, archives of nonconformist churches, solicitors, commercial and business firms, manorial records, maps and plans. Important family collections have been deposited here emanating from the Beringtons of Little Malvern, Hamptons of Westwood, Sandys of Ombersley, and Vernons of Hanbury. Also found here are certain official archives including those of district and parish councils originating in Worcestershire, Droitwich and Evesham Boroughs, and records of schools, poor law unions, and some hospitals. The City's original charters are to be found at the Guildhall, High Street and may be inspected there on application. A list is available at St. Helen's. St. Helen's also holds a collection of archives relating to Edward Elgar, various artificial collections, and an excellent local history library.

Conditions of admission and access	No prior appointment is required, but because of heavy demand, researchers are advised to book microfilm readers in advance, should they anticipate their need. Inquiries concerning administrative matters, genealogy, new deposits, inspections of records, talks or displays should be made to the Head of Record Services at the Headquarters address. Those concerning local history should be directed to the Assistant Head of Record Services at St. Helen's. None of the material may be removed from the premises.
Hours	10:00 AM - 4:45 PM, Monday; 9:15 AM - 4:45 PM, Tuesday-Thursday; 9:15 AM - 4:00 PM, Friday. The offices are open through lunchtime, but are subject to ad hoc closing, depending on staff availability.
Duplicating facilities	Full-size and microcopying facilities are available. Cost and time necessary for processing vary, depending on the size of the work to be copied.
Other services	Brief questions by mail or telephone will be answered, but those requiring more extensive research must be dealt with by the inquirer. Lectures, exhibits, and paleographical assistance

are offered by the staff. There are indexes and
guides and explanations of their use available for
the researcher's use as well as a collection of
works on local history. An ultraviolet lamp and
microform equipment are provided.

Publications   Annual Report; All (or Some) of What You Need
to Know About the Hereford and Worcester County
Record Office; catalogs and guides which are available for consultation in the record office, but are
not at present published in a form which could be
widely available.

YORK

Institution   Borthwick Institute of Historical Research
See: YORK, University of York, Borthwick Institute of Historical Research

YORK (map)

278 Institution   University of York
Address   Borthwick Institute of Historical Research
Gurney Library
St. Anthony's Hall
Peasholme Green
York YO1 2PW

Telephone   0904 642315

Holdings   The Gurney Library is a working library for use
in connection with the deposited archive collections.
The library contains resources in English ecclesiastical history, particularly of the northern province,
archive and ecclesiastical administration, canon law,
and palaeography. The institute is the record
office for the archives of the Archbishopric of
York. As well as being the repository for the
parish records of the York Archdeaconry, the
Institute also has printed, typed and photo-type
copies of registers, and copies of monumental
inscriptions in some Yorkshire churchyards. Also
kept are poor law records, including accounts of
the overseers, church wardens' accounts,
constables' accounts, highway surveyors' accounts,
and rating assessments. There are also records
of parish charities and schools which include
deeds, accounts, and correspondence. Parish
register transcripts begin in the late 16th century
and one (York, St. Denys) in 1558. These cover
a very large area and are a popular source among
genealogists. Probate records of the Diocese of
York, of the northern province and of the various
peculiar jurisdictions within the diocese, are kept.
Wills are found here also. Family and estate

deposits, school records, hospital papers, and
business archives are also held. Of special importance is the political and diplomatic correspondence found in the Halifax Papers. It should be
noted that the Institute is a recognized repository
for specified classes of public records, for manorial
and tithe documents and for ecclesiastical records
(York).

Conditions of
admission and
access

Visiting scholars are welcome to use the collection,
but an appointment in advance is essential for
those intending to work on the archives. Inquiries
should be made to the Director. The material may
be used only on the premises.

Hours

9:30 AM - 1:00 PM, 2:00 PM - 5:00 PM, Monday-
Friday. The institute is closed on public holidays,
for a short period at Easter and Christmas and the
week of the August bank holiday and the preceding
week.

Duplicating
facilities

Photographs, photocopies, and microfilms of the
archives can be obtained under certain conditions.

Other services

Brief postal and telephone inquiries are answered.
The institute can undertake, for a fee, to make
certain categories of searches among the records
(i.e., to search common sources for specific items
of information). Details of the scope, conditions,
and charges for this service are available. There
is a reference library, the Gurney Library, which
contains works on archival study, publications of
local record societies and most record offices.
Typescript and photocopies of parish registers
and transcripts are found in the library. Reference help is provided to researchers.

Publications

The Borthwick Institute of Historical Research pub-
lished the following Series: BORTHWICK PAPERS
(Previously St. Anthony's Hall Publications), of
which the following are in print: The Beginning
of the Parochial System, by G. W. O. Addleshaw,
No. 3, 3rd ed. (1970); Historians of York, by
J. Biggins, No. 10 (1956); Diocesan Administration
in Fifteenth-Century England, by R. L. Storey,
No. 16, 2nd ed. (1972); Archbishop Geoffrey
Plantagenet and the Chapter of York, by D. Douie,
No. 18 (1960); Norfolk Church Dedications, by
C. L. S. Linnell, No. 21 (1962); The Records of
the Admiralty Court of York, by J. S. Purvis,
No. 22 (1962); A. F. Leach as a Historian of
Yorkshire Education, by W. E. Tate, No. 23
(1963); The Labourer in the Vineyard: The
Visitations of Archbishop Melton in the Archdeacon-
ry of Richmond, by R. M. T. Hill, No. 35 (1969);
Beneficed Clergy in Cleveland and the East Riding,
1305-40, by D. Robinson, No. 37 (1970); The

Last Four Anglo-Saxon Archbishops of York, by
Janet Cooper, No. 38 (1970); Christopher Wyvill
and Reform 1790-1820, by J. R. Dinwiddy, No.
39 (1971); The Reformation in York 1535-1553,
by D. M. Palliser, No. 40 (1971, rpt. 1979); The
Jews of Medieval York and the Massacre of March
1190, by R. B. Dobson, No. 45 (1974); The First
Spasmodic Cholera Epidemic in York 1832, by M.
Durey, No. 46 (1974); The Revival of the
Convocation of York 1837-1861, by D. A. Jennings,
No. 47 (1975); The Oxford Movement and Parish
Life: St. Saviour's Leeds 1839-1929, by W. N.
Yates, No. 48 (1975); York Civic Ordinances 1301,
by M. Prestwich, No. 49, (1976); Jonathan Gray
and Church Music in York 1770-1830, by N. Tem-
perley, No. 51 (1977); Dearth and Distress in
Yorkshire 1793-1801, by R. A. E. Wells, No. 52
(1977); Marston Moor 2 July 1644: The Sources
and the Site, by R. Newman, No. 53 (1978);
William Cumin: Border Politics and the Bishopric
of Durham 1141-1144, by A. Young, No. 54
(1978); Education and Learning in the City of
York 1300-1550, by J. H. Moran, No. 55 (1979);
Yorkshire Nunneries in the Twelfth and Thirteenth
Centuries, by J. E. Burton, No. 56 (1979); The
General Strike in York, by R. I. Hills, No. 57
(1980); Defamation and Sexual Slander in Early
Modern England: The Church Courts at York, by
J. A. Sharpe, No. 58 (1980); Confiscation and
Restoration: The Archbishopric Estates and the
Civil War, by I. J. Gentles and W. J. Sheils,
No. 59 (1981); Inland Fisheries in Medieval York-
shire 1066-1300, by J. McDonnell, No. 60 (1981);
Poverty and the Poor Law in the North Riding of
Yorkshire ca. 1780-1837, by R. P. Hastings, No.
61 (1982); Pastoral Structure and the Church
Courts: The Hexam Court 1680-1730, by M. G.
Smith, No. 62 (1982); Building Craftsmen in Late
Medieval York, by H. Swanson, No. 63 (1983);
The Victorian Church in York, by E. Royle, No. 64
(1983); Charity Schools and the Defence of Angli-
canism: James Talbot, Rector of Spofforth 1700-
08, by R. W. Unwin, No. 65 (1984); The Develop-
ment of the Fire Insurance Business in Yorkshire
1710-1850, by D. Jenkins, No. 66 (1984).
  BORTHWICK TEXTS AND CALENDARS: 1. A
Guide to the Archive Collections in the Borthwick
Institute of Historical Research, by D. M. Smith
(1973); 2. A Calendar of the Register of Robert
Waldby, Archbishop of York, 1397, ed. by D. M.
Smith (1974); 3. A Handlist of Parish Register
Transcripts in the Borthwick Institute of Historical
Research, by N. K. M. Gurney (1976); 4. Arch-
bishop Grindal's Visitation of the Diocese of York
1575, ed. by W. J. Sheils (1977); 5. The Cartulary
of the Treasurer of York Minster and Related
Documents, ed. by J. E. Burton (1978);

6. Ecclesiastical Cause Papers at York I: Dean and Chapter's Court 1350-1843, by K. M. Longley (1980); 7. A Supplementary Guide to the Archive Collections in the Borthwick Institute of Historical Research, by D. M. Smith (1980); 8. A Calendar of the Register of Richard Scrope, Archbishop of York, 1398-1405, Pt. I by R. Swanson (1981); 9. Ecclesiastical Cause Papers at York II: Files Transmitted on Appeal 1500-1883, ed. by W. J. Sheils (1983); 10. York Clergy Wills 1520-1600: I Minster Clergy, by C. Cross (1984); 11. A Calendar of the Registers of Richard Scrope, Archbishop of York, 1398-1405, Pt. 2 by R. Swanson (1984).

BORTHWICK WALLETS: Sixteenth and Seventeenth Century Handwriting, series 1 and 2 by A. Rycraft (1969); English Medieval Handwriting, by A. Rycraft (1971); Sixteenth and Seventeenth Century Wills, Inventories and Other Probate Documents, by A. Rycraft (1973); The Reformation in the North, by W. J. Sheils (1976); Medieval Latin Documents, Series 1: Diocesan Records and Series 2: Probate Records, by D. M. Smith (1979, 1984).

OCCASIONAL PUBLICATIONS: Catalogue of Portraits at Bishopthorpe Palace, by J. Ingamells (1972); A Guide to Genealogical Sources in the Borthwick Institute of Historical Research, by C. C. Webb (1981). Borthwick Institute Bulletin, 1975- Annual. List of Deposited Registers (typescript).

YORK (map)

279 Institution   York City Archives
     Address   Art Gallery Building
                      Exhibition Square
                      York YO1 2EW

     Telephone   0904 51533

     Holdings   The collection contains city charters dating from
                      the 12th century and city house books or Council
                      Minute Books commencing in 1476. These include
                      proclamations, writs, letters to the city,
                      ordinances, regulations concerning the running of
                      the city and its inhabitants, and business done at
                      Council meetings. Chamberlains' rolls and books
                      which contain city accounts, are held. The books
                      begin in 1445-54 and survive with only a few gaps
                      from 1520 until 1835, when the office of Chamber-
                      lain was abolished. They contain some original
                      receipts and bills as they came to the chamber-
                      lains. The rolls are audited accounts and exist
                      from 1396/7, continuing in 1433-1835, again with
                      gaps in the earlier centuries. There are also rolls

of the Bridgemasters for the Ouse and Foss
Bridges from the 15th to the 17th century, and
some rolls of the Mure Masters' (who were responsible for the City Walls) exist for the 15th century. In addition there are lists or rolls of freemen
of the city which go back to 1272-1671. There
are also Guild records and Court records. Court
records include Quarter Sessions with Minute
Books from 1559 to the present, business records,
deeds of property, some family collections, poor
law and health records, plans relating to property
in York, and City of York Corporation Town
Clerks' and Departmental records, 19th and 20th
centuries.

Conditions of admission and access	The office is open to the public and appointments are not required for use of the records on Tues- day, Wednesday and Thursday. Use of the material on Monday and Friday is, however, by appointment only and at the convenience of the Archivist. The collection must be used on the premises. Inquiries should be directed to the Archivist.
Hours	9:30 AM - 12:30 PM, 2:00 PM - 5:30 PM, Tuesday- Thursday; by appointment at Archivist's con- venience, Monday, Friday.
Duplicating facilities	Photocopying is done for searchers by staff, but not on the premises so there may be some delay. Microfilm copies can also be arranged. Not all original documents can be copied.
Other services	Staff is available to help researchers and brief telephone and postal inquiries are answered, but there is an hourly fee charged for detailed searches through original documents. A small collection of reference books is also provided. Microform equipment and an ultraviolet lamp are available.
Publications	Catalogue of the City Records, by William Giles (1908); York City Archives, by Rita J. Green (1971); "Richard III and the City of York" (1983).

APPENDIXES
AND
INDEXES

ALPHABETICAL LIST OF INSTITUTIONS

The institutions covered in Chapter 2 are listed here by their names, and indexed to entry numbers. Special libraries within larger establishments are also included. Some organizations which have an official title and are also known by a popular name (e.g., the Royal Commission on Historical Manuscripts is frequently referred to as Quality Court) are given both ways. Finally, many agencies are found more than once with their titles in the proper form and in inverted order as an additional aid to their location.

ASSOCIATIONS AND SOCIETIES

Genealogical Societies abound in Great Britain and may be a source of information for the visiting scholar. Some have libraries worthy of note, and if so, they are included in Chapter 2. Many provide lists of agents who will investigate genealogical records for a fee or provide other services beneficial to the researcher. The addresses of some of the associations change with the officers of the organization and therefore may not be accurate at present. In those cases the address given is at least a starting point for contact with a particular group. Record offices and libraries can, in most cases, furnish up-to-date information.

Aberdeen and Northeast
    Scotland Family History
    Society
647 King Street
Aberdeen   AB2 1SB

The Alderney Society
The Old School
Alderney, Channel Islands

Ancient Monuments Society
Hon. Secretary
33 Ladbroke Square
London   W11 3NB
Tel. 01 221 6178

Association of Genealogists
    and Record Agents
c/o G. B. Greenwood
2 Buckhill Road
Walton-on-Thames, Surrey

Association of Teachers of
    Family History
56 Marlborough Road
Slough   SL3 7LH

Avon
    See: Bristol and Avon Family
    History Society

B.I.C.C. Research and Engg.
    Genealogical Society
38 Ariel Way, Woodlane
London   W12 7DX

Bath Heraldic Society
9 Newlands Road
Keysham, Bristol

Bedfordshire Family History
    Society
17 Lombard Street, Lidlington
Bedford   MK43 0RP

Belfast Library and Society for
    Promoting Knowledge
Linen Hall Library
17 Donegall Square North
Belfast   BT1 5GD

Beresford Family Society
93 Oakleigh Drive

Orton Longueville
Peterborough   PE2 0AR

Berkshire Family History Society
Purley Lodge Cottage
Purley Lane
Purley-on-Thames   RG8 8AT

Birmingham Jewish Genealogical
   Society
25 Westbourne Road, Edgerton
Birmingham   B15 3TY

Birmingham and Midland Society
   for Genealogy and Heraldry
92 Dimmingsdale Bank
Birmingham   B32 1ST

Bradford Family History Society
9 Ghyllwood Drive
Bingley   BD16 1NF

Braund Society
Meadows Side, Slade
Northdown Road
Bideford   EX39 3LZ

Bristol and Avon Family History
   Society
119 Holly Hill Road, Kingswood
Bristol   BS15 4DL

British Association for Local
   History
43 Bedford Square
London   WC1B 3DP
Tel. 01 636 4066

British Association of Cemeteries
   of South Asia
76½ Chartfield Avenue
London   SW15 6HQ

British Records Association
Hon. Secretary
The Master's Court
The Charter House
Charterhouse Square
London   EC1M 6AU
Tel. 01 253 0436

The Brooking Society
37 Church Mead, Keymer
Hassocks

Buckinghamshire Family History
   Society
18 Rudds Lane, Haddenham
Aylesbury   HP17 8JP

The Business Archives Council
Denmark House
15 Tooley Street
London   SE1 2PN
Tel. 01 407 6110

The Business Archives Council of
   Scotland
Glasgow University Archives
The University
Glasgow   G12 8QQ
Tel. 041 339 8855, ext. 7516

The Butler Society
Kilkenny Castle
Kilkenny, Co. Kilkenny

Cambridgeshire Family History
   Society
56 The Street, Kirtling
Newmarket   CB8 9PB

Caraher Family History Society
71 King Street
Crieff FH7 3HB

The Catholic Archives Society
Hon. Secretary
c/o 4A Polstead Road
Oxford   OX2 6TN

Catholic Record Society
Flat 5, 24 Lennox Gardens
London   SW1X 0DQ

Cave Family History Society
10 Tinkers Lane, Sawtry
Huntingdon   PE17 5TF

Central Middlesex Family History
   Society

12 Neeld Crescent
Wembley HA9 6LW

Channel Islands Family History
Society
P.O. Box 507
St. Helier, Jersey, Channel
Islands

Cheshire
See: Family History Society
of Cheshire; North Cheshire
Family History Society

Clan Lindsay
16 Dalziel Drive
Glasgow G41

Cleveland Family History Society
1 Oxgang Close, Redcar
Cleveland TS10 4ND

Clwyd Family History Society
27 Mile Barn Road
Wrexham LL13 9LX

Cornwall
See also: Devon and
Cornwall Record Society

Cornwall Family History Society
Chimney Pots, Sunny Corner
Cusgarne
Truro TR4 8SE

Cumberland and Westmorland
Antiquarian and Archaeological
Society
68 Santon Way
Seascale CA20 1NF

Cumbria Family History Society
32 Granada Road, Denton
Manchester M34 2LJ

Dalton Genealogical Society
2 Harewood Close
Reigate RH2 0HE

Derbyshire Family History Society
15 Elmhurst Road, Forest Town
Mansfield NG19 0EV

Devon and Cornwall Record
Society
7 The Close
Exeter EX1 1EZ

Devon Family History Society
63 Old Laira Road, Laira
Plymouth PL3 5BL

Doncaster Family History Society
7 Sherburn Close, Skellow
Doncaster DN6 8LG

Dorset Record Society
c/o Dorset County Museum
High West Street
Dorchester DT1 1YA

Dorset
See also: Somerset and Dorset
Family History Society

Durham
See: Northumberland and
Durham Family History Society

Dyfed Family History Society
175 Penybank Road, Penybank
Ammanford SA18 3QP

East Herts Archaeological Society
(no address available)

East of London Family History
Society
50 Grange Park Road
London E10 5ER

East Yorkshire Family History
Society
9 Stepney Grove
Scarborough YO12 5DF

Eastbourne and District (Family
Roots) Family History Society
22 Abbey Road
Eastbourne BN20 8TE

English Catholic Ancestor
Hill House West
Crookham Village (nr. Aldershot)
  GU13 0SS

Essex Archaeological Society
11 Plume Avenue
Malden CM9 6LB

Essex Family History Society
48 Walton Road
Frinton-on-Sea CO13 0AG

Falgrave Society
210 Bawtry Road
Doncaster DN4 7BZ

Family History Society of
  Cheshire
5 Henbury Rise, Henbury
Macclesfield SK11 9NW

The Federation for Ulster
  Local Studies
Knockbawn, Knocknadona
Lisburn, Co. Antrim

Federation of Family History
  Societies
31 Seven Star Road
Solihull B91 2BZ

Felixstowe Family History
  Society
4 Riby Road
Felixstowe IP11 7QB

Folkestone and District Family
  History Society
100 Orchard Valley
Hythe CT21 4EB

The Folklore Society
Hon. Secretary
c/o University College London
Gower Street
London WC1E 6BT
Tel. 01 387 5894

Genealogical Society of LDS
399 Garrett's Green Lane,
  Sheldon
Birmingham B33 4OU

Glamorgan Family History
  Society

The Orchard, Penmark
Barry CF6 9BN

Glens of Antrim Historical
  Society
Lemnalary House
Cornlough, Ballymena, Co.
  Antrim

Gloucestershire Family History
  Society
Hollington House
74 Woodfield Road, Cam,
Dursley GL11 6HF

Guild of One-Name Studies
14 Charterhouse Buildings
Goswell Road
London EC1M 7BA

Gwent Family History Society
18 Greenway Dr., Griffithstown
Pontypool NP4 5AZ

Gwynedd Family History Society
Cwmarian, Penysarn Fawr,
  Penysarn
Anglesey LL69 9BX

Hampshire Genealogical Society
12 Ashling House, Chidham Walk
Havant PO9 1DY

Harleian Society
Ardon House
Mill Lane
Godalming, Surrey

Hastings and Rother Family
  History Society
520D South View Court
Old London Road
Hastings TN35 5BN

Heraldry Society
28 Museum Street
London WC1A 1LH

Herefordshire Family History
  Society
255 Whitecross Road
Hereford HR4 0LT

Hertfordshire Family History
Society
6 The Crest
Ware SG12 0RR

Highland Family History
Society
York Cottage
1b Drummond Road
Inverness IV2 4NA

The Hon. Society of Cymnro-
dorion
118 Newgate Street
London EC1A 7AE

Huguenot and Walloon Gazette
Association
Malmaison
Church Street
Great Bedwyn SN8 3PE

Huguenot Society of London
67 Victoria Road
London W8 5RH

Huntingdonshire Family History
Society
14 Horseshoes Way
Brampton PE18 8TN

Institute of Heraldic and
Genealogical Studies
Northgate
Canterbury CT1 1BA

Irish Genealogical Association
162A Kingsway, Dunmurray
Belfast BT17 9AD

Irish Genealogical Society of
Great Britain
The Secretary
The Chaloner Club
59-61 Pont Street
London SW1 0BD

The Irish Genealogical Research
Society
Glenholme, High Oakum Road
Mansfield

Isle of Man Family History
Society
3 Wesley Terrace
Douglas, Isle of Man

Jewish History Society of
England
33 Seymour Place
London W1

Kelso Family
The Manse, Huntley Road
Bambridge, Co. Down BT32 3B5

Kent
See also: Northwest Kent
Family History Society

Kent Family History Society
17 Abbots Place
Canterbury CT1 2AH

Lancashire
See also: Manchester and
Lancashire Family History
Society

Lancashire Family History and
Heraldry Society
Copstherds
Copster Green
Blackburn BB1 9EW

The Lancashire Parish Register
Society
c/o The John Rylands Library
Deansgate
Manchester M3 3EH
Tel. 061 834 5343

Leicester
See: University of Leicester
Genealogical Society

Leicestershire Family History
Circle
25 Home Croft Drive, Packington
Ashby de la Zouch LE6 5WG

The Library Association
7 Ridgmount Street/Store Street

London WC1E 7AE
Tel. 01 636 7543

Lincolnshire Family History
  Society
47 Newland
Lincoln LN1 1XZ

List and Index Society
The Secretary
c/o The Public Record Office
Chancery Lane
London WC2A 1LR

Liverpool and District Family
  History Society
11 Lisburn Lane, Tuebrook
Liverpool L13 9AE

Local Population Studies Society
17 Rosebery Square
Rosebery Avenue
London EC1

London
  See also: East of London
  Family History Society

London Record Society
c/o Leicester University Library
University Road
Leicester LE1 7RH

Macclesfield Heraldic Society
2 Orchard Close, Cheadle
Hulme

Manchester and Lancashire Family
  History Society
3 Lytham Road
Manchester M19 2AT

Mansfield and District Family
  History Society
2 Millersdale Avenue
Mansfield NG18 5HS

The Manx Society
c/o The Manx Museum
Douglas, Isle of Man

Middlesex
  See: Central Middlesex Family
  History Society; North Middle-
  sex Family History Society;
  West Middlesex Family History
  Society

Midland
  See: Birmingham and Midland
  Society for Genealogy and
  Heraldry

The Names Society
7 Aragon Avenue
Thames Ditton

Norfolk and Norwich Genealogical
  Society
22 Chestnut Hill
Norwich NR4 6NL

North Cheshire Family History
  Society
2 Denham Drive, Bramhall
Stockport SK7 2AT

North Middlesex Family History
  Society
15 Milton Road, Walthamstow
London E17 4SP

North of Ireland Family History
  Society
29 Grange Park, Dunmurry
Belfast BT17 0AN

North West Kent Family History
  Society
190 Beckenham Road
Beckenham BR3 4RJ

Northamptonshire Family History
  Society
83 Southampton Road, Far Cotton
Northampton NN4 9DZ

Northamptonshire Record Society
Delapre Abbey
Northampton NN4 9AW

Northumberland and Durham
    Family History Society
33 South Bend, Brunton Park
Newcastle-upon-Tyne NE3 5TR

Norwich
    See: Norfolk and Norwich
    Genealogical Society

Nottinghamshire Family History
    Society
35 Kingswood Road, West
    Bridgford
Nottingham NG2 7HT

Oliver Society
Blain, Blainslie
Galashiels TD1 2PR

O'Mahoney Records Society
c/o The Irish Times
Dublin

Oxfordshire Family History
    Society
10 Bellamy Close, Southmoor
nr. Abingdon
Oxon

Peterborough and District Family
    History Society
511 Fulbridge Road, Werrington
Peterborough PE4 6SB

Post Office Headquarters
    Genealogical Society
27 Havley Bell Gardens
Bishops Stortford CM23 3HA

Powys Family History Society
The Plough
Blakemere HR2 9PY

Presbyterian Historical Society
    of England
86 Tavistock Place
London WC1H 9RR

Presbyterian Historical Society
    of Northern Ireland
Church House

Fisherwick Place
Belfast BT1 6DU

Redundant Churches Fund
St. Andrew-by-the Wardrobe
Queen Victoria Street
London EC4V 5DE

Rolls Royce Family History
    Society
25 Gisburn Road, Barnoldswick
Colne

Rossendale Society for Genealogy
    and Heraldry
183 Bolton Street, Ramsbottom
Bury

Royal Commonwealth Society
Northumberland Avenue
London WC2

Scots Ancestry Research Society
20 York Place
Edinburgh EH1 3PY

Scottish Genealogical Society
21 Howard Place
Edinburgh EH3 5JY

Scottish Record Society
University of Glasgow
c/o Scottish History Department
Glasgow G12 8QG

Scottish Tartan Society
Museum of Scottish Tartans
Comrie

Sheffield and District Family
    History Society
58 Stumperlowe Crescent Road
Sheffield S10 3PR

Shropshire Family History Society
15 Wesley Drive, Oaken Gates
Telford TF2 0DZ

La Société Guernesiaise
Courtil à l'Herbe
Route des Bas Courtils

St. Saviour, Guernsey,
Channel Islands

Société Jersiaise
The Library
The Museum
7 Pier Road
St. Helier, Jersey
Channel Islands

Society of Antiquaries of London
Burlington House
Piccadilly
London W1V 0HS
Tel. 01 736 0193/437 9954

Society of Genealogists
14 Charterhouse Buildings
Goswell Road
London EC1M 7BA

Society of Lincs. History and
   Archaeology
Family History Section
135 Baldertongate
Newark NG24 1RY

Somerset and Dorset Family
   History Society
Bru-Lands
Marston Road
Sherborne DT9 4BL

Southampton Record Society
c/o Southampton City Record
   Office
Civic Centre, Room 101
Southampton SO9 4XR

Spalding Gentlemen's Society
The Museum
Broad Street
Spalding PE11 1TB

Suffolk Genealogical Society
30 Gowers End, Glemsford
Sudbury

Surrey East Family History
   Society
370 Chipstead Valley Road
Coulsdon CR3 3BF

Surrey West Family History
   Society
Bradstone Garden Cottage
Christmas Hill
Shalford GU4 8HR

Sussex Archaeological Society
Barbican House
Lewes BN7 1YE
Tel. 079 16 4379

Sussex Family History Society
44 The Green, Southwick
Brighton BN4 4FR

Swinnerton Society
33 Bridgnorth Road, Stourton
Stourbridge DY7 6RS

Talbot Research Organization
142 Albemarle Avenue, Elson
Gosport PO12 4HY

Tay Valley Family History Society
11 Turfbeg Road
Forfar DD8 3LT

Tyrrell Family History Society
283 Forton Road
Gosport PO12 3HO

Ulster Genealogical and Historical
   Guild
66 Balmoral Avenue
Belfast BT9 6NY

Ulster Historical Foundation
68 Balmoral Avenue
Belfast BT9 6NY

University of Leicester
   Genealogical Society
Students Union
Mayors Walk
Leicester LE1 7RH

Waltham Forest Family History
   Society
1 Gelsthorp Road
Romford RM5 2NB

West Middlesex Family History
    Society
17 Croft Gardens
Ruislip   4HA 8EY

Wiltshire Family History
1 Cambridge Close, Lawn
Swindon   SN3 1JO

Windsor, Slough and District
    Family History Society
Flat 26 "in the Ray"
Ray Park Avenue
Maidenhead   SL6 8DH

Woolwich and District Family
    History Society
4 Church Road
Bexleyheath   DA7 4DA

York Family History Society
1 Ouse Lea
Shipton Road
York   YO3 6SA

Yorkshire
    See also: East Yorkshire
    Family History Society

Yorkshire Archaeological Society
Family History and Population
    Studies Section
4 Woodside Park Avenue,
    Horsforth
Leeds   LS18 4TF

<u>Appendix III</u>

MAPS

This section contains maps of towns where the institutions described
in Chapter 2 are located. They were supplied by the record offices,
libraries, or County and City Councils involved. Not every institution was able to provide a map, but those that could were most
enthusiastic about their inclusion. Permission was readily granted
to use those from record office brochures or, where necessary, to
make sketches from them. In some cases, hand-drawn maps were
provided. It seems to be generally recognized that when an individual is in unfamiliar surroundings, a map can be a great comfort
and a help in locating an address.

There are also maps which show county boundaries for England,
Scotland, and Wales before April 1974, and a map which gives the
boundaries after the local government re-organization which took
place at that time. There is also a county map for Northern Ireland
and for the Republic of Ireland. Finally there is a map of the
Greater London Area which shows the location of selected London
Boroughs.

Since the maps came from diverse sources, they are inconsis-
tent in form and scale and many had to be re-drawn for the sake
of clarity. Because of space limitations the maps are necessarily
quite small and a magnifying glass may be required to use some of
them.

I am deeply grateful to the individuals and organizations who
furnished these maps and for their help in compiling this Appendix.
The enthusiasm from the institutions for this aspect of the guide
was very encouraging and most gratifying. My heartfelt appreciation
and thankful acknowledgment is given to the following:

> City of Aberdeen; City of Aberystwyth; The Alderney Society
> and Museum; Bath City Council; Bedfordshire County Council;
> Belfast Education and Library Board; Berkshire Record Of-
> fice; City of Birmingham; City of Bristol Clerk's Department;
> British Library; Cambridge University Library; Canterbury
> Cathedral Archives and Library; Cheshire Record Office;
> University College Cork, College Calendar; Cornwall Record
> Office; City of Coventry; Cumbria County Council, County

Secretary's Department; Derbyshire County Council,
Derbyshire Record Office; Devon Record Office; Dorset
County Council, County Record Office; The City of Dublin;
Dyfed County Council; City of Edinburgh; Essex County
Council and Essex Record Office; Essex Record Office,
Southend Branch; Glamorgan Archive Service; City of
Glasgow District Council Libraries Department, The Mitchell
Library; Gloucestershire County Council, Gloucestershire
Record Office; Hampshire Record Office; Hereford and
Worcester Record Office; Hull City Council, Hull City
Record Office; Humberside County Council; Institute of
Agricultural History and Museum of Rural Life; Royal
Borough of Kensington and Chelsea Borough Librarian and
Arts Officer; Kilkenny Tourist Office; Leicester Record
Office; Lincoln City Council and Lincolnshire Archives
Office; London Borough of Greenwich Local History Centre;
London Borough of Lambeth; London Borough of Lewisham,
Local History Centre, Borough Leisure Services Officer;
Greater Manchester County Record Office; National Museums
and Galleries on Merseyside; Northamptonshire County
Secretary's Department, Northampton Record Office; North-
umberland Record Office; City of Norwich; Nottinghamshire
County Council, Nottinghamshire Record Office; Mr. C.
Lewis, Department of Geography, University of Nottingham;
Oxfordshire County Record Office; Department of
Geographical Sciences, Plymouth Polytechnic; Portsmouth
Central Library; Public Record Office; Royal Commission on
Historical Manuscripts; City of St. Helier; The Shakespeare
Centre; Shropshire Libraries, Local Studies Department;
South Humberside Area Record Office; City of Southampton;
Staffordshire County Council, Staffordshire Record Office;
Suffolk County Council; Surrey County Council; Tameside
Local Studies Library; Tyne and Wear Archives Department;
University of London; University of Ulster; Walsall Library
and Museum Service; Warwickshire County Council; West
Sussex Record Office; West Yorkshire Archive Service; City
of Westminster Libraries, Archives Section; City of York.

The Counties Of
ENGLAND AND WALES

Before April 1974

SCOTLAND

Before   April   1974

GREAT BRITIAN

AFTER APRIL 1974

Country Boundry •••••••

Shetland Islands

Orkney

Outer Hebrides

Western Isles

Inner Hebrides

Highland

Grampian

Tayside

Strathclyde

Central

Fife

Lothian

Borders

Dumfries and Galloway

Northumberland

Tyne and Wear

Isle of Man

Cumbria

Durham

Cleveland

Lancashire

Greater Manchester

Merseyside

N. Yorkshire

W. Yorks.

S. Yorks.

Humberside

Gwynedd

Clwyd

Cheshire

Derby

Notting-ham

Lincoln

Powys

Shrop-shire

Stafford

Midlands

Leicester

Cambridge

Norfolk

Dyfed

Hereford and Worcester

Warwick

North-ampton

Bedford

Suffolk

W. Glamorgan

Mid Glamorgan

S. Glamorgan

Gloucester

Oxford

Buckingham

Hertford

Essex

Avon

Berkshire

Greater London

Somerset

Wiltshire

Hampshire

Surrey

Kent

Devon

Dorset

W. Sussex

E. Sussex

Cornwall

Isle of Wight

Scilly Isles

Channel Islands

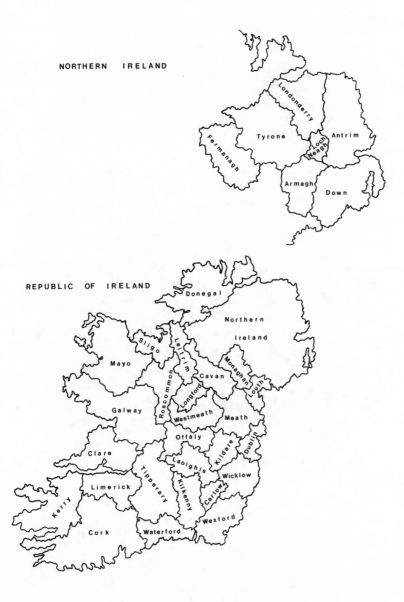

NORTHERN IRELAND

REPUBLIC OF IRELAND

GREATER LONDON AREA
Location of selected boroughs
(M4) Highway numbers

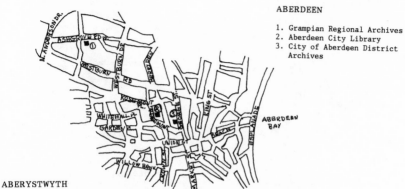

ABERDEEN

1. Grampian Regional Archives
2. Aberdeen City Library
3. City of Aberdeen District
   Archives

ABERYSTWYTH

1. Public Library
2. Cardiganshire Area Record
   Office
3. Royal Commission on Ancient and
   Historical Monuments in Wales
4. National Library of Wales

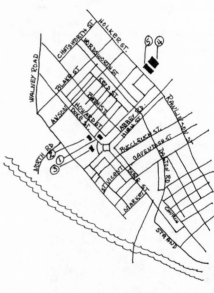

BARROW-IN-FURNESS

1. Record Office
2. Car Park
3. Bus Station
4. Train Station
5. Car Park

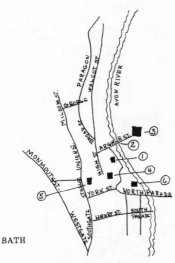

BATH

1. Record Office   4. Bath Abbey
   (Guildhall)   5. Roman Baths
2. Pulteney Bridge   6. Parade Gardens
3. Laura Place

BEDFORD

1. Library
2. County Hall (Record Office)
3. County Offices
4. Parking Lot

BELFAST

1. Belfast Central Library
2. Belfast Library and Society
   for Promoting Knowledge

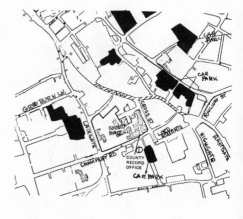

BEVERLY

1. Humberside County Record
   Office

BIRMINGHAM

1. Record Office
2. Town Hall
3. Museum
4. Cathedral

BRADFORD

1. Record Office

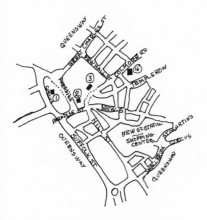

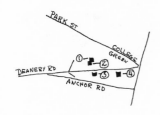

BRISTOL

1. County offices
2. Bristol Record Office
3. Library
4. Cathedral

BURY ST. EDMUNDS

1. Record Office

CAMBRIDGE

1. Record Office
2. Westminster College
3. Jesus College
4. Magdalene
5. Museum
6. University Library

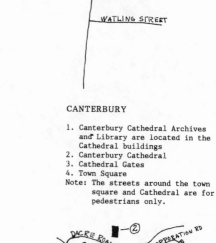

CANTERBURY

1. Canterbury Cathedral Archives
   and Library are located in the
   Cathedral buildings
2. Canterbury Cathedral
3. Cathedral Gates
4. Town Square
Note: The streets around the town
      square and Cathedral are for
      pedestrians only.

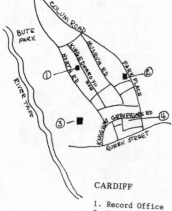

CARDIFF

1. Record Office
2. Museum
3. Cardiff Castle
4. Car Park

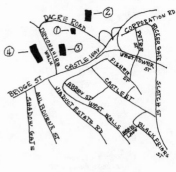

CARLISLE

1. Record Office
2. Car Park
3. Car Park
4. Car Park

CARMARTHEN

1. Record Office
2. Castle

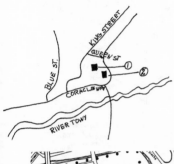

CHELMSFORD

Essex Record Office
(County Hall)

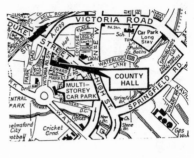

CHESTER

⭐ Cheshire Record Office and
Chester Diocesan Record Office

● City Record Office

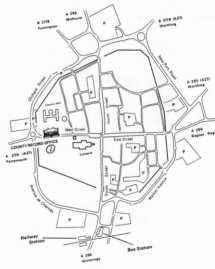

CHICHESTER

1. County Record Office

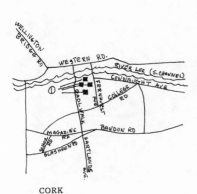

CORK

1. University College, Cork

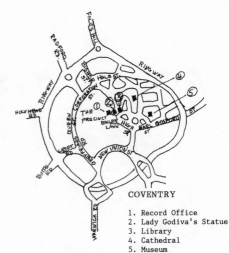

COVENTRY

1. Record Office
2. Lady Godiva's Statue
3. Library
4. Cathedral
5. Museum

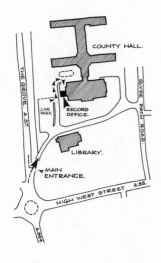

DORCHESTER

Dorset County Record Office

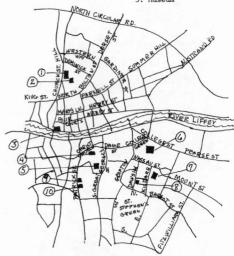

DUBLIN
1. King's Inn
2. Register of Deeds
3. National Archives
4. City Hall
5. Castle
6. Trinity College
7. National Library
8. Royal Irish Academy
9. Marsh's Library
10. St. Patrick's Cathedral

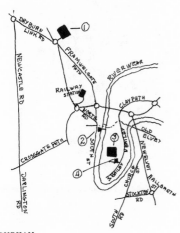

DURHAM

1. Record Office
2. Durham City Library
3. Durham Cathedral
4. University of Durham
   Department of Palaeography
   and Diplomatic

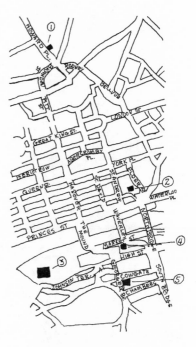

EDINBURGH

1. Scottish Genealogical Society
2. Register House
3. Edinburgh Castle
4. City Chambers
5. National Library of Scotland

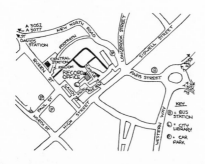

EXETER

Devon Record Office

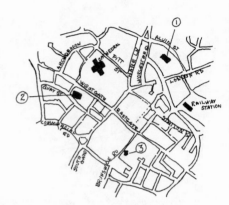

GLASGOW

1. The Mitchell Library
2. Charing Cross Station
3. Anderston Bus Station
4. Central Station
5. Queen Street Station
6. George Square
7. Anderston Station
8. Buchanan Street Bus Station
9. St. Georges Cross Underground Station

GLOUCESTER

1. Record Office
2. Shire Hall (recent records)
3. Library

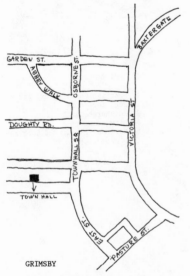

GRIMSBY

Humberside Area Record Office (Town Hall)

Guildford Muniment Room, Quarry Street, Guildford. In the same buildings as Guildford Museum, about 10 minutes walk from Guildford station.

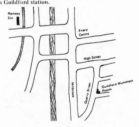

GUILDFORD

Surrey Record Office,
Guildford Muniment Room

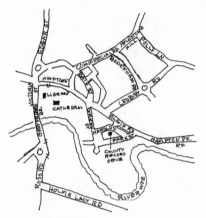

HALIFAX

West Yorkshire Archive Service
(Central Library)

HEREFORD

Hereford and Worcester County
Record Office, County Library,
Hereford City Library, Cathedral
Library

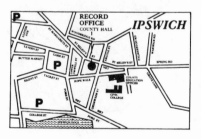

IPSWICH

Suffolk Record Office

HUDDERSFIELD

West Yorkshire Archive Service
(Library)

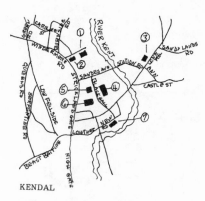

KENDAL

1. Record Office 5. Bus Station
2. Car Park   6. Car Park
3. Train Station 7. Car Park
4. Car Park

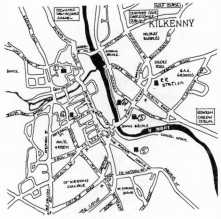

KILKENNY

1. St. Canices Cathedral
2. Kilkenny County Library
3. Kilkenny College
4. St. Mary's Cathedral
5. Kilkenny Castle

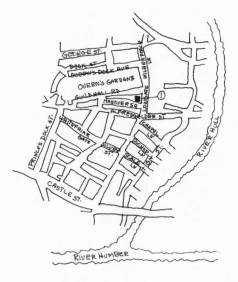

KINGSTON UPON HULL

1. Record Office

Surrey Record Office, County Hall, Penrhyn Road, Kingston upon Thames. About 15 minutes walk from Surbiton and Kingston stations. Bus route 281 from either station.

KINGSTON UPON THAMES

Surrey Record Office

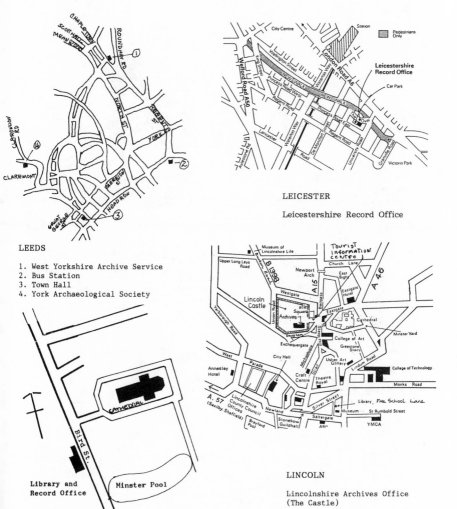

LEEDS

1. West Yorkshire Archive Service
2. Bus Station
3. Town Hall
4. York Archaeological Society

LICHFIELD

Lichfield Joint Record Office

LEICESTER

Leicestershire Record Office

LINCOLN

Lincolnshire Archives Office
(The Castle)

LIVERPOOL

1. National Museums and Galleries
   on Merseyside Archives Department
2. Liverpool City Libraries
3. Maritime Records Centre

LONDON

1. British Library
   (See also: University College
   London and University of
   London Library Map)

LONDON

1. British Library India
   Office Library and Records
2. Imperial War Museum
3. Waterloo Underground
4. Lambeth North Underground
5. Elephant & Castle Underground

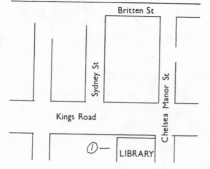

LONDON

1. Chelsea Library

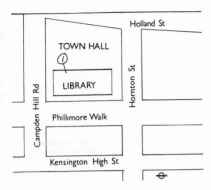

LONDON

1. Kensington Central
   Reference Library

LONDON

1. Lewisham Local
   History Library

LONDON

1. London Borough of Greenwich
   Local History Library

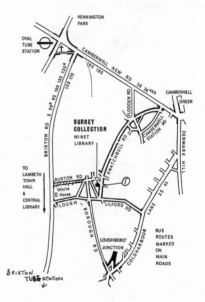

LONDON

1. Minet Library
   Lambeth Archives Department

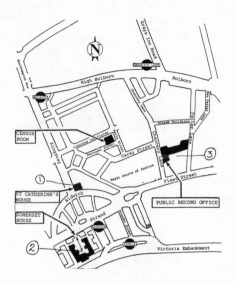

LONDON

1. Office of Population Census and
   Surveys (St. Catherines House)
2. Principal Registry of the Family
   Division (Somerset House)
3. Public Record Office

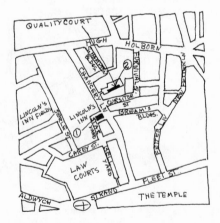

LONDON

1. Lincoln's Inn
2. Royal Commission of Historical
   Manuscripts (Quality Court)

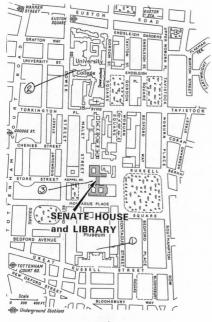

LONDON

1. British Library
2. University College London
3. University of London
   Library (Senate House)

LONDON

1. Westminster City Libraries
   Marylebone Library

LONDON

1. Westminster City Libraries
   Victoria Library

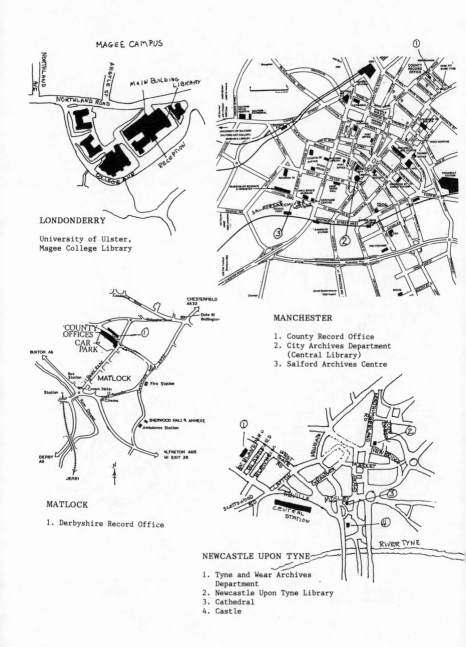

LONDONDERRY

University of Ulster,
Magee College Library

MATLOCK

1. Derbyshire Record Office

MANCHESTER

1. County Record Office
2. City Archives Department
   (Central Library)
3. Salford Archives Centre

NEWCASTLE UPON TYNE

1. Tyne and Wear Archives
   Department
2. Newcastle Upon Tyne Library
3. Cathedral
4. Castle

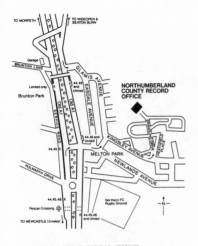

NEWCASTLE UPON TYNE
(Melton Park, North Gosforth)

NORTHAMPTON

Northamptonshire Record Office
(Delapre Abbey)

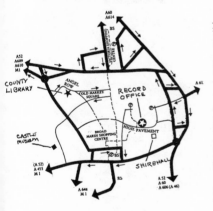

NOTTINGHAM

Nottinghamshire Record Office
Southwell Diocesan Record Office

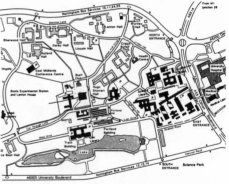

NOTTINGHAM

University of Nottingham Library

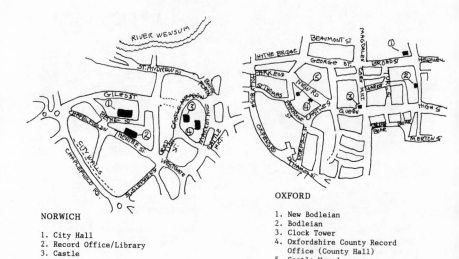

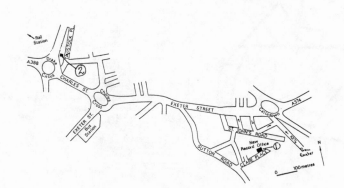

NORWICH

1. City Hall
2. Record Office/Library
3. Castle
4. Shire Hall

OXFORD

1. New Bodleian
2. Bodleian
3. Clock Tower
4. Oxfordshire County Record
   Office (County Hall)
5. Castle Mound

PLYMOUTH

1. West Devon Record Office
2. West Devon Area Central Library

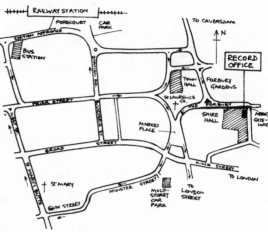

PORTSMOUTH

1. Guildhall Square
2. Portsmouth Central Library
3. Museum
4. Portsmouth City Record Office
xxx Ped. Bridge

READING

Berkshire Record Office

READING

University of Reading
Library
Institute of Agricultural History
and Museum of Rural Life

ST. HELIER

1. La Société Jersiaise
2. Judicial Greffe
3. Sealink

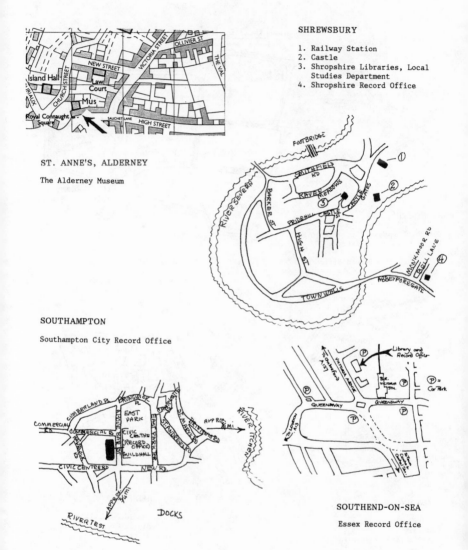

SHREWSBURY

1. Railway Station
2. Castle
3. Shropshire Libraries, Local Studies Department
4. Shropshire Record Office

ST. ANNE'S, ALDERNEY

The Alderney Museum

SOUTHAMPTON

Southampton City Record Office

SOUTHEND-ON-SEA

Essex Record Office

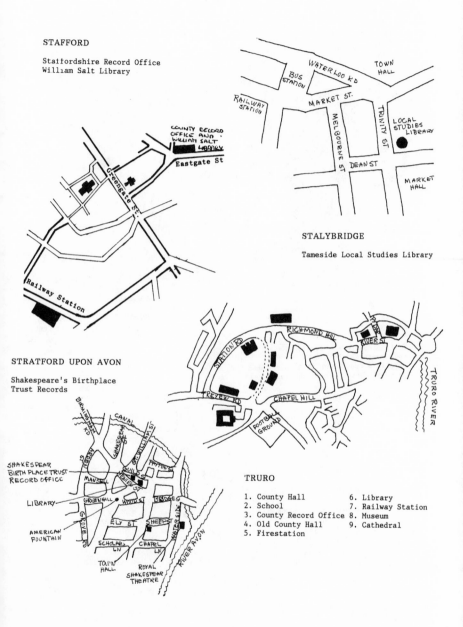

STAFFORD

Staffordshire Record Office
William Salt Library

STALYBRIDGE

Tameside Local Studies Library

STRATFORD UPON AVON

Shakespeare's Birthplace
Trust Records

TRURO

1. County Hall
2. School
3. County Record Office
4. Old County Hall
5. Firestation

6. Library
7. Railway Station
8. Museum
9. Cathedral

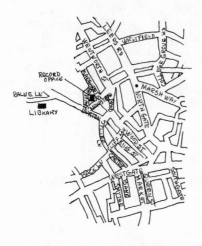

WAKEFIELD

West Yorkshire Archive Service
(Headquarters)
Wakefield Department of Archives and
Local Studies (Library Headquarters)

WALSALL

Walsall Library and Museum
Services Local History Centre

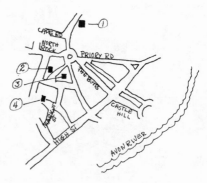

WARWICK

1. Warwickshire County
   Record Office
2. Library
3. County Departments
4. Museum

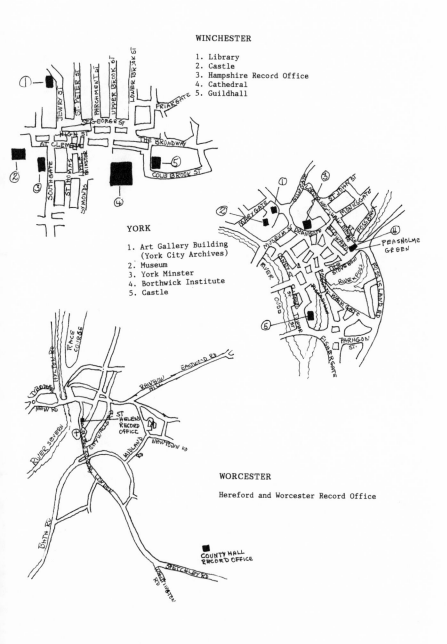

WINCHESTER

1. Library
2. Castle
3. Hampshire Record Office
4. Cathedral
5. Guildhall

YORK

1. Art Gallery Building
   (York City Archives)
2. Museum
3. York Minster
4. Borthwick Institute
5. Castle

WORCESTER

Hereford and Worcester Record Office

DONEGAL
  Letterkenny

DORSET
  Dorchester

DUBLIN
  Dublin

DUMFRIES AND GALLOWAY
  Dumfries

DURHAM
  Darlington
  Durham

DYFED
  Aberystwyth
  Carmarthen
  Haverfordwest

EAST SUSSEX
  Lewes

ESSEX
  London Borough of Barking
    and Dagenham
  Chelmsford
  Colchester
  Southend-on-Sea

FIFE
  Dunfermline

GALWAY
  Cashel
  Galway

GLOUCESTERSHIRE
  Gloucester

GRAMPIAN
  Aberdeen
  Forres

GREATER LONDON
  London Borough of Barnet
  London Borough of Camden
  London Borough of Enfield
  London Borough of Greenwich
  London Borough of Hackney

London Borough of Hammer-
  smith
London Borough of Haringey
London Borough of Havering
Hendon (former Borough)
London Borough of Hounslow
Kensington, Chelsea
London Borough of Lewisham
London
London Borough of Newham
London Borough of Richmond-
  upon-Thames
London Borough of Southwark
London Borough of Tower
  Hamlets
London Borough of Upper
  Norwood

GREATER MANCHESTER
  Bolton
  Leigh
  Manchester
  Middleton
  Stalybridge

GUERNSEY, CHANNEL ISLANDS
  St. Peter Port

GWENT
  Cwmbran

GWYNEDD
  Bangor
  Caernarfon
  Dolgellau
  Llangefni

HAMPSHIRE
  Andover
  Portsmouth
  Southampton
  Winchester

HEREFORD AND WORCESTER
  Hereford
  Kidderminster
  Worcester

HERTFORDSHIRE
  Hertford

SOUTH GLAMORGAN
  Cardiff

SOUTH YORKSHIRE
  Barnsley
  Doncaster
  Rotherham
  Sheffield

STAFFORDSHIRE
  Burton-on-Trent
  Lichfield
  Stafford

STRATHCLYDE
  Airdrie
  Ayr
  Cumnock
  Dumbarton
  Glasgow
  Hamilton
  Lochgilphead

SUFFOLK
  Bury St. Edmunds
  Ipswich

SURREY
  London Borough of Croydon
  Guildford
  Kingston-upon-Thames
  Sutton

TAYSIDE
  Comrie
  Crieff
  Dundee

TYNE AND WEAR
  Gateshead
  Newcastle-upon-Tyne
  North Shields

WARWICKSHIRE
  Stratford-upon-Avon
  Warwick

WEST GLAMORGAN
  Swansea

WEST LOTHIAN
  Bathgate

WEST MIDLANDS
  Bilston
  Birmingham
  Coventry
  Dudley
  Walsall
  West Bromwich
  Wolverhampton

WEST SUSSEX
  Chichester

WEST YORKSHIRE
  Bradford
  Halifax
  Huddersfield
  Leeds
  Wakefield

WESTERN ISLES
  Stornoway

WILTSHIRE
  Trowbridge

ALPHABETICAL LIST OF CITIES BY COUNTRY

ENGLAND

Andover
Aylesbury
London Borough of Barking
    and Dagenham
London Borough of Barnet
Barnsley
Barrow-in-Furness
Bath
Bedford
Berwick-upon-Tweed
Beverley
London Borough of Bexley
Bilston
Birkenhead
Birmingham
Bolton
Boston
Bradford
Bristol
London Borough of Bromley
Burton-on-Trent
Bury St. Edmunds
Cambridge
London Borough of Camden
Canterbury
Carlisle
Chelmsford
Chelsea
Chester
Chesterfield
Chichester
Colchester
Coventry
London Borough of Croydon
Darlington

Derby
Doncaster
Dorchester
Dover
Dudley
Durham
London Borough of Enfield
Exeter
Folkestone
Gateshead
Gloucester
Gravesend
London Borough of Greenwich
Grimsby
Guildford
London Borough of Hackney
Halifax
London Borough of Hammer-
    smith
London Borough of Haringey
London Borough of Havering
Hendon
Hereford
Hertford
Heywood
London Borough of Hounslow
Huddersfield
Huntingdon
Hythe
Ipswich
Kendal
Kensington
Kidderminster
Kingston-upon-Hull
Kingston-upon-Thames
Lancaster
Leeds

Leicester
Leigh
Lewes
London Borough of Lewisham
Lichfield
Lincoln
Liverpool
London
Lydd
Maidstone
Manchester
Margate
Matlock
Middlesbrough
Middleton
New Romney
Newcastle-upon-Tyne
London Borough of Newham
Northshields
Northallerton
Northampton
Norwich
Nottingham
Oldham
Oxford
Plymouth
Portsmouth
Preston
Ramsgate
Reading
London Borough of Richmond-
    upon-Thames
Rochdale
Rotherham
Scarborough
Sheffield
Shepway (District)
Shrewsbury
Southampton
Southend-on-Sea
London Borough of Southwark
Stafford
Stalybridge
Stockport
Stratford-upon-Avon
Sutton
Taunton
London Borough of Tower
    Hamlets
Trowbridge
Truro

London Borough of Upper
    Norwood
Wakefield
Walsall
Warwick
West Bromwich
Winchester
Wolverhampton
Worcester
York

IRELAND

Cashel
Cork
Dublin
Galway
Kilkenny
Letterkenny
Limerick

NORTHERN IRELAND

Armagh
Belfast
Londonderry
Portadown

SCOTLAND

Aberdeen
Airdrie
Arbroath
Ayr
Bathgate
Brechin
Comrie
Crieff
Cumnock
Dumbarton
Dumfries
Dundee
Dunfermline
Edinburgh
Forfar
Forres
Glasgow
Hamilton

SUBJECT INDEX

The subjects covered in this index include individuals, families, estates, collections, and places not found in the name of the institution nor the town under which it is located. Titled individuals are placed under the title and the person's name inverted. This does not extend to physicians or to military rank. Subject terms (e.g., geography, politics, textiles) are found only if the library's collection is considered significant. The names of publications not listed in the Publications Section of each entry are also provided. Churches, church parishes, and dioceses are not usually mentioned, but will be found occasionally if they are very important. The term "wills" is listed only for the Principal Registry of the Family Division, and such words as "deeds," "photographs," "maps," etc. are not included. The reference in this index is to entry number unless it is preceded by a "p.," in which case the reference is to page number.